Active Voices
III

Active Voices
III

James Moffett

with
Patricia Wixon
Vincent Wixon
Sheridan Blau
John Phreaner

BOYNTON/COOK PUBLISHERS
HEINEMANN
PORTSMOUTH, NH

Boynton/Cook Publishers, Inc.
A Subsidiary of Reed Publishing (USA) Inc.
361 Hanover Street, Portsmouth, NH 03801-3912
Offices and agents throughout the world

Library of Congress Cataloging-in-Publication Data

Active voices III.

    1. Readers (Secondary) 2. School prose, American.
I. Moffett, James. II. Title: Active voices 3.
III. Title: Active voices three
PE1121.A185 1986   428.6   86-23300
ISBN 0-86709-113-4

Printed in the United States of America

10 9 8 7 6 5

Acknowledgments

Our first thanks go to those students who essentially wrote this book. Their names appear in the Contents and at the beginning of their contributions.

To their teachers and schools we are, of course, greatly indebted for affording these young authors the kind of education that made a collection of such range and quality possible. Though the bulk of the writing came from some schools connected with the Oregon Writing Project and the South Coast Writing Project in Santa Barbara, California, much came from other parts of the country—New Jersey, Massachusetts, Illinois, New York, Alaska, and Arizona—and from other parts of California, including some schools active in the Bay Area Writing Project.

The Oregon teachers were Vincent Wixon, Jim Martin, Sandy Speasl, Linda Bowman, John Ruff, and Bill Ferguson of Crater H.S. in Central Point; Patty Wixon and Marjorie Nichols of Eagle Point H.S.; Ana Larson, Jan Markee, and Betty Wittner of Sprague H.S. in Salem; Don Vondracek, Robert McBaine, Kathy Williams-Bowen, Penny Therien, and Terry Wells of Ashland H.S.; Ruth Lanham and Jim Proehl of Brandon H.S.; Andrea Stine of Hermiston H.S.; Marilyn Savage of La Grande H.S.; Paulann Petersen of Mazama H.S. in Klamath Falls; and Grant Pine of Bonanza H.S.

The California teachers were Jack Phreaner, Marjorie Luke, Joyce Kent, and David Holmes of San Marcos H.S. in Santa Barbara; Robert Ganahl, Elizabeth Mills, Tom Kiddie, Susan Huber, Lynn Conger, and Zelda Emma of the U.C. Santa Barbara credential program; Andrée Licoscos of Santa Maria H.S.; Mark Schlenz of Santa Inez H.S.; Roderick Schmidt and Warren Arnold of Cabrillo H.S. in Lompoc; Shirley Holgate of Thousand Oaks H.S.; Deborah Ventura of Nordhoff H.S. in Ojai; Gerry Camp of Monte Vista H.S. in Danville; Laury Fischer of Washington H.S. in Fremont; Jim Hahn of Armijo

H.S. in Fairfield; Art Peterson of Lowell H.S. in San Francisco; John Nicholson of Tamalpais H.S. in Mill Valley; Elizabeth Cornell, Marsha Jacobson, and Nancy Steele of Lick-Wilmerding H.S. in San Franscico; Joe Lawrence and Patricia McKenzie of Rio Americano H.S. in Sacramento; and Susan Whitelock of South Torrance H.S. in Torrance. Of the many selections from San Marcos H.S. a considerable number first appeared in *San Marcos Writes*.

An important contribution was made by Don Lasko and Steffi Poss of Columbia H.S. in South Orange-Maplewood, New Jersey. Some of the selections from there first appeared in their local two-volume collection, *This Is Just to Say*, and in *The Columbian*, the school newspaper.

For a number of selections written by students of the Navajo nation, we are grateful to Eleanor Velarde of Rough Rock Community School and Rock Point Community School in Arizona and to Peggy Kaveski, Dan McLaughlin, Rita Faruki, and Kathy Kuencer of Rock Point. These pieces were first printed in *Rough Stones Are Precious Too*, edited by Eleanor Velarde and supported by the Navajo Curriculum Center, in *Echo*, and in the school newspapers.

Some selections are reprinted from *Mosaic*, a community studies publication project directed at South Boston H.S. by Katie Singer, one issue of which was edited by her and another by her and David Donnell, Dan Terris, and Michael Tierney. The authors' teachers were Katie Singer and Ron Pesatura. Other selections are from *Science, etc.*, published at Herndon (Virginia) H.S. under the direction of Ann Sevcik.

Two community newspapers granted permission to reprint items. We thank Ray Elliott, editor of *Tales from the General Store*, in Oblong, Illinois, for letting us use three articles done by students at Oak Lawn H.S. and Hinsdale South H.S. and the *News-Record* of Maplewood, New Jersey, for permission to reprint a series of three articles by John Shue of Columbia H.S.

Our gratitude also to some individual teachers in various other places: Johanna Mosca of Grace Dodge Vocational H.S. in Bronx, New York; James R. Bird Jr. of the Spence School in Manhattan; Walt Kirsch and Ellen LaGow of Naperville (Illinois) Central H.S.; Joe Morgan of Glenbard South H.S. in Glen Ellyn, Illinois; and Nancy Vait of the English Bay (Alaska) School.

James Moffett
Mariposa, California

Contents

To the Student

Students in grades 10-12 wrote this book, which is meant to sample for you the wide variety of kinds of writing done in our world. By using for this collection only the work of people your age we wanted to show that what is written out of school can be written in school— and that what your peers can do you can do.

To get these examples we didn't run a contest or save top papers from years of classes or search out aces among schools and students. We drew from certain schools where teachers were willing to widen the range of writing and of learning methods. We felt confident that students writing from real experience and interest, and benefiting from workshop commentary from their classmates, would supply us with plenty of enjoyable material to choose from.

So in selecting from their work we aimed to make this, like any other good book, a pleasure to read. May their writing entertain you while indicating what you might do yourself.

Before each kind of writing you'll find some general directions. These are meant to give the main idea of each kind and to say roughly how to do it. The kinds of writing themselves are gathered into five major groups:

NOTATION (Taking Down)
RECOLLECTION (Looking Back)
INVESTIGATION (Looking Into)
IMAGINATION (Thinking Up)
COGITATION (Thinking Over and Thinking Through)

The words in parentheses are simply another way of naming the groups so that we have a couple of handles on each.

These groups indicate the different ways a writer turns up material and works it up into a composition. So each represents a source and a process for working with that source. The first group, for example, NOTATION, consists of writing down events and ideas more or less when they occur, as in diaries and journals. These are very important because things written down at first for yourself may be written up later for others.

The next group, RECOLLECTION, is based on memory. Shaping our recollections results in autobiography (author-centered) or memoir (other-centered). Memory is a vast, rich storehouse of experience and knowledge important for writing.

INVESTIGATION depends on inquiring beyond accidental experience by deliberately observing things, visiting places, interviewing people, and consulting sources of information stored in print and other media. This investigation results in new knowledge written as reportage and research.

For the material of the fourth group, IMAGINATION, the writer invents people, actions, places, and things by going in imagination beyond the actual firsthand and secondhand experiences acquired through recollecting and investigating. This results in plays, stories, and some kinds of poetry, which are ways of revising reality so as to illuminate it.

For the last group, COGITATION, the writer again goes beyond actual experience and factual information, this time by reflecting on them, generalizing from them, and relating them to each other to understand them better. This results in various kinds of articles and essays, organized by ideas, not events.

Within a group, the order of examples is meant to bring out connections and differences among the various kinds of writing so that they can make each other clear. You wouldn't necessarily write in the same order, sequentially over a period of time, and in any case you wouldn't have time to write every type illustrated. Some students can try some kinds, and other students other kinds. The main thing is to experience writing in all five groups and to understand some of the connections among types even though you won't do them all. In this way you can find out what sorts of writing exist, what each does best, which come easier or harder for you, and how you relate to each.

The organization of this book brings out how kinds of writing correspond to kinds of thinking. Whether or not you see yourself as doing much writing later in your life, you probably want to develop your thinking ability and extend your knowledge. A kind of writing is going on all the time in your mind as you experience things, recollect them, recombine them in imaginative ways, and reflect on them. By processing experience these ways, you're constantly making your own knowledge; it's part of being human. Writing gets your thinking outside and highlights it so you can become more aware of it, bounce it off other people, and take charge of your own growth.

Any material is fair game when writing is opened up across the whole range. At any moment, look inside, look around; stuff is everywhere. But don't count on remembering it all. Do what nearly every writer does—keep a notebook of possible material. You'll find it much easier to start composing if you have a notebook full of jottings on this and that—observations, random thoughts, dreams, memories, images, overheard conversations, story ideas, or the stray phrase that for some reason intrigues you. Writing begins with the discovery of subject matter you care about. You don't have to stare at a blank page and scratch your head. Store up *too much*, and work from a position of plenty rather than scarcity.

Knowing the kinds of writing and how they relate to each other is, of course, only part of the picture. The rest—the actual processes of composing—concern what goes on *inside* you as you think and write and what goes on *between* you and your teacher and classmates or some other audience. Writing is personal *and* social.

Take the *inside* part first. As a writer, you need to be conscious of what you feel and think when you experience, recall, or reflect on something. (Keeping a notebook helps you capture some of all this.) What's on your mind? What's under your mind? You can find out by taking a little time each day to sit still and relaxed in a quiet place, close your eyes, and focus attention inward in one or more of the following ways:

- Let your mind roam wherever it wants but witness it like a bystander instead of being swept away obliviously.
- Or try to slow down and perhaps even suspend the inner chatter and buzzing. What comes into your mind then?
- Or review the day's events. How do you respond to them?
- Or choose some subject you want to understand better, perhaps some problem you want to solve, and focus just on that by concentrating on some image or phrase or idea that represents it for you. Such a subject might be one that recurs when you try to still or witness your thoughts, or it might just be some situation, person, object, place, or idea that attracts you. Follow through in this way by giving full attention to whatever is already asking for more attention.

Inner material is not necessarily about *you*; it's what you think and feel about *anything*. It's the main source of what you can write about. If you learn to tune into it and cultivate it, you'll not only find writing easier and more satisfying but you'll probably understand yourself and your world better.

Now the *between* part. Unlike many writers who toil alone, you have ready access to an appropriate trial audience—your classmates. You and they don't have to be experts to help each other. And you don't have to play teacher. All you have to do is to respond as readers and listeners. If you can keep reasonably good track of what you're thinking and feeling as you read or hear a composition, you can help the author a great deal to know how close she or he came to the mark. In return, your partners will give you the same useful feedback before you revise so that you can benefit from a realistic trial before handing compositions in to the teacher or publishing them in some way. Most writers do a draft, try it out on whatever audience they can scare up, and then revise (usually more than once). Of course, your teacher provides very important feedback, but he or she rarely has time to respond between drafts as well as after the final version.

Here are several ways that members of a small workshop group can help each other with a draft:

1. Depending on the kind of writing and on other circumstances, you can all either read aloud your own drafts, read aloud each other's, pass around your papers to read silently and discuss later, or pass out copies to annotate as you read silently.

2. As you read or listen to a paper, think of a title for it and jot this down on a scrap of paper and compare later with others'. (The author should have a title but not place it on the paper.)

3. Let the author say what he or she wants help with or is wondering and worrying about.

4. Describe what you thought or felt at various points in the draft without necessarily advising.

5. Ask the author questions on what you don't understand or are curious about.

6. Play with other possibilities. Tinker. Ask the group creative what-if questions about someone's draft. What if things were changed around or expressed in some other way?

Working with classmates has other advantages too. Help can begin even before the drafting stage, when you're trying to get started. Telling a story to someone or talking over some tentative ideas can be useful ways to sort out your thoughts and decide how to proceed, especially if both you and your listeners ask questions.

While thinking of your workshop group as an immediate audience and your class and teacher as a still wider readership, consider as you write who else you might be addressing. Where might the finished piece *go?* What might it *do?* Scripts, for example, or how-to directions, are meant to be performed or carried out. Many other compositions, like stories and poems, serve well as material for rehearsed readings. Nearly all the types of writing in *Active Voices III* are publishable somewhere because they illustrate what can be found in various publications. A number of the selections in this book were previously printed in local publications, as indicated in the Acknowledgments. Consider local newspapers and newsletters and regional or specialized journals. Look and ask around. Exchange suggestions with classmates.

Now read and enjoy. See how some other senior high students have done kinds of writing practiced in the world at large. Try your hand and practice too. Be a writer among writers.

Notation

(Taking Down)

Journal and Diary

Writer's Journal

Keep a lightweight notebook handy and write down in it any time all sorts of ideas and events that interest you enough to want to save. Put in the date whenever you write in it. Carry your notebook between home and school as much as you can so you can write down things as they come to you—your reactions to events, your feelings and moods, observations of what is going on around you, stories you imagine, dreams, memories, lists and plans, and so on.

In this general writing journal you can store a treasury of ideas and experiences to re-run and make use of later. Some of this material you may want to read as is to certain persons, or let others read it on their own. You can choose what you let anyone, including your teacher, read.

Like professional writers, you can pick things out and re-write them—fill them out, change them around, and polish them up for others to enjoy in various ways. Putting a lot in your journal notebook will keep you rich in ideas and material to use for all of the other kinds of writing to follow in this book.

Journal Entry
Jaycee Hunter

March 17
At the rest home where I work, age is the "in" thing. After being there for a while, I have been dulled to the word *age:* it means nothing, just time. The aged are people, personalities, someone interesting to talk to. I know a ninety-five year young lady who gets up every

1

morning and plays the piano with some 100 songs she has memorized over the years. She can't walk but, boy, can she play.

I don't look forward to age, but it doesn't frighten me any more. The saying that life is what you make it applies all the way to the, well, finale of life. Some day I may take care of a ninety-year young man with a Mohawk haircut. Who knows! I'm just going to squeeze life for all it is, all the way to . . . the finale.

Journal Entry
Desiree Webster

December 8

Today's weather is pretty good. It's the first time in the past two weeks it hasn't rained off and on all day. *It's really strange: when it rains I always seem to be in a good mood, but when it's sunny or nice I get depressed.*

The rain has always reminded me of a new beginning or a renewal of life. I guess because it seems to wash away fog and dirt, and a rainbow always shows up afterward. Even though the rain makes mud and a large mess if you work outside it still it's kind of a renewal.

The sun, on the other hand, just sits there. It tans or burns you, but it doesn't seem to stand for or do anything. There's just this huge bright round thing that sits in the sky and soaks up water. The only interesting thing about the sun is that every 100 years or so there is a total eclipse and it's almost like night.

Journal Entry
Lea Rademacher

December 8

College is a scary subject for some people. This is due to the fact that they are not ready for it. They are not prepared to leave home and the security of familiar surroundings. To these people, college poses a threat to their happy, safe life. They are afraid that they will lose what they have. The possibility of losing a loved one while they are not close by upsets them. Possibly, they are afraid of losing a boyfriend or girlfriend. They feel that if they leave, their "spouse" will lose interest in them because they are not always there. Afraid that someone else will come along and fill in their shoes, thus taking away a life that one loves and cherishes. When a person thinks of all of this, and realizes that it is the reason that they are afraid of leaving, they can use this knowledge in order to put it into proper perspective so that they will no longer be afraid.

Journal Entry
Deanna Dunham

December 5
UFOs have supposedly been seen all of the world. On one occasion a man named Loyde D. Wrinkle had the experience of seeing a UFO. Loyde told the police about his experience, but the police didn't believe him. So Loyde went to a psychologist and was put under hypnosis. He started his story the same way as he did when he spoke to the police.

Loyde went on to say that he was in bed one night and he heard a weird noise and saw a greenish-colored light outside his window. He went outside to see what it was. To his dismay a space ship was hovering over him. The door of the spaceship opened, and he was taken inside. There, five female "martians" looked him over and went into another room. When they came back one of them had a gun of some kind. The female fired at him, and he was paralyzed.

Rewritten Journal Entry

Select an entry, or a portion of one, from your writer's journal and compose on the basis of it any kind of writing that you think will interest some other people. Expand or re-cast some idea, image, or event into whatever form seems appropriate—a true story, fiction, essay, poem, or script, according to the kind of value you feel the material has. Or if you are working within the framework of one of the four kinds of writing represented in the following four sections of this book, browse through your journal and select some entry that naturally lends itself to Recollection, Investigation, Imagination, or Cogitation.

[To illustrate the process, the following samples include both the original entry and the composition based on it.]

Journal Entry
Josh Bloom

Friday May 9
I was staring at my bookcase today—looking for inspiration and I noticed three books stacked next to each other which at first seemed

to clash. After gazing at them for several minutes, I realized that the only thing among them which clashed were their subjects.

It doesn't really matter how *Alice's Adventures in Wonderland*, a Pablo Picasso art book, and *Birdy* (by William Wharton) got on the same shelf, but it seems that it is only proper that they did.

Alice's Adventures in Wonderland is a book that is enjoyed by people of all ages because it is not a book for intellectual stimulation or deep thought analysis. Rather it is a book which was written for pure enjoyment. Lewis Carroll was able to preserve, all his life, his ability to imagine as a child does; and that is why the book is so successful.

Pablo Picasso was a man, like Lewis Carroll, who also was able to preserve his child-like creativity. Picasso wanted to express the simplicity and spontaneity which children show at the age of 5 or 6, when they are at the apex of their creativity. They want to express the world as they perceive it and are less concerned with attention to detail than with the expression of their feelings. This is why Picasso's works are so marveled at.

Birdy is the story of two young boys, one of whom becomes obsessed with birds and with flying. The ability of William Wharton to understand and convey the creative and complex mind of a child is awe-inspiring.

I used to have that creative mind. We all used to have that creative mind. It is at the moment we enter formal school that our child begins to disappear.

Until this winter, I had a birdfeeder on my windowsill. I would spend hours sitting at my desk—motionless and silent—watching the birds and letting my mind be drawn into the mind of one of these creatures. My mind would revert to that of a child and I was able to imagine and perceive things in a way I had not been able to since I can remember.

My mother told me to remove the birdfeeder from my window this winter for two reasons: first, she had a dread of all cats, and it made her nauseous to see the one or two cats that would wait in the bushes in the hopes of catching an unsuspecting bird; and second, the birds had a habit of relieving themselves on the side of the house as they flew up to the feeder.

Since I removed the feeder, I feel very empty. I can no longer see through the eyes of a child. I miss waking to singing birds at my window every morning. I miss a feeling of closeness to nature that I used to have. And I miss the moments of meditation and relaxation which the birds brought me every day.

The Day Before Graduation

JOSH BLOOM

When I leave my bedroom on September first, I will be leaving it permanently. There will be a time when I walk out my door that will be the last time I leave my room. I will wonder how many times I have walked in and out of that passage and whether it is an even or odd number because even numbers give me a feeling of comfort and completion while odd numbers tend to be erratic. My brother will creep into the room as mice infest an abandoned building. I will be leaving to sleep in a bed that sags to the floor in the middle, in a room that has been lived in by hundreds of students before me and does not reflect anything about them.

It is not only my room as a self-portrait that I will miss; it is my room as a part of myself, like the back of my hand. I have never counted the paces from the door to my bed, but I could walk the distance blindfolded as I do every night after I brush my teeth and turn out the light. When I am reading in bed, I see out of the corner of my eye an unusual-shaped spot on the wall near my pillow. It's dark gray but not black and about a quarter of an inch at its broadest point. I hit the spot regularly with the palm of my hand thinking it is a bug. I have been meaning to do something about it for years, but I suppose I can bear hitting it for a few more months.

And then there are all those little things that annoy me: the set of encyclopedias that all fit on one shelf but three; the almost invisible scratch in the birch and walnut chest I made at camp; the slant of the cornices that cover the shade rollers; the wheel in my swivel chair that falls out when I lean back too far; the stone in the fish tank that has never seemed in quite the right place; the desk lamp that flickers when the cord is knocked; the digital clock that clicks every minute and still keeps me awake at night; the cork squares that buckle from the wall in the summer because of humidity; and the one spot where the floorboards creek beneath the carpet which lies between the typewriter stand and the bookcase.

I have often wondered if the museum posters on my walls reflect myself or an image of myself that I want to portray. I just recently decided that all but one reflect my true likings, and I am going to remove the one that does not. That one is from the Kremlin exhibit at the Met from Moscow which "pseudo-cultured-I" dragged my mother through while both of us pretended to be fascinated when in fact we were probably both bored to tears. And in my room is an accumulation of papers of a lifetime, individually nothing more than busywork, but collectively equalling Knowledge, with a capital K.

My bookcase is probably least reflective of me directly, containing mostly my father's books, but *Birdy* is on one of those shelves and if it stood there alone it would sufficiently represent me. It was the cause of the birdfeeder that remains on my windowsill, and while it was one of only three books I ever read for pleasure, it was the best. As for the other books, they represent a part of me that feels a closeness with my father and in that way are reflective of me.

I wonder what the floor looks like by the wall at the side of my bed, onto which I have been brushing the nail clippings of a lifetime. I often wonder how many: how many pages I have scrawled upon my blotter, how many times the shades have been lowered and raised, drawers opened and shut; I wonder how many more months it will be before I stumble upon the recharger to my calculator which I haven't been able to use since I lost it a year ago. But besides all I think about physically in my room, there are the endless memories that every single remnant recalls, from the shriveled balloon hanging on the wall to the caricature of myself right near it. I see anger in the door I've slammed perhaps too frequently and tranquility in the ceiling fixture I stared at and daydreamed through for eighteen years. But covering the tie rack is a red gown and black square cap hanging from my closet door, and it casts a glow over the entire bedroom.

Journal Entry
Maxime Champion

January 8

The 20th century is probably the century the most important in the history of the world. The technology, the computers, the nuclear power and all kinds of things which are supposed to help our life becoming easy.

The twentieth century is also the century of the rock 'n roll music. This movement of all the youth to the rock 'n roll music is not even one century old. It's new and gives more answers than any other kind of music. It's made to go with our new kind of life, fast, too fast, with new choices, stress, drugs, etc.

That's one of the reasons why no one under the age of 25 is interested in classical music and I think that's sad.

The other reason is: they want to be different from their parents, they hate culture, they want an all different world, another world, their world. Music helps them a lot, the singers are leaders, heroes.

Have you ever been to a rock 'n roll concert? It's extraordinary and energizing.

Amazing because people accept and want drugs, wildness and sadness.

Music is like a mirror where you can see what people think, where you can see all the tensions and the problems a country has.

If you like an example: in the 60s it was an after war period, the whole world just went out of a long period of horror. When they went out of that everybody was happy of a new beginning. The music told us that.

I'm afraid of the world now because when you listen to the music we have, the future doesn't seem very bright.

The Match That Started the Fire

MAXIME CHAMPION

One morning in my French public school, the music teacher complained about "graffiti" written on her class-room door. Didier, a fourteen year old boy, laughed along with the whole class, but the teacher blamed him because of his school reputation. She ordered him to wash off the "graffiti," but Didier, knowing he wasn't guilty, got angry and started arguing. Jumping out of his seat in the back of the room, where all the goof-offs sat, he ran up to the teacher; they faced each other arguing loudly, and he picked her up by the collar and plopped her down on the desk.

The incident, although not a daily occurrence, does happen frequently in French public schools today. In France teenagers, representatives of French society, show a growing lack of respect for the establishment. The Rock and Roll movement was the match that started this fire of unrest. Music is like a mirror in which you can see the state of a society. You can hear a country's tension and problems in its popular culture.

World War II was a difficult period for my country, France; we lost about everything—people, honor, and hope. When the 50s came, the after-war period, people felt that something was wrong, that there was a feeling of hopelessness. Then came the Rock and Roll period, which isn't only a music movement but more like a life style. Teenage dress and hair style brought about an attitude that parents did not want to accept. This movement was a solution that might have led to a bright future. Instead of following national heroes, the youth were more attracted to popular heroes—movie stars as well as musical performers. Shortly after the war, French economy became strong again. The war still lingered in the minds of the older generation but it no longer affected everyday life.

In the late 60s, the students revolted against the educational system. Led by their popular heroes, they wanted more freedom in the way they dressed at school and their subjects and the teaching style. They wanted to think for themselves and to see both sides of an issue. Students felt so strongly that they marched in the streets and shut down the whole city of Paris. The popular leaders guided the young people's minds.

The results of the student revolution have been both good and bad. Students no longer feel so frustrated or inferior in regard to their education system. They have attained much of what they wanted, but they have also created problems. Student power has brought them responsibility, but it has also made them feel like kings, who don't always show respect to the establishment. The popular leaders created an anger that has led to a change in life style.

Anything that happened in France can happen easily any place else. It's just a matter of time. When you listen to the popular music of France today, the future doesn't look too bright. A popular French song by H. F. Thieffaine warns of the tensions of today's society:

> We are the mad fantasies of a computer/ With his blue eye scrutinizing our brain./ I'm looking to the needle going down in our skin.

Will the fire that was started by the Rock and Roll movement ever be put out?

Diary

Keep a diary for a number of weeks, making at least four or five entries a week. Allow ten to fifteen minutes to write down whatever seems important for that day or the previous one. This is meant to record events and how you feel about them. It can be general or you can use it to focus on some special pursuit or aspect of your life. Write with enough explanation so that you (and possibly someone else, if you want) will be able to understand it later. This kind of journal allows you to develop some subject a long way gradually without trying to write about it all at once and without knowing where you're going to take it.

You can invite others to read it as you go and give responses and suggestions. Select parts that stand well alone and present them in some way to others, re-writing if necessary. Or summarize some of it for others. Often the complete diary, or a slightly edited version, is readable and interesting enough to deserve an audience for its own sake, whether or not you summarize it.

Changing Expectations

PATRICIA BÖCK
[selected and edited by the author]

Tuesday, Jan. 1
Pressing problems going into the new year:

—Dad didn't take a picture of the Christmas tree

—I haven't got the energy to do my English
—I've gained 5 lbs.
—I've got a crush on John

Friday, Jan. 25
Tonight I had the dinner course of Key Club's Progressive Dinner Party at my house. It was fun—Scott is such a nice guy. We played Trivial Pursuit over dessert at Michelle's house. Big shot Mike Hathaway was actually in my house. I hear he wants to go to UCLA. It fits him, he reminds me of someone from *Animal House*.

Monday, April 29
Election Day (Friday) is quickly approaching, and I'm terrified. I hung up my stenciled posters that say "Vote Pattie Böck for Sr. Class Prez." I'm worried my speech is all wrong. I watched *Adam* on t.v., and I felt awful. I think the missing and abused children need help. Police only found Adam Walsh's head, they had to identify him by his teeth. His parents got some important legislation through Congress, but we need to do more. I have to somehow make a difference.

Wednesday, May 8
Well, I found out—I didn't win. Mom was supportive—but Dad was being real down and said, "You didn't win?"—like a question and a statement. I'm really glad about Leo winning though. He beat a really "popular" girl. His winning was almost like a revolution. He really deserved it.

Thursday, May 9
Last night, Shirley Chu died. I'm not sure from what, but I know it was a disease that she had for a long time. She was Class President last year and a cheerleader. I wasn't friends with her, but I feel very sorry for her family and friends. Now I feel dumb for being upset about losing the election; at least I'm healthy.

Saturday, August 17
Today I went to the library to check reference books on colleges. Stanford's my first choice, then UC Berkeley or Davis. I'm so afraid of not getting accepted.

Tuesday, August 27
Today I took Mom to the dentist—she had a wisdom tooth removed. It took 4 hours (she had roots in her sinuses!). A boring way to spend my last day of freedom before school starts, but I think she did appreciate it.

Tuesday, Sept. 3
Today is Dad's 49th Birthday! I lost 4½ lbs this week! My new jeans *don't* fit me, they're too big—Yea!

Friday, Nov. 1
Thank goodness this week is over. These college deadlines are

suicidal. In a way, I think Pete likes me. Karen says I should be more assertive. He thinks I'm domineering—oh the hell with him! I went to a Howard Jones concert with Karen at UC Davis. Fantastic!

Sunday, Dec. 15

Last night was the big AFS Christmas Party. Jeff and his friends D.J.-ed the dance. My house survived, but I'm not so sure about Mom! She keeps looking around the house to make sure there's nothing missing. I had a *great* time!

Monday, Dec. 23

Mom and Dad's 21st Wedding Anniversary! As usual, I didn't have anything special planned for them. It would be so much easier to get over my crush on Carlos, that cute freshman at UC Berkeley, if he were ugly!

Wednesday, Jan. 1

It's 2 am. Earlier this week my Mom bet me $100 to my $10 that Tio Jorge and his family were coming from Argentina on New Year's Eve. Well, she was right. At about 7 p.m. the Allens came. I thought it odd that Jimmy parked the car down on the street. Twenty minutes later the doorbell rang and I went to go get it. Meri told me not to get it—to let Dad do it. Right away, I knew something was up. And there they were: Jorge, Coca, Matias, Federico, and Natalio—all dressed up in Santa suits. Oh those crazy Argentinians! Later they showed me a picture of Dad when he was 18. He was looking in a mirror, and on the dresser was a silver tea set that had belonged to Grandma Yolanda. And guess what they brought me—a tea set! A family heirloom, and it goes to me! Matias is 17 and very big; he looks about 20. Matias flirting with Meri while drying the dishes (he in Spanish—she in English!). At about 2 a.m. our "surprise" guests went back to San Francisco in the silver s-t-r-e-t-c-h limo, with a t.v., bar, phone, etc. I am *so* happy they're here! Finally, some family at the holidays! Jimmy was his usual *rich* and gorgeous self. Meri is 25—she and Jimmy are getting married this year (after 4 years of "living in sin"!). Wow! what a night! Family I haven't seen in 10 years, and a motley assortment of good friends. If that's some kind of an omen, then it's going to be a great year!

Baseball and Related Matters

CAROLYN ROSEN

April 29

This is the first journal I ever kept (or at least I am going to have to keep). All my other attempts at writing down my thoughts on some daily basis were always abandoned.

Since this is supposed to have an over-all theme I've decided for that to be baseball. For a girl, that is a pretty odd thing to write about. Most other girls don't know a lot about the subject or it doesn't interest them enough to want to learn. I, on the other hand, have been raised to love the Yankees.

You see, I was seven years old when my father first took my sisters (not Kathy since she was too young at the time) and me to Yankee Stadium. It was August, being Pammie's birthday. The game happened to be a double-header *and* bat day. The Yankees were playing against Milwaukee and won both games. It was probably all these factors added up that made me take an instant liking to the game.

Perhaps I wouldn't like the game as much if my father didn't have season tickets to the games for the past six–seven years. At first, he had only two tickets, but when the Yankees moved to Shea Stadium for two years, my father then had four tickets. I remember how Lisa, Pammie, and I used to fight over whose turn it was to go to the Stadium with Daddy.

Anyhow, it was probably at my second or third game back in 1972 or 1973 when I first noticed and began to root for my hero, Thurman Munson. The way I first noticed him is kind of unusual. At the time, I used to watch the reruns of the show, The Munsters. The main character's name is Herman Munster. Well, when I heard the announcer say over the loudspeaker, "The catcher, Thurman Munson" I thought he had said Herman Munster. In any case, I started to root for Thurman. It kind of turned into an obsession with me. As I grew older, I was able to better appreciate his talents and ability. However, I will write more about him later in the journal.

Now, to get to the present-day Yankees. This past vacation I went to four games (and would have gone to more, given the opportunity). They were all really exciting, at least to me. I wasn't allowed to go to opening day but wish I had been. Eric Heiden was there to throw out the first ball. He sat very near our seats, also. The only consolation for not being there was that my sisters got me his autograph: TO CAROLYN, ERIC HEIDEN. They would have kept it had it not said TO CAROLYN on it. I tacked it up on my bulletin board. I guess it's almost as good as being there (though not quite).

Well, I have to go to sleep now. Till tomorrow.

April 30

Well, I'm not really in a mood to write right now, but I know that if I skip a day I will never be able to keep this journal properly. The reason I'm not in a writing mood is because I have a lot of problems (worries) at present.

Though the Yankees are not part of my reasons or worries, they didn't help any tonight. While I was struggling through all of my homework for tomorrow (including studying for two tests), I was listening to the Yankee game on the radio. Things went from bad to worse for them. In the second inning alone, they gave up six runs. Several times they had chances to score some runs, but they always managed to strand players on the bases. To give an overall view of the game, here was the situation in the ninth inning. The score was 7-4 in favor of the Orioles. By some miracle, the Yankees got the bases loaded with two outs. Who steps up to the plate but Reggie Jackson. Naturally, he breaks his bat and flies out to end the inning.

I really should not blame Reggie. The playing conditions were terrible and all the Yankees contributed to this loss. It's just that I'm in such a low mood I have to let it out on someone.

As I am writing, I keep looking up to think about what to write next. Every time, my eyes fall on my poster near my bed. I never tell people about this poster because if they knew about it, they would only kid me about it. (Of course, people who have been to my room know about it, but otherwise, no one knows of it.) It's a poster of Thurmon Munson. I got it about a year ago before he had died. He was most likely the closest thing I had to an idol. However, I would never (and still don't) tell people how I looked up to him. Being a girl and a teenager, having a baseball player who is not terribly good looking for an idol is pretty unusual. Most girls my age have movie stars, rock stars, etc. as idols. At least, I think they do. In any case, that's the reason I'm embarrassed about Thurman. It makes me different from other people and that adds to my insecurities about myself. Thurman, of course, is not the only reason I feel different from other people my age, but it all adds up. Whenever I tell my parents my insecurities and how I would like to change and be like some of the other girls my age, they generally say, well why don't you change then? However, I don't really want to change, or perhaps I'm just scared to. In any case, I always feel hypocritical about what I really want. Maybe I don't even know what it is. I do know, though, that I'm very innocent about the things people do, say and act. I get extremely shocked at times about how cruel some people can be to others. For this reason, I'm very sensitive and am hurt very easily. That's probably why I fear being different because if I am different, I worry about how other people think about me and the kind of things they will say to me. For instance, when I heard of Thurman's death, I broke down and cried. Some of the girls at my camp teased me for having cried and for even having become so attached to a person I have never met. That only added to the hurt I already felt.

Well, now it is really late. I have to get to bed. Will write tomorrow.

May 1

Today I am in a lot better mood than I was last night. In fact, I think writing things out helped me to better understand my feelings. I think perhaps that I might like to write about some of the memories I have concerning Thurman and the Yankees.

Probably the happiest memories I have concern the play-off and World Series games. After a twelve-year interlude, the Yankees had finally gotten another division championship in 1976. By this time, I was a true Yankee fan (perhaps fanatic) for around 4-5 years. I was so thrilled, and my enjoyment of the game increased considerably when I went to my first play-off game. That year, I ended up going to two of the three games played at the Stadium. The most exciting game for me as well as millions of other baseball fans was the fifth (and final) game. I remember feeling at the top of the ninth inning that we had won it, having a 6-3 lead over the Royals. Then tragedy struck. George Brett of the Royals hit a 3-run homer, which tied the score. Though things seemed pretty gloomy, there actually was some hope. Due up were two home run hitters: Chris Chambliss and Graig Nettles. As everyone knows, Chris Chambliss hit the very first pitch over the right field wall. Very dramatic, to say the least.

The World Series that year against Cincinnati are not very happy memories for most Yankee fans since the Yankees were swept 4-0. However, to me, they were very special. You see, "my" player batted an outstanding .529 for the series. This was the highest ever by a player on a losing team. (By the way, "my" player is naturally Thurman Munson.) I have always taken special pride and pleasure when Thurman would play or hit well. It was almost as if I had accomplished that achievement myself. Though I was a true Yankee fan (and still am), Thurman was the most important thing to me concerning baseball.

May 2

It's very late now but I know I should write. Today, a terrible accident occurred. My former seventh-grade English teacher (and now my sister's) was killed in a car accident. When I found out, I was shocked and very sad, but it was nothing compared to how I felt when I found out about Thurman. It makes me wonder what kind of person I am, for I knew my teacher well, but I had never had the opportunity to meet Thurman. Yet I was more, by far, upset over Thurman's death.

Thurman died on August 2 (which happens to be my mother's birthday). I was at camp, and on that certain day, I had just returned to my bunk following dinner when I was told. The girl who told me was a devoted Boston Red Sox fan so I refused to believe her. She told me to run next door and ask Abby (a girl who lives in Maplewood and is a Yankee fan) if it was true. So I raced next door and found Abby fiddling with her radio. I asked her if it was true and she said she didn't know and was trying to find out. I raced back to my bunk and began to fiddle with dials on our bunk radio. I finally located a news channel.

Then the announcement came over the radio: today, Yankee catcher Thurman Munson was killed in a private plane crash in Akron, Ohio. I fell apart and burst into tears. However, the girls in my bunk didn't understand my feelings towards Thurman. At first, they tried to comfort me. Then one girl said I was acting as if he was my grandfather or something and that it was kind of ridiculous since I had never met him and he didn't care at all about me. That hurt me a lot. However, I stopped crying, knowing the other girls agreed with her. For the rest of the summer I tried to never cry about him again, but he was always in my thoughts.

Even now, though, I still think of him every day, and being home where they understand me better I cry sometimes late at night or if I see him on T.V. when they are showing past Yankee years. This is going to sound sort of corny and stupid, but I sort of talk to him at times. By talking to him, I am able to get out my feelings. It is actually a type of self-psychiatry.

May 3

Today was an absolutely beautiful day. Thought I didn't do anything special, I did go outside to try and get some sun. At around 3:00 I went in and heard the end of a Yankee game which they won 7-3.

Tonight's topic is going to be superstitions. I am an extremely superstitious person, especially concerning the outcome of a Yankee game, test, and day. For example, when I go to a Yankee game the following occurs. First, I must wear certain clothes (the same going for days I have tests in school). If the first time I wear a certain shirt or shoe, etc., the Yankees lose (or have a really dreadful day) I tend to avoid wearing it again. Pretty soon, I know which shirts are lucky and which are not. Once we arrive at the Stadium we park in the garage near the Stadium (not for luck, but for convenience). However, once out of the car, I generally try to walk down the same staircase as always in the garage, and then out the same gate. I then must enter the Stadium through gates 6 & 7 (I think that's the number; however, I've been there so often I just know which gate it is). Once inside the gate, my father then buys a scorecard, gives me money, and I buy a large container of popcorn. Next, we proceed to our seats. We (or at least I) enter through entrance 13-11. An usher takes us to our seats (though we know the way by heart). In the box of 8, we own seats 5, 6, 7, and 8. I must sit in seat 6, with my father in seat 7. (He is also pretty superstitious.) Once the game starts, I then go through my little chants and sitting positions. If I am sitting in a certain manner and the Yankees are doing well, I try to remain in that position, even if after a while I start to become uncomfortable. As for my chants, I have them for some of the players when they go up to bat. My most famous one is a series of four "walk-em's" before each pitch when Thurman was up. (He himself had his own routine with hitting his bat on the plate, readjusting his batting glove, touching his batting helmet, jerking his head, and then swinging his bat.) Probably the most memorable case of superstition could be found in the first baseman (not a Yankee) Mike Hargrove. Before batting he would do a series of three menacing swings, step into the batting box, do some swings, and *finally always* tug (or hitch up) his pants.

I should start writing earlier so I won't always have to stop because I am tired. In any case, will write tomorrow.

May 4

When I started this journal, I was skeptical as to whether I would be consistent with my entries. So far I have made sure I do. Tonight, for instance, I have come down with a stomach virus of sorts which has made me very sleepy. I was toying with the idea of skipping the journal for tonight, feeling sick and all. However, I felt sort of guilty about doing it since I know I am well enough to write.

My sister was just up in my room and we were discussing numerous things, in particular school and Mr. Potts. It made me start wondering why such men as Thurman and Mr. Potts die at such a young age. When they still have so much to offer in the fields of sports and education. I guess I will never know the answer. I try telling myself that Thurman "was better off" dead since it was reported that he would have been paralyzed for life if he lived. But why the accident in the first place? Why do countries fight wars which only end in killing numerous people? Why did the Holocaust occur? I wish I was able to be given simple answers to these questions, but I feel I never will. It is hard for me to comprehend why a supposedly loving God would let these things happen. I also don't understand why *people* let these things happen. Why do people listen to and believe in such people as Hitler and the Ayatolla Khomeini? Why do certain countries feel it necessary to be the ultimate world power and thus wars result? Why do countries that have power feel it necessary to impose their beliefs on lesser countries when it sometimes only results in civil war for the less powerful country? In fact, why are people not able to get along with each other and establish peace? These are questions that I will probably never know the answers to. I guess there are a lot of things in life which I will never understand or be given a logical explanation. A lot of things just are, I guess. One cannot explain why some people are more fortunate than others, why they are more intelligent, have more power, more money, more happiness and good fortune. One can only wish that they will be one of the lucky few and live a decent life, possibly being able in their lifetime to help make life easier or better for another individual.

Now, I don't want people to think that I am this sweet, wonderful girl able to help or at least willing to help people all the time, for I'm not. There are a lot of times when I have only made life miserable for a person and even sometimes don't regret it.

Oh, well. It's late and I'm sick and should get some rest. Till tomorrow.

May 5

Tonight I don't have much time to write. It's late and I have to get to sleep because there is school tomorrow. I wish I had the time to really think about things now but I don't.

Since I am not going to be writing anything "deep," I might as well talk about yesterday's baseball game. The Yankees creamed the Twins 10-1. I would say that part of the reason behind the clobber was because for once the team had a unifying cause. You see, the game previous, the Twins' pitcher had thrown a ball very close to Reggie (Jackson). Well, Reggie naturally shook it off. However, yesterday Jerry Koosman threw two consecutive pitches right by Reggie. Reggie, of course, got really mad at the pitcher and then the catcher. He had to be restrained by the third base coach. The next thing he did was hit a long home run. All the Yankees came out and congratulated him. You just don't fool around with Reggie. Well, to show his support, our pitcher Tommy Underwood hit their catcher with a pitch (not deliberately, of course!). To make things seem more incredible, our catcher, Rick Cerone, hit a three-run in-the-park homer. Now, Rick Cerone is about one of the slowest players we have. To sum it up, I can only say it was a great game. The kind you would love to see (if it is your team that is winning). However, it was the fact that the whole team was so together for once. The Yankees are always being knocked down by the press, their feuds almost making front page news. Well, for once, it was their unity that did it. The only sorrowful note on the whole game was when I looked at the other teams. The American League team with the best percentage is the Oakland A's, who are managed by none other than Billy Martin. It is that kind of a thing that can put a damper on a good day. Oh, well.

Promise to write more comprehensive and coherent thoughts tomorrow.

May 6

At this moment I am in agony. However, I shall overlook my private sufferings, sacrificing myself so I can keep this journal on a daily basis. What, you say? Why am I in pain, you ask? Well, today I went through a very traumatic experience. That's right! I went to the dentist and had a cavity filled. I will only elaborate on the event by saying that before I entered that office I had not a pain in the world, and now I am probably near death (I feel melodramatic tonight), for if a tooth and gum could double over in pain, mine would be folded in eighths!

So much for the dramatics. I actually don't know why I am in the mood I am with a very difficult, major math test tomorrow. (Well, that got me out of my mood, sure enough.)

Tonight the Yankees are in Milwaukee, but since I didn't listen to the game I don't know the outcome, nor can I give a follow-up story on the new-found Yankee unity. Therefore, I thought I might write about some of my happy memories of previous baseball games which naturally mostly all include Thurman.

My greatest memory involving Thurman was the third game of the 1978 play-offs against K.C. That was the first game played at the Stadium (for the Series), with the two teams coming in tied 1-1. Now, during the play-offs and World Series, all season ticket holders get double their regular amount of seats—their original ones and the others together on the third deck. Well, with the seating that night, I was put in the upper deck on the third base side which made it possible for me to see my father since our season ticket seats are on the first base side, near the Yankee dugout. As it happened, my seat was very good. In any case, Catfish Hunter was pitching for the Yankees. The game started by the K.C. third baseman, George Brett, hitting a towering home run. He then hit two more home runs his next times at bat. Fortunately, though, the Yankees were also scoring runs but never taking the lead. During that game, there were also several questionable calls. (From my seat, which had a fairly good view each time, I would have made the reverse call.) I don't remember the order of the calls but they were the following:

1. Mickey Rivers (CF—Yankee) had apparently made a spectacular running catch, but the umpire ruled that the ball hit the ground, with the consequence that the batter got a double and a runner scored.
2. A K.C. Royal, who had just gotten a hit and was running to third for the triple, was called tagged out. From my view (this play I had the best view to make a decision), he was safe at third.
3. Lou Piniella (Yankee) ran home from second on a single but was called out at the plate. Again, he looked safe.

All those calls were turning points in the game, but in the end they didn't count. Here was the situation. It was the bottom of the 8th and Yankees up. They were losing by a run. A player had reached first base, and Thurman walked to the plate. The K.C. manager then decided to change pitchers and called in Doug Byrd to pitch to Thurman. Now, this pitcher was quoted before the game that the manager always brings him in to face Thurman and that Thurman always hits off of him. So what happened? Thurman hit a long, towering home run to left-center field. He killed the ball, for it went at least

420-450 ft.! He gave the Yankees the win, for they were able to hold on to the lead. The most exciting part about the home run for me, though, was when all the crowds of people were standing and cheering, I was able to look down and find my father, who flashed up a big smile and O.K. sign. I was so pleased, for then I knew that my father understood how I felt that moment about Thurman and how I have always felt about him. I hope before this journal is done I will be able to write about the letter my father wrote to me after Thurman died, for it was truly beautiful.

Well I have to go now. Will write tomorrow.

P.S. I just wish that I had had a bottle for my feelings about that game, for it just doesn't sound the same when I write it, though it does arouse the same feelings.

May 7

I have been trying to think about what I have written in this journal so far because we are to later write an essay based on something that stands out. However, though I do mention some aspect of baseball, there doesn't seem to be any unifying thought. I have written about my idol, my feelings about him, my memories of him, the factors around his death. I have also written about the Yankees now-a-days—their games, etc. I have further written about my feelings about myself and things that have happened that day in school, home, etc. If read as I wrote it, this journal doesn't seem to have a connecting train of thought. Oh, well, it is what I have written and I will just have to work with it as it is.

At present, last night's entry concerning my memories of Thurman has stood out in my mind. Just thinking about him can still make me upset. This sadness most often occurs when I just try to remember how he was before a game. I can picture him and his movements so clearly in my mind. He seldom took batting practice, probably because it was unnecessary. He was known as one of the best clutch hitters around. His batting was probably the best feature in his career. In any case, near the end of the other team's batting practice, the Yankees will come out in pairs and throw a ball back and forth. Well, I can remember pretty clearly Thurman throwing with someone. He is laughing and joking around. He is even jumping up every once in a while to exercise his legs since he has to crouch, being a catcher. As it went, he would continue this mood till when the Yankees would take fielding practice. I can even remember once when during the throwing time, he had to go into the dugout. On his way in, he would tease and joke with the other players, sometimes intercepting their throws. As it is, I like to remember him like that, for I could see how happy he was and how much he loved baseball. I guess it's from having seen him that way that the press remarks about him always hurt so much. Thurman was known to (and probably did) hate the press, for he was actually a private man. They would always pester him. However, I feel that in a way the press are punishing him for doing what he liked—being a baseball player. In other words, he had no right to be so private because of his choice of profession. I happen (I guess sort of naturally, for I always back up and argue for Thurman) to agree with Thurman about privacy.

Well, I have to go. It's late and actually I am pretty depressed from events that occurred today. Till tomorrow.

Oh, by the way, the Yankees won yesterday AND today! At least one cheering thought.

May 8

Today I am in an O.K. mood. That is to say, I am not terribly depressed nor am I terribly happy. My day was slightly cheered by the fact that my math teacher curved our test, for I received an A-. When she returned my paper to me, I actually could not believe it. I wish my father would call tonight so I could tell him. Presently, he is in Mexico City on a business trip, and he called us last night. Unfortunately, I was terribly depressed at the time, and I fear I only succeeded in depressing him. (However, I did tell him about the Yankees and Reggie, which made him very happy. He found it hard to believe that they beat Mike Caldwell, a noted Yankee killer.) I truly wish I hadn't done that now. For you see, my father then likes to be able to talk my problems out with me. I remember once that my father once called home from the business in the afternoon. During the course of the conversation, I told him how depressed I was. Well, when he got home, he was all ready and set to have a talk with me. However, by that time, I had cheered up some so we just talked about things in general.

My depressions are not only caused by events in school. I have a "friend" who frequently makes me look down on myself or worry over things. Whenever I tell her something exciting that happened to me or something that was really good that I did, she almost always either tops my story or tears my good thing pretty much to pieces. Furthermore, this year I have been sick fairly frequently. Since she is a supposedly good friend, I always call her about the school I have missed. She will always tell me how *she* goes to school *all* the time with a cold and a fever, implying I should not "pamper" myself. She has also told me a lot of my illnesses are psychological and that they are caused by my improper eating habits. As for the subject of missed work, she informs me that I have missed an awful lot, will never be able to make it all up, and that my teachers think it very odd that I'm ill so much and students and teachers are making nasty comments. I feel that almost anyone who is ill and then received the above information has reason for depression. With me, I am very work-conscious, and one time in particular I became extremely upset because I thought I would never be able to make up the work. Well, my father came home and had a long talk with me. After speaking with him, I was very cheered up. (I have a lot of these talks, most likely more, with my mother, also. The only reason I am not writing about them is because I felt I would concentrate on just one parent tonight.)

Probably the best display of my father's understanding of me is a letter he wrote to me at camp from Europe which I received around a week-2 weeks after Thurman had died. I feel like I would like to copy it just in case I was ever to lose it or it tears from handling since it is on air mail stationary.

[The letter, omitted here, ends with, "Walk him, walk him, walk him, walk him."]

To me, that was one of the most beautiful letters ever written by a person. . . . The letter displayed my father's understanding of me— my feelings, emotions, thoughts. For me, the four "walk him's" at the end were most significant, for they had almost become my private words for only Thurman. I would repeat them at the games all the time and even when listening to the radio or watching TV. I always felt that Thurman knew I was saying them, for I felt like he would always respond to them.

It's getting late, but at least I will sleep happily, for having reread the letter has put me in a nice mood. Till tomorrow.

Diary Summary

Write an account of the material covered by the diary. Eliminate the dates; summarize so that you blend things into one continuous whole. Feature what seems most important to you and what you think will most interest some audience you have in mind. You are free to cut and add material and to reorganize according to your purpose as you look back. Fit the length to whatever the main subject seems to require, and choose your audience accordingly.

The Things I Never Realized Within Myself

JENNY ENCINAS

In the diary I wrote I found that I wrote things that I would like to say aloud but never do. If I was confused or curious about something I would write it down as if I were talking to somebody. I mostly talked about school and my grades. I always worry about my grades so I talked about that the most.

I found that when I wrote things I only explained or talked about the "surface" of them. As I went back and read through my writings I found that the subjects I talked about were the subjects that are hard for me to talk about to people. Usually I never really said exactly how I felt. In a few I did. But I found it's hard for me to talk to people. I can't even write it down on paper.

I also found in my writings if I was in a fairly good mood I could write more easily. But for quite a few I would just be blank. I couldn't think of anything to write. When I'm in a good mood I talk more freely, say what I feel because it makes me feel better than holding it in.

In my writings I talk quite a bit about other people. I noticed that all I wrote about were the bad points. I think it is because I always keep these feelings to myself and I wanted to talk about them, but had no one to talk to because it sounds like I don't do anything wrong. But I see and look at my mistakes; the people I talked about act like they don't notice they are making mistakes.

In my writings I found that it's even hard for me to—well, I guess you could say hard for me to talk to myself. It was like I was afraid to write things down and realize that that is how it really was. I think of things to write, but when I get in class ready to write, sometimes I just go blank and have absolutely nothing to say. That's when I found my writings making no sense at all. I would drag things on, or change subjects real fast.

In almost all of my writings I talked to someone, not myself, but to someone that I wished were there, someone I could talk to freely. I was only able to do this sometimes because I knew nobody else would see them.

In some of my writings I wrote things that no one else would even expect to be interesting, but they interested me. I talked about boring things that interested me, things that I couldn't talk to people about because I have a different outlook on things. (Most things anyway.)

My writings helped me somewhat to open up myself and also to others. I'm glad we had these writings because I find it easier to realize what really goes on around me.

Recollection
(Looking Back)

Memories

Look around at your surroundings until something you see reminds you of an event or person or place from your past. Write it down. What does that memory in turn remind you of? Keep the chain of memories going. Write pell-mell as a sort of notation for yourself later without worrying about completeness or correctness. Get down a lot of material to choose from later.

With the help perhaps of partners with whom you talk over these notes, you can now go a couple of ways: one is to pluck out a single memory that seems to have promise and expand it by jotting down more details. A second is to look for threads or themes across a number of apparently jumbled or unrelated memories and make notes on the continuity or connections you now see.

Now compose a memory piece comprehensible and interesting to some audience you fix in mind. Use your notes, but feel free to go as far beyond them as you need to do justice to the memory or memory thread that has emerged. Starting to compose may trigger more details or more ideas about a theme. Try out a draft on partners and revise for a final version to print up with other memories by you or others, or deliver as a reading to some audience.

This activity may result in one of the kinds of writing that follow this one, or in a poem or essay.

[The notes are shown for only the first two examples, but the other memories were also composed from notes.]

Notes
Ian Phair

" Stay There, I'm going to call Mr. Castellanos, the administrator "

Stubborness

frustration   anger

Grey   (argument)   "You want to bet"

Al (head of sports equipment room)

"you're always hassling me"

Losing My Cool

IAN PHAIR

"Hi, Al!" I greeted our school's sports manager, the day after I had broken my arm. Al and I didn't get along; he refused to recognize the fact that I'm on the school basketball team despite the fact that I'm one of the tallest boys in school. Numerous times he has hissed viciously at me when I asked him to open the gym so that I could get my backpack. Anyway, I approached him unwillingly now and only because the coach had ordered me to check out my uniform and bag. Al started to jump up and down like an angry little monkey, screaming and screeching about how no coach would send a player by himself to pick up a uniform. I informed Al that on this point he was wrong and that although this might seem a bold and daring move, I had come to get my uniform—alone. Al yelled that I was being unreasonable. I apologized and again requested my uniform. Al hotly replied that if a player claimed he was sent by a coach the player must be lying; Al would happily bet money on this issue. Al asked, "How much money do you have?" Now it was my turn to jump around in a fit of anger. Shouting about his stubbornness, I stomped out of the equipment room as I called him a "smart ass!" I realized immediately what a mistake I had made. Al grabbed me by my coat and pushed me against a bag of basketballs. At any rate, I have an appointment tomorrow with my counselor to discuss alternatives to a three-day suspension.

Notes
Steven Weisman

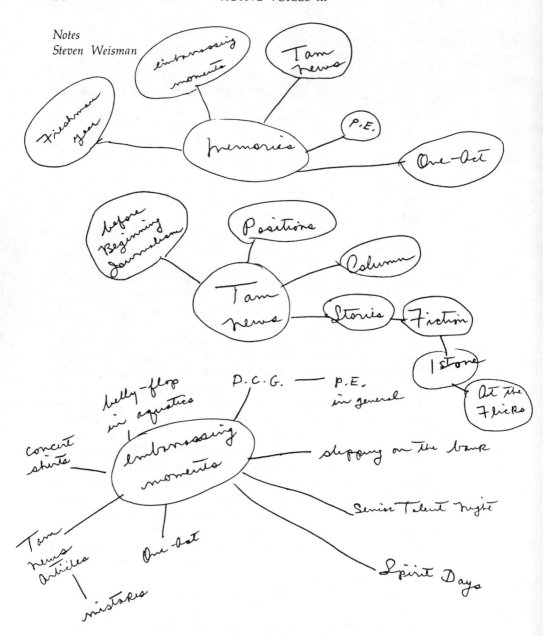

What Kind of Idiot?

STEVEN WEISMAN

    I stood atop the senior bench and watched the rain fall around me. Two students, unidentifiable due to their bulky jackets, the scarves that encircled their necks, and the umbrella one of them held over both their heads, descended the front steps en route to Kaiser Hall. I watched them as they stared at me out of the corners of their eyes, obviously wondering why I was standing there letting myself become saturated while cover was just a short distance away. Being a spectacle was something that, not long ago, I could not have handled. But, now, even though I received more strange looks and giggles from other passers-by, it didn't seem to bother me.

My mind drifted back to another rainy day, four years earlier, when, as a freshman, I had been in a slightly more agitated state. At lunchtime I had passed timidly through the mob that was grouped underneath the large tree trying to avoid the drizzle which seeped from the sky. Picking Safeway as my destination, I tried to make my way through the crowd, only to find it continually blocked by large bodies; swarms of people gathered directly in my path. In frustration I turned to the front lawn, a far more accessible route. Five steps down the grassy slope I felt my feet slip out from under me. In one instant, as my feet lost contact with the ground, I became painfully aware of what was happening to me and what that meant. My back and rear slapped the ground and I slid helplessly a few feet on the sodden turf. I did not even want to turn around. The comments soared at me like the wind that was arrogantly blowing me in the face. "Nice move!"

"Ahhh freshman!"

"Total freshman!"

"Ha! Your back is sooo drenched! What a burn!"

I winced in pain and humiliation while the rain, as if on cue, began to pour down on me.

Water, though seemingly innocent, always managed to have a little fun at my expense. If not in the form of rain then in some other, say a swimming pool. I remember the anxiety and fear with which I looked forward to taking aquatics in my sophomore year. The class was destined to be a nightmare.

Not having the ability to dive, I dreaded that section of the class in which we would learn how to. When the time arrived to learn the basic technique of this skill, I was forced into the swimming pool to make up tests I had missed on the breast and butterfly strokes. After decisively failing both tests, I made my way to the diving pool, where the entire class had just completed their first dives off the low diving board and awaited further instruction from the teacher. I thought the teacher must have been a sergeant in the Army because of the strict and orderly fashion in which he commanded his class. "All right, all right, listen up!" And then as he noticed me standing off to the side trying to be inconspicuous he muttered, "Why don't you just go ahead there, son." I felt as if I were going to be sick.

"O.K.," I reasoned to myself, "everybody can dive. It can't be that hard. Confidence. If I'm just confident and pretend like I know what I'm doing, I can do this. Eh heh . . . right."

The class seemed too quiet. They were paying too much attention to me. I struggled to maintain composure. I climbed onto the board, took a deep breath, ran forward, and with all eyes upon me, soared into the emptiness of open space. With my body in mid-air, I tried to let my head lead the way and to point my feet up in the air, but neither part of my body responded. I hit the water in the shape of an awkward curve, my stomach taking the majority of the impact and creating a loud slapping noise as well. Even under three feet of water, I could hear the people above erupting with laughter. In great physical pain, fully submerged in water, I focused on the drain at the bottom of the pool and wished it would suck me up.

Water was in my eyes, my hair, under my skin. It had started to rain even harder. As I stepped off the senior bench and started to climb the front steps, heading for shelter, I wondered, "What kind of idiot would consider minor embarrassments, like slipping on the front lawn or belly-flopping in aquatics, to be major life catastrophes?"

And as a friend passed me saying "Hey, you fool, what the hell were you doing out in the rain?" I wondered, "What kind of idiot would stand out in the rain for an hour?"

I thought, "My kind of idiot, the kind who knows that everybody's an idiot once in a while."

Ginger's Way

MIKE MEUNIER

I was sitting in my room watching TV when I heard a horn honk. When the horn persisted I got up and looked out the window.

My dog was doing it again. I pulled the shutter open and moved my chair so I could watch the show that was going to take place.

The car was a sky-blue station wagon, and my dog was sitting directly in front of it. The owner backed up a few feet and started to go around it. Ginger got up and moved directly in its path again and sat down. She tilted her head and let her tongue out a little bit.

This happened about once a month, or whenever my dog thought she needed more attention.

I myself never understood if she liked the cars, the driver, or creating trouble in general.

The car now backed about 30 feet and started around her again, blasting the horn, and the driver flinging his arm out the window.

She got up and again placed herself in the front of the car. Now the driver put the car in park and got out, advancing towards her in an aggressive fashion.

I guess you would have to see my dog to believe her. She is a pure bred Golden Lab, and can look very cute at times, as she did now.

Anyway, the man walked up as if to kick her, and she just stood there with her tongue hanging out, her head tilted sideways, and her soft brown eyes looking into his, and I guess she won his heart.

She called the jerk's bluff, and now he was trying to coax her over to the side!

I sat back down and began laughing. If only he knew.

I myself think my dog has a sense of humor and enjoys teasing people. She consistently does something like grab your left shoe while you're putting your right one on. She then stays just out of your reach until you corner her, and then she playfully rolls over and wags her tail so you can't really spank her.

She went with him and sat there wagging her tail until he got into his car again, and she then got in front again.

This time he got out and slapped her butt about 10 times until she moved and got back in his car. . . then she got in front again.

By this time I was rolling. He just backed up and started going, and this time she moved out of his way.

I don't think he would have stopped for her that time.

As he disappeared around the corner Ginger started wagging her tail and walked over to the neighbor's house.

A Past

ERIC STONE

It was a house reincarnated. My family moved out to an old, run-down, turn-of-the-century farmhouse, and it took to life. It wasn't cared for before, so it didn't care; but we cared then, and it returned the favor. We did everything to put it back on it's feet—painted, rebuilt, added on, and loved. It was on the verge of death before we moved in, a regular fire-trap of eighty years. It was still marked for fire when we moved in, but it never hinted a flame.

We were happy, but happiness never stays the same and always alters its shape. The house sensed it first, with long calm creaks of wood against nail in wind. There was trouble. My parents got in fights, and I saw my dad cry for the first time, just weeks after a new addition had been put onto the house. The fights only went on. They separated, and we moved into town and then out of town a year later.

The house was loved until we moved, and it knew we were leaving. Others moved in. They didn't love the house like we did so they moved out, two months later. They couldn't resell the house we'd loved. After three months on the sales block it burnt down, flat.

I heard by phone a week later, and part of my past was gone with it. The wood against nail had gone with our love and the wind.

The Stranger Who,
I Pray, Is Not Watching

KRYSTEN CRAWFORD

The phone would ring perhaps just once, or maybe twice, but never more. My stepmother would pick it up with an inquiring "Hello?" After, she would turn to those of us near and wave us out of the room. So I would leave. She would begin to ask questions I never wanted to hear, and I knew the woman on the other end of the line would answer those questions with words, luckily, I never had to hear. For a year and a half my stepmother worked as a volunteer counselor for the Rape Crisis Center.

I had always known the threat of sexual assault existed but had always managed to push the thought out of my mind. When my stepmother began her work and, eventually, I was told about a few of her cases, my awareness increased, but not enough.

Then one day, about a year ago, I was walking home from school. I had walked past a man who I noticed was watching me, but I had thought nothing of it. As I turned on to the street leading to my home, a car drove slowly past me and stopped several yards ahead. The driver turned and looked at me. I stopped. It was the same man I had seen watching me earlier. Instinct, I suspect, told me to turn around and head in the opposite direction. And so I did. The car did the same. Once again he passed me, still watching me, but slower this time. Frightened, I turned up a nearby driveway and watched as the car drove up the nearest road and disappeared. I waited about three seconds and then ran home. I had been lucky.

Was the man simply trying to harrass and frighten me? Or was he intending to attack? Had I over-reacted? The answer to these questions I do not and will never know, but I sense I didn't over-react. I believe my fears and suspicions had been valid.

I related the story to my family and attempted to portray the episode as nothing serious. I even tried to convince myself of that. But in the next few days I found myself terrified of walking to school or anywhere else alone. I was constantly looking over my shoulder and even running. I did everything possible to avoid walking alone.

A few months later I attended the self-defense classes for women at the Center. There, I met women who hadn't been as lucky as I. I was taught the myths and truths of sexual assault and given the evidence about how society has been conditioned to accept rape.

Several weeks later the Center sent two representatives to my school. For one week I heard more data, more facts, and more ways to fight back. I became disgusted at the way my classmates joked and laughed at everything told us. I also became increasingly frightened.

Everywhere I went, the thought of some man jumping out at me would follow. Everywhere I went, whether it was to the movies or the store, the thought of being attacked would flash for a fraction of a second in my mind even before I left my home. Everywhere I went I felt unsafe.

Now, at the age of sixteen, nothing has changed. I don't believe I'm paranoid. I'm just aware. More aware than anyone else my age, and I hate it. I hate hearing stories, or being warned to lock my door, or not to leave the window too far down. I want to fight back.

I am afraid that for the rest of my life, I will be frightened.

The Crumbling City

KAREN BABER

I wheeled my brother's ten-speed across the hot asphalt towards the dorm, his new home.

Marc going to college? How could the time have slipped away so soon? It seemed like just yesterday we were seven and ten and promised each other never to grow up. How could he break the Peter Pan vow?

I set one of his many cartons of books on the bed and glanced around the tiny room. Surely he couldn't prefer living here. The teddy bear I had given him years ago caught my eye and reminded me of our earlier days.

Being the only children of an unhappy marriage, we learned to care for each other and be the parents our mother and father couldn't always be. Marc had bandaged my scraped knees acquired from vigorous games of hop-scotch and even had given them an occasional kiss-to-make-it-better when they were especially painful. He taught me how to read my first book and carried me all the way to kindergarten the day the worms were on the sidewalk. The nights they'd yell at each other we'd sneak into each other's rooms and have long talks about chemistry sets and animal heaven.

We unpacked some sandwiches and started to eat our "last supper" on the leaf-covered park picnic table. It took three swallows of grape soda to get the food over the lump in my throat. The entire meal's conversation was awkward and unbearably tedious.

We'd never had trouble communicating before. People had always told us we were the closest brother and sister they knew. We laughed together through out favorite Neil Simon play and cried together on the train ride to Grandpa's funeral. On hot summer days we'd pack our dog and all our snorkeling equipment into the Datsun and head out for the refreshing Little North Fork River. I'll never forget the little boy who mistook us for a couple and was amazed to learn we were siblings. "You mean you talk to your sister?" he asked. Marc only laughed in reply.

During the long ride home the two of us would try for three-part harmony, which usually ended with a sour note and a fit of giggles. We'd open all the windows and invite the neighboring cars on the highway to listen to our personal renditions of all the Simon and Garfunkel songs we could think of.

I gave him one last hug and ran back to the pick-up where Mom and my stepfather were waiting. I didn't cry, but I felt the way I had the day our miniature mud city crumbled in the first rainstorm. Only this time Marc wasn't there to give me a consoling punch and say, "Nothing lasts forever."

Big Enough

NANCY FLAGG

After what seemed a thousand years of watching, I was finally going to attempt it. My parents considered me big enough. The skis looked gigantic to me, but the water was warm and smooth, so why not?

I remember the patient directions Dad gave to me as he helped me put on the skis. Dad said, "Keep the points of the skis out of the water, and keep them straight. Don't try to get up too fast, let the boat pull you a little first. Just relax and let Karen and me worry about the rope."

With a forceful pull the boat tore the rope out of my hands. I felt the water rush past my ears. Before I knew what happened, I was face down in the water with both skis off and floating away in opposite directions.

I tried again and again. Each time the rope was snapped out of my hands. Dad kept giving directions, and Karen kept putting on the skis for me. Resolutely, I decided that I was not going to let go of the rope no matter how hard the boat pulled. Gripping the handles as hard as I could, I gave the signal to go. My arms were pulled out straight with a huge jerk, but I held on. I felt the water rush by me with a tremendous force. Suddenly, I was on top of the water, with wind surging by me. I felt only a strange hammering on the bottom of my feet. Then I realized I was skiing. Amazingly, the wake of the boat looked gigantic, and the people in the boat looked small. Soon after, a small wave sent me into a sprawling nose dive, but I had water-skied on my sixth birthday.

Perception of Perfection

GREG SUTHERLAND

I remember walking into the store. There were so many people browsing here and there, looking like they were doing something important. In reality they had absolutely no idea of what they were doing. I noticed all these indecisive people as I walked. I knew where I was going.

The record department looked so far away, and I had so many aisles to maneuver, but I got there so fast. I guess that kind of thing happens when one becomes as excited as I was. I wasn't really conscious of my legs or any other part of my body, for that matter. I just wanted to get there.

I reached into my pocket, pulled out the bill, and glanced hurriedly at Alexander Hamilton's face to make sure I had enough. Satisfied with my financial status, I looked for the object of my obsession. It was not difficult to find, and I quickly pulled it out to gaze at it one more time before buying it. It just goes too fast. Walk in, find a record, buy record, walk out. I wanted to delay it just a little bit, so I stood there in the Fred Meyer record department for a minute or two, holding what many critics had described as one of the best records ever made.

By now it was almost 4:30, and I wanted to get home and listen to it alone. The cashier and I looked at each other for a few seconds. It wasn't exactly a searching, imploring kind of eye she gave me, but rather, she seemed to be saying, "Well, buddy, are we gonna stand, or are we gonna do business?" It was only a fleeting glance, though, and after that she smiled pleasantly, especially when tap-tapping the six dollars and ninety-nine cents into the digital cash register. In exchange for my Hamilton came three Washingtons and a useless Lincoln cent. Still, I walked out feeling extraordinarily blissful, and as the mechanical doors closed, the indecisive people lingered.

Home seemed so far away as I lowered myself into my Datsun, but once again, I got there surprisingly fast. I kept looking over at my passenger in the brown paper bag, frequently checking to see if it was alive, as if something horrible was going to happen to it. I drove slowly to prevent sudden stops. I wasn't going to let anything hurt it. As I drove up the driveway, I felt a sense of accomplishment. I had purchased the album *and* I had brought it safely home.

Almost immediately I was in my room. I threw down my sweater. I put my keys on the desk. Then, I looked happily at the brown paper bag, carefully slid the album out, and filed the bag in the trash can. I held the plastic-covered masterpiece for a moment, realizing I would never see it like that again, but I boldly ran my recently-clipped thumb-nail along the right hand side, forever cutting the album from its plastic womb. After throwing the static-filled covering away, I turned my full attention to the album itself for the first time.

I sat down next to my stereo to study the colorful cover. It consisted of almost fifty famous people, some instantly recognizable, some not, staring right at me. Some of the photos were in color, some black and white, and all of them were small and bunched up close together. There were trees and colorful flowers and a faded blue sky. And, of course, in the middle of it all, were The Beatles, standing directly behind a large drum containing the title *Sgt. Pepper's Lonely Hearts Club Band*.

I turned the cover around and found the lyrics to all the songs. I already knew them by heart, having listened to the album before on several occasions, but now it was mine. It was *mine*, I wouldn't have to return it to the library the next day, nor would I have just a couple of days to listen to it. No. It was mine now. This fact made me want to hear it even more. I carefully (Oh! How carefully!) took it out of the sleeve, and I held it.

There is nothing more "brand new" than a new album. The sunlight seemed to crystalize on the glossy black surface, and a burst of brightness shot up at my eyes, playfully blinding me for a split second as I moved the record in my hands. The grooves were clean and free of scratches. There was no dust or dirt to speak of. It was perfect; it was beautiful; and it was mine.

I guided it gently toward my turntable and placed it in its comfortable little cradle. I pushed the lever to automatic start and closed the stereo awning. I could not see my record any more, but that did not bother me. I knew it was there, and I felt safe because my record was safe.

Then I lay down on my bed and listened. Every word, every note, every beat was absorbed by my enraptured ears. It was a truly fantastic piece of work, and as I listened, I felt more and more like I was reading a classic novel. I noticed that the album cover opened up like a book, and that the record consisted of a group of songs that told a story. There was a beginning, a middle, an end, and an epilogue.

The story seemed to be about loneliness and how people deal with it. At various times, I felt happy, sad, relieved, depressed, helpless, and comforted. I listened to it over and over, and I was fascinated. How could a record have such an effect on me? It built up emotion like a movie; it got more and more optimistic as it went (with a few depressing parts scattered here and there) until the ending, which was so dramatic and so crushing. My mind was spinning. I felt as if I was in another land filled with yellow skies and scarlet red rivers. And then, suddenly and dramatically, it all ended in a loud and rapid flurry of cacophony that made me feel so small and lonely with the quiet universe swimming around me.

I was still on my bed when the needle put itself back. It was almost 11:00 p.m. I was at a loss for words or action. I simply sat up in my bed thinking and listening to the quietness. If I had turned on the radio or gone to sleep, it would have ruined everything. My heart was beating rapidly. I thought of the day's events. I tried to think about lots of things. But try as I might, I couldn't. All I could think about was *Sgt. Pepper's Lonely Hearts Club Band*. It was mine now.

Autobiography

Autobiography: Incident

Tell an incident that happened to you some time in the past, an incident being a specific occurrence that took place only once, on a certain day or mostly on one day. Think of who might want to hear or read this, and where or how.

Murderer

BRENT DEAN

I loved days like today, the warm sun, a slight breeze, and the sounds of all the other kids making the most out of recess. The day was made even better by my victory over the fourth grade tetherball champ. Now I was the hero of all my third-grade classmates.

As I sat on the lawn rolling in pride, three girls came over to me. One was crying, the other was about to, and the third was looking deep into my eyes. It really gave me a weird feeling. I asked what was wrong as the third girl sat down beside me. She explained that the chicks they had raised from eggs had fallen off the table and were going to die. She said they weren't supposed to be playing with them so they didn't want to tell the teacher. Since I was known for my way with pets I guess they thought I would know what to do.

They took me to the room where it had happened. When I got there they showed me the chicks, which they had put in a shoe box. All three were just about dead. It made me sick to see them twitch and jerk as the blood came out of their mouths. All I could think of was when my dad had to shoot a rabid dog. His words stood out in my mind. "No animal should suffer unjustly. Sometimes it's hard, but it's man who must see that they don't." I decided it was up to me to see that the chicks suffered no more. I went to the teacher's desk and got her scissors. We went to the field behind the school and prepared a grave. As the third snap of the scissors sounded, the only thing that kept me from getting sick was the fact that the chicks had stopped jerking; they were just lying there at peace at last.

The next day at school I was sitting in class when I was pulled out by the teacher of the three girls. She was really mad, but I didn't know why.

"You little brat, what's wrong with you, what in heaven's name would make you do such a horrible thing?" I didn't say anything, she had it all wrong, it wasn't a horrible thing, it was right.

"Why did you want to kill those poor little chicks, they never hurt you, why?" Kill? I didn't kill those chicks. I put them out of their misery. What's she talking about? Her yelling made me start to cry. She was turning everything around. Why couldn't she understand?

"You're a murderer, a murderer. Do you know where murderers go? They go to hell, and you're going to burn there for what you did." Why can't she understand? My dad knows what's right. If I could only tell her, but all I can do is cry, and listen.

"A murderer, that's what you are, a little murderer."

One More Chance

LEROY BAKER

It was my second year living in the Big Apple. I was only ten. We had come from Georgia. It was real nice coming to a city with so many good things to see—the Statue of Liberty, the Empire State Building, the Twin Towers, the United Nations and, most of all, millions of people. It seemed like everyone was in a rush to get somewhere.

My first day of school was a real drag. I had thought all people just spoke one language until I found out I was wrong. I was real scared. I didn't know what to say or do. In a couple of weeks everything turned out exactly right when I got used to the school.

One night my mother was making a cake but didn't have any frosting, so she sent my sister and me to the store. I know my sister was scared to go out so late. I was a little afraid too.

Then it happened. These two boys jumped us, but I wasn't about to give up the money that my mother worked hard to get. I began fighting like there was no tomorrow. My sister started crying and ran into the store.

The owner of the store came out, and one of the boys pulled out a gun and fired it. I really don't know how he missed. He was only about seven feet away. It was funny because I thought it was a cap gun. I never told my mother because I know she probably would have had a heart attack.

One thing I found out is that, living in New York, you always have to be prepared day or night, inside and outside your house.

Brother's Story

PHALLA KEN

I am Cambodian. I come from Cambodia. I left my country because of war. I love my country. I always dream, and when I put my head on the soft pillow tears come down over my cheek. I miss my country, I miss my people, I miss my place where I used to live. I can't forget what happened to my life during the war. I miss my brother very, very much because he saved my life one day. I have been separated from him for ten years now.

In 1975, during the Communist regime, my life was very bad. One day the Khmer Rouge separated me and my brother from my parents to live in the young team far away from the city. They wanted my brother, me, and the others to work for them. They wanted me to work from 4 a.m. to 11 p.m. They just gave us a little bit of food to eat. When I picked my food I cried.

One day my brother and I were very hungry because we didn't have food for two days. So we tried to find something to eat. In the night time around 12 o'clock, my brother woke me up and he said, "Let's go to find something."

"What are you going to look for?" I asked.

"We are going to the field to pick some rice," he said.

I was afraid. I said, "We don't have much time, brother." He pulled my hand and ran to the field.

It was very dark. I couldn't see anything, so I didn't know where the Khmer Rouge were. When my brother and I reached the rice field, we didn't know that a Khmer Rouge was waiting there. We picked the rice and put it in our pockets, and I heard the sound of the gun right behind me.

I turned over. I saw a Khmer Rouge standing and pointing the gun to my head. He called me and my brother to come out.

We were really afraid. Our bodies were really shaking. He told us to sit down, and he walked around. We didn't know what he wanted to do. He walked behind me and hit me over my neck and knocked me down with his gun.

My brother jumped over him and punched him on the face and then the gun fell from his hand. My brother picked up the gun and hit him until he died. My brother put water on my face and carried me back home.

Two days later my brother was very worried about killing the

Khmer Rouge, so he ran away without telling me a word. I miss my brother so much and I don't know where he is now. I always loved my brother but after this incident my love for him grew even more. I appreciated his bravery and brotherly love very very much

Wonder Woman Strikes Again
VICKI BILIK

It was Monday, the first day of kindergarten after Easter vacation. School had gone well that day. I arrived early that morning with a little baggie full of left-over jellybeans in my lunch and a complete repertoire of stories for my friends, ranging from what the Easter Bunny brought me to the egg hunt in my grandmother's backyard.

The day had gone well. I had convinced all my classmates that I had received the biggest Easter basket of all of them, and I even succeeded in trading a mere two jelly beans for an entire marshmallow bunny. I was shrewd and unfeeling in my business affairs. So, there I sat in front of the school waiting for my mother and contemplating the day's victories. All of a sudden, a sparkle caught my eye. I looked down and there they were, my brand new, black, patent leather shoes, the pride of Miss Bradey's kindergarten class. I had got them to wear on Easter Sunday along with my brand new dress. I was so proud of them.

As I sat there admiring my prized posessions, I felt a shadow fall upon me. I looked up and there was Jeffery Wilson. He thought he was so cool just because he was in first grade and I was only in kindergarten. For absolutely no reason at all he looked down and sneered.

"Those are the ugliest shoes I've ever seen!" Then if that insult to my precious shoes wasn't enough, he leaned over and *spit* on them.

I felt the tears rush to my eyes, but I held them back. I wasn't going to let that beast know how deeply he had hurt me.

Suddenly I became aware of something heavy in my right hand. Of course! My Wonder Woman lunch box! Wonder Woman wouldn't let me down. I reached my right arm back and then swung forward, Wonder Woman hitting Jeffery in the face with all her might.

"That'll show that creep!" I thought.

Just as I watched Jeffery go crying into the boys' bathroom, my mother pulled up in the station wagon. I got in the car and relaxed against the seat. Defending one's honor is very hard work, you know.

Now You See Her, Now You Don't

RANDY ROCK

When I was just a little kid around the age of two or three, I went everywhere with my mom. On the day I best remember the two of us were going to a big store, and my mom was shopping for clothes for herself. I found this really boring and was tempted to wander around but didn't want to get lost.

Then I found something I'd never seen before. It was a mirror over by the dressing rooms, but it was not an ordinary mirror. This mirror was one you could examine yourself in to see how you look, and it had a whole bunch of mirrors that moved. At certain angles you could see many images of yourself. I thought this was all neat and forgot all about my mom.

I was having fun seeing about a hundred or so of me and moving the mirrors back and forth making different ones appear. I discovered I looked pretty cool walking into myself. What an illusion as I could now see my mom's reflection in there too along with all mine. I thought how cool it is to be able to play around while keeping my eye on my mom so I wouldn't get lost or left there. So I was watching her in the mirror when she got up and left in about 200 different directions.

I turned around and she was gone. Then I ran around the corner and nothing, then around the other corners and still nothing. I looked everywhere close by and found nothing but people who looked like giants to me then. I went back to the mirror and where she had been and I couldn't find her anywhere.

Then a thought started to go through my mind. What if my mom left and went home without me? What if she forgot all about me and I never . . . . got home, if I didn't start to look all over for her. But if I looked somewhere else and she came back looking for me and I wasn't there she might not know where I was and we wouldn't be able to find each other, or when she did she might be mad and I might get into trouble.

Well, as I was thinking of all this I climbed up on a nearby chair and sort of went into a state of hypnosis and was about to doze off when all of sudden, "Come on, it's time to go home" was blasted in my ears. It startled me, but then I was glad to see her even though she was laughing at me for jumping in the air off the chair. Then we were walking out the door and I asked her where she was and she explained that she was paying for things and now they were ours.

Well, I was certainly not going to let her get off with leaving me there all alone and not have her buy me something. So as usual I had her buy me something to eat, and since it was summertime the best thing I could think of was hitting A&W Drive-In on the way home. So I put down a hamburger and then an ice cream cone. What an adventurous day I thought as I sank my teeth into my ice cream cone, back in my cheerful mood again.

Money

THO NGUYEN

Would you believe that I had the chance to be rich, yes, very rich when I was only nine? It is hard to believe but it is true.

Like other boys, I always wished to be rich, healthy, talented . . . just dreams. One night, I fell asleep and dreamed about having some money. About eleven o'clock, many things like books and notebooks seemed to fall on my bed suddenly. I woke up immediately, and money, yes, money, was all over my bed. I looked around right away; nobody was in the room but me. Very quickly, I wrapped those bills—later, I found out they were about a half million dollars—in my blanket and then ran to my dad's room.

I knocked on the bedroom door and got no answer. After a while, I dared to call him and said that I wanted to talk to him. He answered me that this was not the time to talk and he'd "kill" me if I did not go back to sleep. I then got angry and ran into his room and threw the blanket filled with money on his bed. I know that you can imagine how surprised he was at that time. Then we stayed up almost all night, my dad and I.

The next morning, I went to school in a daze. When I came home, my dad told me that he had already returned the money to the neighbors. He also told me that they were business people who didn't want to pay taxes to the government and wanted to hide their money. Those people stuffed their illegal items into my house in the little holes under my roof; the money then dropped on my bed. My dad told my neighbors that they had to change; if not, my dad would tell the police the truth. My dad was a most important person who was respected by those neighbors. Finally, they changed their business and became good common citizens of our nation.

Neither Here Nor There

AIMÉE O'LEARY

The elementary school dance was to take place in three days. My best friend Julia and I were discussing the dresses we planned to wear. Julia proclaimed that she was positive that Mike would ask her to the dance, and I was inwardly hoping that my secret-pal gifts were having an effect on Jay so that he'd ask me too. Every year our Valentine's Day dance was an event that we girls at the Cambridge Heights Elementary School talked about endlessly.

The commotion surrounding me was all part of the ritual. All we girls were planning our outfits for this formal sixth-grade affair. We were typical girls hoping to get asked by our dream boys. Lisa Heckle approached us and bubbled, "Hi guys! Tell me all about your dates! I'm going with none other than Jim O'Neal! Have the two of you got dates?" Fortunately, before we could answer, Mrs. Arellanes came in, and our conversation abruptly ended. Julia and I breathed sighs of relief at not having to admit to Lisa that we had no dates.

While Mrs. Arellanes took attendance, Julia voiced her thankfulness: "Aimee, Lisa would have told *everyone* that we were dateless!" I nodded in agreement. After attendance was taken, Mrs. Arellanes announced, "We won't be collecting homework today; instead, we'll be seeing a movie about civil rights."

Instantly, the classroom roared with excitement. Movies were special because we got to see them with all the other sixth-grade classes. Mrs. Arellanes rapped on her desk for order and explained to us that the film concerned civil rights and the struggle that some people had to go through just to get them. She said that the film was in remembrance of Martin Luther King Jr.'s birthday.

As Mrs. Arellanes talked, students turned to look at Ruth, a dark-skinned black student, as if to monitor her reaction. I stiffened instinctively, knowing that they would turn to scrutinize me next, since I was the only other black student. I felt their eyes boring into my back, and I blushed hotly, hating my pale yellow skin color, and embarrassed because they had noticed it.

Mrs. Arellanes instructed us to go quietly to the multi-purpose room and sit at our assigned sections. I rose from my seat next to Julia, now recovered from my shame. Some of our friends walked with us, and as they giggled about one of the boys in our class, I saw Ruth walking alone with her head proudly in the air.

I had never liked Ruth. Unlike me she wasn't bright, and everything about her was stereotypically black; she had kinky hair that stuck to her head like a pack of wool and a jutted jaw filled with buck teeth which were engulfed by protruding, full lips. She was far ahead of the rest of us in physical development and she always smelled of a heavily musty scent. She didn't fit in anywhere, and her isolated presence made her all the more noticeable. Whenever people spoke of her, I became embarrassed and uneasy.

Julia cut into my thoughts by asking where I wanted to sit. I shrugged indifferently and she motioned for us to sit in the back. We sat down amidst the amicable chattering of friends and got comfortable. The multi-purpose room soon darkened, and it became virtually impossible to see through the blackness. Nevertheless, we searched the crowd for familiar faces. As I strained to look around I saw Ruth sitting alone at a table.

She sat staring at the blank movie screen. Feelings of guilt that I didn't understand stirred deep inside of me. I dismissed them angrily: Why did she always have to sit alone looking so self-satisfied? What made her so wise that she, too, couldn't wish that she were blonde and blue-eyed? Instead, she always sat proudly alone, never pretending for one minute that any white boy was going to ask her to the dance or to be his girl. She seemed to be laughing at me—at my ignorance in believing that I could, through self-denial, make the color of my skin irrelevant.

As she sat stoically with her lips pressed firmly together, I imagined her jeering, "No matter how white you think you are, no matter that your momma's white—you always gone be black to them."

I hated Ruth intensely at that moment. I wanted to fly at her and slap her shiny black face so that she wouldn't think that she knew so much—she didn't know anything.

The movie came on then. It showed King and black people marching through the streets arm-in-arm by the hundreds. It pictured policemen beating them murderously without hesitance. In sharp contrast, it showed churches full of black men, women and children coping with racial hatred as best they could. The narration on the movie said that King had been arrested hundreds of times, his home firebombed, his family threatened—all because of his fight against racial injustice. The film depicted the sacrifices of black people from imprisonment to the pain of physical violence and death. I saw the strength of a race in their willingness to die for equality.

I have never in my life felt so much shame. For years I'd denied my blackness, thinking that if I ignored my color, whites would ignore it too. I'd expected to be accepted as white if I projected myself as being white. I had channeled the frustrated energy of suppressed self-hatred into despising the black race; as a result, I'd wanted no part in their heritage. Suddenly, my pride wasn't in my genetic whiteness, it was in my distinctive blackness.

I sat rigidly in my chair, the hardness of the seat pressing into my back. Forcedly, I turned to look at Ruth. She was no longer the defiant girl I thought her to be. She slumped in her chair, her body shaking, tears flowing freely and unashamedly down her face. I wanted to reach out to her, to accept a part of myself, but I couldn't move. I felt that I was trapped in a mold with no freedom of movement. Each breath I drew became increasingly difficult. Thick, stinging air filled my lungs suffocatingly. I wanted to bolt out of the door into the cool security of the mid-February morning, as far away from this threatening situation as possible.

We should have comforted each other in some way; a simple meeting of the eyes would have been enough—words would have been too burdensome—but I sat there stupidly, afraid that if I moved, my white classmates would stare at me.

Instead, I wept, partly for Ruth, but mostly for myself. You see, I knew that tomorrow I'd be pretending again—talking with Julia about the dance, and how I knew I would get asked. Like before, if ever my fantasy was endangered by my pretend boyfriend calling me a "nigger," or a snobbish girl teasing me about my afro, I'd put on my mask and hide behind the barrier it conveniently made between me and my classmates. I'd push the memory of today aside, desperately trying to erase my blackness, knowing all along that I couldn't be a whole person until I was strong enough to face my dual identity. My problem wasn't just accepting that I wasn't white—it was realizing that I wasn't black either, rather that I was somewhere in the gray middle.

Autobiography: Phase

Tell what you did or what happened to you during a certain period of your life covering months or a year or so— some phase. Allow plenty of wordage to do justice to both what happened and what made it a phase, that is, a period having its own beginning, development, and end. This could become an installment in a full-dress autobiography comprising all the phases up to now, or it could be offered separately.

Making Do

DOYA TENIGIETH

As a child living on an Apache Indian Reservation, I had a lot of problems, but in recent years these problems have been solved. When I was only a child, my parents forced me to assume big responsibilities. I am the second to the oldest in my family. I have an older brother Ricky, a younger sister, Sue, and two younger brothers, Paschal and Fitzgerald. Both of my parents were heavy drinkers. Whenever my parents got paid, they spent every cent they made at the nearby bar.

Because my parents would waste their money on liquor, we would always be broke. The electric company shut off our lights, so we had to use candles or go to bed early. With hardly any food in our home, Ricky would hunt for fish, birds, squirrels, rabbits, or some wild turkeys. Even if it were winter, I had to cook outside because the stove and the oven didn't work. Ricky always chopped wood for the fireplace so we could keep the house warm. Sue, who was about seven, would watch three-year-old Paschal and one-year-old Fitzgerald. Because we had no milk for Fitzgerald, I would make him some wild tea to drink. Because we had no money, I had to wash our clothes in the river. It took a long time to dry the clothes on a winter day, but somehow we managed to keep ourselves and our clothes clean.

My parents would be gone for a couple of days after each payday. When my folks came home drunk, my Mom usually would have bruises all over her body, and my Dad would have scratches on his face. If I didn't take care of my brothers and sister, I would get whipped with my Dad's belt. If Ricky didn't bring home any meat, he would get whipped badly by my dad.

One time Ricky went to the Bureau of Indian Affairs to talk about this situation with a couple of social workers. They sent Sue, Ricky, and me to an Indian Boarding School, while Paschal and Fitzgerald went to an orphan home. A month later, my uncle Chris decided to take care of Paschal and Fitzgerald, and the children were then released to him. After eighth grade graduation, I applied for the Indian Placement Program of the Mormon Church. On this program, I would stay in a foster home.

Right now my sister and I are on Placement. My sister is in Ridgecrest, and I'm at Santa Barbara. Ricky dropped out of high school, while Paschal and Fitzgerald are attending school on the reservation. We are separated from each other now, but I am sure all of us will remember our youth and the kind of struggles we went through. The problems of my childhood are solved, but I am afraid that they will remain in my heart forever.

Weekend Morning

DIA DUSETTE

The alarm, a shrill siren assaulting me every morning, wakes me at 5 a.m. sharp. I am instantly up and running toward the gleaming surface of the refrigerator door. Armed with yogurt and my ice-skate bag, I crawl into my sweats, closing the gate behind me. I jump into HER van, banging my head. And, at the uncivil time of 5:15, we are off and heading toward two hours of physical torture.

The ice-skating rink's lights shock my heavy eyes as I uneasily view the newborn-smooth ice. Three familiar figures are already at the well-worn "barre." I wordlessly join them. We make a motley crew, four half-asleep girls, as we go through our morning routine. Yet, by the end of "pliés" our muscles are warm and graceful. Each girl views herself in the mirror, concentrating, as SHE raps offending limbs that ruin the "line."

In ice-skate dresses and skates, we dutifully trot out onto the ice twenty minutes later. Absolute silence, intended for concentration, pervades the rink as we trace identical figure eights, marring the ice's smooth surface. Small mistakes, in timing or distribution of weight, are easily heard against the rhythm of others' clicks and scrapes. Eventually the boring and time-consuming figure eights are over. We relax, in an uncharacteristic lack of grace, for the five minutes SHE has allotted us. Candy bars and quick energy food disappear into our energy-starved cells.

Then the music blares from the crackly speakers as we draw numbers. Pulling second, I resignedly go to the corner of the ice to practice individual moves. Ten minutes later it is my turn to take the ice. My music blaring, I take a few practice laps to warm up. SHE starts the song over, pulling a scratch across the record. My mind is wiped clean and blank as I run through the memorized routine: prelude to jump, jump, and smooth landing as my head drops back and my legs pull me into a sit spin. It is as though I am experiencing each move for the first time. The absolute rightness of the move fills me with a sense of peace and an unbelievable sense of pride.

Out of breath already, I dread the next five routines. My elbow, red and aching, is a persistent reminder of what even a "minor" fall can accomplish. Even the most well rehearsed move can result in disaster, during a moment of inattention. Every jump, spin-turn or twist is accompanied by HER rasping voice calling out corrections, improvements, and, very seldom, praise.

At 7:45 I crawl into HER van that serves as a daily schoolbus. Cleaned up and dressed in schoolclothes we look like a normal, though unusually alert, group of students. I fly into class and my seat as the tardy bell sounds. Mumbling good mornings to my classmates, my eyes grow heavy. The last of my sugar-high leaving, my muscles are drained of energy. My head drops to my desk, at its customary time of 8:07, and the voice of my teacher drones through my dreams.

* * *

My dream rudely slips away. It is 5:30, half an hour past the usual beginning of my morning drills. I struggle to get out of bed. Reality entering my brain, a tear winds its way down my face. It has been over four months since I last skated, but a two-year habit is hard to break. I roll myself back into my blanket, pressing my useless cast-encased leg against my body, and fall into a deep, dreamless sleep.

The First Time

ANITA FRONEK

There's a first time for everything. That pretty well summed up the night Amy, my best friend, and I went to a party—my first drinking party. I felt a little funny about being there, but when the drinks were passed around, I had my first beer. Then a second and a third, and before I knew what had happened I realized I was drunk—for the first time in my life!

Amy and I had to be home at 1:00 a.m., because we had told our parents we had gone dancing at the local disco and that's what time it closed. Both of us didn't drive yet, but a friend drove us home. On the way I got us lost. Since I didn't drive I wasn't too familiar with the streets, and that combined with the drinks, confused me for some time before I finally recognized a street I knew and could direct the driver to my home.

I was embarrassed by the whole situation, but what was worse was the fear. I was scared to go home because I didn't want my parents to know I was drunk. I tried to imagine how they'd react, but I couldn't. The whole situation was beyond anything I'd ever contemplated before. Another first, but just the beginning.

I wasn't at all surprised to see the lights on in the house, when we finally pulled in at 1:30. But the reminder that my parents were waiting inside paralyzed me with dread. I'd have rather stayed lost.

I did say goodbye and forced myself out of the car. By the time Amy and her friend were backing out into the street. I was closing the door. In the few minutes it took to lock the door and turn out the light, I had decided to play things cool. So I faked a relaxed, casual "Hi" and quickly went to explain why I was late. When they accepted that without comment, I felt a little more secure. So far so good.

They asked about the dance and I gave them a complete report filled with descriptions and anecdotes. They sat and listened. My plan was working.

"Were there a lot of guys there?" Mom asked.

"Yeah," I said keeping the voice steady.

We talked a little longer on the details of the evening. But I stayed across the room so that my breath wouldn't give me away. A few minutes passed before I said goodnight and headed for my bedroom with an exhilarating surge of relief.

For the first time since my childhood, I had lied to my parents and had gotten away with it. Or had I? As I lay in bed waiting to calm down enough to drop to sleep, I kept replaying the living room confrontation over in my mind. Did Mom and Dad suspect the truth? Did they know I'd been drinking and just let it slide? Not likely.

But was my act really good enough to fool them? Or was it just that they wouldn't expect me to do anything like that? I fell asleep still wondering. I just couldn't be sure.

The next day, away from the emotion of the experience, I decided my parents didn't suspect. I did get away with it! That thought gave me an unusual feeling of satisfaction—a feeling of freedom. But at the same time I felt a twinge of guilt about doing something my parents wouldn't approve of and then lying to them about it.

However, my uneasiness wasn't enough to keep me from going to another drinking party again the next week and the week after that. Soon the partying and drinking became a regular part of my weekly routine. And so did the lies to my parents.

The pattern continued for months with never a clue that my parents suspected a thing. I'd lie about where I was going, who I was with, and what we did. By the end of my 8th-grade year I was confident in my ability to deceive my parents.

Then came a night when I was too drunk to go home. But I had to because it was a weeknight and I had school the next day. I called my mom up and asked if I could stay a little longer at my friends. It was already 10:00 p.m. and I knew what the answer was. Mom didn't argue, just insisted I come home immediately. I expected a big blow-up when I walked into the house, but instead my parents talked to me quietly and calmly explained why they set up a curfew. They warned me about what could happen to a young girl like me out at night by myself, but when they started warning me on drugs and alcohol I became uneasy and tense, because I thought they knew. Actually all they wanted was to warn me. I listened and I nodded. And when they finished I lied and told them I knew they were right. I apologized for being late and promised it would never happen again.

But instead I was just more cautious. I cut the amount I drank and stopped drinking long before I went home. Also, for several months I made a careful habit of getting home by curfew. It bothered me a lot that my folks were losing faith in me. Growing up, I had always wanted to do things for them; we were so close. Now I was lying to them and disobeying them every week. And while I wasn't ready to give up doing what I wanted to do and living the way I wanted to live, I hated the way I was hurting my parents.

Some things still went on like always. We'd eat our meals together and we'd talk about some things that didn't matter. But there was always a barrier between us. I never talked about my friends because that was a point of tension. And I knew Mom would never approve of the pot and everything else we did. Boyfriends and dating were another area we couldn't discuss.

When I got away from the confrontations and from the emotions of specific incidents and objectively thought about my relationship with my parents, I realized the communication gap was largely my creation. They tried, but I couldn't communicate about the things I knew would hurt them.

But early in my freshman year I made things worse. I told my parents I was spending the night at my friend's, which in part I was. Our plan was to go to the movies. My friend's mom would drop us off, and there we would meet our boyfriends. We saw their truck and got in. Then proceeded to get stoned.

Meanwhile, all this time my parents were parked right across from us learning what their daughter did when she was supposedly at her friend's. We didn't know that at the time. We all got the munchies, so we drove to the nearest Seven Eleven store and were just going in the door when my parents drove up, shining their headlights in my face. It didn't occur to me that my parents would follow me, and when they showed up I was quite surprised. I felt as if everything was spinning around. I don't know why I was so scared, I've dealt with worse happenings before. I guess it was all the guilt that had built up, and the pot was making me feel lightheaded. Next, everything happened so fast I can hardly recollect. I remember, though, my father's voice ordering our boyfriends to never see us again, while my mom ushered my friend and me into the car.

The ride home was worse yet. No one spoke a word. I was still trying to get over the shock of my parents' arrival, but now my head was pounding. I calmed down a little and tried to rationalize the situation. Why did my parents follow me, I wondered. They always used to trust me. I didn't find out till we had dropped my friend off at her house and were home seated at the kitchen table. Then mom pulled from behind her a folder. With a closer look I saw it was my diary. I felt as if the walls were closing in on me. For if my mom had read it she would know the lie I was leading. It turned out she had. She read it again, out loud to my dad.

While my mom went on reading, I sat shamefaced and sullen. Dad just kept nodding his head. When it was over they gave me a lecture on how hard it was to be a parent and how hard I was making it for them. Then they clamped down on freedom, and I had to come directly home from whatever ballgame, movie, or any other entertainment I went to. And while the significance of what they said didn't sink in for quite some time, I remember one of my parents saying, "Ellen, we've always had so much faith in you. Now the trust is broken." Starting then, I got the third degree every time I came into the house. "Where'd you go? Who were you with? What'd you do? When did you leave?" I had to account for every minute. The grilling got so intense I sometimes felt guilty when I wasn't being grilled.

I felt like a terrible daughter. And I didn't feel like a very good person either. The more I thought about how I was hurting my parents, the more I realized I was hurting myself. I was doing things when I was drunk that I didn't really want to do. I didn't know it at the time until I had sobered up and by then it was too late. There were so many incidents, so many things I did that I hated about myself. It began to get to me. I pulled back on the partying and the drinking and tried to get my life under control. Yet I knew I was the same person, the same me I didn't like. I blamed it on my best friend Amy. I shouldn't have, but it seemed she was against my going straight. I thought she would understand and help me, but at every opportunity she would tempt me, and I would give in. On the outside it looked as if I was straightening up, but I knew deep down inside that as long as I hung around with Amy, I would always be tempted. So I found new friends, and though Amy and I once in a while hang around together, she knows better than to ask me if I want to go to a party. For the answer would always be no.

That day my relationship with my parents began to change. I know they've seen a difference in me, and I've become more open with Mom. I tell her what I'm thinking. But the biggest difference is my openness with what I do with my friends. When I come home from a game or social occasion, I want to tell her all about it because there's nothing to hide.

It took only a few nights of drinking and missed curfews to destroy my parents' faith and trust. Rebuilding it is taking a lot longer. But the trust is returning. And I'm learning it's a mutual thing. As I share with my parents about my life they share with me about theirs.

I feel good about myself—for the first time in a long time.

Full Autobiography

Write the story of your life. It can be as long as you like, but since it's impossible to tell everything, think about what you might want to select and emphasize. "Full" means that all of your life is covered but not that all of it is covered in the same way. Some parts you may want to summarize briefly; other parts you may want to tell in more detail. Do you see your life as a series of phases? Will certain key incidents capture the main things about different periods or aspects of your life? Combine long-range views and close-ups in whatever way best tells your story.

You might put together some pieces you have already written—revised, if necessary—and write continuity for them as well as new material. Or start from scratch. (For reasons of space, the samples to follow here illustrate shorter forms this can take.)

Growing Up

ALEXANDRA STODDARD

It had been a long day. Actually it had been a long month. Life hadn't been the same since the family's newcomer. I was sitting in my parents' room on the foot of the bed watching them get dressed to go out for dinner. I yawned. My mind flashed back to two weeks before. My little sister had been trouble from the beginning. I wet my pants the moment I found out it was a girl. I was sitting and waiting in a coffee shop with Dad drinking lemonade when the pay phone rang. Dad jumped up. I shook all over and my stomach hurt. I knew that was it. The child had been born. Now it was her first day home. Flowers lined her path to the newly decorated nursery, and balloons and gifts were everywhere. When I got home with my babysitter from my walk in the park, I walked into the room to find my mother breast-feeding this red, bald creature. Dad was taking pictures. I looked at the baby nurse. She was a big Swiss woman. I couldn't stand her at first glance. Instead of joining my happy family, I wandered about the house.

Now I was relieved that they were going out to dinner. The "addition" had been put to sleep, and I was at ease. I said goodbye to them at the door and proceeded to pad across the apartment to the nursery. It was September and it still didn't become dark until late. I opened the door slowly and walked in. I quickly shut it behind me.

I could hear her sleeping in her crib, quietly breathing in and out. I sat down in the rocking chair next to the window. The six o'clock light shone in on the floor. I thought to myself, how stupid it was that someone could go to bed when it was still light. I would always wait till after dark. Slowly I looked down at my white keds. I had on pink shorts and pink socks and a white short-sleeved shirt with a Peter Pan collar. I touched my soft, curly golden hair and stared at my sister's bald head through the bars of the crib.

I stopped rocking and stood up. I walked very slowly towards the crib. I made sure not to wake her up—at least not yet. She was lying on her stomach with her head turned away from me, under a light blue blanket. I looked at her chubby calves and ankles and studied her fat wrists. Then I looked at mine. I picked up her arm and sank my teeth into her wrist. I couldn't bite that hard because of her babyfat. She squirmed, then opened her mouth and let out a sob. I grew scared. Scared of that awful nurse with the white hair and weird teeth. I quickly put the blanket over her, and she soon fell back asleep. Nervous, I stole out of the room and down the hall to mine. I tore off my clothes, put on a nightgown, and hid in bed. Finally I fell asleep. Some time later my father was sitting beside me on the bed, stroking my hair and smelling of cigar smoke. My mother walked in, talking a mile a minute. I pretended to be asleep while my father interrupted her. "The nurse said Alexandra went to bed early."

Mom just stood there, and then said, "Alexandra bit her baby sister."

* * *

Dear Diary,

Ninnie's dead. I couldn't tell you for a few days. I couldn't face it until now. A bad time to face it, her funeral was today. "Wear the summer dress," I was told, and a blue flowery thing was thrown at me early this morning. I was a blank the whole car ride up to Connecticut. Relatives gathered in a small room off the chapel for coffee and donuts. There was a quiet murmur which filled the room, and I looked at a girl standing near the door and wondered if she was my cousin. Next we met Father Jonathan—a quiet, young priest, homosexual, I believe. The girl turned out to be my cousin. Yes, she and I were my grandmother's favorite grandchildren. We studied each other as we all walked into the chapel and sat down. She was a pretty girl. Simple but beautiful in a soft way. She had brown hair and eyes.

The service was touching, people spoke of what a wonderful woman she had been. I sat in the front row with my mother and sister. My cousin sat behind me with her brothers and parents. I heard her crying, but I kept my tears to myself. At the end of the service I heard the organ begin to play. I recognized the song. It was the theme song to "The Sting" by Scott Joplin. I knew she had requested it because they used to play it at school when we marched out of assembly. She always loved it so. Oh, I cried so hard. All of her pain-filled months of cancer, killing me slowly, seemed to occupy me. Almost as if the pain and suffering needed another place to go. All of a sudden I missed her so badly. I needed her. Everyone was marching out and I rose slowly from my seat. I turned around to face this girl, whom I had never spoken to. We were both crying as if a special understanding filled the two of us. We hugged each other. "We were her favorites," she whispered. "I know."

* * *

"It's early," I think to myself. I look out the window from atop my bunkbed. "It looks like it's been raining," I perceive, but quickly remember it never rains in California. It was the sprinklers, I conclude. I wonder why I didn't sleep longer and roll off the top bunk. Once on the floor I stretch and yawn, then walk slowly into the bathroom. I look at the clock, it's 6:30 a.m. "Whoo, it's early for you, Drange," I say as I look into the mirror.

I think back to the night before. The cold, glassy-blue eyes, the streaked blonde hair, a beautiful Australian accent kept telling me how beautiful I was; a witch came for dinner. I feel cozy in this room. I belong here. I look at my sleeping sister, she looks beautiful. The humidity of the early morning has covered her forehead with a soft layer of perspiration, and along her hairline the blonde locks begin to curl. She didn't like last night either.

I picture the city, and a bubbly joy fills me. I am so happy to be here. I can see perspiration under my Mickey Mouse tee-shirt. It reminds me of Manhattan in July. Footsteps interrupt my train of thought. I go to the door to say good morning to my father, wondering why he would be jogging this early. My ears focus on the sound, and I realize it is the sound of high-heeled shoes. I rush to the window in time to see her leaving. She trips down the front steps in all her glory. The hair is rumpled, and she looks awful. She gets into her Mercedes Benz and drives away. "Too bad"—my smile like vinegar. There is a dry rectangle on the driveway—my friend the sprinkler hadn't gotten under her car. "You didn't think of everything, Dad."

* * *

"Mom, stop taking my temperature, it feels funny under my tongue." She shoved the thermometer in my mouth quickly and jumped up to answer the phone. "Hello . . . yes, . . . oh no—that's terrible . . . how is her mother? Is everybody else all right? . . . yes, I'll tell her, she was such a sweet child, . . . Well, thank you for calling, goodbye." I watched my mother's every move. She turned to me, her face covered in terror. She stared at me for a long time. Soon she forced a smile and said, "Let's see how your fever is." I took out the thermometer and swallowed. I told her I was going to call Rebecca and asked where the class list was.

"You can't call Rebecca . . . she won't be home . . . . Today on the class trip to the museum she ran in front of a fire truck during a red light."

"Did it knock her over? Did she cry? . . . Mom!"

"She's dead, Alexandra."

"No, she's not," I said and got off her bed. I walked out of the room, and as I meandered down the hall I heard her mention something about how she should have waited for the light to change, isn't it a shame, such a beautiful, young child, and finally how hard she knew it would be for me to accept this. I found the class list and went to call Rebecca. I dialed her number. I felt familiar and expected her to answer in her friendly lisp, yet at the same time I was scared. Her mother answered in tears, and I hung up. I went into my room, and even though it was only five o'clock I got into a nightgown and lay in bed until I fell asleep finally—four hours later. I had tried to fall asleep before Daddy came home so I wouldn't hear Mom tell him. I didn't sleep well.

The next morning I got dressed and came out of my room. I was quiet through breakfast and all the way to school. I didn't see Rebecca all day. I looked everywhere for her. Nobody smiled. I saw her little sister playing in the sandbox, and I went up to her. Cheerfully I asked her, "Where's Rebecca?" The little girl turned to me matter-of-factly. "She's in heaven," she said.

* * *

"Aunt Hid is coming over, and you can go with her to the garden and gather some flowers." Kick, kick. My heavy legs burdened by sandals hit the sides of the stool. The dish of milk with bananas floating on top is taken away because only the cereal was eaten. Suddenly my soft skin is attacked by a hot cloth. "Honestly, your face gets so messy, Alexandra."

"Grandmommy always says messy," I return.

"Because, little girl, you are. Your great-aunt is coming over and you don't want cereal sticking to your cheeks; ask your mother, I'm right."

"She's right, Sweet-pea."

Suddenly Aunt Hid is standing in the doorway. She looks the same, her smile sweet. But something tells me to run—quickly, far away. I run up the stairs as she's saying "hello." My mother sprints after me, catching up with each stride. I reach my room and stop. She stands behind me out of breath and says, "What do you think you're doing, young lady. You come down and show your manners right now."

"No, I'm staying here. I don't want to see Aunt Hid."

"Come, Alexandra."

"No!!!" I scream, and before she can grab me I dart under the bed. I keep screaming until she shuts the door and goes away. I feel safer under the bed. Soon there's a knock and Daddy walks in. "Alexandra, I don't know what's wrong, but you're acting very strangely. You love Aunt Hid, why don't you want to see her?"

"No, I won't, leave me alone." The door is closed again. I get up and look out of the window. I see Aunt Hid walking on the front lawn with my grandmother. The slow walk, her hair in a bun. So old. I love her, but I cannot be with her now. I have to stay away from her. At sunset I checked the window again. I saw her walk home to her house across the street. I stared and calculated how much time it would take her to get to her front porch, in the door, and up to her room. It seemed a long time until I saw the light turned on in her bedroom.

Mommy came into my bedroom and told me to get into bed. I wasn't allowed any supper, she told me. Not after the way I had treated Aunt Hid. I felt sad but not guilty or ashamed. I fell fast asleep. In the morning they told me that Aunt Hid had died in her sleep.

* * *

"Wake up, girls, rise and shine, I'm getting married today!" I took my time getting out of bed, and I wandered into the T.V. room. No sooner had I seen one commercial when Shaw-mai came into the room. She looked at me with her soft eyes and said, "None of that, you can't be late for the wedding." She clicked off the set and took hold of my hand. She led me back into the room where I found the dresses—

matching yellow, ugly dresses we had bought at Cerutti just for the occasion. I hated the smocking on the chest and no sleeves. They were so uncomfortable. Laid out on the bed, they reminded me that I had to get ready. "The dress goes with this day," I thought.

I was putting on my tights when I looked up to see my mother standing in the doorway. "How do I look?" Already dressed in her Halston pale yellow ultrasuede dress and black patent leather sandals, her hair standing in a tall bouffant. She had had it done the day before, for the wedding. I hated the way it looked.

From down the hall I heard my grandmother. She walked slowly towards my mother, who had just caught her from the corner of her eye. Mother turned angrily on her heel. "You're not dressed yet?"

"No, I'm not. Will you just calm down? We're not going to be late. Peter will wait anyway. Lord love a duck, if we showed up tomorrow he'd still be there waiting, holding the ring in his hand with some dumb smile across his face."

"Stop talking like that, Mother."

"Oh, shut up. If you had known what was good for you, you would have stayed married to Brandon. He's such a nice man." Slam. Mom met the door to her bedroom. An inch too close. "Ow—I hate you, don't lock me out of my bedroom!"

Back in my room we were almost dressed. Shaw-mai began brushing our hair. "I'm wearing mine in a ponytail," I quickly added. "But your mother wants you to wear it down. She has specific barrettes for you here," I'm quietly told.

"I don't care, we're doing everything for her, can't I just wear my hair the way I want?"

"What is all that trouble, Alexandra?" Mother walked in.

"I'm wearing my hair in a ponytail, no trouble," I said.

"No you're not! You're wearing your hair down today."

"I hate the way it looks, Mom, what's wrong with a ponytail?"

"I don't care, it's my day, you are wearing your hair down, it looks beautiful. Just do it!" She stormed down the hall and disappeared. I started to cry. I really thought I looked ugly with my hair down. I wanted to look pretty, but I like my hair in a ponytail.

I heard my grandmother come down the hall again, this time to my room. My mother stood behind her. "Let her wear a ponytail," she said. Mother screamed again. I didn't listen to her words. I just went over to the bed. I picked up the "Tinkerbell" hairbrush and started brushing my hair. I got the barrettes off the floor, where I had thrown them, and put them in my hair. I turned to face them at the door. Mother smiled and said I looked beautiful. I looked out the window. "This is going to be a bad day," I thought.

* * *

An abandoned picnic is a few yards away, while a pregnant mother walks with her two-year-old daughter. They are walking alongside a brook. They are holding hands, and the sun shines through the trees, adorning their path with glorious specks of light, which shine on the water. "If the baby is a boy we will name it Christopher," the mother says to the little girl. "What if it's a girl?" the child asks curiously. "I don't know. I want a name that's rare, beautiful, innocent . . . . I can't think of one," she said.

"I like this brook, it's so pretty, Mommy. How come there aren't so many of these around?" her daughter asked.

"Yes, how about Brooke? Do you like that name?"

"Yes, I do, better than mine; if it's a girl can she have my name and you can name me Brooke?" she asked in a naive tone. Her eyes looked up at her mother, and they both smiled. "Will you like me still if you have a little girl?"

"Of course I will, you're you. You're special, and different from anyone else in the world. No one can replace you, Alexandra."

My Family: Letting Go and Setting the People Free

LAURA SULLIVAN

My First Family

When I was four or five I had three brothers and a mother. People told me that my father was killed by a neighbor. The neighbor thought that my father was her husband dressed as Santa Claus. The two of them were fighting (the neighbors), and her husband was also dressed as Santa. When the neighbor came out of her apartment, my father was knocking at the door, and she stabbed him in the back.

That's all I know about my father.

My mother raised the four of us: Edward who is now 23, John, 22, Peter who is 19, and me, 18. She had a hard time because she didn't work. We were too young to work and she didn't have much family in Southie. She lived as the days went. Till this time now I don't know how she managed to do it.

My mother and I shared a room. We slept in the same bed. We had two dressers and we got along. When we had a little disagreement, she would throw me out of her room. I would lie on the floor in front of her room, no blanket, no pillow, nothing there to keep me warm. And I would cry and pretend that I was cold. My mother used to look at me and then yell, "Get your ass in here and go to sleep." So then I would go to sleep.

One day my uncle was down. I was spoiled rotten by him, and he thought I was sweet and innocent.

While he was there, I went in the bathroom and carved a swear word in the soap. When my uncle went in there, he came out mad. He put all my brothers in a line and made them stand there till one of them admitted that they did it.

I was only seven or eight. He asked me if I did it. I said, "No." So finally my oldest brother took the blame.

One fight that me and my brother John had was when I took his gum and hid it on him. He got mad and started hitting me.

When my mother saw that, she gave him a belt and a shoe. She didn't think that that was right for a boy to hit a girl. John still won, but my oldest brother came in and helped me. It made me feel good to know that he was there to help.

My Mother and Cancer

When I was about eight or nine, my mother was running back and forth to the hospital, but I didn't know why.

All that I can remember is how her hair used to fall out in big chunks and her arm started to swell up pretty bad. She couldn't use it. She had trouble picking things up and putting things in high places.

I knew that she had cancer, but I didn't understand or know the side effects. I was scared. I saw how people treated her with care. Everyone that I knew or saw with her treated her differently than they ever did before.

I would go to bed at night and I would sleep with my mother. I would be restless at night because I didn't know what would happen.

I was going to a school right across from my house. I was in the schoolyard before school started when I saw an ambulance in front of my house. I ran over to it, no one was there. Then I ran up three flights of stairs through a metal door which led into my house. There were two strange looking guys with white clothes on carrying my mother out of her room in a stretcher. Down the stairs and into the ambulance she went.

My mother told me to go to school. I told her I wanted to stay with her. She said no.

So my brother John brought me across the street. I stood at the fence which surrounded the school yard and stared. As the tears came down my face, the ambulance pulled away. My teacher, Mrs. Sternes, came over to me and asked, "Do you know who was in the ambulance?" I said, "Yes. It is my mother."

As I was in school that day I couldn't concentrate. I was like 4×4=8, and things like that. I was worried.

After school that day I ran home. I opened the door and it was empty. No one was home, so I sat on the couch and called Kathleen (my aunt) up to see if she knew when they were coming home. She didn't know. She wanted me to go over her house, and I told her that I wanted to be alone.

As soon as I hung up the phone I fell fast asleep. When I woke up, Kathleen was there and she brought me over to the hospital to see my mother.

My mother was just lying on the bed. By the time I got there, so many people were there that there wasn't any room so I could see and talk to her.

I just stared. She was almost bald and very pale. She had machines on her to keep her alive longer. The thing that I can still see is how her eyes looked. They had a look like she was scared. Her eyes looked as if she was punched. She had dark, dark circles under and over. They looked terrible. She looked terrible.

My oldest brother Eddie took me and put me on the bed beside my mother. She looked at me and said that she was glad there is one girl in the family. Then she said to Eddie, "You boys better keep a good eye on your only sister."

That's when I knew something was going to happen to her.

I said to her "What about you? Where are you going?" And as she held my hand she said, "I love all of you kids, and look after one another. Wherever you kids go, keep in touch with each other." That was the last time I heard her. My brothers just looked at me and stared.

The next day came and it was Saturday. When I was in the room with her, she didn't realize that I was there. She had all kinds of machines on her to keep her alive, but it didn't work. She was pronounced dead at 2:00 p.m. My family was all in one room. There was a doctor there trying to talk to us kids about our mother's death. She explained why she had died.

At the funeral, my family, my mother's friends and even my first and fifth grade teachers were there.

Splitting Up My Family

I went to live in Pembroke with my Aunt Barbara, but I didn't like it there. I stayed there a week and then Barbara drove us down to Southie and told us to stay where we wanted to. So I went with my Aunt Kathleen. Peter went with me. Eddie and John went to my Uncle Joe's house on Fifth Street in South Boston.

Besides the family splitting up, my mother's furniture was split up. My Aunt Barbara took all my mother's furniture and sold it to people that we didn't even know. I still don't know them. It hurt me that I had nothing of my mother's, not even a picture.

My brother Peter lived with me and my aunt for three or four weeks and then he ran away and was among the missing. Meanwhile my uncle treated my other brothers rotten. He used to come home to his house around 3:30 to 4:00 in the morning drunk and wake them up to yell at them about the past and what they did. All my brothers left there and lived on their own.

I stayed with my aunt, and she told me to stay away from Peter, but it was all right to see my other brothers. Peter turned out to be a trouble maker. He was always in trouble with the law, stealing cars, B&E, A&B, and dealing with drugs and alcohol.

I didn't see any of my brothers for five or six years. It was hard for me, because I was close to them in a way that no one knew about. I loved all my brothers. They cared for me. They always wanted to help me. But we split up. It really hurt me to find out that I had no more brothers.

I always asked people that knew my family if they saw them, and I never got an answer that I was looking for. The answer I wanted was that they knew where they were.

It was getting to a point that I started to look through the obituaries. After a while I lost most of my feeling and didn't care about them as much. People would come up to me and ask me about them, and I would say I don't know or care. But my brothers meant the world to me because I had no one else left in my family but them.

Living with My Aunt

In my aunt's house there was my aunt, Kathleen, and three of her daughters. Nancy is the oldest. She got married and had kids and moved out before I lived there. Peggy was the next oldest, then Patty. Patty is my age, but she is two months younger than me.

Patty and I used to talk, fight and go out together. We got along like real sisters. Peggy always talked to me. She is like my big sister up to this day. Nancy and I talk once in a while.

It was hard for me to adjust to them because I never knew what it was like to have sisters. My aunt and I got along for the first year or two, and from then on it was like the worst time of my life. It felt like everyone was against me. When I came home from school it was as if my head would know what's coming, and I would get a headache. It was weird, because when I got a headache, I knew my aunt would yell. But if I didn't, I was in the clear. We would fight constantly, and it got to a point where we wouldn't talk to each other for weeks. This lasted for like three years of my life, and I hated it.

I had no one to turn to. Her daughter Peggy moved out, and Patty was on her mother's side. I used to get sucked in to do everything. These three years of my life were like the story of Cinderella and the stepmother and stepsisters.

My aunt used to tell me to do all kinds of things like go to the store, clean the room, wash the dishes and stuff like that. After a while I got sick of doing it.

One day after school she told me to clean something while

everybody went out. I felt neglected, because they always did that. Leave me behind to clean. Some days that I had to clean I would make up an excuse on where I would have to go just to get out of it.

It all kept up, so I thought of saying no. But I didn't want to get in trouble for not having any respect for Kathleen. And I respected her for taking me in. I felt as I owed her something for that.

One day we were both in a rare mood, and I came home and she told me to do something. I ignored her, and she yelled for me to do it. I turned around and said, "No!" I just got sick of everyone telling me what to do and walking over me. So I got stuck in the middle of another fight. But from then on it got easier and easier to say no to her. Now we talk and fool with each other, tease and laugh.

My Brothers

When last year came, my brothers started coming around again. Boy, was I happy, because it had been six long years without them, and I missed them.

The first time that I saw my brothers in six years was when my brother John came to my work. He walked in like a regular customer. I looked at him because he was wearing shorts in the winter time. He looked at me and stared. I did not know who he was.

He yelled across Woolworth's, "Hi Laura!"

I just kept looking and said, "Hi?" I did not know who he was. I never saw him in there before.

As he started to walk over to me, that is when I realized that that was my brother.

We went to his van, which was parked out front of Woolworth's. We sat there and talked about what we did in the past good and bad. The fights that we had, and the way I used to get him into trouble. Those were the good things.

The bad thing that we talked about that I did not like was him talking to me about how he would go out and get so drunk that he would not remember half the things that he did.

My brother's friends were there and they seemed nice. They said hi. They were surprised to find out that my brothers had a little sister. I was stunned, because it seemed that they never talked about me before. Come to find out John did talk about me, but his friends did not believe him. They said I was an image.

John had kept in touch with my other brothers, and he told me about them. Eddie, the oldest, was in the service. And Peter no one knew. John gave me his phone number and told me to keep in touch. Since then he has been around every Christmas, and he and my other brother call and come to visit me now that they know my phone number. Thanks to John.

One day I was in my Reading/Writing class. One of the aides came in to get me. I didn't know what for. I was scared that something might have happened to my aunt.

They took me to the main office, and some strange-looking guy was there. When he turned around, I knew who he was. He was my brother Peter.

He looked so different because he used to have silver caps, glasses, and long hair. But when I saw him he didn't have the caps on, no glasses, and he got a hair cut. And he lifted weights. It was a surprise indeed.

He wanted to take me out of school at 9:05 in the morning to get drunk. He asked me if I had any drugs that he could have from me, or if I knew anyone with any so he could get high. I told him no!

When Peter and I talked, it felt as if I never left my brothers. It was like I knew my brothers. At first I didn't know how to feel. But I felt surprised that they were coming around, happy that they were coming around, and confused because I didn't know what they wanted to do with me.

I sat down for a while and thought about them coming around again. I said to myself that I won't get as close to them as much as it takes from me. I won't! I don't want to get hurt like I did six years ago.

I always looked up to them, but now they look up to me because I work, and most of all I am finishing school. They all tell me if I don't finish school they will kill me. But I tell them they should have finished so I would be influenced.

My Family Now

My family now is the one that I am with because they have stuck with me for the past years. Kathleen and her daughters have taught me some things that I wouldn't know if I was with my brothers. Like I wouldn't know what happened to my mother and father without them. My aunt and her daughters are like sisters to me. We talk to each other and laugh, and we have fights. They treat me equal, as in the way they treat each other.

I have to let my brothers go. They moved from me, I moved from them. I could have gone with them, but I had to go on with what I wanted to do. They did too. If I wanted to, I could go with them now, but I can't. I can't live the way that they live, because ever since we left each other, we have been living differently than when we were together. We still keep in touch sometimes, but the longer we don't talk or don't see each other, the harder it is to talk because we lead different lives.

I don't really understand these feelings about kids moving away or staying. Now I can see that a family is being able to let go and set the people free. But not for good. If you were brought up as a family, and if you move away, you're still a family. The people who moved away from me—by dying or moving away, it's okay. It's a part of life really.

Memoir

Memoir of Another Person

*Tell someone else's story as you witnesssed it. This may
be an incident that occurred on one occasion or what someone
you knew or observed did over a longer period of time amount-
ing to a phase in that person's life. Tell about yourself only
enough to recount how you came by the knowledge and how you
reacted to it. You might place this in a collection of your other
memoirs or, if it makes a certain general point, consider how
you might reach an audience that would appreciate that point.*

The Old Man

SUE BRENNAN

Gazing out the window during a break in History, I noticed an
old man standing alone.

Wednesday night while we were working on the *Piper*, the same
old man shuffled in and sat down. "Just so you won't think I'm crazy,
I'll show you my pin," he said. Turning the lapel of his shapeless tweed
coat, he fondled a red kite-shaped pin. "Forty years with the State," he
continued. "Worked as a suveyor. . . . Yep, forty years."

Last year after a tennis match, I recall him appearing looking like
someone's Grandpa, in a white, long-sleeved shirt and a blackbanded
straw hat slightly tipped back. He had shown some of us his pin and
talked emphatically about politics. He had seemed well informed on the
Watergate crisis and had damned the Republicans.

Now he sat forward in his chair, his legs spread apart, bracing his
hands on a crooked wood cane that was taped at the bottom. Peering
over round wire-framed spectacles, he pointed to his left eye, which
was filmy and partially closed. "Lost my eye in World War I."

"Oh?" I replied with interest.

"I don't get around so well these days, have to go to bed earlier
too," he trailed.

Patches of unkept gray hair grew on his neck and face. His brownish gray coat and pants hung limply on his small frame.

"They had me in the State mental hospital for three days, and I didn't like that at all. Some people think I'm a little bit crazy; I'm not all too sure but that they're right. . . . I don't know."

He lives alone; he says his wife is dead and his daughter was shot by his son-in-law. (Others were told the daughter's leukemic husband hit her with a board in a fit of rage.) "My son's dead now too, and my wife. . . . I really miss her. Sometimes I hear her talking to me."

"I played football fifty years ago at U. of O.," rambled this seemingly intelligent man. "One of my friends, a real rabblerouser, I played football with, beat and killed a man. I went to see him at Alcatraz while I was in San Francisco.

"I've worked everywhere in Oregon. On the coast near an Indian settlement; we'd play on the dunes. . . . The guys on the Highway department nicknamed me Hard Rock Simpson, from my name, Rockwell Simpson.

"They took away my guns. My grandson did. They're mine and they have no right to keep them from me," he faltered. "Anything going on at McNary tonight?"

He stayed twenty minutes that night and was anxious for the school play to open the following evening. "You're all going . . . aren't you?" he inquired as he left.

The next day at lunch I noticed the same old man standing alone outside, waiting for someone to talk to.

I'll Never Forget Anna Jordan

DEBBIE VUKOVITZ

Anna Jordan always jokingly identified herself as my father's "girlfriend" whenever she called me on the phone, but I could easily tell, from her strong German accent, who she was.

Born and raised in Minihof, a lovely small village in Burgenland, Austria, she became known as a superb cook when she was just a teenager. She had lost her mother when she was little and, being the only girl in a large family, was forced to cook at an early age. In fact she used to boast that she began to cook as soon as she learned how to hold a spoon.

At the age of eighteen, Anna left Austria for the United States, following John, her boyfriend. They eventually married and lived in Chicago. She had not wanted to leave her family and beautiful Austria because she loved them both dearly, but John meant more to her. Since my grandfather and Anna were from the same village, she was one of our close family friends.

By the time Anna and I became good friends, John had passed away after fifty years of happy marriage and she was well into her seventies. She seemed to have a lot of friends, though she did not have any children. She treated my sister, Amy, and me as if she were my grandmother so that for a long time I even thought she was. She was a sincere large-framed lady with broad shoulders, big bones, and huge fat-fingered hands. Her honest dark brown eyes could penetrate me. She spoke in a rather loud voice with a serious expression that scared me at first, but gradually her unpretentious personality with occasional hearty laughter attracted me. She was full of curiosity like an innocent child and very outspoken, though she seldom hurt anyone intentionally.

I still remember the day Anna Jordan taught me how to make apple strudel. Patiently she showed me how to do everything just right as I stood wide-eyed, trying to copy every detail. When we were finished, I placed our strudels in the oven, and we waited anxiously for them to bake. She asked me to play a few pieces for her on my violin and show her pictures that I drew. Full of delight, she praised me until there was nothing left to praise, and then we feasted on strudel.

The last time I saw her before she moved into a convalescent home was when she invited my family and me over for a goulash dinner. She was pale and her face somewhat swollen. She tried to act cheerful, but I knew there was something deeply wrong. After dinner she showed us her favorite pink dress and said to me contentedly, "Isn't this a lovely dress? I wore this to many, many weddings, even to your parents' wedding. And I'm going to wear this dress when I go to heaven."

We were busy for a long time after that, because my father received an order to transfer to California. I had forgotten about her for a while.

Then, one afternoon in 1979, my family and I had a chance to visit Anna Jordan at the Altenheim German Old People's Home. It was a cold lonely building that smelled of medicine and mold. When Anna Jordan saw us, she kissed and hugged us joyously. Her small room was so warm and cozy that it made me forget the cold outside.

"Oh, great! You've brought your violins," she smiled excitedly. "Will you play something for me?"

My younger sister and I played dozens of pieces. Last of all I played the second movement of the violin "Concerto in A Minor" by Vivaldi, Anna's favorite piece. It was a very sad piece and she loved it. By then her room and the hallway were packed with her friends, and everyone showered us with candies and praise. Anna Jordan looked very happy and satisfied . . . until my father stood up and said, "We really have to go." My mother said, "We'll miss you a lot in California, but maybe you can visit us there soon."

"I hope so," she nodded. "Don't forget to write to me!" reminded Anna.

As I kissed her good-bye, I saw tears well up in her eyes. Stepping out the door, we heard a loud cry. We turned around and found Anna Jordan crying like a little child in an old lady's arms.

"Leave her alone," my father whispered to us. "The longer we stay, the harder it will be to leave her."

Anna Jordan's heartbreaking cry echoed through the lonely dimly lit hallways and seemed to follow us as we walked down the main stairs.

I thought I heard her even after we stepped out of that huge cold building.

Bronwen

CYNTHIA PFOHL

We were always together; people called us twins and got our names mixed up even though we didn't look anything alike. I remember the day I met Bronwen, 6 years ago, the first day of fourth grade. I walked into the room and looked around to see if there were any new kids. The room smelled of fresh paint and new carpet; the rooms had all been rebuilt over the past year and during the summer. The newly cleaned chalkboard stretched across the front of the room and was empty except for our names clearly written in white chalk. My eyes searched for an unfamiliar name, and "Bronwen" caught my attention. I had never heard of that name, and for some reason I thought it was probably a new boy, which would have been nice.

We became friends from the start and spent practically every minute of every day together. The principal of the school at that time happened to be good friends with her and her family, which helped out a lot when we got in trouble. We would give him these sad looks and say we were sorry and swear we wouldn't do it again. It worked almost every time.

The first year of our friendship I was taller, but then all of a sudden she grew—and grew. Pretty soon the kids started calling her "Brawny" for short. She pretended to hate it. She would whine, "You guys, quit it!" It was really funny to watch and listen, but of course I couldn't laugh; we were best friends. We stuck up for each other.

Our first year in high school, ninth grade, we somehow grew apart. My parents were glad to see me hanging around others; they thought Bronwen was too wild. She was wild, but she was my friend. I couldn't stand to see her with others. Even when she hung around someone she knew I hated, I still considered her my best friend—forever. Sometimes she would see me when she was with another friend and come up to me afterwards and say something like, "I wish she would leave me alone. I really can't stand her!" or, "Ya know, she just asked me if she could spend the night at my house. Can you believe that?" I never believed her.

One day in the middle of our ninth grade year she came to school with the top of her hair chopped off about an inch from her scalp; the rest of her long strawberry blond hair had been cut evenly all around just above her shoulders. She told me that she and her mom had gotten in a fight. She got mad at her mom and took the scissors to her hair. She did it to somehow get back at her. Of course she had to keep up her image, so she couldn't tell everyone else that. She told them that she was going punk and that her mom had even cut it for her. She gradually did go punk, and I went along with it.

Bronwen and I went to school together through the ninth grade. There was a party last summer, the day before we moved to Oregon. We had a really great time even though we knew it couldn't last, and I had a feeling that it was a different kind of goodbye and that she didn't really care what happened to me, but she said, "I'll try not to cry, Cynth," right before we both cried.

She hasn't written me a letter yet, but she has called once. I called her several times and she always promised she would write. The last time I called she told me something I'll never forget. She said, "Cynth, I did something—you're gonna be mad; I'm pregnant." I wasn't mad, but I still feel like it's all a dream.

Memoir of a Group or Place

Tell what you remember that a group did one time or did typically. Or tell what used to go on at a particular place. You were there but not central. Whatever feeling or idea makes this memory stand out now may provide the mood or angle to give it in telling others about it. Could this be a feature piece for some newspaper or magazine? Or include it with your other memoirs of people and places.

Woods Hole and I

TOM ROBERTSON

I walked through the living room, the shiny oak floor reflecting my steps as I passed. How many summers have I tread on that cold hardwood? Only my subconscious knows for certain. In spots the varnish had worn off, leaving the planks naked and gritty with sand brought from the beach. The bottoms of my feet shivering, I wandered aimlessly about the room. "No aims, goals, or expectations to live up to," I thought suddenly, "that's what's great about summer, this house, and Woods Hole." The sound of paper shuffling distracted me. My little brother Alex was up early, as usual, reading a thrashed edition of "The Fantastic Four, Issue #67." Sprawled out on the window-box, chin resting in his upraised palm, he was totally absorbed in heroic adventures. Arching over where he lay, dawn's early rays shone through the windows, casting silhouettes of tick-tac-toe boxes while dust swirled lazily in hazy columns of light. The start of yet another typical Woods Hole day: the sun shining, people baking at the beach, the pathways choked with bicycles, a sampling of paradise. But outside the air was still quiet and cold. And the morning was not yet finished.

Rivulets of water trickled down the frosted glass. Looking out, I could see the fog sliding in across the seawall. It encompassed the orderly cobblestones until the wall faded to a line of dark mist, barely discernible as it stretched between the two hills fronting the house. The fog continued on its journey inland, brushing the tops of waving catskill stalks, creeping through the dense salt marsh, leaving a film of briny dampness in its wake. Beyond the seawall lay an angry Atlantic, its waters churning, swells battling one another, throwing snow-like froth to the crests, than subsiding into insipid bubbles. I tried to open one of the windows. Gripping the driftwood-like midsection, I pulled. Years of crusted salt gave way, and the window slid upwards. Like air filling the vacuum when the lid is peeled off a can of tennis balls, the salty environment invaded the house. My nose rankling, the acrid smell cleared my head, collaborating with the ocean roar, which pounded on my ear drums. No longer muted by the closed windows, the roar shattered the quiet and actually coaxed Alex into forgetting his superheroes for a moment to witness supernatural forces happening in the realm of the real.

I stuck my head out the window, squinting my eyes because of the damp breeze, and noticed how small Woods Hole actually was. Most notable of landmarks was the rusty drawbridge. Its steel girders moaned every time the keeper threw the lever, much like a railroad switchman in his tower, to place the gears in synch, grinding it aloft. Up the street a ways sat the corner drugstore and around the way an ice cream shop where flies butt persistently against the screen mesh, intent on stealing some Cookies 'n Cream. A Woods Hole tan may not stack up against one acquired in the Bahamas, but the town fills a need in people which grows into irreplaceable appreciation. It acts as a brake to slow time that otherwise would have slipped uselessly through my fingers. And now I shamefully admit that I am an addict. I'm addicted to Woods Hole.

The morning ferry blew its whistle, a loud and disturbing blast that causes people to stop and listen for a moment. The sound remained in the air for a second as if it was something that you could touch, then dissipated into nothingness. In the harbor, halyards slapped against the aluminum masts, a random melody of chimes, unconnected and free. A red flag snapped in the wind above the shack that masquerades as the Woods Hole Yacht Club. Gusts of wind pushed on the tall hedges leaning out over a deserted path. The green leaves rustled gently like the sound of a wave slowly breaking. Roots from the oak trees crumbled and bent the asphalt paths.

Climbing out through the window, I brushed the sill, my pants made wet with beaded water left by the fog. The razor blue sky cut by the shape of the sun marked the day's beginning. The morning was finished. Suddenly the screen door groaned and then reverberated shut. My little brother walked up giving me a curious look. "Whatcha lookin at?" he asked. "Myself," I replied.

In Church

DANIELLE LACAMPAGNE

Despite the blisters on my feet from my most decent-looking pair of heels, I walked briskly along with the flow of the other late congregation members through the overwhelming, tall, heavy, dark oak doors. I refrained from tugging and pulling at my nylons despite the wrinkles at my ankles and the sagging at my knees. I chose a pew third from the last where I could be virtually unnoticed and secluded.

There was a cold brisk draft coming from the side door, and unfortunately the high ceiling of the spacious church prevented any possibility of retaining heat. The slightest scent of incense flowed through the air, just strong enough to give the day's parishioners a sense of past, sorrowful ceremonies.

Through the stained glass the sun projected softly, blending glowing bright colors near my feet. The images seemed to form some type of abstract art, even though the actual window was a complex portrait of a very serious Saint Augustus. I quickly returned my attention to the more pleasant image at my feet.

The graying parish priest rambled on in French, a language that I could never decipher. His voice was powerful and annoying. His persistent singing along with the chorus was harsh and off key.

I choose an English prayer book and turned to today's scriptures in an attempt to find the true content of today's gospel. "One must turn the other cheek," I read from the beginning. "If only life were so simple," I thought to myself as I returned the book to it's holder.

Near the ceiling of the back wall of the altar, a huge, detailed wooden cross hung. A figure representing Jesus was nailed limp and lifeless to a merciless cross. Bright red stains dripped from the piercing nails at the figure's feet and palms. His forehead bled from the rigid thorns from his crown. This was a rather repulsive representation of the man who was supposedly our savior.

Sitting still was a difficult feat for me. I constantly shifted on the bench in an attempt to find some sort of comfortable position until finally I was relieved by the priest's request to kneel. But soon my knees became weak, and I could feel the strain on my kneecaps. A second request to rise brought even more pain as I tried to stand slowly, stretching my stiff joints carefully.

Today's crowd was typically small, consisting of many elderly women clothed in navy blue stuffy coats, clutching large brown handbags. The women were usually alone. Each of them appeared seriously attentive. The stout old woman only a few pews in front of me had thinning hair with a slight blue tint. Perhaps the blue was a result of a failing attempt to soften her white hair to a grayish tone. Regardless, I decided it was unattractive.

As the priest spoke, a quite distorted echo filled the church. This echo was quite familiar to the typical congregation members. Every Sunday, a retarded man in his late twenties sat with his mother in the first pew, faithfully attempting to repeat after the priest. The echo, which was almost impossible to overlook, presented a rather eerie cast to the mass. Sometimes I tried to imagine what life is like to this man who probably doesn't even know what this mass represents but nevertheless is dragged to it every Sunday morning by his mother, who fears to leave him alone. Perhaps my Sunday mornings were somewhat similar to his.

At the end of the mass I am always among the first to leave. Upon exiting I shake Father's cold, strong hand and force a smile to my face. "Merci, au revoir," I say in my most serious voice and my usual dull accent.

The Laundry Chute and the Sleeping Porch

JULIE VONDRACEK

I awoke slowly, trying to remember exactly where I was. When it dawned on me, I felt a rush of pleasure. I craned my neck towards the opened window; sunny and hot—great! My sister, still sleeping, turned over with a rustling of the pseudo-satin comforters I loved so well.

I went through the events of yesterday in my mind. The four-hour plane ride was long, and the five hours of layovers were hot and boring, but it was all well worth it. We were finally in Schuyler, Nebraska, home of the Cornhuskers and my parents' families. To me, Schuyler was everything you could ever want in a vacation.

The scuffing of feet and murmuring voices upstairs lured me out of bed. I padded up the stairs with my "Angel Baby" doll. A familiar sight greeted my sleepy eyes. Grampa V. was at the table drinking coffee, and Gramma V. was standing over the eggs in her curlers and fuzzy slippers.

"Well, good morning, sweetheart, have a good sleep?" I nodded, indicating that it was the best ever. She asked if I was hungry, and when I answered yes, she got out the six-pack of little cereals that were always handy. These were a special treat that we only got at Gramma and Grampa V's.

The rest of the house began to wake up, and we discussed the day's activities. The grown-ups, it was decided, would take a drive to see my great aunt, and my sister and our cousins could find something to do in Schuyler. About fifteen minutes later our cousins arrived, and with the beginning of our game, pretending to be the Box Car Kids, the rest of the day faded into a happy, giggly bliss.

Thousands of such memories overload my mind. I remember once, when it was about 110° (normal for a Schuyler summer), we fried an egg on the curb. We'll never know if it worked since when we came out to salt and pepper it, we found Grampa had turned the sprinker on it. When the heat got to us we'd go inside and create elaborate skits to amuse and amaze the grown-ups. Or we could spend hours sending messages from the upstairs to the downstairs through the laundry chute.

Then there were the days at Gramma O's. She had a delightful old white house, full of closets and trunks that children just love to play with. We'd begin those mornings with a glass of the most wonderful fresh-squeezed orange juice and end with our nightly firefly catching session. Then when it was time for bed, the happily exhausted kids would tumble into the big overstuffed bed that was set up on the sleeping porch. We'd fall asleep inhaling the warm lilac-scented air, dreaming of the next day. In between we would go swimming at the local pool, or rent P.P.V's (people-powered vehicles) and fool around Schuyler. On special days Gramma and I would make *the* most delicious fresh peach pie to be devoured that night.

The weeks spent in Schuyler were full of childish joys. There were playmates galore, parents rarely reprimanded us, and grandparents lavished love and treasures on us. It was Gramma O's orange juice and her golden bowl with its constant supply of candy; it was Grampa's big camera and his polyester leisure suits; it was Gramma V's familiar perfume and mysteriously ever-perfect hairdo. It was all these things and more through a child's wondrous eyes. It is now my own personal Lost Domain.

We went back there, Mom, my sister and I, a few years ago. My cousin was getting married in Omaha, so we took a drive to Schuyler for a day. Gramma V. had passed away years ago, so Grampa had moved and was living in a small apartment. (Needless to say, without laundry chute.) Gramma O. had also died, and her beautiful white house was sold to some young couple who took the bed off the sleeping porch. The cornfields looked dismal and desolate, and the hot days were just a bother. My cousins are all grown up and living here and there. I've grown up too, but not so much that if I look, really closely, I can't still catch a glimpse of that long-ago paradise, *my* Nebraska.

Going to Market

CARLA WILLETTO

The faraway horizon and the sheep corral were silhouetted against the sky—blue, pink, and orange introduction of the day's sunrise. My cousin David and I had stretched out on sheepskins in the cool hogan on the floor the previous evening. My grandparents were lying motionless on the old squeaky beds by the wall. The door was standing open and a soft breeze caressed me as I rose and stood outside, loving the land and everything on it and above it.

I wore jeans and an AIM T-shirt that belonged to Caroline. Barefooted, I started down the driveway when a soft "shhht" told me to wait a minute. Without a word or a look, I paused as David caught up with me, and we ran the mile to the road and back again. I fed the horse, chickens, and dogs as David carried some firewood into the hogan.

Grandma was fixing fry bread, and the stew was bubbling on the little woodburning stove. She smiled at her young adult grandchildren with their bare feet and shaggy heads. I playfully shoved Grandpa's boots onto his feet, and we pulled him to his feet as if he were old and decrepit. He was old but not decrepit! David and I just stood before him as he looked us over. He nodded at us and said, "Good Navajos" and slapped David's broad bare shoulders affectionately.

The sun opened its arms and enfolded the land with soft morning light, turning the interior walls of the hogan to pink. It was about six o'clock.

After finishing breakfast, David and I set off on Blacky, Grandma's horse. I sat behind David, drumming Blacky's soft sides with my bare heels. We rode with no saddle or blanket, and my handsome cousin guided the horse across arroyos towards Tohatchi. A few of Grandpa's cattle were ranging somewhere out there with some of Grandma's relatives' livestock.

Dew still clung to the underside of the sage brushes. Rabbits scurried and birds flurried. We stopped at John Joe's, and he gave me a horse to use. As we rode along I joked and laughed. David's smile was like the sun that shone on his bronze back. He threw back his head and sang to the perfect blue sky. I had combed his long hair as we had ridden, and now it streamed behind him, playing with the breeze, as we trotted.

As we topped a rise, we came upon the cattle with Chee Manuelito's brand. After chasing off a few strange ones, we rounded up the steers and headed back to the sheep camp. It took us long to get back because the cattle were slightly wild and had a mind of their own, so they moved slower than our horses. By now it was hot. David's back glistened and my horse's body was warm and damp. The dust rose in clouds from beneath the plodding hooves, coating us and our every breath.

We passed the time by singing our herding songs and country-western tunes. Being sweaty and dusty held a certain pleasure for me. I did not wish for cold Orange Crush and butterscotch sundaes. Out here I never thought about those things like other kids my age did. I would rather do what we were about to do now.

We had come to the watering place. The cattle rushed for it eagerly, and I raced David to the trough. There was a small reservoir, a water trough, a windmill cranking away in the wind that had just started up, and a spigot for filling water tanks and washing cars. As the livestock drank, David and I cooled ourselves off by standing under the spigot. We hosed the horses and pushed each other in the mud! But we didn't have much time for playing around. After a final shower, we mounted and drove the cattle across the highway and up Grandpa's drive. I guess it was almost noon because the sun was directly above us.

As we drove the cattle into the corral, Grandma backed John Joe's 2-ton truck up to the ramp. After deciding which ones we'd take, David and I set to work. Cattle are fast when they don't want to get caught, but old Blacky was a pretty good cutting horse. After what seemed like hours, we had five good-looking steers in the 2-ton and we put another one in Grandpa's pickup. Sweat trickled down my neck and my feet were caked with mud and grime. My feet! Our feet! We all laughed! We had been out the whole morning, cut out all those cattle, raced across the corral . . . in our bare feet!

We all went inside the hogan. I washed from the chipped enamel basin while the men ate outside. I even washed my hair. I put on my last pair of blue Wranglers and one of David's western shirts that he didn't know I took. Then I went up to the other house and used the mirror in Caroline's room. I put on the make-up that I'd used very little of that week and went outside. There sat David in the huge red truck, waiting.

"Shhht! Hey, foxy," he said, leaning out the window with an intoxicating grin.

"Hey, foxy, yourself," I said as I climbed in. "How do you like my shirt?"

"Looks like one I used to own but somebody ripped it off about ten minutes ago!"

"Let's go, cowboy!"

"You got it! 10-4!"

We took off towards Crownpoint. Most people sold to the stock-yard near Gallup, but Grandpa had once been cheated there. The Chee Manuelitos had always done cattle business in Crownpoint. Grandpa had known the man who bought our cattle for a long time, since the days when they were both young men with new wives. Now both their families had many grandchildren. That man had never cheated a person, white or brown. So we went east to Crownpoint to do our business. Grandma and Grandpa followed in their pickup.

After half an hour of listening to the radio and modulating with CB'ers on the Midland, we pulled up to a small series of corrals and ramps. An Anglo man came out of a house and greeted my grand-father warmly. The man knew David, too. David introduced me to John McCabe, who was almost as dark as an Indian. His face was etched with lines of hard work and good nature. His extended hand was hard and calloused.

"I have some cows to sell," said Grandpa.

"Let's have a look," replied John enthusiastically.

We let the cattle down the ramp into the corral. They were healthy and strong. These animals had just come down from ranging on the fertile ridge behind Grandpa's place about a week before; they weren't blue ribbon winners, but they were not bird cages either. For reservation cattle they were of excellent quality and condition. John admired the cattle and said he'd take all of them. We went inside the house, where he gave us coffee and paid $200 for one steer and $180 a head for the rest. The grownups visited a long time because they had not seen each other for some time. After a little while, David and I took off in John Joe's truck.

We went to the feed store and bought some grain and pellets. Then we headed for 7-11, where I began selecting some perishable groceries to eat that evening (because Grandma had no refrigerator). Just then a bunch of foxy guys came in and, of course, they knew David. The guys had a long conversation which included me. They tried to talk to me but, as always with boys not related to me, I became outrageously bashful and took off down an aisle. The tallest boy recognized me as a singer at a dance he'd been to recently.

Finally I was able to pay for the stuff and dash for the truck. David trotted out as Grandma and Grandpa pulled up and we all headed for home.

The day was nearing an end. Two hawks sailed towards Chuska Mountain. Small whirlygusts skittered in the distance. Peace, contentment, and fierce love of the land filled me. A soft breeze caressed me as I sang, with David, a song about going home.

Memoir of an Eyewitness Incident

Tell anything you saw happen once that was a brief incident you merely witnessed as a spectator, something of some significance to you but not necessarily very unusual or dramatic. Would this go well with some of your other writing? Or would it fit into the theme or subject characterizing some publication or audience you know of?

Who Is This?

JOBIE GRETHER

I was eating lunch in a small cafe in Jacksonville when the small, old man walked in. Everyone seemed to know him but gave him no special recognition. He approached me and stuck his hand out.

"How's it goin?" Not waiting for a reply he continued, "When's your birthday?" I told him, and he nodded vigorously and smiled, showing his blackened vacant gums. I curiously watched him as he summoned the seemingly annoyed waitress; she got him a mixture of some obviously outdated Tab syrup and ice water with a shiny stainless steel spoon. This intrigued him as he stepped towards the window and held it up to the sun. Giving a grunt, he sat back down and again noticed my presence. Looking around, he requested I read the label on a glass cookie jar that sat next to the ancient cash register. Repeating it three or four times to his contentment, he explained that he never did learn to read, again with a toothless grin. My food arrived and we sat in silence for a few minutes, I eating my burger and fries and he slurping loudly at his drink.

I wondered what type of life this man led. I again looked over and caught myself staring at him. Looking at him noisily sipping on the stained yellow glass, I truly felt sorry for him. He looked up and caught my gaze.

Then as suddenly as he came, he got up, picked up a concealed, rusty coffee can and rushed out the door.

Who was this? What kind of life could this person live? He wanted no compassion, yet this I felt for him. I never saw him again.

In Search of a Continent

ANDREA GOLLIN

The screen in front of the room is pulled down, the lights are dimmed, and the curtains are drawn. A weird sort of harmonious, throbbing music, underlaid with the soft, insistent beats of drums, fills the classroom. A few children in the front titter as they pass notes back and forth, and a boy to the right, near the bulletin board, cracks his gum. As the narrator's voice enters the room, two paper airplanes fly through the air, and several heads drop to their desks. The teacher has furtively slipped out of the classroom and now leans blissfully against the wall in the hallway, inhaling cigarette smoke deep into her lungs.

Several colored maps of Africa appear on the screen and change colors in accord with instruction received from the voice. The tape accompanying the film conveys information concerning such topics as tropical rain forests, deserts, and natural resources. Herds of wild elephants lumber across the screen and are followed by action pictures of lions, tigers, and poisonous snakes. A journey under water displays several species of sea-life feared to be near extinction. Palm trees precede banana trees until the camera is surrounded only by green. A monkey shrieks and, grinning insanely, shakes a few coconuts onto the ground.

The camera and narrator then travel to an African family living in the middle of the desert. These people travel from oasis to oasis in the same manner as was set forth by their ancestors more than two thousand years ago. Untainted by the problems and difficulties of the modern world, these individuals live only to struggle for survival, carrying their few belongings on their backs, and eating worms and insects. The children stand shyly, clutching their thirteen-year-old mother's bare legs with thin arms, bloated stomachs thrust towards the camera and shy smiles on their faces.

The family is left alone to search for the rare oasis in the Sahara desert while the camera probes on in its never-ending quest to define Africa. The teacher re-enters the room following a loud crash. She roughly grabs the child unfortunate enough to have fallen asleep so blatantly, hauls him upright, and dispatches him to the principal's office. The teacher wearily notes that she is finally receiving the class' undivided attention, and shrilly orders its members to pay attention to the film. It's too much for her. She vanishes into the hallway once again, this time to slump limply against the wall as she passes a clammy hand across her wet forehead, wiping the moisture into greasy hair.

The narrator drones through the history of the Kenyan village in which he finds himself. The village, like the underfed nomads previously witnessed, has existed in the same manner for thousands of years and thus is an accurate portrayal of Africa as well as a valuable clue in the hunt for a key to the continent.

The screen features a stereotype of a two-year-old African villager, covered with fat, green flies, but somehow unperturbed. Johnny Smith's mouth drops open, and the pen that he has been using to draw on the back of Susie's neck drops from his limp hand. He shudders slightly, and then giggles. He has glimpsed an ear dripping with fourteen distinct earrings. Johnny laughs outright at the sight of nude bodies balancing pots of water on their heads, and continues with the task of mutilating Susie's neck, whistling contentedly as he does so.

A few women prepare the noonday meal. There is a large pot of monkey soup smoking over some red embers. It is soon ladled into waiting mouths via coconut shells but does not seem to do much good, judging from the life expectancy and mortality rate cited by the speaker. Here again, extended bellies are pushed towards the viewers, those generous Americans.

Cut to trained professionals who are improving the quality of daily life at this very moment. It is innoculation day in a nameless, isolated village. A veritable army of white-clad troopers shove hypodermic needles into a countless number of skinny brown arms while managing to smile reassuringly in the general vicinity of scared eyes. The village medicine man prances around the area, dressed in a jumbled array of paint and feathers. The scene leads to a consideration of religion and customs. A festive celebration entailing the donning of colorful garb and accompanied by much music and dancing serves the purpose.

On to the last stop of the journey in search of the true Africa. It consists of African children learning to read, write and cipher, exactly what young Lincoln learned so long ago. Switch to a more advanced stage, entailing Chemistry. A smiling, nose-ringed girl decants a beaker of clear red liquid into one of orange and carefully scrutinizes the reaction.

The teacher strides back into the room, flicks on the lights, snaps up the screen, and yanks open the curtains, leaving the shades down. Neighbors poke one another out of various reveries as she grimly passes around the composition paper.

Falling Forever

JIM BLAU

I was walking down Daytona Streeet at five on a hot afternoon in July. As I passed the East Church Road intersection, I noticed that people were passing me at a run and seemed excited. My first thought, a rather stupid one, was that perhaps someone famous was in town,

and all the people were running to see him/her. Then I thought maybe
there's a fire down the street. I looked above the apartment buildings
that line the right side of the street for some sign of smoke.

Then I saw her. She was standing on the roof of the Armada
Hotel, at twenty stories the tallest building in the area. A crowd had
gathered at the foot of the building, all faces looking upwards at her. I
was still about a block and a half away, but I could see clearly her
indecisive stance at the edge of the roof, her skirts blowing around her
legs in the soft evening breeze.

The people in the crowd were dumbfounded. Nothing like this
had ever happened before in our town. Don't do it!" a few people
yelled. "Don't be stupid!" shouted a young man in a brown suit. Sirens
wailed in the dusk, getting louder.

She jumped. Like a rag doll, she flipped and tossed in the air,
arms waving. In my mind I can still see her, flailing as if suspended in
the air for one horrible moment. There was an unbearable sound as
she hit the pavement.

People milled around in confusion. "Did you see? Did you see?"
they asked each other. Others wre crying; one was screaming. A
stretcher passed through the crowd to the foot of the building. "Let us
through, please," they shouted above the noise.

I turned around and went home, that rag-doll image seared into
my mind forever.

Memoir of Nature

*Give an account of some action you witnessed in which
people played little or no part, such as some animal behavior or
weather that particularly impressed you. Give your own thoughts
and feelings, however. You may include this in a collection of
your memoirs, to diversify them, or you may make it part of a
booklet of nature memoirs by others.*

Jill

KAREN CAMPBELL

When I was 7, my older sister and I adopted two lovable little
ducks. Jack and Jill were an inseparable pair. I sacrificially gave up my
A-frame playhouse for the two ducks, and a wire fence was set around
the playhouse to serve as a pen, even though the ducks could fly free
of the fence.

One morning, when I went out to the duck's domain, Jack was
nowhere in sight. I called his name so many times that I began to get a

speech impediment. I climbed over the wire fence, squished through the mud, and stepped into the playhouse. The pungent odor of duck-poop hit me with a bang. Within a few seconds my nose adapted to the awful smell, and I scouted the shelter, but Jack wasn't there.

Weeks passed. Jill waddled and fluttered around restlessly. She was lost and confused without Jack. Mom and Dad soon informed us that we were going to move in a few months to a location closer to my dad's job. During those last couple of months, something strange and magical happened. Jill and our Shetland pony became quite good friends. Sometimes we looked out our kitchen window at our field, to find Jill contentedly resting on Rusty's back. They were made for each other. When the time came for us to move, Rusty had to be sold, because there wasn't a place to keep him at our new house.

A man in faded Wrangler jeans and muddy cowboy boots came for Rusty in his pick-up. Tears ran down my face as the man harshly pulled on the lead-rope and shoved Rusty in the horse-trailer. I glanced at the open field, to see Jill fluttering and waddling around angry and confused. Her neck stretched far forward as she tottled, letting out shrill, squeaking quacks. Our family looked at the distraught duck, and then at the horse-trailer.

"How'd you like to have a duck thrown into the deal too?" my father said.

"Why heck, why not? Since the two are so used to each other." The pick-up and trailer drove up 95th street and disappeared over the hill.

Cougars at Bay

SCOTT STEPHENS

About three years ago I witnessed something very few city folks get to see.

I was archery hunting in a remote canyon, known to most people as Fiddlers Hell. This was not irregular at all since Doug Anderson and I hunted there quite often. It's a steep canyon that most people won't dare to venture into.

I don't quite know what I was doing there. I saw many deer and elk and didn't even bother to shoot.

About noon I stopped to rest on a large rock. I was sitting there enjoying the scenery, when I spotted a slight movement in the brush. I was hoping to see a big bull elk.

To my surprise two full grown cougars strolled out into the meadow. They were playing happily, wrestling with each other.

The wind was blowing in my face, and I was sitting above them. As long as I was still I could watch them play.

They played in the meadow for about an hour, and then as if a signal from nature beckoned to them, they raced off. I wasn't quite sure what made them run off. I attemped to follow them.

As I stepped off my rock, I caught a faint sound of braying dogs. Then I knew. Poachers! I thought for sure the cats would be shot.

I ran up on the ridge, leaving my bow lying on the ground. I spotted the dogs. I was shocked. These were not pure-bred hunting dogs used by poachers. Instead, they were a mangy crew of about seven dogs, led by a big redbone. It was the wild pack that I had heard so much about. I spotted the cougars just ahead of the pack. One cougar climbed a tree, the other prepared to fight. With a rock cliff at its back and the pack at its front, it fought.

I ran back to get my bow. When I reached the fight one cougar and five dogs lay dead. The other two dogs ran off. I went up to the cougar. It was a large male. The female was still in the tree.

I never really understood why the male didn't tree, or why the female didn't help.

About three months later I figured it out. In the first place if he had climbed the tree the dogs would have waited for them to starve. And the male fought the dogs to give the female a chance for her life; she was bearing young. I've often gone back to Fiddlers Hell to look for the cougars, but I've never found them.

Memoir Profile

Show what someone was like or is like by telling typical things about their behavior that you know from knowing him or her. Use the subject's actions and habits and words to sketch the main qualities of his or her character or relationship to you.

My Grandfather

JOHN GOSSETT

When I was young I would go to see my grandfather at his shoe store. I can remember sitting and watching him talk to all the people who came in. In his twenty years of business he learned all the regulars' names and something about them. In his years he was very well known and had acquired many friends. Many of his friends were from Elks and Rotary, where he had been president. I guess I never realized how many friends he had until he died. At the funeral there were more than five hundred people. Standing room only.

In his life he had accomplished all he wanted and realized all his dreams. My grandfather was a great outdoorsman. He had hunted and fished year round for fifty years in this valley. When he died he was thought to be the best fly fisherman in Oregon. I can remember the hours he spent casting for practice. I would set a hat on the grass, and he could hit it consistently, up to forty yards away. My grandfather survived a heart attack in nineteen seventy-two. When he returned home he told us that "the Lord doesn't count days spent fishing so I have at least ten years left." He guessed very close. He died last year, only a year off.

I can remember all the huge meals we ate together. Grandad always knew when I was coming, so he would fix a large meal. We usually ate wild game along with corn and crescent rolls. I can't remember ever leaving without being stuffed to the gills.

I was at the hospital when he died; he looked strangely unfamiliar. In life he had a ruddy complexion and dark hair. In death he was cold and pale. There was none of the warmth I knew he possessed. The memory of his death makes little difference to me; my memories are of his life.

Charlie

SANDI RYALS

It wasn't that he was stuck-up or anything; he just liked to be alone. While all the other third-graders from Miss Harvey's room were running down the hall to get the biggest dessert at lunch, Charlie walked quietly with his peanut butter sandwich and green apple to Table Number Seven and sat all the way at the end of the bench with his back against the wall. While all the other kids were scheming how to get rid of their beets so that they could get another wiener roll-up, Charlie would grin broadly and sometimes offer ideas whenever they came to him. He always had good ideas when he felt like talking.

"Ya see here, first ya drink all ya milk, and then open the carton all the way up and stuff ya beets in that there carton and close it up. Got that?" Even though Charlie couldn't run very fast, he could throw a ball pretty far, so Robert Morgan always picked Charlie first on his baseball team. Robert was All Right, Charlie decided, but he was always chasing those dumb girls, or else they were chasing him. Some girls were okay, but most of them were disgusting.

Like Margie Crans. She was always belching. Not just little burps and then an "excuse me," but rumbling belches followed by a hoarse laugh. How sickening.

Nobody really knew Charlie. He was just a nice kid, and even though he was quiet, he was well-liked. Even when Susie Bowles, the most popular girl in school, had a party, she asked Charlie. A lot of the boys would have jumped at the chance, but Charlie said No, he had other things to do. And later while everyone was talking about how great the party was, Charlie noticed there were only six yellow bikes in the bike-racks. When others ran to each other's houses after school, Charlie would walk home by himself. Sometimes a few of them would ask him over to play catch, but they soon got tired of his polite declining. They never questioned his refusals. He was still considered a "good guy" by one and all.

And then one day it happened. The thing he was backing away from came and jumped him. It started out a normal school day. At recess all the kids were goofing around on the monkey bars; Robert Morgan was being pursued by a couple of leggy girls, and Charlie was just walking toward the bars with a boy from another class. Suddenly he knew what was coming and let out a frightened cry. His body was thrown to the ground as if by some unseen force. His muscles twitched violently in all directions, and breath, when it came, came in gasps. . . .

When the seizure was over, Charlie looked slowly up to see a sea of white, open-mouthed faces, not seeing any particular ones. He lay on the gravel for a few minutes, while the silence became so still it almost cracked. He got up slowly and tried to let off a casual laugh, but it caught in his throat as he feebly brushed off his pant legs. He quickly looked down as a tear made its way down his dirt-streaked face, followed by others. As he walked away, he could hear a nervous series of throat clearings, fake coughs, and them the almost inaudible hissing of hand-cupped whispers.

Investigation

(Looking Into)

Writing Up Sensory Notes

Go somewhere that interests you and jot down pell-mell as much as you can record in note fashion of what you see, hear, smell, and touch there. Allow ten to thirty minutes. Don't think yet about what you will make of this; just get down plenty of material for later. Do the same thing at another locale of your choice, or at the same place at different times, if you would like to be sure to have plenty of choices for writing up.

Now look over your notes and see if some fragments especially stand out or if an overall impression, mood, or pattern emerges that would interest some other people. Organize around this by deleting whatever you judge to be irrelevant, by adding things you may remember but didn't record or that you know about from other sources, and by re-shaping and re-phrasing what you keep. This could end up as a story, a sketch, a play, an essay, reportage, or a poem.

[Some of the following samples are notes, and some are compositions based on notes. For publication purposes we have chosen notes that happen to be comprehensible to others than the author, but notes may frequently be so abbreviated and private as to mystify all but the one who wrote them, the only one who needs to make sense of them.]

Notes
Joe Cabler

I'm sitting atop the back porch of our house. From here you can see across our field and view the huge mountains not more than 2 miles away. They are covered completely with trees except for a small barren patch where Dad and I put salt out for the deer. After our monthly hike to that spot deer can be seen through our field glasses wandering around the clearing.

Between the two highest mountains is the last bit of bright sky marking the spot of the sun's evening descent. A few grayish clouds slowly move over the mountain line in a southwesterly direction. The pungent smell of the burning oak and pine in our fireplace drifts with the smoke as it follows the clouds. My sister's champion dairy cow walks lazily among the clear-cut streak of green running, as the creek that it follows, to the nearby pond. The splash of water can be heard in the kitchen as Mom prepares to load the dishwasher. My cat T.M. is rolled up at my feet staring up at me with eyes that look as if they are wishing to receive. A small swallow nibbles and picks carefuly through the seed in our bird feeder. Our neighbors' chickens can be heard down the canyon making their traditional racket at the wrong time.

Notes
Karen Campbell

The neglected lawn is disturbed by the wind, looking like a still, green pond whose waters have been ruffled by a paddle boat on its surface. As the breeze rushes through the trees, the branches & leaves are arched birds' wings in flight against the wind. The wooden shed stands stiffly alone. The boxes, buckets, and yard tools huddle together inside. Outside the rain drips, spitting into the puddles on the walk.

I am the things around me all at once, the placid pond, being ruffled by a disturbance, the birds' wings in flight against the wind, the shed that stands alone, and its muddled clutter that seeks refuge. I am the drops of rain that fall from the sky, and then landing with a splat into a pool of other raindrops. Each is a fragment of feeling.

Notes
Jim Anderson

Getting to this dirty spot on this unique broken bridge was not as easy as it used to be. The trail was overgrown to the point where one realizes that fall can no longer effectively trim back a summer's thick growth. When I think of this broken bridge and am not actually here, I see the fracture as more of a tear than a clean cut edge. Over the edge large chunks of cement lie above and visibly submerged. There is a foam on the water that washes back into the still shallows. It is a white foam tinted with a greenish brown. The idea of a broken bridge reminds me of an album cover by the Doobie Brothers, I think. It looks so out of place here—a grey manmade structure in the middle of a natural area. Why did they not make a park here? It is better that they didn't. If one doesn't know about Bear Creek, or hear the stories of the things that are dumped into it, it looks peaceful enough, but I wouldn't want to drink it. It would look better if a subdivision was not right across the creek, behind a wall of high trees. I remember training Cody here, Jeff's black lab. I remember when Jim and I came here one day and smoked half a pack of cigarettes. That was five years ago. I haven't really spent any time with him since that year. Any time to speak of anyway. I rode Doug's motorcycle near this bridge once and crossed when I was dove hunting. How I can shoot those things confuses me. For what is lost, the hunter really doesn't get much. I was here before a concert a little more than five years ago, with Steve, my cousin. I wonder what these cars coming over the overpass think when they see a kid out here stooping over something with a something in his hand. They probably think I am one of those legendary Bear Creek Transients. A small child could panic here under all this shrubbery; it looks like a trapping nightmare. I would suppose winter is very cold here. The frost must hurt the leaves and stalks of the things that stand up against the coldness with a numbing sting. In the summer you wonder where the snakes are and hope one doesn't slide over your feet as they pass invisible beneath your knees, blocked by the high thick weeds. The bridge and the straight line of pine trees hiding the freeway are the only artificial things in my immediate surroundings. I remember wading up the creek with the sand settling in my sneakers with the training buck in my hand and Cody by my side. She was still a pup and sometimes I would have to carry her, shivering. But that was in the late fall, with the fog. In the summer the creek seemed a little lower and the cottonwood white flakes blew down and floated in the water, which seemed more like syrup in the summer. It doesn't look like syrup now, it's still a little thin and it splashes & gurgles. I've seen muskrat here. When will this grey bridge fall? I'm really not sure if I was even alive when this bridge was in use. I can't remember ever seeing it. And I-5 was always here so I guess that answers my question. A swarm of gnats or mosquitoes, like the cottonwood flakes, are massing near the right corner and moving up and down. How do they do it in a breeze? All the little trails on the far side of the creek where I used to hunt grasshoppers and lizards with Mike are almost gone. Kids these days must find better things to do. I expect it will be getting cold.

Notes
Peter Nicholson

camelia bush—green cool waxy leaves
trash bag—hot
blossoms—damp withered sweet smell

```
sunlight—broken
earth—dry hot
dead leaves—rustle
ivy
stones
twigs
lips—parched salty
snake—garter, black red yellow still
        pink tongue
```

Snake

PETER NICHOLSON

I crouch beneath the cool, green camelia bush. My hand relaxes, and from it slips the hot trash bag into which I had been stuffing damp, withered blossoms. Sunlight drops through the camelia's waxy leaves, splinters through my hair onto my cheeks. Silence. The sweet, cloying aroma of the fallen blossoms hangs in the air, mixing with the dry smell of the hot earth. Rustle of dead leaves. Without moving my head, my eyes run over the ground across ivy, stones, twigs—there.

A shape as still as a twig, but rounded, full, living. It is a garter snake, poised with its head above the ivy in a puddle of sunlight. Ebony, coral and maize, it rests immobile. Flick. Its pink tongue darts out and back in a motionless mouth. I lick my parched lips, working my tongue slowly over their salty, chapped curves. My eyes follow the curve of its body trying to find its end, but once it dips below the ivy I am lost. The snake pivots its head, and I stop thinking. Quickly, it drops to the ground and slithers through the ivy. I stand up and look down at where it should be, but it isn't. I prod the leaves with my foot, but there is no answering movement.

The Pick-Up

KELLI KIMPEL

At a small oakwood table near the bar stools, a macho male, around twenty-five years old, sits scanning the bar and restaurant. After some time of not finding worthwhile prey, his eyes feast upon a young blonde wearing a sparkling tube-top and velvet black pants, ordering a "strong margarita." Casually floating her way, he winks and flashes a million-dollar smile.

"Let me buy you a drink," he says in a well practiced Paul Newman voice.

"Thanks anyway, but I [giggle] already bought my own."

Persistently, he and his size-too-small Calvin Klein jeans stay seated on the red-cushioned bar stool. He downs a couple of White Russians while carefully combing his mustache. After an unsuccessful attempt at picking-up on the blonde, his attention is about-faced toward a brunette with a new permanent and dress with slits everywhere imaginable. He approaches her with one hand stroking his chest hairs above his V-necked shirt, and one hand whisking his feathered haircut out of his face. He asks her to dance while in front of her; he does a few of the newest disco steps in place.

She replies, "Hey look, man, my boyfriend's in the john, and when he comes out you better be gone."

Without hesitation, he finds the door and on his way out winks at the waitress, "Don't worry, baby, I'll be back."

As the Tide Rises

ANTHONY RANDALL

The water slowly climbs up the shore as the giant, yellow sun settles into the far, green water. The green waves dance up and down on its face as if trying to extinguish it. The long brown beach stretches for miles in each direction then slowly slopes to the horizon. Pieces of driftwood are carelessly littered up and down the beach front.

A sand crab's tracks lead wobbly to a shallow but spacious tide pool. The little rock edges contain a small portion of a captured tide from the high noon waters. The rock ledges contain small cracks with all sorts of little sea creatures in them, most of them so small that they must remain in hiding for fear of being eaten by a bird. On one edge are tracks from a bird who was trying to get a free and easy meal by eating the small animals or the little portions of broken off seaweed that float in the pool.

On the bottom of the shallow pool a snail shell moves at a pace above that of a normal snail. It stops in front of a small green plant. Slowly a crablike creature appears from within the shell and gobbles up the plant. The moment the plant is eaten the hermit crab dashes back to his home. Another snail shell moves along a little rock ledge, but this time it is being pushed by its original owner.

There are two sea anemones in this pool, one on each side. They face each other as if preparing for the last showdown. Their tentacles flow back and forth with the wind-caused currents, always in a hopeful search for unsuspecting prey. A piece of a dead plant comes swirling by and is immediately sucked up and surrounded by the tentacles before being drawn into the mouth

In the most remote corner lies a dark shape, as if in hiding from an unknown enemy. In the light this creature would prove to be very colorful but not very active. It is the sunflower star, one of the biggest and most beautiful of the sunflowers. It has anywhere from nineteen arms and can grow to over two feet in diameter. This one has about twelve arms and is about one-half foot in diameter.

Out of the water on one side of the tiny pool lies a small mussel shell. Its purple- and white-streaked cover is hard and dry because of its long disuse. Once this shell was a home and a source of great protection for the small yellow mussel. Now it is a piece of ocean debris, waiting for the next tide to ride it higher onto the rocky seashore.

On the higher rocks of the pool walls are quite a few barnacles. Most of them sit half submerged in water and half drying in the ocean air. The larger specimens that cling to the upper surrounding rocks are sharp and will easily cut anything that comes in contact with them. These barnacles range in color from a light brown to a light orange. You will find barnacles hooked to a lot of things but most frequently to the rocks and mussel shells that lie in or near the tide pool.

Out of one of the large cracks slides a yellow prawn on its way to dine on the smaller animals who inhabit this temporary home. Its feathery gills move back and forth as if in a giant wind. The prawn slowly crawls one way and quickly darts back across the pool at an almost invisible little fish. The fish tries to get away, but the prawn grabs it in its two front claws and snaps its back. Slowly but surely the prawn makes his way back to his home and gets ready for a big dinner.

Now that the sun is setting many of the sensitive animals start to show themselves. From under one rock alone come four flat, brown ribbon worms. They crawl to and fro searching for food or some discarded material left by some other inhabitant of this home.

The last animal to see before the sun disappears is a bright purple sea urchin. Its round body is fitted almost perfectly into a hole in the rock. Its long narrow legs stretch out to find an evening meal.

Then all hopes for further discovery are over as the tide rises and the sun disappears.

A World at Peace

JOHN CONRAD

It's a cool misty afternoon at the far end of the Goleta pier. Several seagulls hovering above add color and life to the otherwise dull gray skies. The pier is alive—surprisingly crowded with people from all walks of life.

Glancing to my right I notice a young Hispanic couple with two small children having a good time. The parents want to leave soon to get an early start for dinner, but the kids are begging to stay just a while longer.

"Are you enjoying yourself?" I ask one.

"Yes," he replies happily, "I've caught three fish."

That's three more fish than anyone else has caught since I've been here, I think; maybe it's beginner's luck.

"Have you been fishing before?" I inquire.

"Yes, we come almost every weekend," he says, completely destroying my theory.

Looking to my left for a moment, I notice a young couple all bundled up to protect themselves from the cold wind. They have three poles in front of them but they don't appear to be having much luck. I doubt if fishing is foremost in their minds now anyway, judging from the smiles on their faces.

Directly behind, there are two different sorts of people. One is an aged fisherman type wearing a woolen ski-cap, old blue windbreaker, and worn jeans. His face is wrinkled and unshaven, just the kind you'd expect on an old man of the sea. It's strange to think he was once young like me. I wonder how he got into his present situation.

Two young men, probably students at UCSB, are also behind me. They've been talking quite a while about many things, but now the conversation has turned to disputes involving the countries of the world. They both seem very concerned about the threat of war and what can be done about it.

Glancing away, I look around the pier again, and a thought comes to me. There are so many different types of people here but there are no disagreements. No one is worried about what other people are saying or how many fish they're catching. Well, if the attitude here spreads there might be hope for the world yet. Maybe all the countries will eventually exist together peacefully just as the people are doing here on this cool, misty afternoon at the tip of the Goleta pier.

Through the Frost

KELLIE HAMILTON

The ducks chatter harshly at me as I approach the small pond. They are frightened by the crunching of the brown leaves under my feet. Squatting, I study them through the frost-covered wires of the sagging fence. They stretch and shiver, their reflection on the water in the pond interrupted by small patches of icy crystals, frozen in geometric designs. Occasionally, tiny bubbles rise to the surface and pop, making ripples in the water. The ducks begin to feed at the far edge of the pond, but they are startled by the barking of a nearby dog. One of the mallard drakes loudly scolds the dog while the others continue to eat, bobbing and shaking their heads as they swallow. The white rings on the necks of the males make them look like Catholic priests with their white collars on. The brown-speckled females visit each other as they wander through the white, frozen weeds, nibbling at the roots. By now, my nose and ears are numb from the cold, and my legs ache from squatting. As I rise to go, the ducks start their chattering again, warning me to keep my distance.

Under the Sun

JULIE KENASTON

The long, rectangular loft was close to half-filled with hay. Fine fragments from the bales explode in clouds of dust at each footstep, giving rise to a dry, musty smell. Crevices between the thick, splintering floorboards are filled with stale, acrid hay and dust; bits of bailing twine lie on the floor among the loose hay. The tin barn roof magnifies each sound, especially the moaning of the sultry wind coming through the broad opening that overlooks the sundried pastures. The slight breeze does nothing to relieve the stifling heat of the loft but brings on a scent of the parched grass, and sere, humid air.

The cracked ground is fervid to the touch; the insipid grass, brittle; and yellow starthistles line the fences, thriving in the scorching rays of the intense summer day. Killdeer rove feverishly under the hot sun, and horses pace impatiently, heads hung low, dehydrating in their thick fur. Some chickens, feathers puffed, squawk pitifully as they traipse discontentedly to the water tub in hopes that the cool liquid will assuage their parched throats. An enormous pile of dirt clods and manure interrupt the barren scene, the lumps slowly crumbling away in the afternoon warmth. Sheep roam the field continuously, discontentedly bleating their protest of the heat to the flaming ball of fire above.

Reportage

Participant Reportage

Do a sketch of a place or activity that you know as an insider, as one of the participants. Tell what you did and witnessed at some typical or especially informative time. The subject might be a job or sport or pastime of yours—something you habitually take part in with others. This means looking on your familiar activity as a fit object of investigation. Tell what happened on this occasion so as to give an idea of what happens there most of the time. This will result in one kind of feature article.

911

KIM FAUSKEE

It's a shining November morning with the dew covering the ground as I walk into the crew quarters for 911 ambulance. I'm greeted by the sounds of snoring and coughing. The last shift was busy with eleven calls, three of which were during the middle of the night.

As I sit down to read about the calls, my partners arrive. They are Paramedics Curt Dalton and Layne Hicks, both of whom have been working for two years. They walk through the door noisily, waking up the other crew. A few rude comments are made, and the other crew members try to go back to sleep.

The next thing on the agenda is to check out the ambulance and then go to breakfast. About thirty seconds after we get to Farmer Boy, our toners go off and the dispatcher tells us to respond to a vehicle accident with injuries on Modoc: a car has run into a power pole. When we get there, Curt yells to be careful because of downed power lines. A man says to me that he's the driver but is unhurt. Soon the fire department arrives, and the situation is brought under control. On the way back to breakfast Curt says, "Boy, I thought we had the big one."

The rest of the day is spent running a couple of non-emergency calls and cleaning up the quarters. After dinner we go back to quarters, where Curt plays his guitar and Layne reads a magazine. When the emergency phone rings, Curt copies down an address and says: "Let's go, we have a heart attack call."

The streets are busy with Saturday night traffic. The city fire department is there when we arrive and advises us that they have a fifty-two year old male, pulseless and non-breathing and they are performing CPR. Curt tells me to set up an I.V. and hook the man to the E.K.G. monitor, which I do quickly because in this situation a few seconds can determine life or death. Layne calls Cottage Hospital on our radio, and they advise us to administer the appropriate drugs and apply shock at 400 watt seconds. We all feel great when the man revives. Curt says that he wishes this happened in all cases, and we all agree.

We get to sleep the rest of the night and are awakened the next morning by the new shift kicking to get the door opened. The first words they say are, "Boy, what an easy day you guys had! Where are the keys to the ambulance, so we can go to breakfast?"

Working for the Army

PATRICIA BÖCK

"You know what athlete's foot is, right? Well, mistletoe is what astronauts get."

I looked at him like he was a Martian I couldn't understand.

"Thanks, Patty. I get the point. Hey look, it's your turn to ring the dumb bell now."

"Hey, no problem."

Mike Coyle handed me the shiny metal bell that we had been ringing constantly since noon. He said that the bell was driving him crazy; I really didn't notice it much. The two of us had talked about my future, the usual questions about my college and career plans. When he found out that I want to be a lawyer he explained to me how he became a lawyer and tried to justify lawyers charging a hundred and fifty dollars an hour. (He didn't convince me they were worth it, but he sure got me more interested in law!) I was about to ask him where he had gone to school when a boy about seven years old came running up to the red Christmas Kettle of the Salvation Army.

"Do you take checks?"

"Yeah! Sure! Just make it out to the Salvation Army."

Mike and I couldn't believe it. People had been dropping in dollar bills and small change that was left over from their shopping at Long's, but we didn't expect anyone to give us a check.

The little boy came running back from a blue pick-up truck with a check in his hand. Mike took it from him and folded it in half to fit in the slot, but not before he took a look at the amount. It was for a hundred dollars. I couldn't believe it. Mike bent down and looked the little boy straight in the eyes.

"Tell your parents thank you very much—and Merry Christmas, son."

Mike and I were quite proud of ourselves. I was wearing the "I'm working for the Salvation Army today" pin and Mike had on his Fairfield Kiwanis jacket. We made quite a team.

We spent the next hour talking about the Kiwanis Crab feed-in January and why anyone would want to live In Green Valley. (He doesn't, I do.) We sometimes stopped in the middle of a sentence to say thank-you and Merry Christmas to old ladies who made the big five-cent donation. Mike kept telling passersby that they should "give till it hurts," but I was grateful for every donation, big or small.

At about one-thirty a large woman in a dark blue suit and the traditional Salvation Army hat came marching up to our kettle. She was being followed by about twelve kids aged 4 to 9. She introduced herself; she had an ugly German name like Hildegarde or Inga, I can't remember which. She informed us that she was going to lead the children in singing Christmas carols. She yelled at the children to form a line; they refused. The sun was too bright, they didn't like it shining in their eyes. Inga handed out sheets with the Christmas carol lyrics on them. One little boy whined that he didn't know how to read. A little Asian girl named Emily said the same.

"Well, just pretend that you know how to read!" Inga snapped at them.

Mike muttered something under his breath. I didn't hear him. "What?"

"I said, she must be a sergeant in the army,"

I couldn't help laughing. Inga certainly didn't have a winning way with children. The children struggled through "Joy to the World" and "Away in a Manger." Little Emily loved stepping on the walkway that opened Long's automatic doors. But Inga didn't think that was as funny as Emily did.

"Emily!!!"

Emily pulled her skinny leg off the walkway and leaned against the wall. The kids were obviously getting bored. Inga made one final attempt to get the kids to sing. They started "We Wish You a Merry Christmas" nice and loud; even Emily was singing.

"And a Happy New Year."

Inga was apparently pleased with this last song and told the kids to go back to the van. Inga told Mike that she would be back at three o'clock to pick up the kettle. She thanked Mike and Kiwanis, and me and Key Club, for our time. We told her we were glad to help.

Shortly after our carolers had left, three little boys came out of Long's. The oldest boy dropped a few pennies into the bucket. The two younger boys followed the oldest one, carrying small plastic shopping bags. Suddenly, the littlest one came running back towards us. He was trying to put a nickel into the slot but he couldn't reach it. Mike picked him up and let him drop the coin in. As soon as Mike put him down, he ran to catch up with the others. Mike and I resumed our conversation, I promised to call to remind him about the next Key Club meeting, and he gave me his business card with his law office number on it. Well, our time was almost up. Mike turned around, and we saw one of those boys come careening around the corner. He had run all the way back just so he could drop his donation into the bucket. We heard the quarter click against the many others that were already in the bucket. He turned and ran towards the other boys, who we could no longer see. Our last benefactor slid around the corner like he was running bases in Little League. His was the last donation for our shift, and at three o'clock sharp Inga came to pick up our bucket. I realized then that Ms. Depesto of T.V.'s *Moonlighting* was right when she said that "Kids and Christmas make the rest of life more bearable"; they certainly do.

The Hornet

PAT LEWIS

It's seven in the morning on a foggy Saturday and time for another day's work on the *Hornet*. Today's fishing expeditions consist of two half-day boat trips. The first trip is from 7:00 a.m. to 11:45 a.m. It's now time to let the waiting people on the boat. While they are boarding you can almost feel the anxiety of the unskilled fisherman.

The first spot we tried was off the coast of Shoreline Park, fishing for halibut. The first fish caught was a twenty-inch calico bass, weighing about four pounds. While the passengers are fishing, the first deckhand and I go around and ask people if they want to enter the jackpot. It's a little game that we play. Everyone puts two dollars in a bowl, and the person who catches the biggest fish collects all the money. The first halibut caught was about 35 inches and weighed 15 pounds. There were two other halibut caught, but they were under the limit of 22 inches so we had to let them go. As the captain fires up the engines to move to deeper water, the passengers pull up their lines and put on different-sized hooks and weights.

It's about 9:00 a.m. as we reach our designated spot, and we haven't had any problems with sea sickness yet. We are now fishing for deepsea bass. About an hour passes by, and all the fish that the passengers have caught have been mackerel. The captain tells the passengers to pull up their lines so that we can move to deeper water. The passengers start catching calico and johnny bass and still a lot of mackerel.

It's 11:30 and time to head back to the docks. The jackpot winner is a middle-aged man, the one who caught the 35-inch halibut. As the people leave the boat, you see that they walk on the ground as if they were still on the water.

It's 12:00 and time to prepare for the second half-day boat. The first deckhand lets the people on the boat as I prepare the bait tanks for another exciting afternoon trip.

The first spot that we tried was again off the coast of Shoreline Park. As we left that spot there were three halibut, two calico bass, and a few mackerel caught. We started heading out to deeper water, and I noticed that the water was getting rougher. We reached a spot four miles off shore and fished for red snapper. At the beginning the passengers started catching mackerel, but as they got deeper, they began pulling the massive red snapper, and the jackpot really began to take effect on them.

The ocean started to get too rough about 4:00, so the captain decided to head in. A few passengers were getting sick. The swells reached a height of nine feet.

We reached the docks around 4:45. After all the passengers are off, the first deckhand and I have the job of scrubbing the boat.

Visit

Go somewhere that you would like to report on for a journalistic feature—a locale that's colorful or significant, a place where things important or amusing or typical take place. Observe, move around, and take notes until you feel you have enough material to do justice to whatever impelled you to choose the place. Use your notes now to render it according to what it most seems to have to say. You might submit this to a newspaper or magazine.

Morro Bay's First

JAMES DVORAK

The thousand watts of never-ending juice shock Morro Bay on this Friday night as the small oceanside town has its first punk gig.

Inside the poorly lit Vets Hall swarm about 200 punks, misfits, and posers. Their adrenalin is ready for the next band.

"Hi, Morro Bay," says the guy on stage wearing a hooded shirt that covers his head. He looks like a boxer right before a fight.

The guitarist and bassist are tuning their instruments. The bass player is a young dark-skinned kid, a skinhead with Dumbo ears. The guitar player's hair is different. Patches of hair are missing from various spots on his head.

The always smiling drummer sits patiently behind his percussion set waiting for their set to begin.

Two long-haired hippies hang a peace banner on the yellow curtains at the back of the stage.

"Start playing!" yells out some guy in a green sweat shirt. I think he is the one that put the gig together.

Ear-piercing noise suddenly bursts out of the amps and into the stale smokey air. The crowd's attention was suddenly focused toward the stage as the guitarist ground out hard-hitting riffs, the bassist rumbled the floors with low booming energy, the drummer pounded out an intense rythmic beat, and a singer spit out his harsh stimulating vocals into the mike. Together they're known as Armistice.

The crowd takes notice and slowly moves closer to where the insanely fast music originates.

The music stops and the singer takes off his shirt. Now I get a good look at his tough, stern face.

"'Just to Think.'" He announces their next song.

Suddenly ear-ringing noise blasts from the amps as the vocalist leaps four feet into the air, landing on his knees, and then desperately spews out some meaningful lyrics while holding the mike with both hands, as if he were praying.

The uncontrolled crowd turns itself loose to the blaring music. A human whirlpool forms and snakes around as fast as the music will take it.

Sweat drips off the singer's brow as he pounds the stage with his fist. A skin bumps into him but then turns around and violently hurls himself back into the crowd.

The pit is a fury of leather jackets and mohawks.

"Just to think! Just to think!" The music goes on. A young kid about 12 years old runs past the possessed singer and dives into a dense human pile of arms and legs.

Suddenly the music stops! A soft round of applause fills the air where the intensely wild music once was.

The exhausted singer wipes his brow then says, "Do unto others as they do onto you: if you're nice to them, they'll be nice to you."

Armistice—a band with a message.

The Emergency Room

ROBERT EMERSON

It is 8:00 on a Saturday morning, the beginning of another shift in the emergency room. Dr. Crane sits down at this desk and checks the patient list from the midnight to 8:00 shift. An incredible twenty-two patients were admitted last night, and three of them are still being treated. Dr. Crane goes to check on one of these three.

Bill, a senior at a local high school, is the victim of one of the six traffic accidents that occurred last night. He has had stitches put in below his left eye and on the eyebrow above it. Aside from these two lacerations he is not badly hurt. In order to determine if there are abrasions on the eyeball itself, Dr. Crane puts a liquid called Fluoresine into the eye. He turns the overhead light out and shines a fluorescent penlight on the eye. The eye is bathed in cool blue light, and two yellow spots appear over the pupil. These are the abrasions, small but dangerous. Healing ointment is squeezed into the eye; it is patched and Bill is sent home to recover.

Another doctor peels off his white rubber gloves, tosses them into a nearby trash can, and walks to his desk to fill out his own reports. He has been sewing since midnight without a break and he looks it. His eyes are bloodshot with dark circles around them and bags of skin hanging like oriole's nests beneath them. The poor man will only be able to sleep for a few hours, because his next shift begins at 5:00 p.m.

The ER is quiet for now. The nurses are cleaning instruments, changing the beds and grabbing a much needed cup of coffee. The silence is broken by the occasional paging of a doctor over the loud-speakers and bursts of noise from the large radio used to contact paramedics. The telephone buzzes, and the receptionist answers it with a bright and crisp, "Emergency Room, may I help you?" Then the brief respite is over and the waiting room is suddenly full again.

Over the next hour five patients are seen, including two people with lacerations. The first is a little boy whose eyebrow has been cut by a key ring thrown at him by his brother. His eyes are red, and he is whimpering a little as he lies down on the bed. His father is with him, and Dr. Crane tells a joke to ease the tense atmosphere. "You know, most of our lacerations cases occur when parents faint watching their kids get sewn up!" The father laughs and promises not to faint.

Dr. Crane begins the suturing procedure by anesthetizing the wound. He sticks a syringe full of fluid in the cut and moves it around until the wound is insensitive. The boy tenses his legs, clenches his hands and tries not to cry. His father comforts him with a reassuring pat and smile. The doctor now washes the wound with a Q-tip soaked in iodine and begins sewing. Two stitches and a band-aid later, the child is ready to go home.

Dr. Crane now approaches the second lacerated patient. The man is a surfer who has been hit on the head by his surfboard, which has left a large, ragged wound. The doctor uses the same procedure as before, but before washing the wound he uses scissors to cut some tissue so the cut will heal without much of a scar. The man tells the doctor that he is the only surfer where he works and the other guys always "bug" him about his hobby. He doesn't know how he will live this accident down. He talks on and on, about his job, his friends, surfing, anything he can think of to keep his mind off his wound.

Dr. Crane is having trouble putting the suture through the skin because the wound is on the scalp, which is very tough. After bending the end several times, he finally gets it through. He makes the first stitch using an instrument tie. The doctor wraps the suture around the forceps several times, grabs the end of it and pulls it through the loop forming a stitch. The laceration requires six such stitches, and just as the last one is finished another patient is wheeled in the door.

The new patient is a large, swarthy man with a pot-belly. He is in a wheelchairs and his neck is wrapped in blood-soaked towels. The nurses carefully lay him on a bed and remove the towels, revealing two bloody, gill-like slits, one on each side of his neck. The patient has tried to commit suicide by cutting his throat with a razor blade. Dr. Crane scrubs his hands, puts on new gloves and comes to examine the man. Although there is a great deal of blood, close examination reveals that the man has only cut a minor vein on one side of his neck. The doctor parts the skin on the neck and exposes the cut vein surrounded by layers of yellow fat, large purple muscle and bright red blood. He stops the bleeding by tying off the ends of the vein and then begins the two-hour job of sewing the wounds shut.

As Dr. Crane is preparing to leave after finishing this last patient, another doctor passes through the ER. "What have you been doing today, Dr. Crane?" he inquires. "Just the usual, saving lives and stamping out disease," Dr. Crane replies as a wide grin spreads across his tired face.

Beach Show

KIM SVOBODA

The day was gorgeous and clear with just a few clouds in the sky. The islands were visible through a light haze, and the sail boats' masts were matchsticks lined up in perfect order.

A shiny black car, a Clenet, was parked along the curb, at the beach show. A dozen people were gathered around it.

"How much does that cost?"

"About $40,000."

"Oh, my gosh! $40,000. Where's it made?"

"Right here in Santa Barbara."

Many tourists with cameras slung over their shoulders admired the car and near-by paintings, especially one with two large rocks jutting out of the ocean. Between the two rocks stretched a clothes line pinned with bright colored shirts, a subject which amused the spectators.

A few yards down the sidewalk a little boy sat quietly on his mother's lap while being sketched by a lady wearing a coolie hat and a shirt decorated with a beautiful red dragon. Carrying paintings, dogs and children, rollerskaters whizzed by on multicolored wheels. Bikers and joggers rode and ran along the path. One jogger said, "I think it's better running on the grass." In the parking lot another biker rode his bike backwards. Near the path, seagulls were flying and swimming in a dirty stream, paying no attention to a sign that said, "Danger no swimming."

Across a green lawn, many people were dancing to Greek music, a barefoot man in blue striped overalls leading the way. "This is just like in the old country." Nearby, a man in an orange helmet straddled his bike and watched the dancing, obviously pleased. Another man juggled some balls while some happy children did some handstands.

A motorcycle sat next to the curb with a sticker: "Nobody for President in '88." Quotations on tee-shirts ranged from "YES" to "Lover Boy" and "I Love Real People." Two of the slogans captured the day perfectly, but many people probably never noticed. They said, "There's Something for Everybody Here" and "The Promised Land."

The Courts

BRENT LYNN

Two men talk to each other in the crowded waiting area at Los Positas Tennis Courts. One of them, a tall middle-aged man clothed in an expensive green sweatsuit with white stripes—even in the eighty degree heat—leans against a post. His dark-haired partner, also clad in an Addidas sweatsuit, is wearing blue ski glasses and sitting on a bench.

The tall man says, "Psychologically, I have improved my game tremendously over the past few months."

"Really," replies blue ski glasses. "I feel I'm mentally stronger too and that makes a huge difference in those pressure situations. By the way, did you see McEnroe play Borg last month?"

"Of course. That was a fantastic match, but don't you think that Borg could've won if he had kept the pressure on McEnroe? . . . How do you like your new Prince Graphite?"

"It's a heck of a racket." The dark-haired man pulls the expensive racket out of its cover and starts adjusting the strings. "The stiffness of this frame gives me a lot of power, but I still have the control of a wood. You know, I tried a bunch of different, cheaper rackets, but I figured it was worth a few extra bucks to buy a racket of this kind of quality and. . . ."

"Hey, look! Courts two and five are both open. I think we should take five; it has a better angle toward the sun."

"That's true. Besides, two has less wind resistance."

Both men open up new cans of balls and take several minutes to stretch out. On the first rally, a ball goes into the next court. "Sorry about that," says the shorter man to the girl who hits the ball back to him. "I angled my racket too much to the left." On the next rally the ball flies over the fence.

Without taking off their sweats, the two men chase balls for five minutes. Then they agree that "it's impossible to play good tennis in such hot weather," and walk off the court.

"Don't you think that Santa Barbara's heat makes indoor courts here a must?" asks the man in green.

"Definitely. People just out here to get a suntan don't really care about the weather factor, but serious players. . . ."

An Unknown Trauma

CHELLI HEISLER

Looking around at all of the people, I see a boy looking at kites in the toy store, a couple looking at rabbits in the pet shop, and two girls working in the hot dog stand. They have the ugliest uniforms I have ever seen. They are striped blue, red, yellow, and white. I would never wear shorts out in public if my thighs were as fat as the one squeezing the lemons for lemonade. She must be embarrassed. The metal tub she is using reminds me of one we used to bathe our dogs in. The lemons go slosh, slosh, squish. A drop flies upwards and shoots her in the eye.

The mustard they put on the hot dogs makes my mouth water, Before I know it, my stomach is whispering, "Please feed me." I decide on a glass of lemonade. There are chunks of lemon floating around in it. I take a drink and taste the tartness. It is so cool that it makes my head hurt. Some of the wax on the cup falls off and lands in my mouth. It is rough.

Two black girls walk by, and I strain my ears to listen. "I really don't give a damn about it," one of them states.

"Me neither. She can go ahead and kill herself. I don't care none." They are dressed all in black and look like they don't care if a person lives or dies. They climb the stairs and are soon out of reach for me to hear them.

An older couple sits down beside me. He has a gray sweater around his shoulders. She has her hair in rollers and is wearing a flowered dress. "Henry, do you want a hot dog?"

"What?" He says, barely audible.

"A hot dog. Henry, do you want one? Pay attention."

"Yeh, I suppose so."

Two blonde girls, about junior high age, stroll casually by. One is dressed preppie, the other is a Val. "Ohmagod! Totally *awesome*. Did he really say that?"

"And more. You're not going to believe this. Guess who he's going out with?" This conversation sounds interesting enough to listen to, but they too walk away.

A young woman, nicely dressed in a taupe colored dress, brings her little daughter over by me to sit down. The little girl has long, blonde hair and is wearing blue Oshkosh B'gosh overalls. The child is about three years old. "Now, Lisa, you sit here while Mommy gets you a hot dog."

"Sure," she lisps. Like any normal child she can't sit still. She turns around and picks up wood chips that are abundant in the planters. She puts one in her mouth and begins chewing on it.

Her mother glances over at her and sees what she's doing. Running to the little girl, she grabs her hand and slaps it. "No, no, Lisa. You're such a bad girl. I should have left you with your grandma when I had the chance."

"I sorry, Mama."

"Just shut up and come on. I can't do anything with you around. You're a little brat, I wish your Dad would take care of you." As she drags her past me, a tear runs down Lisa's cheek.

I can't be sentimental about this. I only wish I had the courage to say something. But I don't. The old lady returns. "Here's your dog, Henry."

"Huh?" he says.

"Your hot dog. Henry, pay attention."

The two black girls are coming down the stairs. "So, I say to her, 'Girl, you're full of it,' and that's the truth."

"Yeh, no one can handle that much coke."

"I don't care if her whole brain gets fried."

As they pass, the two blonde girls walk by. "So, he really does like her."

"Gnarly. I mean, like, you know." And they giggle.

Everything goes on as before. The girls in the ugly uniforms make lemonade and hot dogs, while nearby the old lady is trying to get her husband to remember he wanted a hot dog. It seems the only people who care what happened to the little girls are she and I. A trauma began and ended in the span of five minutes, and nobody cared.

Oral Stories

Ask older relatives or friends to tell some of their memories of their youth. Write this down in their own words by recording, transcribing, and editing, or by taking notes and going over these with the person after he or she finishes. Keep the words of the speaker, who should be the "I" of the memories. But you may add a short introduction, if you want, telling who the person is. Capture the manner in which the person speaks. Edit out your questions, if any, and any false starts, confusions, and repetitions, unless you feel that these are important for some reason. Transcribing and editing may be much easier with partners, so you can discuss decisions.

Read your story to others. Make a collection of them with other students.

An Authentic Indian Canoe

BETSY HARPER

My grandfather loves to tell us tales of his younger days, and we love to listen. Of all stories my favorite starts when he and two of his friends were in their late teens:

Tom, Bill and I were crazy about fishing, hunting and just hiking. We frequently went up on Old Holland Hill where Bill's uncle was a ranger in the national forest there. One day we stopped by to visit him after a day of fishing. He was trying to move a large redwood that had been blown down. When he saw us he grinned. "Boys,".he said, "if you can get this tree out of here it's yours." We were thrilled. Another friend of ours had a truck so we got him to help us in exchange for half the tree. Boy, was that a job. We had to split the tree and take it out in two loads.

We decided to use our half to make a dugout canoe like the Indians did. None of us had ever seen one made and had no idea how to go about it, but we set to work. It was many weeks later that we finished. It was great. We hauled it up to one of the lakes in the mountains and left it there. The canoe worked great, but it was definitely too heavy to haul back and forth. When we weren't using it we kept it tied up under some overhanging trees. That old canoe stayed there in that lake for years. We all used it whenever we could. When your father got big enough I would take him up there too. He learned to row and fish in that old dugout canoe.

One day when your father was a teenager we went up there to the lake to fish. The canoe was gone. We couldn't find a trace of it anywhere. For years I wondered what happened to that darned canoe. One day your grandmother and I stopped in to visit a new Indian museum. Boy, did I ever get a surprise. In a corner sat that same canoe. We looked it over really good. It was without a doubt the same canoe. The delineation of the canoe described it as an authentic Indian canoe. We got a good laugh out of it, but we didn't tell the museum, and the canoe has been sitting there for several years now. No one seems to have realized it was not made by Indians. Somehow, without even knowing what we were doing we seem to have produced an authentic Indian relic.

There Was No Train Home

As told by DAVE CONNOLLY to RANDY CROWLEY,
JAMES FIGUEROA, STEPHEN ROBEY, and LILLIAN COLON

I got there as Tet was starting. Tet is the lunar New Year. It has a lot of significance. Our New Year is a party; theirs is closely woven to the growing of crops, which is their life.

In the Tet of 1968 the National Liberation Front and the North Vietnamese Army hit every major city in South Vietnam. They hit every province capital. We were caught completely unaware. In the two months that followed there were more than 25,000 American casualties: 4200 dead, over 20,000 wounded and 800 missing in action.

I was there two days after Tet started. When I came into the Bien Hoa Air Base there were rockets impacting on the airstrip. We were hustled out of the planes and handed flak jackets and guns, and we ran to revetments, 55-gallon drums of concrete that they had just thrown all over the airfield.

Those first couple months I was there, it was an honest-to-god war like the one my father fought. We were fighting an army. But after Tet was over we started with search-and-destroy.

After securing the cities we went into the countryside and paid the people back for helping the Viet Cong. We'd take these people off their land that their ancestors had been living on since before Columbus landed in America.

We had almost complete license to kill. The day I got there, I was told I was to kill gooks and I could kill any gook I wanted.

In a normal operation we would be combat-assaulted into a landing zone early in the morning. Then we would move on foot to the nearest village. If they had any prior knowledge of our operation, which they usually did, we would take fire as our helicopter landed. The approaches to any village held by the National Liberation Front were mined or booby-trapped.

I never walked for any length of time near any inhabited village without encountering mines. Some were designed to take your foot off. One was an American invention from World War II called a "Bouncing Betty," which was a mine with a small charge under it. The small charge would blow, and that would throw the mine about waist-high where it would blow. By the time we got to this village where we were supposed to coordinate search-and-destroy, we had already lost people.

Even if this didn't go on, you knew the villagers would be sullen and uncooperative, and you'd just take the place apart piece by piece. You'd always find rice, ammunition, grenades. You'd find bomb factories, not huge, probably a little corner of the hut that they had covered with boards. And you'd see the sardine cans laid out to be filled with gunpowder.

And then the killing would start. If anyone moved you were scared absolutely crapless. You shot them. It didn't matter who. If they moved quickly, you shot them.

At that point we had already come to realize that we were on our own, completely on our own. Our officers were no older than we were. I was nineteen, and the officer in charge of my company was just twenty. The lieutenant was nineteen, eight months older than I was.

We were alone, and there was nobody tighter than the friends you grew up with there. Everyone was bro. It was black, white, yellow, red. It didn't matter. We were all little kids and we were there by ourselves and between us we couldn't come up with a reason for being there. And our officers couldn't come up with a reason for being there. It really wasn't discussed and decided openly, but we were going to go home. Even if we had to kill everyone we met, we were going to go home.

A lot of the problem, a lot of the guilt that Vietnam veterans face now, is that they performed these jobs, search-and-destroy, knowing full well we shouldn't have been there. You couldn't desert, there was no train home.

It was a war of silence. It was a war of quick movement. In the jungle, you fired at any sound. You fired at any light. Any movement. Without hesitation. You knew that if you didn't fire you were going to die.

You didn't care who you were shooting at to start with, because they were all gooks. That was just drummed into you. They were all gooks and you were there to kill gooks.

It's harder for a normal person to kill someone if you see that person as a human being. It's a lot easier to kill a "gook" than it is to kill a Vietnamese person. It's easier to kill someone if you see them as being a number. Especially if you're rewarded for a lot of numbers. We had a program within my regiment that the squad with the highest body count for the month would be sent to a rest and relaxation town. We had to pay our hotel bill, but the regiment would pay our bar bill. They kept a big tally board up—they marked down every person, every body, every count.

There was a maxim in the military that said, "The only good gook is a dead gook and any dead gook is automatically VC." Any dead Vietnamese is automatically the enemy. They went down on the tally sheets that came back to America to prove that we were winning the war. That's how the war was gauged.

It didn't matter if they were armed. It didn't matter if they were men. Or women. Or children. If they were dead, they were Viet Cong.

There were people who would shoot whenever they had a chance. The majority of people were there to survive. A weekend in a rest and relaxation town only meant it would take you two weeks to sweat all that beer out when you were back humping the bush.

It was usually 110° in the jungle. I carried nine to twelve canteens of water for myself always. You were roasting all the time. You ate salt tablets more than anything. You were always hungry, always.

The Army's big boast is how they can keep an army in the field supplied indefinitely with their helicopters. But once you were out in the fields, the best way to get your butt kicked was to call in resupply helicopters. It was going to take them an hour or two. Plenty of time for the Viet Cong to set up rocket launchers and drop everything they had on you.

We had c-rations. But you couldn't eat them. They're really high in preservatives, and the ones we ate were manufactured when my father was at war. They tasted that bad too. You lived off whatever you could. You took or you bought rice balls from the villages. You ate dog, cat, rat, snake and monkey.

Mostly you lived on c-ration candy bars. cigarettes, water and salt tablets. And dexadrine from the medic's pouch.

The clothes would rot off your back after a while, from the perspiration. You'd come in after an extended operation and ask them for a new shirt or a new pair of pants, or boots. Boots were like gold. And they'd send you to the dead pile. Whoever got killed, they'd strip him and dump his stuff in a pile. You'd root through that and find something that wasn't too bloody.

During the rainy season it rained hard enough so you couldn't see your hand when you put it in front of you. It rained for a couple of hours a day, in the morning and again in the afternoon. You'd be up to your knees in mud. But at least it slowed the war down. He couldn't move in that stuff either. The war didn't stop but it slowed down.

Family Anecdotes

Retell in your own words some incident that is told in your family about one of its members. Ask relatives to recall some story that is passed around because it is comic or dramatic or otherwise memorable. If the story isn't already familiar to you, write it down right after your hear it. If it is familiar, write it down from memory, perhaps reinforced by another's retelling.

Exchange one or more of these with others and make a book of them.

A Smelly Snake

MARY NIELSEN

I heard many stories from my relatives that I liked. But the one I liked best came from my grandpa, or Sid as you will come to know him in the following story.

Sid was raised in South Carolina. His family lived on a small farm consisting of a barn, a pasture, and a worn-down house. They raised a few animals such as cows, pigs, and chickens.

This story happened over fifty-five years ago when Sid was about ten. Sid, as well as his brothers and sisters, had certain chores to do each day. Sid's chores consisted of feeding the animals, cleaning the barn, and bringing in firewood for the evening.

On this day for some unknown reason he forgot to bring in the wood. During dinner his father reminded Sid that he had to go out and get the wood. In the country there were a few wild animals around. It was a dark, gloomy night, and Sid was scared to go outside. Sid tried hard to persuade one of his brothers to go with him, but nothing he said would make them go with him.

Sid began doing his homework, hoping everyone would forget about the wood. It wasn't long though before he was reminded of what he had to do. Sid slowly bundled up, for it was cold outside. He walked quickly to the barn, where the wood was kept. He walked cautiously through the door, making sure it was empty. He quickly gathered the wood to be taken into the house. As he was turning to leave he noticed a snake in the corner. He stood terrified as the wood slipped out of his hands. Unaware of what he was doing he grabbed a shovel.

Being scared of snakes, he stood back and began hitting it. Sid hit the snake over and over again. When he was finished beating the snake he wanted to make sure it was dead. He cut the snake up into a hundred little pieces.

Proud of his victory he picked up the wood and ran back to the house. Sid burst into the door and began telling everyone what happened. He was awarded an extra piece of pie for dessert for his bravery. It took Sid a while to get to sleep because he was so excited. But he finally fell into a sound sleep.

Before Sid got up his father went to see this snake Sid had killed. Sid was awakened by his father's laughter. He got up to see what was so funny. By the time he got dressed and reached the kitchen where his father was laughing hysterically, everyone was up. It took them about fifteen minutes to calm his father down. Once he was under control he sat down and tried to gather his words. By now the suspense was killing Sid, and he was ready to scream. Finally his father began to speak. "Sid," he said, "I hate to be the one to tell you, but last night you beat a cow pie to death."

"Samples, Anyone?"

JAN GRAINGER

One day early in the spring of 1951, Doris Betts awoke, her stomach churning with excitement. This was her first day working at Sears and Roebuck department store in Ventura, California. She dressed in a blue gabardine suit and matching blue patent leather shoes and purse. As she waited for the bus she thought of what her mother told her years ago and still believed it. "Cars will never last, they are just a fad."

After checking in she found that she was assigned to the "bargain basement." That was fine with her. Maybe there would be fewer people down there. Doris reported to her supervisor and was assigned to the candy counter. Candy counter, oh no, all that weighing and measuring. Her excitement was turned to fright. She was introduced to the woman who was to work with her and train her. She seemed very nice. Her name was Julie.

Julie showed Doris all the different candies and how to use the scales and the cash register. It all seemed easy enough. After a few customers Doris seemed to have the hang of things. Julie said it was time for her coffee break. Off she went, leaving Doris with the candy counter and a few words of encouragement.

Fright seized her. All by herself? On her first day. She wasn't even sure what to do if she made a mistake. Should she call the supervisor? What if there was a robbery? She really did want to do a good job and impress Julie when she got back. That was when she spotted the samples, or what she thought were samples. Whitman Samplers. She had never seen them before. The boxes seemed rather large for samples, but the box said they were. So whenever anyone would ask for a sample, out she would bring the two-pound box of Whitman Samplers. On discovery of the dwindling amount of boxes, she went into the storeroom. After requesting more of the Whitman Samplers she was congratulated on her success in selling so many boxes. Immediately following was an inquiry of how she had been able to sell so many boxes.

Sell? All color drained from her face. Mass confusion took over. What was she to do?

The incident was then reported to her supervisor. Doris was called into his office, where she received specific details on what were to be sampled and what were not. Because of her lack of supervision, experience, and intelligence she was not held responsible for the price of fifteen to twenty boxes of Whitman Samplers.

Interview

Choose some person you would like to interview for his or her special knowledge. Tape-record or take notes. Plan some questions according to what you want to know, but be prepared to follow up the responses with new questions you hadn't planned. Write up the interview by summarizing and paraphrasing to convey to someone interested in the subject the main things you learned. Use quotes for flavor and accuracy. Perhaps show a draft to the interviewee to check for accuracy and emphasis.

You may specialize this assignment by choosing a person —or two people, as it worked out for one of the writers in this section—in a career you want to know more about and are perhaps considering for yourself. Direct questions toward what the career requires and what it's like. With other interviewers plan a booklet covering a number of careers that would be interesting to people not yet settled on career plans.

Tribe Can Better Use Powers Given to It Under the Treaty of 1868

EILEEN HOLIDAY

Modern Navajo history begins with the treaty of 1868. This treaty was introduced to the Navajos on June 1, 1868 at Ft. Sumner. I interviewed, over the phone, Dr. Robert Young, a professor of Linguistics at the University of New Mexico and co-author of the Navajo Dictionary. I asked him questions about the treaty, which is referred to by the Navajos as the "Naaltsoos Sani." He told me that most of what the treaty said is today meaningless but that the treaty did recognize the Navajo tribe as a sovereign nation. This has had, and continues to have, important consquences on the reservation.

Dr. Young told me that there were five major points of the treaty. First, the Navajo tribe agreed not make war against the United States, any other Indian tribes, or anyone on the outside.

Second, the Navajo tribe agreed to turn criminals or w   ⁻doers, that the Navajos caught, over to the United States government.

Third, the United States made the original boundaries for the Navajo Reservation. The first reservation—which had much less land than the present reservation boundaries include—is known as the "Treaty Reservation." It extends along the Arizona and New Mexico border to the San Juan River, and westward over to Chinle and Canyon De Chelly. "It includes 3.5 million acres and made a rectangular shape. The tribe agreed to relinquish its right to occupy any territory outside of this reservation," said Mr. Young.

This meant that the Navajos who lived outside of the reservation had to move within the borderlines of the treaty reservation. Before they moved to Ft. Sumner, the Navajos had occupied about 20 million acres. This was before the treaty was signed. The reservation that the United States established was a much smaller area than the land the Navajos lived on before. "However," said Dr. Young, "Navajos were so anxious to leave Ft. Sumner that they bought the idea of a treaty that really took much of their land."

A fourth point stated in the treaty of 1868 was that an agent was to be established on the Navajo Reservation to administer tribal affairs. This meant that the agent was to work with the tribe's government as well as the government in Washington. This Indian agent was known as the reservation Superintendent.

A fifth point raised by the treaty was that any member of the Navajo tribe who wanted to engage in farming could get land from the United States government to do so. Navajos had to make an application to be able to receive as much as 160 acres of land. If the Navajos accepted the idea of farming, the government would provide land, seeds, tools and other equipment necessary for farming.

While these five points may have been important to the Navajos earlier, the treaty's main effect when it was first signed, and still today, has to do with sovereignty. Sovereignty means having the power to govern. Dr. Young said, "I think the treaty's main effect has to do with the fact that only sovereign nations can enter a treaty agreement."

When they first came to America, Europeans treated Indian tribes as sovereign nations. "This meant that sovereign Indian tribes governed their own rights, even if they entered into treaties with the United States. The United States and the Navajo Tribe signed a treaty. Therefore, the Treaty of 1868 recognized, however indirectly, the sovereignty of the Navajo Tribe."

At the same time that the treaty recognized the sovereignty of the Navajos, the United States Congress took jurisdiction over the Indian tribes. In so doing, it extinguished the "external sovereignty" of Indian groups. "That is, Indian tribes cannot under federal law make treaties with foreign nations, such as Russia, Germany, or China," Said Dr. Young.

Yet, Indian tribes do have the power to govern themselves. This power is known as "internal sovereignty," and it can only be extinguished by an act of Congress. "I think this is the most important aspect of the Treaty of 1868. It recognized the 'residual' sovereignty of the Navajo tribe," said Dr. Young. Dr. Young defined "residual" as meaning anything that the Congress has not taken away from the Indian tribes.

I asked Dr. Young a question concerning who really owns the land that the Navajos live on. Dr. Young said, "All the land that the United States has is in fact owned by the federal government. That even includes my house. Now, the land that was set aside for the Navajos by the Treaty of 1868, and all the land that was eventually added to the reservation, is tribal land. This means that the land the Navajos live on belongs to the tribe; but it is held in trust by the federal government, or more specifically, by the BIA [Bureau of Indian Affairs]."

The Treaty of 1868 said that for every 30 Navajo children who could be induced or compelled to enter school, the United States government would build a school. "The tribe, in the treaty, agreed to compel children between the ages of 6 and 16," said Dr. Young. "The tribe and the government attempted to do this, but without much success." Of course, ever since the treaty, the government has assumed responsibility for educating Indian children.

I asked Dr. Young if the BIA today provides services—schools, land management, and law enforcement, plus others—because of the treaty. He told me that the federal government has never taken away certain powers that Indian tribes have, such as the power for Indians to provide their own police services. The tribe, not the BIA, makes the rules and laws for their own police.

In fact, the BIA does not provide services because of the treaty. The federal and tribal governments are providing services for Indians due to certain laws having been passed by Congress since the treaty. The treaty does not mention anything about what the BIA is responsible for doing nowadays.

The Navajo Tribe has many problems dealing with the federal government today. I asked Dr. Young about this, about how he thought the tribal government and its relationship with Washington could be improved. Dr. Young feels that Navajo government could be made more efficient and more powerful and that this would help Indians. "The Navajos could develop a tribal constitution and have it approved by Congress. Congress has the authority to approve a constitution. I have always felt that this would help. But the tribal government has never got around to it."

Naaltsoos Sani might be somewhat meaningless today to the Navajos, but it did recognize the tribe as a sovereign nation. Being recognized as a sovereign nation means having the power to build our dreams, though we might struggle to reach them. By using this power, we can turn around and face the government. If we, the Navajos, get together, we can make our dreams become reality.

Going Beyond Yourself with Alan Ziegler

MICHAEL FERRARO

"My ambition used to be to appear on The Johnny Carson Show, now it's to appear on The David Letterman Show." I can't think of a better quote to reveal an unpretentious writer and an unpretentious person. After reading Alan Ziegler's work I immediately felt a down-to-earth quality that I could easily identify with. Meeting him confirmed this impression.

Of medium stature, with penetrating eyes and brown hair, wearing Levis and a plaid shirt, he made himself a very approachable person. Good, I thought to myself. This was my first interview and I was a bit on the nervous side, but my nervousness cleared away quickly. Another relaxing element was his Upper West Side apartment. We entered a small, book-cluttered room that served as a workroom. From reading his poetry I had almost expected the eclectic taste in literature I found in the books there. Standing next to his typewriter was a stereo and collection of records. I flipped through the latter and again saw a great variety of taste. We sat on the floor and began.

I started asking about his early years. The first thought to come into Ziegler's mind when asked about junior high was "misery." "I did a lot of ground work in junior high—I became a better student and I got involved with the school paper," an interest which would stick with him for the rest of his school years. "But nothing came together; it was just misconnected." Socially things weren't great either. He remembered the school dances ending and being left all alone while "all the 'in' kids went off one way to a place—God knows where. I'm sure there were other 'me's' doing the same thing, and if we had known each other, I'm sure we would have had a good time too."

High school was far better. Things seemed to start coming together for him, especially his writing. This was mostly newspaper writing, though, because he liked the immediacy of the form. Later in college he enjoyed the aura of it all: "I loved working till three in the morning in a crowded office and the sweat and later everyone going out for coffee.

"Well, I almost feel guilty that I liked high school. After graduation, I was one of the few people who, at least outwardly, showed some sadness and regret." At the time he wanted to become a lawyer. "With so many people asking you what you want to be you finally just come up with an answer and they stop asking."

In college he majored in political science but then shifted to psychology. He felt that political science didn't focus on the individual, and therefore the change to psychology was just a matter of going from the outside of people to the inside. "I was interested in what went on inside people, including myself." From psychology he went into writing. "I think my switch into writing poetry was simply a natural extension of the psychology."

At first he felt badly about his creative writing. For the most part it was because he compared it to the students who modeled their poetry after the likes of Shelley and Milton. Later on in college there was a major turning point for him. "There was one guy who wrote a poem that started with or had the lines: 'I know you love him, baby—I can tell by the grass stains on the back of your shirt.' I saw that and thought, Can you do that? Is that allowed?" After that, in the same year, "Someone wrote a poem for William Carlos Williams and it started with, 'Well, Bill, I see you've kicked the proverbial bucket.'" From there on Ziegler found a "natural colloquial voice that could be used." This voice liberated him from the constraints of traditional style.

He remained very interested in politics. The anti-war and student movements "all came to a head at the end of my senior year." A new dissatisfaction began here. "For a long time I was very disturbed with myself. I wasn't able to transfer my political feelings into poetry that worked." By this time he was able to judge his poetry on its own colloquial merits and felt that his writing on any other subject was "pretty good." "But I couldn't write about the things that concerned me politically, and I don't think I can now. I've sort of reconciled that I need to do a different sort of writing if I'm going to write about politics. I really admire certain writers who can, like certain Latin-American writers for whom poetry and politics aren't separate. If I have any regrets, it's that I can't do that."

For Ziegler there is a chemical attraction for poetry. He has to write because of a tremendous desire. "Poetry is sometimes the thing you do when there is no alternative. As you do it, you are in touch with something. It's the same feeling you get when you are running or dancing or any other activity where you go beyond yourself." He finds a great satisfaction in poetry and that that feeling comes whether the writing is a sudden inspiration or a grinding piece of work. "I suppose it's much the same feeling one gets when building a house."

He is not a believer in putting poetry high on a pedestal to live by. "I wouldn't go so far as to say that I write poetry so that someone will read it and be a better person. It's not quite that lofty . . . but there is a secondary effect." He does think that poetry can help people ("Freud and Jung drew on it constantly in helping people understand what they were feeling"), but that expression of feeling should not be the only writing an author does. "Self-expression is fine, but you have to go further to discover about your pain—where it comes from."

"Late One Night," one of the best poems in Alan Ziegler's collection entitled *So Much to Do*, is a very good example of his personal style, a style which is close to the way the mind often works, following a flow of fragmented, disparate thoughts and connecting them. After reading this poem I felt as though I had learned something about him and that he had learned something about himself. Not to mention myself.

"I'd say ninety percent of the poem is literally true. There was no feeling at all, as it was happening, that I was going to write about it, and I'm glad. It was a period of three hours where I was very much alive. My brain was getting filled with a lot of things having to do with my girlfriend, Rod Serling, Tim Buckley (folk singer), this horse (Ruffian), and the people in Sheridan Square.

"I came home the next day and started writing it down almost exactly as it happened, doing the line breaks very arbitrarily. It could have been done in prose, but I just seemed to be pushing the return key at certain times. I don't know much about astrology, but the constellations must have been set in a certain way."

When he finished, he wondered if anyone in the world could possibly be interested in it. The ante had been raised. From writing it down for himself it changed to a poem to share with others. "I called up my harshest critic, a very good friend (and co-editor with Ziegler of *Some* magazine) who doesn't say nice things for the sake of saying nice things and was very capable of being honest. He didn't particularly like that kind of confessional outpouring." Ziegler read "Late One Night" over the phone and when he finished his friend said he was hanging on every word.

Another excellent poem is called "Choreography." It shows how certain people can act and move with a perfect grace and others with awkwardness. Ziegler does not typecast these people as always graceful or always awkward. One isn't always one way or always another; he is both.

"I had a serious technical difficulty with that poem. I was having dinner at the house of a large extended family. As an outsider who had known the family for a long time, I saw them as very graceful people. I was feeling awkward and that I didn't quite fit in. A woman said, very literally, 'Have you got a spoon?' And I was so happy that there was a spoon. So I brought it over and I expected them to say, 'Oh, sit down and join us!' When I got back she was stirring." He started writing in the first person as one of the awkward people who wanted to be one of the graceful people, but it began to look like he was self-pitying, so he ended up with a third-person format which provided greater distance from the experience and worked very well.

He took a sip from his coffee cup, and I looked out the window where the snow was falling heavily on this March day. I thought of the people in his poems and that led me to my next question. Influences.

"Books weren't a big part of me. I was part of the first television generation. I was in the peanut gallery on *Howdy Doody* and I met Clarabelle personally. *Twilight Zone* was one of those shows that stuck." He felt that what held the show together so well was its atmosphere and irony. No matter how bizarre the situation was, he never found himself questioning it. "The grammar of the show was so carefully done that, like any good science-fiction, it drew you in.

"I internalized the way that a writer, or in this case a television show, can alter the familiar." When reading Ziegler's poetry, perhaps one of the first things to stick out to the reader would be a line of irony running through many of them. Sometimes he appreciates this influence, sometimes not. "One of the faults in my writing is, perhaps, an over-reliance on that irony. More so in my earlier work was a reliance on the 'punch-line.'"

As for punch-lines, comedians were also important to him and his work. "What they do is elevate the familiar. They either exaggerate the familiar to a point where it becomes funny or sad or they twist things around. I used to watch people like Steve Allen and his whole crew and then the whole new generation of stand-up comics like George Carlin."

Songwriters were also a very major influence for Alan Ziegler. During college he himself wrote many songs and collaborated with a friend who set them to music and sang them. He liked the poetry of early Dylan music, but that old feeling of "This is poetry?" came back to him. Then came another turning point. Writer Alan Ginsberg came to his college "and repeated a Dylan line and said, 'that's as good as anything I've written' and I was glad to hear that."

Other songwriters important to him were Joni Mitchell, whom he did a paper about, comparing her to the imagist poets, and Neil Young, "Because of the way he never feels that he has to tell you the whole story. Like, 'Down by the river I shot my baby,' but he won't tell you why." He also likes Jackson Browne for the way he puts words together.

He also enjoys the songs of the thirties and forties. They may not have been as artistically free or as "deep" as some of the music of the sixties and seventies, but there was s simple lucid quality about them that stands out. He pointed out a song that Bing Crosby sang during that earlier period that had the line, "In order to get to my house I have to pass your house." Ziegler had an experience like that with an old girlfriend whose subway stop he passed on the way home from work.

Like the rest of us, Alan Ziegler has a fantasy. One of his poems was published recently and he imagined himself on a subway where everyone had a copy of that *New York Times* issue, of course. "I felt like saying, 'Ladies and Gentlemen, will everyone please turn to page C. 2 and read along with me.'"

At the end of the interview I asked him what he'd like his poetry to achieve for himself and others. He said, "James Tate said his ambition was to get a gasp from a stone. I'm more modest. I'd like a person to once and a while say, 'wow.'"

Wow.

Visit Plus Interview

Choose a person and place that go together, like some local character in his or her natural habitat or someone in a key position of some operation. Arrange to interview the person in these habitual surroundings and to look around while you talk. Record or take notes on the interview and also jot down notes on any aspect of the setting or behavior that suits your reason for choosing this subject in the first place. Write an article based on your notes. Weave together the relevant details for setting and action with things the person said. Consider when to quote directly and when to summarize or paraphrase. This could become a character sketch, an atmosphere piece, or a short factual article—some kind of journalistic feature. Decide on an audience accordingly.

A Hobby First, Then a Career

JIM ELLIOTT

It's spring again, time to clean out your house and start to repair all the things that got broken over the long winter. And if you're like most people, you don't have the time or the knowhow to repair or refinish it.

That's where Wendell and Midge Newcomb come in. They own and operate The Strippery, a furniture repair shop in Oblong.

"This all [furniture repair] started out as a hobby," Wendell said, wearing a T-shirt with "The Strippery" printed across the front of it.

"When we got married we both liked antiques, old furniture and stuff, and what we could afford to buy wasn't refinished. So we had to buy it and refinish it ourselves. That's how we first got started, that's how we learned to do it."

It wasn't long, though, before other people heard about their repair work and asked if the Newcombs could refinish, repair and cane their chairs. As time passed, the requests came more and more often and became more and more complicated.

With all those requests, the Newcombs started to work on many other people's furniture. "Maybe in the months along [after we got started] we might have done two or three pieces for somebody else," he said. "And then it just go so more and more people started calling and coming by so we just started doing it. We've done it part-time for about three years, and the last year and a half we've done it full time. So far we've stayed busy."

All indications are that The Strippery will stay busy repairing, stripping, refinishing and caning chairs.

"We do more of that kind of work [repairing and refinishing] than we do chair bottoms," he said. "The first thing we'd do if someone brought in a chair would be to strip off the old finish, unless somebody else already had.

"If we have to repair work, we'd do that next and then we'd put on a finish. We use varnish, it's my preference. So when we buy an old piece, unless it looks good [with paint] I'm gonna refinish it.

"Then the last thing we do, if it's a cane bottom, is put the cane in. That would be the final step. We could have a chair done in a week's time, but that wouldn't be countin' puttin' the cane in."

Standing behind a counter, weaving cane into a chair bottom, Midge said, "Yeah, because I work slower.

"This here is factory-made cane," she said, pointing to the chair bottom she was working on. "It's the easiest and probably the most simple to use."

But there are many different types of cane, from the factory-made press cane to split bottom to old hickery, which is just tree bark.

"That's the kind they used 100 years ago," Midge said, still weaving cane into the chair bottom. "They used bark off young saplings, and things like that. They pulled it off and rolled it together. It was crude, but they refined it. Yep, that was how they did it 100 years ago."

But caning goes back a lot further than 100 years; in fact, it is an art that goes back to India and China in the 2nd century A.D. The craft was brought to Europe in the 17th century by the East India Company. And Midge Newcomb has brought it to Oblong, mostly because she had some chairs that needed to be caned but couldn't find anyone else to do them.

"She's the one who does all the chair bottoms," Wendell said, standing on the other side of the counter watching his wife weave the cane into the chair bottom.

"We were basically forced into doing it because we couldn't find anyone around here to do it. Since we've been in business we've gotten a lot of calls to do this, so she stays busy. If she wanted to do a chair every night, she probably could. But we just done it out of necessity at first."

Taking a break from caning, Midge said, "It's hard work but very rewarding."

"Yeah, each piece is a new challenge," Wendel said. "Each piece is different; you don't run across the same thing in any two pieces. Each one has its own special character."

"Especially old furniture," Midge said. "Old furniture has a lot more character than new. And it takes a pretty good piece of furniture to survive for 100 years. Say something's 100 years old, no telling what it's been through.

"Once we brought in some chairs that were painted, and when we got the paint stripped off 'em, we saw that they'd been in a fire. They were charred underneath, but we couldn't tell it with the paint on 'em. So you never know what you're going to get."

Wendell agreed with her and added, "To me it's fun. Just like if you got something you really enjoy doing, like a hobby, you get to doin' it for your livelihood, too. You just never get tired of it."

Ballooning

MARY STRICKLING

Ballooning was a subject I was interested in but knew very little about. But since I've been working with Al Carver of Big Al's, we've talked about ballooning quite a lot. He had always promised to take me up some time, but we never made any definite plans. So when he found out I was doing a report he invited me to come that following Monday.

Of course I was thrilled. Going up in a hot air balloon isn't an everyday occurrence! But at the same time I was a little apprehensive to be going up hundreds of feet above the ground in just a wicker basket hooked to 24 panels of non-rip nylon.

As long as it didn't rain, the flight would go on. Monday morning I woke to gray overcast skies, but no rain, so the trip was still on. We pulled into the Jefferson flight center around eight in the morning and went around to the hangar in which the balloons were kept. I was introduced to Clyde Pope, who had a share in the Big Al's Corp. and also flew the balloon but would be the ground crew today.

The ground crew would, after the balloon took off, follow the balloon in the car with the trailer. So when the balloon got ready to land they could be right there close to help land and deflate. Usually Al and Clyde alternate on ground crew.

Al and Clyde both had on white flight suits with the colors of the balloon around the legs and arms. These they said were an absolute "necessity." I was glad I had worn my overalls.

So we hitched up the 4' by 8' trailer onto the car, climbed in the car, and were off to the school where we were doing the demonstration.

None of us knew where Lone Pine School was, but by chance we ran into the third partner, Mike, who knew where the school was and led the way there. The advantage of having three partners is the costs are divided by three. An average hot air balloon and equipment runs about $20,000. The Big Al Balloon costs $18,000, so split three ways that's about $6,000 each.

The balloon when fully inflated is about seven to eight stories high and 45-50 feet across. This balloon has 24 panels making up the envelope. Vertically on the envelope is an air vent which is used to let out hot air. Below the envelope is the mouth or the skirt, which is fastened to the basket by wire coils. The baskets are woven wicker with steel wire woven in between. The edge is covered by suede ties with leather thongs.

The only control you have of the balloon is in going up and down. The wind current takes you forward, turns you around, and goes whichever way it wants. There are two coil burners that heat the air and cause the balloon to rise. They are not burning or heating constantly. About every 10 to 20 seconds you pull a chain which fires heat and warms the air. There's a 20-25 second delay between the time you fill and when the balloon goes up. So if you want to fly low to the ground or just above the trees, you can judge when to fire so that when you come to a tree you rise. This skill just comes through experience. In order to go down you don't fire quite as often.

At the school we took the basket with the burners, the fan, and the bag with the balloon out of the trailer and began setting them out.

Each time the balloon is put away, it's put away so when it's unrolled there won't need to be a lot of moving around. The next step is to tie the skirt up where it falls over the burners. (All this time the basket is on its side.) The nylon singes easily, so this must be done right. The hardest part is lining up the metal clamps and sticking the holding pin into the holes when they're lined up.

With that over now we had to fill the balloon with cold air from the fan. The skirt or mouth has to be held open and kept close to the ground so the air won't cause a bubble underneath. While it's filling Al and Clyde go inside and check to make sure everything is all right.

As it starts to fill, it will become upright, so you have to have someone holding the ropes on the sides to keep it balanced. When it's upright, then you blast the burners to warm the air; that usually takes just a few seconds. The air at the top of the balloon must be at least 150° to 200° but no hotter than 250° Fahrenheit.

After a few more blasts we were ready to take off. The takeoff is smooth. I'd always imagined the balloon would be rocky and unsteady. But everything was very smooth. I felt like one of the balloons that little kids might let go of, just gliding up. The only way you can really tell you're moving is to watch the shadow of the balloon or look down. The basket doesn't move at all unless one of the passengers does.

Al's balloon carries three adults or up to 625 pounds! When you're flying around 200 feet above the ground you can hear people talking and all kinds of sounds because the balloon is in the air current and voices and sounds are carried by these currents.

Taking off's a breeze, but landing is a different story. Landings you come down quite fast, and as you hit the ground you have to bend your knees slightly and hang on. On our landing, just before we touched ground the wind caught us and blew us into a tree. When that happens you just hit the floor. That came automatically to me.

There is literally no danger in an air balloon providing it's operated correctly. If the burners were to stop working, or a rip occurred, the balloon would come down about as fast as a parachuter does with his chute open.

The whole trip in the air lasts an hour and a half. The fuel in the two 20-gallon tanks lasts for about two hours. So after an hour and a half you start looking for a place to land. From the balloon you can get a 360° view of wherever you are; it's really a sight to behold. So we then loaded everything up and headed for the airport.

The experience and research on ballooning was not only interesting but a real learning experience. It cleared up some of the fallacies I had about ballooning and taught me quite a lot. It's an interesting sport because each time is so different from the next, and you are never quite sure where the balloon will take you.

Biography and Chronicle

Biography: Phase

Narrate some experience another person went through during several months or years that amounted to a phase of that person's life having something of a beginning, middle, and end of its own. The person may be from the past or the present. Draw from fresh sources such as interviews with the person or diaries or memoirs by or about the person, and indicate in some

way appropriate to your presentation what these sources are.
Bring out the nature of the experience that makes for the phase,
keeping in mind an audience that might be interested in the
person or the experience.

A Taste of the Big Apple

STEPHANIE STEVENS

The sun's light was shaded by the grey clouds stretching out over the city as the skyscrapers stood to greet them. The streets, congested with taxi cabs, double-parked cars, and hurrying pedestrians, were alive with the sound of blaring horns and angered drivers. The sidewalks, randomly decorated with old newspapers and fast food wrappers, were almost hidden by the sea of determined people heading in opposing directions. The people's expressions changed only momentarily to looks of surprise when they had to go around a dark-haired young woman with one small child strapped tightly to her back in a denim gerry-carrier, another clutched tightly against her chest, and the oldest child held closely by the hand, making their way to the subway in downtown Manhattan. Equipped with a supply of disposable diapers and apple juice, Darla Stevens was determined to experience the exciting city of New York, even with three children under the age of four.

In 1970, Darla and her husband, Southern California natives, had just moved from Canada to New York, where the women's movement, to her surprise, was in full swing. Women were opening their own car doors and men were babysitting. Darla moved into a small apartment in the northern tip of Manhattan and discovered life without a backyard; one had to keep children in the apartment at all times. Even the hallways were a risk for three curious, exploring kids.

On her very first day in New York City, her husband already off to work, she found herself with the apartment cluttered artistically with dusty moving boxes, the continuous sound of the nearby traffic right outside her window, and her kids curiously inspecting the new home. She excitedly drew in a breath of New York air and smiled. She wanted to go exploring but needed to go grocery shopping, which was, of course, a major expedition in itself. After loading three kids in and out of the car and into the grocery store, she strapped one child to her back in her worn gerry-carrier and put the other two in the shopping cart. As she turned down her first shopping aisle, she got her first words from a New Yorker. The grocery clerk walked up to her and

said in a distinct New York accent,"So you couldn't bring more kids?!"
Family Circus couldn't find a better caption.

And so it was that she found herself in the most exciting city in
the world, at the inception of the women's movement. With three
young children and a husband who worked both days and evenings,
most of the time on the staff of Columbia University, she took a part
time job herself. Darla had grown up in Los Angeles as an only child
under a strong-willed but doting mother who dominated most of her
early life. Darla earned straight "A's" all through school and was never
a very rebellious child. Nevertheless, she developed independence and
self-sufficiency. It would have been easier to stay home after work in
New York, but she decided to explore the city—even with her young
children.

After many outings carrying the kids on various errands, Darla
decided to convert to a more efficient means of transportation. She
bought a little red "stake-sided" wagon to pull the children in. She
discovered that it fit into subway cars, through revolving doors, and
that street-hardened New Yorkers responded with a helping hand to
maneuver the wagon up and down stairways.

Within a few months, Darla began picking up on the city's fast
pace and began to become a true New Yorker, always dressing casually
(it was the dress-down seventies). She acquired the local accent, and
she began to taste the true excitement of the city's offerings. When
she wasn't working or pulling the little red wagon full of kids to
Central Park, puppet shows, swimming lessons, and the museums, she
occasionally tasted New York's cultural life by meeting her husband on
the subway to spend the evening at the theater or the opera.

Darla loved to explore New York. Nothing was more exciting to
her than sampling with her husband the many things that the big city
had to offer—a cup of Cappuccino at some al fresco cafe in the Italian
district, miniature sailboat races at the Central Park lake, bargain-
hunting on Canal street, artist exhibits in the Soho district, with a visit
to the Bronx Zoo thrown in for the kids.

During her first year in New York, Darla found that people
would help her whenever she was in a difficult situation with the
wagon or her children. The reputation of the "cold New Yorker" was
relatively unfounded as far as she was concerned. However, she also
experienced the darker side of New York and found herself in situations that she never would have encountered in Canada, Colorado, or
California.

On a humid day in March, Darla took her best friend, who was
visiting from Washington D.C., to the theater district in Manhattan.
They walked up the crowded sidewalks in between the famous buildings, stopping only at a cafe to sample the Cappuccino. On the way
back to one of Darla's favorite Broadway shows, a man wearing a torn,
black leather jacket and ripped jeans ran furiously past them, almost

knocking them over. All of a sudden the man turned around and fired a pistol in their direction. To their horror, they heard a bullet whiz by, intended for a policemen behind them. It ricocheted off a building, echoing its shocking sound. The policeman came by, knocked them aside, and chased the perpetrator. During this time, she and her friend were amazed and shocked; it had all happened so fast. This was one of the few times that the blasé New Yorkers on the street stopped to pay attention, but only for a short while.

There were also many risks in exploring New York with young children. An example of this came on a cold day when it was snowing. Darla was taking care of her neighbor's two children and decided to take all five for a walk. She bundled all the kids up and set off for a short trek in the snow with the wagon. After walking no more than three blocks, she saw four teenage boys walk up behind her, the leader eyeing her purse, the others surrounding her and the kids. Her heart started beating fiercely as she clenched the wagon handle and drew it closer. She was defenseless if they decided to mug her or kidnap one of the children. But at the last minute, the dominant teenager in the group suddenly switched his victim to an elderly lady with a cane walking in the snow only ten feet ahead. The knocked her down, grabbed her purse, and all ran up the street, leaving only deep footprints in the snow behind. It had all happened in less than thirty seconds.

After living three years in New York, Darla's husband took a job offer at Lawrence Livermore National Laboratory and they decided to move to Pleasanton, California. On the subway going out to work for the last day, she barely had room to stand behind the closing subway doors because it was so crowded. She was daydreaming about her future life in California while staring at a patch on the shoulder of a man's overcoat no more than six inches from her face, when the subway came to a stop and the doors opened wide in front of her. She couldn't imagine how anyone else could possible get in, but a small, shifty-eyed Oriental man attempted to squeeze on next to her in the absolutely packed subway car. A few seconds later, the man started to get back off because it was too crowded. Darla's first impulse was to look in her purse that had been crushed in between the two of them, and she was horrified to discover that, sure enough, her wallet was missing. As he stepped off, she reached out, grabbed his jacket, and ripped it as he pulled away. The doors closed and the subway train was off.

She was depressed at the thought of having to replace her driver's license and credit cards. Her only consolation through the day was that she had accomplished some retribution for the stolen wallet. However, when she called home to tell her husband what had happened, the first thing her husband said to her was that she had left the wallet on the dining room table. The thought of the Oriental man standing with a torn jacket in the subway station leaped embarrassingly into her mind. This episode has become one of her favorite New York stories, and she hopes that the small Oriental man has gotten some good story-telling mileage out of it, too.

Biography: Life

Recount the central story of another person's whole life in a way that brings out the main features or significance of it. This could be a summary of a person's life to date, an obituary for a newspaper, or the life of someone who lived long ago. Use fresh sources as much as possible that you draw together in your own way—interviews, diaries, letters, autobiography, and memoirs of the person or of those who know him or her, as well as public records. Indicate sources in a way appropriate to your general presentation, if such indications themselves are appropriate. Regional historical societies might appreciate the result and have a journal to publish it in.

What a Life

DENA FELLMAN

Imagine being in a time when there are no automobiles, no telephones, or no electricity, and imagine seeing all of these changes come to pass to the point of seeing a man on the moon and having space shuttles rotating the earth. This is the time span that Esther Glass lived in, and she witnessed all of these incredible changes.

She was born in 1898, in a schtetl (town) named Bolikikva in Russia. This was a tiny town near a big city called Berditenez.

She managed to survive the pogrom, which occurred whenever the Cossacks (horse soldiers) came through the towns and randomly killed people. These massacres were well known, especially in Berditenez. In order to keep her safe from these Cossacks, her mother would hide her in the oven, when she was about eight years old.

During that time, her father ran a tavern. They kept cats inside to keep the mice away. Whenever she was there, Esther would put the kittens inside her dress to keep them from freezing to death because it was so cold in Russia. There was one Russian peasant that would come into the tavern every night and get extremely drunk. Whenever he got drunk, he would sing the same melody over and over again. Esther loved the tune so much that she took it and hummed it all the time. Eventually, she passed it on to her children and so on; it became a family lullaby.

When she was about eleven years old, she became interested in an education, but in Russia, girls were not allowed to go to school. Esther made her younger brother Art teach her everything he learned.

She remembered one day when rumors were going around the town about an automobile coming through. Everybody thought this was the biggest thing ever, so everyone went outside to watch the car go by. Many religious people thought it was the work of the devil.

When Esther was fourteen, a tremendous migration era started. Esther's father had only enough money to go to America by himself and then send for this family later. About one year later, Esther, her mother, her sister, and her brother came to the United States through Ellis Island. There were hundreds of thousands of people waiting to become American citizens. The family joined their father in Pittsburgh, Pennsylvania in about 1912.

Esther's father was working hard, loading trucks. Knowing this would not feed all of them, they all had to get jobs. Since Esther was only fourteen years old and could not speak very much English, she was only able to get a job as a cigar stripper. She earned about $1.00 a day at the most.

It was required for children to attend school until a certain age in America, so Esther went to night school for about a year. A couple of years later, her father received a job offer in Cleveland, Ohio and they moved.

Esther met Sam Levin when she was eighteen and married him a year later in 1917. They met at the Workers Social Affairs, which was an organization for immigrants to meet other people who had something in common with themselves and enable them to reminisce about old times in Russia. In 1918, they had their first child and named her Ruth Rachel. Sam had just opened a hand laundry. It became very successful fast, even to the extent that they had a maid. Jack Manual was born in 1920, Sylvia Gene was born in 1923, and then Sidney was born in 1926.

In 1925, Esther found out some very distressing news about her health. She was diagnosed as having juvenile onset diabetes. Now insulin had only been discovered in 1923, so this disease was extremely dangerous and often fatal if certain precautions were not taken. Doctors warned her about having a strict diet and the possibilities of blindness or amputation of a limb. She became very religious about her eating habits to the extent that she would measure and weigh out her portions before eating.

During this time, they owned a ladies' clothing store. In 1929, the Stock Market crashed and they went bankrupt. They managed to save some of the merchandise. Since those clothes were all they had, Esther had her kids wear them even though they were about ten times too big for them. President Roosevelt was elected in the middle of the Depression and organized the WPA (Works Progress Administration). This organization allowed people to do some sort of labor, whether it was meaningful or not, just in order to provide jobs so these people could make money to survive. At this time Sam learned all about insurance and began selling it because he couldn't earn enough money from the WPA.

They were very poor, so Esther decided to go back to work. She was fed up with welfare because one time when she went to get some money, they gave her practically nothing. She told them that she could not buy any fruits and vegetables with that kind of money, but all they said to her was to go buy onions. She had an idea to start a business. The first thing she did was borrow some money from a friend and some more from a group called the Hebrew Free Loan Association to buy a soda shop next door to a high school. She called it Ma's Lunchroom. Hotdogs were sold for five cents apiece and cigarettes were sold individually for a penny. Esther and Sam worked very hard to make Ma's a success. It became a very popular place for kids, especially when they were cutting school. All of the kids loved Esther so much that they all started calling her Ma. She would let them hide in the kitchen when a truant officer came in. After a while Sam and Esther expanded and took over their competition next door and called it Pa's Lunchroom. Sam worked at Pa's and Esther worked at Ma's.

By the mid-1930s, the school threatened them since the kids were cutting all of the time, so they had to close down, because if the kids were not allowed to go there during school hours, Ma and Pa would lose all their business. They opened another shop in the middle of a black neighborhood, but it wasn't very successful. In 1941, when the war started, Sam was drafted. But since he had four kids and he was forty-two years old the service didn't take him. Instead, he had to work in a factory which was benefiting the soldiers. The government ordered them to close the shop down.

Sam died in 1957, and Esther sort of went into a shell. At about age 60, she stopped working and socializing with her friends; she was very lonely. Her kids were all grown up and had their own families.

All of this time, Esther lived with a fearful disease, diabetes, until her death in 1985. She died because of the things the doctors had warned her about long before. A cut on her ankle spread, causing gangrene and an amputation of her left leg, and blindness occurred. She had lived for at least sixty years with diabetes, which is a medical miracle in itself besides the fact she was eighty-seven years old. The life of Esther Levin was a hard but happy one. Her children, grandchildren and great-grandchildren meant everything to her. Her existence will never be forgotten.

(Sources were interviews with an uncle, Sidney Levin, and my mother, Gail Fellman.)

Kareem of the Crop

JOHN PAUL RAEL

As Lew Alcindor, he tore opponents apart at Power Memorial Academy and dominated the college ranks at UCLA. As Kareem Abdul-Jabbar he has made more field goals, scored more points, blocked more shots, and received more Most Valuable Player trophies than anyone else in the history of the National Basketball Association, and he is still adding to his accomplishments. At age thirty-nine, Kareem is the oldest player ever to play in the NBA; yet his incredible physical talents and endurance allow him to remain one of the most dominating players in the professional game.

Ferdinand Lewis Alcindor Jr. was born in New York City on April 16, 1947. At birth he weighed thirteen pounds and measured twenty-two inches long. Alcindor grew up in the middle class environment of upper Manhattan. Lew's determination to win and his athletic skills were noticed by many people when he was still in grade school. Although he is best known for his basketball accomplishments, his first medals and trophies came in swimming, ice skating, and baseball. As his self-consciousness over his abnormal height increased, he spent more of his time on the basketball court, where his size became his biggest asset. In the eighth grade Lew already stood 6'8" and had become well known among local basketball circles. Hard work and long hours playing his favorite game produced scholarship offers from numerous preparatory schools.

Alcindor chose Power Memorial Academy, a local school, and as a freshman he was placed on the varsity basketball team. It was not difficult for his coach to motivate him to want to be the best. After an extensive training program consisting of rope skipping, handball, and long hours in the gym, an awkward young player became a fine-tuned, experienced player. In Alcindor's sophomore year he averaged twenty-six points a game, and his team went undefeated and won the New York City Catholic high school championship. In his junior year, the dynamic young athlete averaged twenty-six points and eighteen rebounds a game, and once again his team won the Catholic championship. During his senior year, Alcindor averaged thirty-two points per game and set a New York City scoring record for high school players. Also during his senior year Power Memorial Academy suffered its first defeat since Alcindor had begun playing for them. The loss simply provided incentive for this great competitor to work harder. Alcindor dedicated hours and hours of his time to practice, and his team won the remainder of their games as well as their third consecutive championship.

Lew Alcindor left Power Memorial Academy as the most sought-after high school basketball player in the country. The long practice hours and hard work paid off as more than one hundred colleges and universities sought out this young basketball phenomenon. Lew Alcindor decided to continue his studies and play basketball at UCLA.

At UCLA a great player met a great coach. A man who is regarded as one of the best coaches in the history of college basketball, John Wooden, eagerly took Alcindor into his program. Wooden immediately realized the potential of his future center when Alcindor, in his first collegiate game, led the UCLA freshman team to a fifteen-point victory over the two-time national championship UCLA varsity team. That year Alcindor led the freshman team to an undefeated season and set a single-game scoring record for UCLA freshmen as well as most points and rebounds in a season.

His next season, 1966-67, Alcindor became a member of the UCLA varsity team, and in his first game set a UCLA single-game scoring record by pouring in fifty-six points. Teams that played UCLA attempted various types of defense to limit the success of his skills, but none of them worked consistently as Alcindor averaged twenty-nine points and fifteen rebounds a game and led his team to the NCAA championship. Lew Alcindor continued to dominate the college ranks by leading his UCLA teams to two more NCAA championships. He was named outstanding player in each of the three years that UCLA won the collegiate championship. He graduated from UCLA in 1969 with a degree in history, a B– grade point average, and the reputation as a franchise player for a professional team.

In the 1969 NBA draft Lew Alcindor, who had changed his name to Kareem Abdul-Jabbar for his Muslim religion, was the top pick of the Milwaukee Bucks. He had an immediate impact on the professional game and was named the NBA's rookie of the year. Abdul-Jabbar's dominance continued as he led the Bucks to a world championship in 1971 and was named Most Valuable Player in the championship series. Also while playing for the Bucks, Kareem received the league's MVP award for the 1971, 1972, and 1974 seasons. In 1975 Abdul-Jabbar was traded to the Los Angeles Lakers. This talented athlete provided the perfect element for an already solid Laker team. His competitive attitude has led the Lakers to World Championships in 1980, 1982, and 1985. In 1985 Kareem was named MVP and also was awarded Sportsman of the Year by *Sports Illustrated*.

The most amazing accomplishment of this tremendous athlete is that he is still playing basketball. In the NBA, where the average player lasts approximately 4.3 years, Kareem has lasted eighteen years and plans to play for at least one more. At age thirty-nine Kareem is making two million dollars a year to play a game he continues to enjoy. One may say that Kareem Abdul-Jabbar plays just for the money, but he has already made enough money to keep him happy for two lifetimes. It is his love for a great game that keeps this true competitor going.

Anonymous, "Alcindor, Lew Jr.," *Current Biography*, The H. W. Wilson Company, 1967, p. 3-6

Kareem Abdul-Jabbar, *Giant Steps*, Bantam Books, 1983, 336 pp.

Gary Smith, "Sportsman of the Year: Now, More Than Ever, A Winner," *Sports Illustrated*, 23-30 Dec. 1985, pp. 78-94.

Chronicle

Tell the story of what some group did. Members of a team or staff might have collaborated in some organized action, or some individuals might have chanced to undergo some experience together or to weave a web of action through independent behavior. Draw on accounts by participants and witnesses, fusing these in your own words while indicating sources appropriate for your manner of presentation. Many newspaper and magazine true stories are such accounts.

The Bellair Store

VANESSA FAURIE

On May 20, 1844, John Ryan bought Lot 20 for $25 and built a log store. It was destroyed by fire in 1850. The community helped him build a big, new frame building. Thirty-seven years and eight owners later, Amos Fouty bought the store in July 15, 1887.

Son-in-law Frank Harris tore down the old structure, erected the two-story building in the alley and had it rolled into where it stands today. A dozen men have owned or operated it since.

—from "The Story of One Town,"
a history of Bellair [Illinois] by Lucille Randolph

Now only four of those owners or their wives are around to remember what it was like to run the old store. Back then 25 or more people were there some nights.

But not any more. The Bellair store is almost 100 years old, and the mice and the cobwebs use it. There aren't any more cool summer nights when the men around town go to the back of the store to talk or play 42, using nail kegs with boxes over them or hardbacked benches for chairs.

The women don't sit on the long, wooden benches to talk and crochet while others wait at the counters as clerks gather their orders. Kid's don't run and play outside on the porch, either. And no one relaxes on the benches that sat on each side of the front door.

People only did those things at a time when they had to depend more on their neighbors to have a good time instead of on a car or TV. People depended upon each other in Bellair, as they did in many other places during that time.

"O' course, back in those days, we didn't have television, too many radios an' those things," Oletha Matheny said as she remembered when she and her husband, Harold, owned the Bellair general store from 1941-55. "It was more jus' friendliness an' gettin' together an' seein' your neighbors when you went to town."

Matheny sold the store in 1955 when her husband died. "He'd always told me, 'If anything happens to me, don't run this store,'" she said. "That was because it'd be too big a job for me."

But now Matheny sat in a rocking chair on her front porch in Robinson, talking about the importance of general stores to the community.

"Like sometimes now, I go get my groceries an' I don't see a soul I know," she said. "But in the smaller towns, if there was somebody you knowed, then usually you didn't have to be in an awful big hurry that you didn't stop an' visit with people a lot. You see, that was part of it."

Howard Knicely was part of it in the early thirties. He went to work for owner Ray Purcell at the Bellair store evenings before school when he was in high school in 1929, just after Purcell bought the store.

"I started out makin' egg crates for a cent a piece," Howard said. "You know, nailin' 'em. They bought a lot of eggs then. I could make 30 or 40 cases a night."

After nailing crates, Knicely started weighing and buying chickens, handling eggs and testing cream.

"I was testin' for butterfat one time," he said. "You have to stir it to get a good sample. Well, I stirred up a five-gallon can an' got a rat."

Eventually, though, Knicely became a clerk and waited on customers as well as worked at the post office that was in the store. He also pumped gas from the two glass-topped gas pumps out in front of the store. He worked seven days a week at $6.50 a week.

In addition to the gas pumps, a grease rack and a croquet diamond were set up outside. And movies were shown on a screen that was hung on the west side of the store. There were plays and musicals over the weekends on the second floor of the building. A stage stood at the north end, and rows of chairs filled the rest of the floor.

Knicely liked his years at the Bellair store. He got to know everyone as well as making some money.

"I wouldn't know just how to describe it," Howard said, looking back on his job. "It was a good experience, an' I'm glad I did it."

Knicely quit his job in 1935 to go to school. Purcell wasn't left empty-handed, though. He had other help, including his twin sister, Fay, who started working in September of 1933 as a clerk. She didn't leave until 1952 after working for three different owners.

Now living in Mattoon, Fay remembered working from 8 a.m. to noon, then from 5 p.m. until 9 p.m., six days a week. Working at the Bellair store, according to her, meant doing "anything that needed to be done"—from candling eggs to pumping gas.

"An' in the beginning, the gas pump wasn't electric," Purcell said. "The hand pump was on the side of the tank."

She remembered waiting on customers while they all talked. But she didn't get too many chances to visit.

"It was just a little country store," she said. "But we had quite a lot of loafers. It was the folks that was there that did most of the talkin'. And there was always a loaf o' bread or a box o' crackers open, an' they'd buy lunchmeat and make their own sandwiches or somethin' like that. But I'd be up and down waitin' on customers."

During the time she worked in Bellair, Purcell collected newspaper clippings and other things for a scrapbook she started around the time of World War I.

"I just saved anything that was unusual," she said. "Anything an' everything."

One of the things she saved was an old playbill from 1942, announcing an upcoming show at the store. It read: "ALL STAR WEDDING Bellair, ILL. Friday, April 3. Sponsored by the Red Cross. Curtain 8:00. Each character a man—each man a lady. Children 15 cents, Adults 25 cents tax included."

There was also a list of the cast and their characters. People like Art Farley, now mayor of Oblong, played Sally Rand. Harold Matheny, owner of the store at the time, played President Roosevelt, and Riley Chapman was Eleanor Roosevelt.

Some other characters included Shirley Temple, Gene Autry and Carmen Miranda, played by Earl Adkisson, Roy Mikeworth and J. R. McCollough, respectively.

"They had some really good plays," Fay said, laughing. "The times and the people who are still around have really changed since then."

Along with the people who have changed since the time they were in the play, Purcell remembered some changes around town in 19 years she worked there.

"Electricity was put through Bellair while I was there," she said. "That was one thing that was a change."

Before electricity, Delco lights from a battery plant in the back of the store lighted the place.

"I remember the Delco lights very well," she said. "I went back there one time. It wasn't stopped, an' I thought it was the gas main that didn't shut off. It splattered oil all over me."

And the only heat for the store in winter was the potbellied stove. For Purcell, working behind the counters was "like wadin' through ice water." She left her job at Matheny's Bellair store in March of 1952 to take care of her mother, who had burned herself and needed help to get around.

Fay's brother ran the store until 1937. And Ray Purcell and, Ada, his wife of 58 years, still remember the years they spent in Bellair. But because of Ray's hearing problem, Ada did most of the talking during a recent phone conversation from their Gaylord, Michigan home. She also worked in the store.

"I didn't work all the time," she said. "Our daughter, Betty, was quite small then. Ray opened up at 6:30 durin' farm season six days a week, an' sometimes was there till 10 at night. He'd be open till noon on Sundays.

"Everybody'd just visit an' talk about the happenings o' the day. If someone had a problem like an illness or something, that would be mentioned. Or if you could help in any way if somebody needed it, most everybody in the community was willing to do what they could."

People also talked about the big subject of the times—the Depression.

"Oh, they talked about how serious the economy was, like they do today." Ada said and laughed. "Things don't look good today, even. But there's always one or two in a crowd that get too riled up, or someone thinks they know everything. I don't remember that too much, though."

Because of the hard times, people bought a lot of goods on credit. And while the Purcells lost some money, Ada said it wasn't any great amount.

"Durin' the Depression, there was some that could hardly make it," she said. "There was some on WPA. An' the banks were closing.

The Bellair bank closed in 1931. And it was robbed in 1929. But the Purcells had little problems with robberies or break-ins.

"'Cept one time in the winter," Ada said, laughing a little. "Some boys broke in an' stole some rabbits. But that was about it."

There were other aggravations. Vacations weren't a big part of a storekeeper's life. And sometimes running the store could be frustrating with all the work and people.

"At times you'd get a little discouraged," Ada said. "But's that's only natural. Like maybe you'd want to go some place or do something, an' you couldn't get away cause you had to go to the store. It wasn't such a bad thing after all, though. It was an enjoyable time cause you could visit with different people.

"Now in the summer, it got pretty hot in there," she said. "We didn't have any fans. An' in the winter, everybody'd see which one could get the closest to the pot bellied stove. Course that's when we really had the good times 'cause people'd stay at the store longer, an' they wouldn't have to be in a hurry."

The Purcells kept a radio in the store, and everyone listened to the Cardinals' baseball games and music like fiddlers' contests. "Fibber McGee and Molly" and Red Skelton were on a lot, too.

But in 1937, Ray's health wasn't good and he sold the store.

"He did hate to sell out," Ada said. "But he jus' was no longer able to take care o' the responsibility of the store."

In April, Roy and Fannie Johnson, who now live in Oblong, took over the store. Roy has become virtually bedridden because of poor health, but Fannie spoke of the more than four years they ran the store.

"Yes, we bought it in '37," she said holding her hand to the frame of her glasses as if it were helping her remember. "Oh, we sold feed. We sold dry goods, notions, ice cream, groceries, an' just about anything you could name."

Johnson sat back in a chair in her living room and talked about the role she thought the general store played in Bellair.

"Ya see, at the time, people didn't go out like they do today," she said. "Some of 'em didn't even have cars. They depended on the country stores for their groceries, especially.

"An' then, o' course, the social time came in 'cause they didn't have any place else much to go like the kids do now an' take their cars an' jus' run here, there an' everyplace."

But it seemed to Fannie that there were always people coming in and out of the Bellair store during the long week when the store was open from six in the morning until about ten at night and eight until noon on Sundays.

"The store was generally full throughout the day," Johnson said. "We had them old schoolhouse, recitation benches that we would sit on. An' course we had chairs all around an' tables for their dominoes. There never was any time they wasn't comin' in. That's the reason I was near wore out. I wasn't used to stayin' up an' I got sleepy."

Sometimes the store was even open as late as 11 p.m. and midnight when there were 42 tournaments and plays. There were also some musical shows with banjos, mandolins and other string instruments.

A long, rectangularly shaped, two-storied building with 15' ceilings, the store stretched out a 100 feet from the street to the rear exit, where it had built onto it a sprawling one-story shed.

"Oh, it was quite big," Johnson said. "I 'spect on the one side was the main counters we sold over. They was on the west side. Folks come an' give us their order, an' we would write it down in a book. Then we'd gather the things up for 'em.

"But on the east side, we had counters with glass in 'em an' had our notions in 'em, like thread an' needles—little things for 'em to see. Up in front, we had the pop case out in the middle o' the floor. And then they had what you called a pot bellied stove that's always been there that we heated the store with. Course that's where mostly all of our chairs an' benches were.

"We had shelving all along the east side, an' that held our dry goods an' hardware. An' then on the west side, why, we'd have all our groceries. In the back was a meat counter. An' then clear on back we had a little partition where we went back in to do the eggs. Then back just a little was a little place to test the cream."

The eggs that people brought in had to be checked to see that they weren't bad. A box with a hole in the top of it and a light inside was used to see the outline and color of what was inside the egg and check for spots.

"I 'spect we even got some with chickens in 'em sometimes," Johnson said, laughing.

When people sold cream or eggs to the store, instead of being paid, they could be credited with an equal value of groceries and anything else they wanted to buy in the store. It was known as "doin' the tradin.'"

The Johnsons also gave credit to customers, usually on a one-month basis.

"It's not like it is now," Fannie said. "We didn't investigate an' things like that. We knew just about everybody, an' I guess Ray Purcell advised us who to credit an' who not to. It wasn't so established to customers as it is now.

"Well, even when Ray wanted Roy an' me to buy the store, Roy says, 'Well, we don't have the money to buy it.' An' Ray said, 'Well, I think Grandad'll (John Pyane) furnish it.'

"So we went up to John's, an' Roy signed a note at four or five percent interest. An' we got the store on just our note. We was real pleased with all our dealin's in the store. We never lost a lot o' money, but we did lose some."

Like other general storekeepers of the time, the Johnsons kept their credit listings and other accounts in a type of desk made by the Macaskie Company. It was about three feet wide with a straight back. The front slanted down and files folded out to keep individual records.

To get the goods the Johnsons sold, they would place an order to the Hulman Company in Terre Haute every week and pick it up themselves.

"Now we did have our feed delivered," Johnson said. "An' that was from Oblong. From Monte Eagle Mills. But the rest of it was from Terre Haute."

Unlike the Purcells, who never really had a break-in, the Johnsons did have burglars while they owned the store.

"They broke in through the front window once," Fannie said. "It looked like a woman's footstep that stepped in the window. They got a li'l bit of our money, but somebody told us it was goin' to be broke into so we took our money home with us every night or hid it. Got some of the cemetery money, too.

"At the time, peopled gathered in money to take care o' the cemetery," Johnson said, explaining. "Now around here, we have a regular feller to take care of 'em. But they didn't before. They'd use this to hire somebody to mow an' things."

With all the time, the hard work, the break-in, the four years that the Johnsons owned the store were still happy ones.

"I always liked workin' in the store," Johnson said. "We ran another store down here in Oblong. The girls that helped us didn't like for me to be there 'cause I liked to keep it clean, you know, dustin' an' things. Roy didn't make 'em do that too much when I wasn't there.

"An' there was another thing. We had a radio in the store. An' jus' like these soap operas that you see from day to day now, they had them over the radio. Course when I was home, I kinda got used to hearin' 'em. That's one thing I had to give up cause they'd want to listen to the sports.

"That's when I started to get fleshier 'cause I ate chocolate candy," she said and laughed. "But it was just about as happy a time as any."

The Johnsons sold the store in December of 1941 to Harold and Oletha Matheny, who had previously owned a service station for 13 years in Yale. The store was rewired for electricity when the Mathenys took over.

They took over on December 1. Six days later the Japanese attacked Pearl Harbor.

"Everybody in town was pretty upset when war was declared," Matheny said. "I remember they had a farewell party for us in Yale. Everybody thought about the ones that'd have to go to war. It was a lot of the conversation at the time. I can't remember when we got word when some of 'em got killed, but I remember them happening."

In addition to the plays and musical shows, the second floor of the store was also used during the war for dinners for the soldiers before they left or when they were home on leave.

"An' durin' the war, the only time we had the store closed was on Friday afternoons," Matheny said. "We had to haul in most everything we sold from Terre Haute. But things were scarce. People'd expect Harold to be home. An' by the time he opened later in the evenin', they'd be there grabbin' everything.

"We might get a stalk o' bananas or two stalks. That'd probably be the most we'd get because that'd be all they'd allow us to have. They'd be gone jus' like that."

The banana stalks hung in the back of the store by the meat counter. Occasionally, they'd last a few days. But because things were hard to get, that wasn't often.

Matheny remembered selling things like sugar that was kept in a drawer behind the counter. They would scoop whatever was ordered into sacks. They also sold flour in sacks that women made dresses and other things from.

"Actually, it was quite pretty material," Matheny said, holding a pillow slip with pink flowers as an example. "This is the only one I have left."

The flour and sugar were stored up on the west side of the store. Up in front near the window on the same side was a six-door ice cream case. Next to it were two candy cases, one with a curved-glass top sitting on top of a long, rectangular glass case. Both bowl and bar candy were sold.

Across the small aisle in the middle of the store stood the Coca-Cola cooler. The six-ounce Cokes and seven-ounce 7-Ups stood up to their necks in cold water on the left side; the Pepsis and RCs were on the right with the flavors in the middle.

Behind the pop case, there were bread and cookie racks. The store was a familiar sight to many. Mable Elliott, who still lives in Bellair, remembered what the store was like from a customer's point of view.

"They had square boxes of cookies in the racks," she said, remembering the general-store ways of selling different items. "They bought 'em that way. There was a metal frame with glass in it to show the cookies. Course some of it got broke out.

"The lid was on a hinge. They would put this on the box, an' then they'd open it jus' like a lid. When you wanted cookies, why, they'd get in there an' get 'em out an' weigh 'em.

"They even had a vinegar barrel you'd pump your vinegar out, along with sellin' nails, bolts, brooms an' mops an' everything like that. Had chicken an' hog feed. An' they sold coal oil or kerosene, too."

Oletha Matheny remembered the kerosene.

"Yes, we had that old crank kerosene," she said. "If you wanted a gallon o' kerosene, you turned a crank an' the kerosene came out. If you wanted five gallons, you turned it to five gallons.

"My daughter, Sharon, wasn't very old an' Harold's brother and wife was there, an' they had a little grandson, Larry, with 'em. I think the funniest thing was when they were playin' once, an' they were hollerin' down in the tank. It'd have a hollow sound, an' they was havin' fun. First one an' then the other would holler.

"Well, Sharon had her head down there a-hollerin', an' Larry turned the crank an' got her head soaked with kerosene. I don't know how long it took to get that smell out o' there. It's funny to look back on, but it wasn't funny at the time."

The old crank telephone hung on the west wall behind the Macaskie desk about the middle of the store. Both were central to the operations of the general store.

"On the old crank-type phones, everybody's'd ring, an' they'd all listen so you couldn't talk about your neighbors, that's for sure," Matheny said, laughing. "Other people really used it more than we did though. If they didn't have a telephone, they'd just come an' use it."

When the Mathenys ran the store, much of the credit kept in the Macaskie desk was for oil field workers, who were paid twice a month.

"Harold'd laugh an' say, 'Your payday is my payday,'" Oletha said. "But we scarcely lost any money. That's the kind of credit we did. We didn't let people have it long term, and we usually knew when we were going to get our money."

Competition between stores in the area was another fact of life for the general storekeeper. As Matheny said, "General stores was quite common. You always had a little competition."

Some of the competition were the huckster wagons that drove around the country. It was like a grocery store on wheels. Goods were stacked on shelves on both sides of the back of the truck or wagon. Orders were placed at the back as the huckster stopped at each farmhouse, buying eggs and even selling ice cream.

Each store usually had its own customers, though. But Oletha remembered a time when they got a sudden rush of new business at their service station in Yale.

"There were a couple of little boys that never had any money to spend," she said. "My brother-in-law, Cecil, was livin' with us at the time, an' he felt sorry for 'em. So he bought some pop for 'em an' those little boys went up town an' said, 'There's free pop down at Mathenys.'

"I think every kid come runnin' down there," She said, laughing. "They didn't realize Cecil had paid Harold for it."

But for Matheny, running the Bellair store was an enjoyable time in her life, even though they didn't have time to take vacations.

"That was something that we should've done but we didn't," she said. "As I look back on it, it was a lot o' work. But everbody worked that way. We were together an' that was the happy part of my life."

Matheny sold the Bellair store in 1955 to its last owners, Bill and Ruby Ritter, who had run Ritter's store three miles northwest of Bellair for 20 years.

During those last 15 years, the Bellair store wasn't as much a gathering place as it used to be. People still came by to visit, but then there were better roads and supermarkets and people were traveling more.

According to Ruby Ritter, now Ruby Hickox, who still lives near Bellair, there weren't as many people in Bellair any more—either they died off or moved away. The store was changing, too, though.

"We rearranged the counters to make 'em look more like the modern check-out counter," Ruby said. "That's when we took one o' them counters out an' put the lunch counter there. You know, we did a pretty good business around lunch time then."

With the addition of the lunch counter, the Ritters sold most of the same goods as the owners before them. And they also gave credit.

"A little too much sometimes," Ruby said, laughing. "But we got away from the credit by that time.

"Had a fella that was workin' on a drillin' rig up around Moonshine that came in an' told me he forgot his checkbook. He wanted to know if he could have some gloves an' just a few items. An' he told me he'd leave me his watch cause he'd be passin' through the next day, an' it'd be his guarantee.

"Well, I let him have the stuff. When he came back for his watch, why, he got quite a bit more stuff. He gave me a check for it an' picked up his watch. An' his check bounced."

She laughed and said, "I lost it all. But I don't think it was over $10 or $15."

The Bellair store still had a kind of reputation for having whatever people needed.

"If there was things you couldn't find somewhere," Rudy said, "people say they'd come to Bellair to find it."

People couldn't say that after 1970, though. Bill Ritter died in October of that year. Ruby had a sale just after Thanksgiving and the store was an empty shell, holding fading memories of a time gone by.

"A fella from Oblong wanted to buy the store complete an' put in an antique place," Ruby said. "He wanted my house, too. An' at the time I didn't know what I wanted to do. He was kind of interested in it, but he didn't want the store unless he could have my house, an' I didn't want to sell it.

"Other than that, I didn't have any other chance to sell the place. I wonder sometimes if I should've sold it to him."

After her husband died, Ruby was glad to get out of the business.

They had planned on selling out that summer, anyway, because business was dropping off.

"But I always enjoyed it," Ruby said of her 35 years in the general store business. "I missed the store. I missed seein' people an' talkin' to people. Sometimes I get a little homesick, too. I hated to see the store leave there. And I hated to be the one that done it."

Case and Profile

Case Study

Choose some person whose story typifies the experience of some other individuals such as a runaway teenager or middle-class person reduced to welfare, and tell what that person did or underwent. A case may present an instance of a current social phenomenon, a kind of personal behavior, or a feature of history. If the person is alive, you might interview him or her and others involved as well perhaps as seek out letters, journals, newspaper accounts, records of public agencies, and other documents that would have to be consulted for a person of the past. Or do in the same way a case study of a group.

Though basically a narrative, your case might include background information about whatever the case exemplifies. Think of your audience as people concerned with this subject matter. Perhaps make a case book with others who are writing cases.

Self-Sufficiency Costs Money

FLORIAN JOHNSON

If Reagan were a Navajo, he probably would think that President Reagan was mistaken about his decisions on cutting the budget. Reagan is misunderstanding us. We need support through government services to become independent.

Let's have Ronnie take Willie Chee's place. Willie Chee lives in Senostee, New Mexico on the Navajo Reservation. Since Willie lives in an underdeveloped area of the United States, opportunities are limited and infrequent.

Every day Willie struggles to take care of his family and herd his sheep. He went to school at Albuquerque Indian School for only three years. He didn't go back when his grandparents grew old and weak. No one in his family was able to stay and herd the sheep. He had to take on that responsibility. Because he didn't get a high school diploma, he couldn't get a job that would financially support his family.

Willie gets assistance from various government programs. Willie views the assistance as resources which help him meet his family's needs. Every month Willie's family gets food stamps and a General Assistance check. Mrs. Chee gets a check from the Women, Infants and Children (WIC) program for her youngest daughter. With less than the total income from these checks, Willie knows his family would not have enough to meet daily needs.

Survival is an important issue to Willie. Uranium tailings were left piled on land where his sheep graze. For many years, he has bugged the federal government to clean up the uranium tailings. His sheep have grazed near the tailings and are beginning to die. His family is afraid that the sheeps' sickness could be transmitted to them. Willie learned about a uranium task force studying the tailings removal. He went to Window Rock to see what could be done. A group of people from the task force came out to his place and started to survey the area. When the Indian Health Care Improvement Act (IHCIA) was vetoed by President Reagan, several government programs were not re-funded. One was the uranium task force. The task force stopped surveying the area around Willie's hogan. Nothing more has been done.

The windmill which pumped water up into the tank where his family drew its water broke. The IHCIA used to provide funds for repairing broken windmills. Willie is worried that the windmill will not be fixed and water will become scarce for his family and animals.

When his three-month-old daughter got sick, he took her to the Indian Health Service in Shiprock. The doctors couldn't do much for his baby's sickness. The hospital was not equipped to handle his baby's neurological disease. The doctors sent the baby to the IHS hospital in Albuquerque, New Mexico. The doctors told Willie he could also have taken her to the private hospital in Farmington, which had the needed staff and equipment to treat his daughter's sickness. He couldn't take her there because he lacked money and insurance. When his daughter became sick with pneumonia, she was again taken to the hospital in Shiprock. His daughter suffered during the long drive to the hospital. Willie wondered why a hospital couldn't be built closer to home. He found out the IHCIA used to fund new equipment for improved services and new construction for medical facilities. Because the act was not re-authorized, there is no money to build new hospitals.

Willie views other government programs as opportunities members of his family can take advantage of to better their standard of living.

Janet, the oldest daughter, got a scholarship in order to go to medical school in Utah. She became worried about her medical scholarship for the second half of her junior year when the Indian Health Care Improvement Act was vetoed by President Reagan. The act had a provision to fund scholarships for medical students. She got her scholarship back when the Indian Health Service (IHS) picked up the scholarships. Now she is worried about her senior year. Will IHS fund her again?

Kevin, the oldest of all the children, worked under the Comprehensive Education Training Act (CETA) program in Tohatchi until 1983. The CETA program ended. Kevin wanted to work under a new program called the Job Training Partnership Act program (JTPA). Most of the JTPA jobs the employment office in Shiprock listed were in towns off the Reservation. Kevin thought that the JTPA program was more restrictive than the CETA program. In the JTPA program Kevin had to work at an already-established business. Kevin would have to leave home and go to a city because there weren't enough businesses on the Reservation to hire the Reservation's unemployed. The family needs Kevin's help with household chores. Kevin wanted to work close to home. If he stayed, he would remain unemployed.

November 6 came around. Reagan was re-elected. Willie is worried about President Reagan's budget. He thinks Navajos are affected when social programs are cut. Even a two-percent cut hurts since most of the programs were designed to help the people survive. Reagan's budget cuts threaten their survival.

Reagan needs to understand that Navajos need government financial support as the first step to "pull(ing) ourselves up by our own shoe strings," as M. N. Trahant, the editor of the *Navajo Times Today*, said. The government should cooperate with us so that we will become self-supporting.

Internment of U.S. Citizens

TRACI TAKEDA

Imagine yourself a youngster living with your family in Sacrament Your days are filled with playing tag with friends, helping out around the house, and otherwise enjoying your seemingly endless childhood. Suddenly all of this is taken away. In a matter of days your schoolmates and hometown are replaced by armed military personnel and barren flatlands. For the next six years, these are to fill your childhood with fear and confusion.

It is Sacramento, California, 1941: Mr. Kintaro Takeda, his wife, Shizue, and their four children lead an average life. Being of Japanese-American descent, they choose to reside in Sacramento, a city highly populated with Asians. Kintaro manages a small fish market while his wife tends to the house and their children—Walter, eight, Toshiko, six, Susumu, three, and Osami, one. They are neither rich nor poor but are content with a simple lifestyle. As World War II rages on, the Takedas attempt to carry forward through the turmoil.

But on December 7, 1941, an event took place that changed their lives and future; the Japanese bombed Pearl Harbor. In a venture to protect and secure the United States, President Franklin Roosevelt signed Executive Order 9066 on February 19, 1942. Requiring that all people of Japanese ancestry living on the West Coast be evacuated into relocation camps further inland, the order brought much mental as well as physical harm to those involved.

Though he was only a young boy at the time of internment, Susumu still recalls the tragedy to this day. Allowed only one suitcase per person, Susumu and his family were forced to abandon many of their belongings. While being loaded into cramped freight cars, he took one last look at the familiar city of Sacramento and boarded to be taken to a new and alien environment. During the time of internment, the Takedas were relocated three times: to Walegera, California; Tule Lake, Louisiana; and Minidoka, Idaho. Each place looked the same; each left memories of barbed wire fences, sentry towers, and armed guards.

As soon as they arrived, the camp residents were herded with many other families into barracks. They were forced to live like animals and allotted only a fourteen-by-sixteen foot space per family. Susumu remembers being limited to only a pot-belly stove for warmth, a bare bulb for light, and the small, uncomfortable cots they slept on. There was to be minimal privacy here; the walls were made of thin plywood, and the tarpaper covering was considered insulation.

While in Tule Lake, the Takedas were blessed with a ray of hope and happiness. Shizue gave birth to a daughter, the fifth and last of her children. Retaining basic family structure was an ongoing effort. Susumu's father worked in the kitchen as a cook; his mother tended to his brothers and sisters. He, along with the other "camp" children, went to school, formed friendships, and tried his best to accept this as his new home. Outside, Susumu played with his newfound friends, but the air remained uneasy as the familiar sight of armed guards loomed.

In Tule Lake, many aliens were being taken in by the F.B.I. for questioning. One day, three agents arrived at the barracks. Susumu stood in horror as he watched his father being taken away. No one knew why or where Kintaro was being taken; no one bothered to tell his family. Several weeks had gone by before Kintaro's return, but there was no word of his well-being during this time.

Perhaps one of the most tragic disasters brought both grief and relief to the Japanese prisoners. On August 6, 1945, the United States dropped the atomic bomb on Hiroshima, thus ending World War II.

One by one the camps were closed and the families were released. The Takedas moved to Caldwell, Idaho to begin putting their lives back in order. Shizue and her eldest son, Walter, worked in a labor camp as farm hands. Kintaro supported his family while managing a local store. The year of 1948 marked the Takedas' re-entry to Sacramento. Their lives were free from the barbed wire fences and guards, but the next five years of their lives were to be filled with open and direct hostility. The Takedas found themselves faced with those who still held the Japanese-American citizens responsible for the war. They had to endure awful prejudice and bitterness upon their return. Susumu says, "I'll never forget being refused food at a restaurant in Nevada during our trip home in 1948. It took many years before I felt comfortable in a restaurant or hotel for fear of being refused service." The Takeda children also recall being constantly watched and followed by suspicious store clerks as they shopped.

These experiences left many invisible scars on the lives of everyone involved. While almost forty years have passed, nightmares from the camps still haunt my father and his family. After his return to Sacramento, he finished high school and chose to attend the University of California at Berkeley, School of Engineering. Because his parents were still trying to recover from their financial losses, Susumu worked throughout his four years of college to pay his tuition. After graduating in the top one percent of his class, he married my mother and together they moved to San Ramon, California to start their own family. There is nothing said about those years in the camps, and the subject is still very difficult for my grandmother, uncles, aunts and father to talk about.

(Sources were my father and my uncle.)

Profile: Person

Like a sketch, a profile shows outlines. It answers the question, "What is she or he like?" Interview the person or people who know or knew the person. Read what others have written about him or her and look at what your person has done or is doing. Use as many sources of information as are available, and go for detail. Your subject may be of interest because already known or because, if unknown, he or she is accomplishing something interesting or simply is an original person. What are the **traits** *of this person? Organize your profile by these traits, illustrating each by anecdote, quotation, observation, and factual information. Capture the essence of the person as you perceive it. Submit your piece to a publisher whose readers might want to know about the person or about* *the activity she or he carries out. Or include it in a collection of other articles treating the subject that your person is associated with.*

James Weinstein:
South Orange Trustee

JEFF SCHAFFER

Jimmy Weinstein is a 23-year-old Republican who also happens to be a graduate of Columbia High School [Maplewood, N.J.]. "Politics always was my interest, national or anything else." During high school he was the Treasurer of the Student Council and Business Manager of the *Columbian*. He was "always working for one or another losing Republican campaign," and often spoke at BOE meetings. At Columbia University, he majored in American History. Having been elected as a College Senator he represented the undergraduate school in the University Senate.

Immediately after graduation in 1984, he went to work in Washington for the national Republican Congressional Committee. The committee was in charge of the support for the 435 Republican campaigns.

After one month, however, Jim was offered a position helping the Dean Gallo campaign in the eleventh congressional district.

"I thought I'd do my stint in Washington, but it made a lot more sense to do something in my home district on a well run congressional campaign; and I don't regret in the slightest leaving Washington D.C."

His job entailed "making sure 17 bundles of mail totaling almost two million individual pieces got out in the correct sequence, printing on the correct paper, and all the details that went into making sure they got produced within the $350,000 budget. I was prepared for this somewhat in Washington, but not at all in college."

After Gallo defeated 22-year-incumbent Joseph Minish, Jim's political career was ignited. He had won himself a reputation as a hard worker who got things done.

"If you have credibility as being sincere or as one who gets things done it doesn't matter either way. I would like to get a reputation as one who gets things done; and, in that way, people will believe me. That's the measure for the success of a politician."

Right after the election he was hired by State Assemblyman Bob Franks. Franks, who represents Maplewood, had Jim handling political work, running his reelection campaign, and doing legislative work, special studies, and some writing. Jim still holds this job.

In addition, nine months ago he was to run Congressman Gallo's

Livingston office. Jim handles the local press relations, relations with local elected officials in the 12 towns in the district, and represents Gallo at various functions.

Last year Jim ran for his first elective position. Although in high school he felt he would someday run for the Board of Education, he ran instead for the position of Trustee of South Orange. Jim knew that South Orange had a substantial amount of issues in last year's election. People voted not on service to community but rather on position to issues. "That's why I won," expressed Jimmy.

"People heard from me five or six times. I was in the newspaper, in the mail, and I was in front of the bagel store every Sunday morning."

Jim's honesty is unbounded. He is a staunch Republican and a serious person. When talking with him, one realizes that every sentence is well thought out. He takes positions on everything. Every theory and stance has been reached systematically. He very rarely tones down what he has to say. In fact, even when it may not be necessary for him to give answers, he tries to. This is most evident by his conduct at trustee meetings.

"Many times, what you'll see with politicians is that they'll give you some kind of bland pap. I try to get into the issue somehow. If it's a legal matter, I won't talk or a personal matter, I won't talk. Generally, if it can be detrimental to the village later, I won't talk."

Jim senses that people see right through it when someone is trying not to give them answers.

"It's a hell of a lot easier to say to someone, this is what I can do; this is what I am going to try to do; and if I don't do it, then call me and ask me why I didn't do it."

He is all too aware of policitians' favorite expressions such as "I hear your concerns," "I sympathize with you," "I understand your concerns," "I hear you." He feels that one has to add, "I understand your concerns, and this is what I will try to do about it"; or "I am restricted in this way by the law"; or, to say bluntly, "I sympathize with you, but I have seen cases like this before, and nothing can be done." However, he realizes that politicians do not usually bother to do this. They have this "forced sincerity" and have been very successful.

One may think that the above is an exaggerated method of attack. If one were actually to practice what Jim preaches, it would seem that he would not get elected. However, Jim is earnest in his beliefs.

"I think that the people of South Orange would find it very unacceptable if I were not to be frank. . . . I doubt very much that I will not be reelected in '89. I think that at this level people reward you for hard work more than anything else. . . . If I lose, I lose. I will be 26 and I can sit out for 20 more years and still be a young politician."

Jim is Chairman of the Public Safety Committee of South

Orange. Jim commented on the steps being taken to combat the recent racial difficulties that our town has faced.

"We have stepped up the patrol cars, sent fire vehicles on patrol, informed South Orange residents to keep their lights on more often, since light deters crime, banned the sale of spray paint to minors who do not have a parent accompanying them, and are currently receiving new types of sophisticated equipment to catch these criminals. With lots of cooperation, one too many coincidences, or one lucky break, we are going to catch these guys."

Jim noted, however, that one cannot place the blame on kids at this time.

Jimmy Weinstein has admirably begun his political career. He is the youngest elected official in the state and has already established very impressive credentials. Perhaps he is following in the footsteps of Democrat Peter Shapiro.

"I like Peter. One should have friends on the other side. Peter is probably one of the hardest workers, save Tom Kean, in the state of New Jersey who understands your concern and can make you believe he will do something."

"It's kind of neat to say I was the youngest ever elected official in South Orange, and the state of New Jersey. That's a distinction which is nice to have. To have the blood and vinegar at such a young age is incredible. New blood causes the change. The best thing about politics is constant change bringing in new ideas."

Perhaps Jim's high school yearbook quote as well as his college yearbook quote can best summarize the intentions of this young man.

"If nominated I will run. If elected I will serve."

Robert Kennedy: What Could Have Been

AIMEE GROVE

Neither a genius nor a saint, Robert F. Kennedy was a creative individual with a vision of a better world. "Some men see things as they are and say 'Why?' I dream of things that never were and say, 'Why not?'" he was fond of quoting. Outspoken where others were evasive, brash where others were subdued, and restless where others were complacent, Robert exceeded his brothers in courage and passion. He was ambitious—not for himself, but for those he dubbed "the suffering children of the world." Although he was born into a world of power and affluence, he was obsessed with the plight of the poor, the hungry, and the blacks, whom he dreamed of uniting in a majority for change. He was impatient to accomplish so much so fast; to reconcile the races, end the Vietnam War, abolish poverty. An idealist with the discipline and determination to achieve his goals, he could have made it happen. Had time and fate permitted, Robert Kennedy might have changed history.

Robert Kennedy, who could never shuck his boyish nickname "Bobby," was essentially an enigma—a dangerous opportunist to some, a pop hero to others. Because he felt simply, fought fiercely, and lived by action rather than words, he was often mistrusted and misunderstood. To his enemies, he was a shrewd politician exploiting his brother's legend. As an active participant in some of the most controversial politics of the era—McCarthyism, the integration of the University of Mississippi, the opposition to the Vietnam War—Bobby was, indeed, an easy target for attack. Businessmen and conservatives interpreted his every move as an act of ruthless ambition. Many doubted his sincerity in public affairs.

In the eyes of his supporters, however, Bobby was a man of incredible compassion and empathy, a champion of the desolate and disinherited members of society. Embraced by blacks for his policies, which recognized their need for power and pride rather than sympathy, he was called the "blue-eyed soul brother." With his long hair, wiry frame, and undeniable charisma, Bobby became a teen idol like James Dean or Frank Sinatra—a candidate of hope for the disillusioned youth of the sixties. His speeches drew crowds of "Bobby boomers" who cried and yearned to grasp a piece of their hero.

Bobby's magnetic presence particularly attracted children. They flocked to him with innocent fascination, and he, in turn, treated them with attention and respect. None of his infamous brusqueness surfaced in the presence of children. He could stand on his desk for an hour to explain the workings of the government to a roomful of schoolchildren. As a father of nine, Bobby enjoyed a unique communion with all young people, who, like him, were creatures of intuition, rather than deliberation. In a riotous crowd, he could discern a small child's face, pluck her from the chaos, and give her a hug, oblivious for that moment to the turmoil around him.

Bobby Kennedy, for all the raucous adulation and bitter animosity he evoked, was, after all, a man, not a myth. Beneath his rugged image, he was a shy, alienated man, less extroverted or confident than any of his brothers. He stammered, his hands trembled and twitched, he often spoke in a Bostonian monotone, and his handwriting was small and squiggly. Yet these flaws brought him closer to the American public. Despite his inherited fame and fortune, he could be identified as a common man—a politician with a scarred face rather than a slick mask.

Like any public figure, Bobby made mistakes in his youth which later tarnished his image. As JFK's campaign manager in the 1960 election, he earned the "ruthless" reputation which would later prove a detriment to his political career. Decidedly unscrupulous campaigning methods were used; delegates and political rivals were threatened. Bobby told his campaign workers, "It doesn't matter if I hurt your feelings. It doesn't matter if you hurt mine. The important thing is that we get the job done."

Some of Bobby's policies shifted as he matured, undermining his sincerity in many people's minds. As J.F.K.'s Attorney General, for example, he participated in the early decision to escalate the Vietnam War by increasing American forces from 800 "advisors" to 1600. He would later strongly denounce this action. A dedicated civil rights advocate, Bobby admitted of his early years, "I never lost any sleep over the Negroes before."

Critics labeled him as "rash," "unpredictable," and "scheming," but they failed to recognize the events which shaped and molded Bobby's policies. Concrete experience educated him in a way Harvard never could. He discovered poverty and hungry children during his presidential campaign in desolate West Virgina. He learned gradually, through the struggle of the Southern Negro, of the importance of civil rights, witnessing first hand the brutal beating of the Freedom Riders in Montgomery, the integration of the University of Mississippi, and violent voting discrimination against black men in the South. Through his experiences, Bobby developed a special sensitivity to the black movement and a strong conviction that children were the most innocent victims of injustice. He saw with his own eyes the magnitude of inequities present in the richest nation on earth. And he vowed to fight to rectify them.

As Attorney General, Bobby functioned primarily as a pioneer for John's more controversial ideas. He acted as an ombudsman, deflecting criticism of the White House while testing new policies. As a result, the brothers were forever separated in the press, with Bobby as the rebel and John as the saint. Bobby's single greatest contribution to the Presidency, however, was his ability to discuss frankly, advise, praise, or contradict John when others may have side-stepped him. He was an honest counselor, friend, and sounding board for the President during some of the nation's greatest crises, his emotion-laced style a perfect foil for John's intellectual cool.

It was during these years that distinct differences in style and substance surfaced between Bobby and John. While John possessed the keen intellect and clear perception of a scholar, Bobby's best decisions and brightest concepts sprang from intuition. His most moving speeches were impromptu; his unrehearsed address to grieving Indiana blacks on the day of Martin Luther King's assassination is considered one of his best.

Bobby had a quick temper, a deep, brooding personality, and an utter emotional immersion in politics; John observed the problems of the world from without. Although he sought to abolish poverty and

racial discrimination, John did not feel a compelling personal identi-
fication with their victims as Bobby did. His empathy overwhelmed
him. After visiting a Native American reservation, he sat in silence for
an hour before bursting into tears. When he traveled into a coal mine
in Lota, Chile worked mainly by Communist party members, he
emerged exclaiming, "If I worked in this mine, I'd be a Communist
too!" John's manner embodied a joyful warmth; his soul exuded opti-
mism and happiness. Bobby, on the other hand, felt too deeply to enjoy
life so easily. His drive and immense capacity for emotion, both love
and hate, would not allow him John's peace.

Two characteristics dominated Bobby's personality more than
any others: competitiveness and religion. He pushed himself with
Puritanical discipline in everything he did. Second was never good
enough for a Kennedy, but Bobby, who did not possess the natural
grace or athletic prowess of his brothers, struggled all of his life to be
the best. As the "runt" of the Kennedy litter, he was forced to try
harder than his siblings. At four years old he taught himself to swim
by diving into a lake and swimming back to shore unaided. As a
diminutive football player at Harvard, he compensated for his lack of
strength with unwavering tenacity and perseverance. As a senator, he
accomplished things by working longer and harder than his opponents.
Thus, as Bobby grew older, he had little tolerance for people he saw as
"lazy" or "undisciplined." In fact, he often criticized Eugene McCarthy,
his Democratic rival, for being "indolent." He said, "He sleeps while
those marvelous kids work for him. He won't even study the issues
they care about."

A moral and very Catholic personality shaded Bobby's political
and personal opinions. The most devout of the brothers, he once
dreamed of becoming a priest. At twenty-one, he received a reward
from his parents for abstaining from alcohol or cigarettes, a check for
$1000. As he matured, his black-and-white, good-and-evil view of the
world blurred very little. Though technically a liberal, Bobby Kennedy
often took a moral conservative stand on personal issues. For example,
he refused to give *Playboy* an interview because one of his children
"might see that magazine." He also urged a year's moratorium on
cigarette advertising. His catholicism reinforced other parts of his
character—his self-motivation, his sense of public responsibility, and
his loyalty to his family and his constituents.

The turning point in Bobby Kennedy's political career arrived in a
morbid form on November 22, 1963, when a bullet robbed him of his
leader, idol, and friend, JFK. The assassination shattered him, sending
him into an anguished withdrawal for months. As a religious man, he
grappled with a philosophical and emotional dilemma of the order of
death in the universe. "The innocent suffer—how can that be possible
and God be just?" he wrote during his mourning period.

The assassination awakened in Bobby a sense of fatality, and a skepticism for the future. "I can't plan," he said. "Living everyday is like playing Russian roulette." Along with this fatality came a compulsive urge to dare the elements. Whether he was scaling the 14,000 foot Mt. Kennedy, or canoeing down the piranha-infested Amazon river, or traveling through riotous crowds void of armed protection or trained bodyguards, he constantly taunted the odds.

When he emerged from his haze of shock, Bobby found himself the unlikely successor to the throne of the family dynasty. No longer smothered by his brother's shadow, he was finally free to forge an identity of his own. He realized that he had the power and the desire to continue the programs and achieve the goals John had initiated. In a speech at a West Berlin university, he told students: "The hope President Kennedy kindled isn't dead, but alive. . . . The torch still burns, and because it does, there remains for all of us the chance to brighten the future. For me, that is the challenge that makes life worthwhile."

Given the family tradition, perhaps it was inevitable that Bobby would follow on John's path to the Presidency. Explained JFK while still a senator, "Just as I went into politics because Joe died, if anything happened to me tomorrow, my brother would run for me in the Senate. And if Bobby died, Teddy would take over for him." But Bobby bided his time, hoarding his political strength for the time in which the public would be most receptive to him and his causes.

By the middle of 1968, Bobby had begun to struggle with his instinctive sense of loyalty to the Democratic party and his obsessive drive to become the leader of the "underclass." When Eugene McCarthy announced his candidacy, Bobby felt confused and guilty for staying out of the race. His indecision paralyzed him, until President Johnson's popularity began to sag, which mobilized him to announce his candidacy. This decision to run represented Bobby's final metamorphosis from politician to leader.

Bobby's eighty-one day campaign was furiously fast-paced, chaotic, and in many ways, strange. He severed all ties with President Johnson and chased Eugene McCarthy across the nation, challenging his traditional liberalism. People gathered about him like a faith healer wherever he went, especially in the ghettoes and on the college campuses. Bobby said, "We're going to win this election in the streets!" At the same time, he suffered harsh criticism and rivalry from other party members. Even Harry Truman said of him, "I can't see any qualification he has for leading a nation."

When President Johnson dropped out of the race, Bobby temporarily lost his sense of direction and driving purpose. He lost the Oregon primary, and the prospects looked glum. But Hubert Humphrey provided a moving target, a formidable opponent. Bobby finally gained a new sense of himself, and this confidence attracted votes. By June 6, 1968, he had captured South Dakota by a 50% share, and

California with a 46% share, leaving him with 198 critical delegate
votes. At his victory speech in the Ambassador Hotel in Los Angeles,
Kennedy and his supporters were ecstatic. His final words from the
rostrum: "I think we can end the divisions within the United States,
the violence."

And then, in the hotel cafeteria, next to a hand-lettered sign,
"The Once and Future King," the hopes and dreams of millions of
Americans were eliminated once again. Bobby Kennedy was killed at
the height of his glory, on the road to the White House.

Bobby left behind him an incomplete journey to a new world of
peace, void of poverty, starvation, and racial discrimination. The underclass of the society had been robbed of their leader with a single
hollow-nose slug. As Jack Newfield of the *Village Voice* put it, "The
stone had rolled to the bottom of the hill."

Bibliography

Anonymous, "For Perspective and Determination," *Time*, June 14, 1968, pp. 22-
    27.

Barrett, Laurence, "The Politics of Restoration," *Time*, May 24, 1968, pp. 22-
    27.

Kriss, Ronald, "The Shadow and the Substance," *Time*, September 16, 1966, pp.
    32-36.

Newfield, Jack, *Robert Kennedy: A Memoir*, E.P. Dutton & Co., Inc., New York,
    1969.

Schlesinger, Arthur, Jr., "Robert Kennedy: The Lost President," *Esquire*, August
    15, 1978, pp. 25-52.

Profile: Enterprise

*Choose some enterprise that interests you or a readership
you have in mind—a factory, laboratory, farm, office, service
agency, or other enterprise. Make at least one visit to observe
the operation and to talk with people there. You may need to
make several visits to see all the phases of the operation or to get
all the information you need from people connected with it
(some of whom may be elsewhere). Take lots of notes or
recordings and possible photos as well for illustration. Ask for
brochures or other material put out by the enterprise or written
about it elsewhere. Are there still other sources of information
that you can draw on?*

*Assemble this information to create a profile or full
picture of the enterprise. Interweave direct observation with
secondhand information and decide when to quote and describe
and when to summarize and generalize. Organize by phases of*

operation or by **traits of the enterprise so that your reader**
learns what it's about and how it works.

Consider this as one kind of feature article for a news-
paper or magazine. Or make a book of profiles with other
students doing this assignment.

Get Thee to a Nunnery!

CINDY KENNEY

Dedicated to every person
who, like me, wonders what
nuns laugh about.

If you have faith
    as a grain
of mustard seed . . .
    nothing will be impossible
to you

Matthew 17:20

Sister Mary Judith:

Let's see, when did I decide to become a nun? Well, when I was in
high school, a girlfriend and I used to joke around about becoming
nuns, then suddenly it wasn't a joke any more. My family was shocked
but finally realized that I meant business. I visited a few convents and
decided on Dominican Sisters. They were very helpful and urged me to
go out in the world and get a job, my own apartment and go out on
dates. They don't want naive high school girls going straight into the
convent without being out in the real world first. I really learned a lot
about myself and how to stand on my own two feet.

After two years I returned to the convent and made my promises.
It was a real cultural shock for me. I had to do a lot of things for the
good of the community that I would have rather not done. Getting up
at 5:45 a.m. is still tough for me, and I'd rather not eat at the hours we
have, but I'm only one out of 120 sisters who live here. It's part of the
sisterhood, and if it pleases God then that is all that matters. I guess
there are bound to be a few unexpected inconveniences. It's like a
mother with a new-born baby. She thinks it is cute and cuddly, but
then she realizes she has to get up at 3:00 a.m. to feed it. (Laughs.)

HOW DO PEOPLE REACT TO YOU, KNOWING YOU'RE A NUN?

Well, right now I'm attending Cal. State Hayward. This is my last year (raises her eyes up), praise God, and as far as I know, I'm the only nun there. Most people are very polite and a lot of them come up to me and ask for advice or just want to talk, knowing I'll listen. It's funny because I go jogging every day, and the school gave me a locker to keep my gym shorts in. I change into my shorts and jog around the campus, and boy do I get strange looks when I take off my running clothes and put on my habit.

WHAT DO YOU FEEL ABOUT THE LIBERAL NUNS WHO DON'T WEAR HABITS ANY MORE?

Mmmmmm (pause) I think our habits are very important for us and the rest of the world. I see them as a sign—a sort of a message to others that God is alive and well in the world today. Even if they don't believe in God, they know that I do. I think it's a big part of being a nun, and they're okay with me. Gosh, they've changed a lot since the first Dominican Sisters. Just recently we've gotten these new tailored habits. Later on you can see the older sisters who still have the oldfashioned habits. They don't like changes, even subtle ones.

WHY DID YOU WANT TO BE A NUN?

That's a good question. I suppose my prior experience with religion influenced me and I had a feeling that it would be best for me. I have always felt that I have a personal and loving relationship with God. I guess we just hit it off!

* * *

I sought to hear
 the voice of God
 and climbed the topmost steeple,
but God declared:
 "Go down again—
  I dwell among the people."
   John Henry Newman

Donna Martin:

Why did I quit? (Laughs heartily.) Because politics became too big, and I felt I could do more good on the outside. Holy Family, where I was a sister for fifteen years, used to be very conservative, but then it went completely overboard. Most of them don't wear habits any more, except for the older ones.

It wasn't until my last year that I noticed all of the garbage. I saw some—not all, but some—nuns driving around in fancy cars and living in fancy apartments, acting like the world was supposed to wait on them. They have no respect for the older nuns who are in their communities. I have one special friend at Holy Family who calls me once in a while just to talk because no one there will talk to her. She gets very upset that the girls she has taught to become good nuns will not give her some of their precious time to talk with her. She calls me instead, and I talk to her or take her somewhere. It's very sad, very sad.

DO YOU FEEL THAT MANY GIRLS GO IN WHO DON'T BELONG THERE?

Well sure. Plenty of them don't know what they are getting into. For many of them and even people who aren't nuns, religion is a sacred superstition. They go through all of the motions and find out that they don't really believe in God. Sometimes their families push them into it, or they may go into a convent hoping to escape their families. Some of them are actually afraid of men, and they don't always realize it until it's too late. They literally shake around priests even. I remember once while I was showing some sisters around the communes where I worked at in West Berkeley, a few men walked by stark naked and you never saw women squirm and shriek like they did. I just had to laugh at them. I guess it didn't bother me because I was in the Navy for fifteen years and then graduate school, and I'd seen my share of naked men.

DO VERY MANY NUNS LEAVE THE SISTERHOOD?

I don't think a lot of them do, but there are those of us who have decided that it just wasn't right for us. Some of them realize that they want a husband and family. They get out because they want SEX! They shouldn't fool themselves, that's why you've got to know yourself and not use the convent as a place to escape the world. I decided that I could do more good out here and I think I do a good job at the Adult School. I'm still a religious person, but I just don't wear a habit or live in a convent. It wasn't for me.

* * *

We live within the shadow
     of the Almighty,
sheltered by the God
     Who is above all gods.
          Psalm 91:1

There it was in big white letters, "Dominican Sisters, Queen of the Holy Roses College." I turned left and proceeded slowly up the thin, curving road until I saw it. There amor   he trees, nestled in the hills like a well-guarded egg, was the conv   As I drew closer the butterflies in my stomach flew wildly about, bumping into the acid-lined walls that grew tense with each rotation of the car's engine. Inside my car I felt safe, like gold in an armored car, but still the thought of having to get out and actually enter into that unknown world of holiness made me feel nervous. It would only be a few days until I would have to return here and attempt to get an interview from the friendly young nun who called and agreed to show me around.

For right now, though, I could just sit here alone in my car and imagine what went on inside of that beautiful old gothic building. The yard surrounding the convent was well cared for and set a heavenly scene. It reminded me of the Garden of Eden, but instead of a babbling brook it had a sprinkler system that sent cool water spraying over the green grass and a spectrum of flowers. The parking lot was empty except for a small white Pinto covered with bumper stickers like "Holy Names College, God loves you!," "Saint Mary's College," and others, displaying the fact that its owner was probably a devout Catholic.

As I sat there, taking in as much of the area as I could, I caught a glimpse of what looked like an angel floating between the trees below the lovely stained-glass windows of the convent. As the figure drew closer, I saw that she was not an angel but an elderly nun walking slowly towards me with the help of a wooden cane. My heart began to do flips, and I just knew she was coming to ask me why I was sitting there staring at her and her home. Much to my surprise, she walked right past me without even looking at me to see me watching her. She crossed the parking lot, and through my sun-streaked, dirt-covered windows, I saw her walking into what must have been the convent's cemetery. When I could no longer see her I took one last look at the place and put away my notebook and pen. Starting up the engine was awful! It seemed so loud that I thought the whole world must have heard it. The roar of the engine broke the silence like the wail of a baby in the dead of the night. Driving back down the same narrow, winding road, I could have sworn I heard bells ringing. I slowed down the car to quiet it down, but I must have imagined them because I could only hear the faint roar of the cars driving along Mission Boulevard just a few yards away. That was my first visit to Dominican Sisters, and who knew what lay ahead?

* * *

"They don't understand that we have to get out of ourselves. We can't sit forever and listen to our arteries harden. We have to get out of our little nunny world."

Sister M. Charles Borromeo

Hesitantly I rang the doorbell, thinking how strange it was that a convent would have one. I took a deep breath and tried to build my confidence by thinking I was on a "mission from God." The sudden opening of the door and the smiling face which said to me, "Hello, Cindy? I'm Sister Mary Judith," made me think twice about this project. Struggling to find my own voice I said, "Hi," and stepped into what must have been the main building, which was equipped with an office, library, printshop, storage rooms, and who knows what else behind those doors.

During my well guided tour, my hostess laughed like a normal twenty-four-year old college student and talked like one too! Looking for those wonderful status life details I scanned her face and clothes searching for something interesting. Well, her skin was clear and smooth and her small delicate nose held a pair of modern, plastic-rimmed glasses, through which her plain, brown eyes peered out at me. Nothing peculiar about her face. Aha! her clothes are definitely different, and that thing on her head is no summer bonnet. She held her head high, and upon it was a plain black veil which covered all of her light brown hair, except for the feathered bangs upon her fore-head. With her hands casually in the pockets of her modern tailored habit of white, she talked on about the books in the library and some historical facts about the Dominican Sisters' origin. As she walked, her modern, wedge-heeled shoes squeaked as if she had been out in the rain. She moved with a casual but purposeful gait and acted like a woman proudly showing off her home.

As we entered the newly built, million-dollar dining room, she explained that the old one had to be torn down and that they may not have the money to pay for the new one. One of the main donors for the building could not give the money for some reason, and now they had to pray for new donations. Below the dining room was the sewing room, where Sister Conrada was trying to prepare the new habits before returning to Germany for a short vacation. Sister Mary Judith introduced me as a senior from American High School and told her that I was writing a paper on nuns. Like a grandmother wanting to dress up her grandchild, she asked me what size I wore and if I was going to be entering soon. Sister Mary Judith laughed and said, "No, no, Sister Conrada. We don't even know if she's Catholic. She's just here for a visit." I could feel the blood rush to my face, and I timidly said I was Catholic but that I didn't need a habit made. Feeling like an escapee, I left the room with Sister Mary Judith, saying, "Nice meeting you." Boy, was that a little white lie. I almost expected God to strike me dead.

Next we moved down to the basement floor. Sister Mary Judith explained to me that a family had come to them for help and after-wards wanted to thank them, so they donated a pool table. With an embarrassed guilt she told me it was a fluke, and not the usual donation, but as we entered the room two nuns were playing pool. Not expecting this, Sister Mary Judith giggled and said, "Now all we need is a keg." One of the other nuns said, "What for?"

"What do you think a keg of beer is for?" laughed Sister Mary Judith. They all giggled, but I sensed a feeling of dislike towards the comment from the third nun. She was the Principal. Her face was strange, and her features were almost manly, making her seem stern and tough. She contemplated hitting the cue ball at one angle and then moved to a new position and sent the ball marked 6 rolling into the right corner pocket with a thud. Reminding me that this was a fluke, Sister Mary Judith said her goodbyes, and we climbed the stairs and went out a side door to the outside.

* * *

It is good to say, "Thank You" to the Lord, to sing praises to God who is above all gods.

Every morning tell Him, "Thank you for your kindness," and every evening rejoice in all His faithfulness. Sing His praises, accompanied by music from the harp and lute and lyre. You have done so much for me, O Lord. No wonder I am glad! I sing for joy.

Psalm 92:1-4

We're going to pray where? I guess Sister Mary Judith doesn't want me down in the pews with the other sisters, so she's taking me to the choir room. Wow, there's a great view from up here and it's pretty nice. Oh no, she just genuflected. Should I do it too? I know that I'm supposed to at my church, but what will she think of me? Will she snicker at me, or will she be impressed that I know what to do? Well, here goes. Kneel slightly and make the sign of the cross like you've done so many other times. There now, that was easy. I don't even think she saw you. What's that? It sounds like a guitar, and yes, now I see her. One of the nuns is playing a guitar and like angels from heaven their voices fill the chapel and send goose-bumps down my spine. They sound so lovely and quietly strong that I begin to wonder if one of the requirements of becoming a nun is to have a good voice. That's ridiculous! They probably just get a lot of practice, and the acoustics of the chapel make them sound better than they actually are. I feel pretty strange having Sister Mary Judith sitting so quietly next to me, while the others are singing. Maybe she wished she could be down there with them, or perhaps she likes not having to go through all of that formal stuff. They look like pop-up dolls as they sit up and down while one of the sisters leads the Mass. They read along with her in those little prayer books, like the one in Sister Mary Judith's lap. I just realized how much my head hurts. I've never had such a headache, and I keep swallowing for some reason. I bet she can hear me swallowing. It's so quiet up here, except for the low hush of voices below, that I can hear her breathe, so surely she can hear me swallow. Rrriiinnnggg, rrriiinnnggg! Hey, that's a telephone. I can't believe how loud the phone is in here. Oh how terrible! Now I remember that when I called, the sister at the other end told me, "Well, I'll have to see if anyone is interested and have her call you back later. Right now we are in the middle of prayers." Uuuggghhh! You dummy! YOU called right when they were singing and praying and conversing with God. You made the phone ring just like it is doing now and boy was it loud! Now what are they doing? Oh I see. Everytime they say "The Father, Son and Holy Spirit," they bend over, straight-backed, and it looks like they are kissing the pew in front of them. They all look so calm and holy. It's hard to believe that they do this every day, and I don't even know it. Of course they don't know about me either, but it all seems so peaceful, and it must be nice to think about God so much. If I only took the time. Now that I look at the place, it's really very plain, not at all like Holy Spirit where I go to church. There are rows of dark wood pews that form an aisle, where surely no bride would walk. Above the simple table-like altar is a large replica of Jesus on the cross. There are no elaborate statues of the Virgin Mother, or saints, only small fairly simple stained-glass windows of venerable Dominican saints. Really, though, I wouldn't expect it to be very elaborate anyway because nuns seem to have a frugal image and don't seem to be into having fancy chapels. Looks like it's over. They're beginning to shuffle out. Sister Mary Judith rises and gives her angelic grin and motions me out of the pew. Shoot! This time I know she'll see me if I genuflect. Go ahead, it's okay. No, no, don't, you'll look stupid. She'll think you're showing off. Forget it, it's too late now, she's already past me and moving towards the stairs. She probably thinks you're a heathen or just plain disrespectful. That's the breaks, you're leaving now. Noise, beautiful noise. My head is beginning to feel better already. I guess I just can't handle the peace and quiet here because I'm so used to the chaotic atmosphere at American High School.

* * *

A Basic Day

This was a basic day—a day of plain and wholesome living, a balanced day of work and play—of getting and of giving.

Today was such a basic day as Heaven's patterned after, with simple lives that live a way of quiet love and laughter.

Helen Lowrie Marshall

Food. How could I think about eating when my stomach is turned completely inside out? What else could I do but follow Sister Mary Judith and the others into the modern dining hall and take my place in line as they mumbled a before-dinner prayer. We stood in line like you'd do at any other cafeteria, only no one pushed and shoved or took cuts in line. The sign near the food said "Chicken Cacciatore," and I could tell this would be a fun experience. I knew that I wouldn't like it, it sounded so foreign. I'm a very picky eater, but what could I do? I put a little bit on my plate and some salad, white rice and a roll. Sister Mary Judith said that I must be awfully nervous because I ate so little. I tried to tell her that I was a picky eater and that I always eat this much, but she wouldn't listen.

When we sat down she introduced me to the other nuns at the table and explained my purpose. They were all quite young and friendly, but I couldn't help feeling scared and out of place, considering I was the only person in civilian clothes. Conversation was light. They discussed food, old times when they first came to the convent, and their plans for next year. It was all very nice, and although I wasn't hungry I managed to eat a little, and actually the chicken was okay. When we had all finished our dinners we moved back into the kitchen and stacked our plates for this week's clean-up crew.

Smiles and well wishes from the other sisters made me feel warm, and I sensed a true kindness towards me in them. I thanked them and said goodbye and Sister Mary Judith and I walked towards the main building where I first entered. It seemed as if I had come to know her almost personally as we stood there saying thank-yous and good-byes. Walking out through the heavy, dark wood doors, I felt greatly relieved to see my car in the parking lot, ready to take me home. I had finally begun to get a picture of a nun's life in my mind, and some of my questions had been answered. Still, I was glad to be going, and I couldn't help but feel a flutter of those butterflies as I glanced at the convent one last time.

Factual Article

Traditional Lore

Find out who in your locality knows how to do or make something according to a tradition that has been passed down in the family or community. Visit and talk with that person or group, watch them do what it is they have learned how to do, take notes, and write this up so that your readers will learn exactly how their craft or procedure is carried out. You may need to make several visits or talk with several people. Sketches may help. Recapture that lore and make sure that it continues to be known even though the practitioners of it may be dwindling. Your account might be partly narrative but should be organized whatever way best brings out how the thing is done or made. Some of the lore might concern why this is done and how it fits into the culture and life of the community in which it survives.

The result might well suit a local newspaper or magazine as a feature article. Or it might become part of a collection of other "oral history" pieces on the locality done by other reporters.

There's More to Butchering Than Killing a Hog

CRAIG JOHNSON

In the vacant lot between the general store and the bank building, the unmistakable smell of wood smoke hung in the air. A cold wind fanned the flames below two large, cast-iron kettles.

Men and boys dressed in overalls and heavy coats gathered around the flames, holding out their hands to the heat. They moved when the wind shifted directions, trying to escape the steady stream of gray smoke and soot given off by the burning wood.

The sun had been up for a few hours. And although some of the people who were standing around in huddled groups had been up for a while, the day had just begun.

The muffled crack of a single .22 caliber shot being fired momentarily silenced the onlookers. Two hundred thirty-five pounds of Yorkshire hog hit the ground.

People close by backed away slightly as the hog's body convulsed spasmodically and its legs kicked wildly. Someone pointed to where the cut to bleed the hog should be made.

"Oh no, I ain't goin' to touch 'im yet," Lafe Graham, an experienced hand from rural Oblong who had volunteered to help butcher the hog, said. "I had a deer kick a knife out of my hand one time."

Several minutes passed before the hog lay completely still. Forest Richards, Sidell, who has gutted hogs all his life, then stuck a knife in behind the hog's ear. He twisted the blade until the jugular vein and carotid artery were torn open.

Gurgling hollowly, blood gushed out of the cut and onto the ground. The blood foamed and thickened quickly in the cold air.

Most of the people who witnessed this seemed unmoved by, even accustomed to, the sight. A few, though, turned away from the scene to the amusement of some people watching who had previously seen a hog bled for butchering.

Richards and Graham, with help from others, sliced down the back of each hind leg to expose the tendons. They used a hayhook to pull the tendons away from the leg and inserted a gambrel stick.

The gambrel stick, a branch about two or three inches in diameter and a foot and a half long, had the ends whittled to a blunt point and a notch cut near each end.

"You turn the notch up so it won't slide off the end," said Clyde Purcell, a long-time Bellair resident who remembered butchering his first hog at a neighbor's house when he was a boy nearly 70 years ago.

With some help, Richards and Graham lifted the hog on a raised, wooden platform that rested on logs about two feet high. Leaning against one end of the five-by-ten-foot platform was a 55-gallon drum held at an angle by a chain and boomer.

By now the onlookers had unconsciously divided themselves into two groups—those who had seen a hog butchered before and those who had not. Those who had stood around and talked softly among themselves, offering an occasional bit of advice or a word of encouragement. The rest watched apprehensively, unsure of what would happen next and whether or not they wanted to see it.

Someone stepped toward the cast-iron kettles and quickly dipped the fingertips of one hand into the boiling water. Without speaking, a few more men did the same.

"She's hot enough," one of the men said.

The others shook their heads and agreed that the water, which had been pumped and carried from the well across the street, was ready. They scooped the steaming water up in buckets and poured it into the metal drum.

Two men firmly grasped the gambrel stick and let the hog slide into the hot-water-filled drum. After dunking the carcass a few times, they removed it from the water and turned the hog around.

Using the hayhook for another purpose, Richards and Graham pushed it through the hog's nostrils and secured it in the tough cartilage of the animal's snout. Then they scalded the other half of the hog.

When they finally removed the hog from the water, they laid it on the platform. Someone scattered a few handfuls of ashes from the fire over the carcass.

"Well, 'at jus' helps the hair come off better," Paul Tomaw, Sidell, said. "The acid in it, I reckon."

Several people helped scrape the bristly hair off the hide, using knives, although an attempt was made to scrape with a small, sharpened bell. Clumps of the stiff, wet hair fell between the planking of the platform and collected in piles below.

In areas where the hair wasn't coming off easily, someone placed a piece of burlap and poured hot water over it. After most of the hair was removed from the right side, two men flipped the animal over and scraped the left side before dragging it to the hanging post.

Hung by the gambrel stick on a two- by six-inch board, the hog's head dangled a few inches above the limestone road pack that surrounded the base of the post. Atop the eight-foot post were crisscrossed boards so that as many as four hogs could be hung for gutting.

Graham, a cigar clinched between his teeth, knelt down on the ground near the hog's head and used a sharp butcher knife to cut through the head just behind the ears.

"You got to hit right between the vertebrae to get it off," Graham said, calmly feeling for the correct spot to chop.

His hands were hidden inside the practically-severed head. He twisted and pulled on the head until it cracked loudly and snapped off in his hands. What was left of the blood inside the head slowly dripped onto the stones.

"It's all yours," Graham said, handing the head to Harold Elliott, Bellair, who placed it in a bucket of cold water.

Both men used the hog's ears as handles when they carried the head.

A couple of the onlookers walked away, seemingly revolted by the sight of the decapitated animal. Some watched with apparent disinterest. Others seemed to force themselves to watch and pretend to be unaffected by the relative nonchalance of the beheading. And still others gazed in what looked like fascination.

The hog was left to cool a while. While it was hanging, someone took a knife and scraped off the remaining hair. During the lull in the activities, several people stopped to look at the hog's head staring up out of the bucket.

An hour or so later, Tomaw prepared to gut the hog, a job handled by Roger Walden, Porterville, with Mike Kessler, Hardinsville, sharing his years of experience.

"I worked in a packing plant for eight years," Tomaw said. "But it was a lot different than this. We killed a thousand to fifteen hundred hogs a day and each guy had his job to do. I never did do one like this."

Besides meaning that only one man would do most of the gutting, it also meant that the hog would not be skinned as is the common practice in slaughter houses.

"We have hog roasts all the time," Graham said, waiting for Tomaw to make the first cut. "We usually skin 'em. The reason they're doin' it this way is to render the lard out of the hide."

Assisted by Graham and Richards, Tomaw started at the top of the underside of the hog and cut all the way down the hog's belly and cleanly sliced the layers of flesh and muscle to expose the innards. He cut a circle around the anus, freed the large intestine and then tied it off with a piece of string.

The front of the rib cage was hacked in two to allow easier access to the viscera. Using his fingers as a guide, Tomaw carefully cut loose the entrails to avoid slicing into the intestine. This was important because the intestine was full.

"It's warm in there, anyhow," Graham said, holding up the loose intestine.

Tomaw cut free all the organs, and the elastic-like entrails rolled out of the hog into a bucket. Some heads turned to learn the cause of the loud plopping sound made by the entrails falling into the bucket.

Steam rose from the bucket and from the clean-looking cavity of the gutted hog. Several people smiled broadly and congratulated Tomaw and the others on doing a good job.

"Couldn't tell you'd never gutted a hog," one man said. "That looks like you'd been at it all your life."

"Well, I just wanted to give 'er a try," Tomaw said. "I didn't know if I could do 'er or not. These boys [Graham and Richards] here gave me a lot of help."

With the gutting completed, Elliott sifted through the bucket full of bloody entrails and removed the heart, liver and sweetbread and put them in a bucket of water. At the same time, Graham used a hacksaw to saw down through the middle of the backbone, splitting the hog's carcass in half.

After the hog had been hanging for another hour, the two halves of the hog were laid on the platform. Graham, Richards, Tomaw, Elliott and the others took turns cutting the meat. They removed the tenderloins from next to the backbone, cut apart the spareribs, removed the hams and shoulders and cut the bacon from the sides.

Even though the meat cutting was almost as bloody as the gutting, few people seemed bothered by it at all. They casually looked on as though the platform were a supermarket meat case.

The chunks of fat for the cracklings and lard were thrown into the cast-iron kettle and cooked down, with Purcell stirring the mixture with a lard paddle. The chunks were put into a lard press and squeezed together, the lard draining into a waiting lard can.

All that remained after the lard was rendered was the cracklings. Nearly everyone gathered around for a few bites of the crisp, crunchy, hot pork rinds.

Elliott used an axe to cut the hog's head in two, splitting it right between the eyes. He saved the brains to fry and said the hog's head would be used to make mincemeat.

After several onlookers cut the extra chunks of meat and threw the lean pieces into a metal dishpan for sausage and the fat pieces into another pan for lard and cracklings and ground the sausage, the hams, shoulders and sides were carried inside the store to be cured.

Some people drifted inside to watch the curing process; others lingered around the fire, talking and reminiscing a while longer.

"I've butchered a lot of 'em," Purcell said, standing by the dying fire, his hands jammed in the pockets of his overalls. "My folks used to butcher all the time, and we'd help the neighbors. Neighbors'd all gather in, you know, and butcher at one neighbor's house one day, maybe four or five or six hogs. Next day we'd go to another neighbor's house."

Several men nodded in agreement.

"Yep, that's the way they used to do it," Walter Whittaker, rural Lawrenceville, said, sitting in a lawn chair near the fire. "But this is the most people I ever saw at a butcherin'. Must 'o been 50-100 people here."

How to Make a Cradleboard

ARLENE NEZ and VINCENT JOHNSON

While driving to Chinle, Peter Benally, a well-known cradleboard maker, talked about the necessary things you have to do if you want to make a cradleboard. "You have to go to Chinle and get a cutting permit," Peter told us. "A long time ago a cutting permit was not necessary. You just went to the forest and cut a tree, but now it's different." Peter went on to tell us that if you don't have a permit and a ranger sees you cutting a tree, you either pay for the tree or go to jail.

We went to the Bureau of Land Management Office, and a worker there asked Peter several questions. After a few minutes of typing and writing, we had our permit. Then Peter explained the second step. "Now we go to the mountains and find a good tree." He told us that you have to find a red cedar that is tall and straight. There are some trees in the mountains a few miles south of Navajo Community College. We moved up into the mountains until Peter spotted a tree that looked good, and then he measured it to make sure that it was a good tree because it had no large branches on the lower part of the trunk.

After Peter was satisfied that we had chosen a good tree, he told us what to do next. "You have to clear the brush and limbs from around the tree," Peter said. He said to clear around the tree because you might trip and fall over a branch and injure yourself with the saw or you could hit your head on a limb.

"After clearing the brush from around the tree, you cut the cedar tree down," explained Peter. When he was ready to cut the tree, he didn't cut it all the way through; instead, he made two diagonal cuts on one side of the tree down low to the ground. Then he made another cut on the backside of the tree. This lets you fell the tree in the right direction. After the tree was down, he cut off the small limbs and branches.

"After cutting the limbs off, you measure the trunk and cut it into 30" and 32" sections," explained Peter. Peter cut three sections from the trunk. He then cut down a thin cedar tree which would be used for the rainbow. He cut one 28" section from this small tree.

After all the sections were cut, Peter told us to carry them to a

large, dead log nearby. "You place a section on the log at the spot
where there is a curve or dip in it," said Peter. He put one 32" piece
against the log and then placed a little stick between the log and the
section of cedar so it wouldn't roll when he began cutting the pieces of
cedar trunk into boards. He said it's better sometimes to put two holes
in the ground and to put two large sticks in the holes. This makes an X
and you can put the log in this to help hold it. "Then you cut the logs
into boards about one inch thick," Peter told us. He cuts the logs into
boards with his chain saw. First he cuts down the middle of the log but
he doesn't cut it all the way through. Instead, he makes a shallow,
straight cut so that when he cuts deeper in the log the chain saw won't
cut crooked.

He cuts two boards out of each log. He doesn't use the outside
pieces because they are too small. He takes the middle two boards to
make the bottom of the cradleboard and to use for other parts too.

After the boards dried for a few weeks, we returned to visit Peter.
He said that the next step was to cut out the pieces for the cradleboard. He has patterns for all the pieces of a cradleboard, and he drew
around these patterns while holding them on the boards that he had
cut out of the cedar trees a few weeks earlier. He also marked where
the holes should be drilled. These holes were for the leather that holds
the cradleboard together. Peter told us that it is very important that
you use only cedar when making a cradleboard. You should never use
two different kinds of wood. You can't use wood from two different
cedar trees to make the two back boards of the cradleboard, but you
can use wood from other cedar trees for the rainbow and the other
small parts. He said that he doesn't know why this is so, but it's just
that way.

When he put the patterns for the back boards on a piece of cedar,
he told us, "I put the pattern in the middle of the cedar board so the
board has both red and white colors. I do that just to make it look
pretty."

Then he drills the holes in the boards. He uses a small hand drill
since there is no electricity at Peter's house. The holes are 3/16" in
diameter.

After tracing the patterns and drilling the holes, Peter told us
what the next step was. This was to cut out all the pieces with a hand
saw. He cut the bottom boards out first and then the foot board and
the broken rainbow pieces. He cuts them out with a crosscut handsaw.

After he cut all the pieces out carefully, he planed the small pieces
with a jack plane. He planed them down from about one inch to ⅜" or
½" thick. While planing the boards, Peter stopped often and checked
the boards to make sure they were straight and even by closing one
eye and sighting down the edge of the boards. At one point he stopped
and pointed to a place in the board where the wood had chipped out.
"If you plane the boards when they aren't dry enough, they will chip

out like this. When it is dry enough the wood will plane smoothly and it won't chip."

When the small boards had been planed smooth enough, he took a piece of sandpaper and smoothed the boards. He used a file to round the edges a bit.

When he finished planing and sanding the small boards he was ready to plane the large boards for the back of the cradleboard. He took the boards to a shed near where he planed the small boards. In the shed Peter had a bench and a small piece of tree trunk to sit on. The bench is about four feet long and two feet high. It is about one foot wide. This has a wooden block nailed at one end to keep the board that he is planing from sliding around. When he finished planing the large back boards he sanded them. He uses an electric sander to save time. He goes to his daughter's house to do this because she has electricity. "When you sand these boards by hand it takes a long time and you get really tired. Sometimes you don't finish on time."

After a month or so, Peter told us to go to his daughter's home to work on the rainbow. Peter said, "It is necessary to sand the rainbow real thin to about ¼". If the board is still thick it won't bend. If it's thin it will bend easily."

After sanding the rainbow, Peter told us what the next step was. He put the rainbow under hot water in the kitchen sink and let the water run on the board for a little while. He did this so the water would soak in the board, making it easy to bend.

After several minutes he began to bend the board very slowly so it wouldn't break. While he was doing this, somehow the board cracked a little. Peter said, "The board cracked because there was a knot there." Then he just turned the board over and let the hot water run on the other side. Then he bent it slowly again back and forth until it was in the shape of a rainbow.

Then he said, "You tie both ends together with a strip of cloth to hold the board in a rainbow shape until it dries. After the wood is dry it will stay in that shape."

Then Peter puts the rainbow away and lets it dry for several days. It is probably better to let it dry in the sun, but he just left it in his daughter's house since it was cold and wet outside.

After the rainbow had dried, we were ready to tie the boards together. He used very thin strips of leather to join the boards. He uses a square knot so the boards won't come untied.

The first boards he tied together were the "earth" and "dark sky" boards. Then he tied the "broken rainbow" to these on the back side to make the two back boards stiff. Then he added the "short rainbow" and he tied it to the place where the baby's feet rest.

Finally, he tied on the rainbow. He ties the rainbow and the bottom boards together in a certain way.

After all the boards were laced together, he had his daughter sew

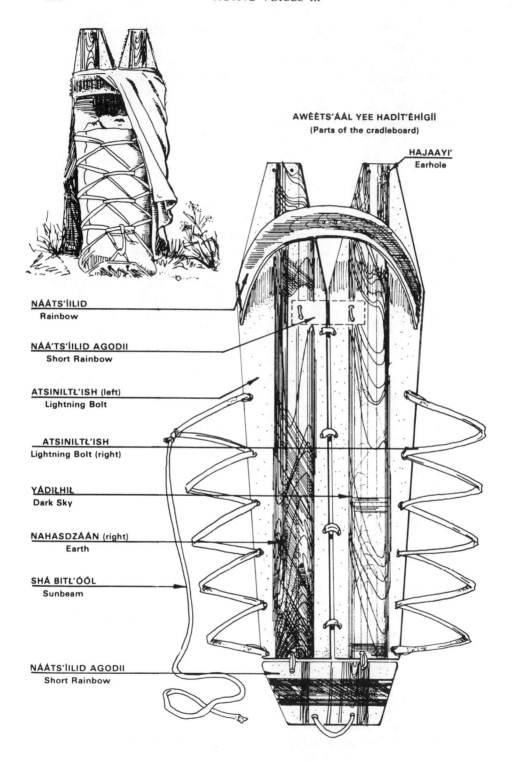

AWÉÉTS'ÁÁL YEE HADÍT'ÉHÍGÍÍ
(Parts of the cradleboard)

HAJAAYI'
Earhole

NÁÁTS'ÍILID
Rainbow

NÁÁ'TS'ÍILID AGODII
Short Rainbow

ATSINILTL'ISH (left)
Lightning Bolt

ATSINILTL'ISH
Lightning Bolt (right)

YÁDILHIL
Dark Sky

NAHASDZÁÁN (right)
Earth

SHÁ BITL'ÓÓL
Sunbeam

NÁÁTS'ÍILID AGODII
Short Rainbow

1" wide strips of cloth. These make the "lightning bolts" which are attached to the sides with string in order to form the "sunbeam," and this is laced through each of the lightning bolts.

When the cradleboard was all finished, Peter still had one more thing to do before he showed us how to put a baby in the cradleboard. He put some red stuff called *chííh* on the cradleboard. It is made out of a certain kind of sandstone which you have to dig out from under the ground. This special rock can be found near Black Mesa and Rough Rock. After you dig it up, you have to grind it up and mix it with lard so it will be sort of sticky. Peter took this *chííh* and touched it around on different parts of the cradleboard.

I didn't really understand this part so I asked a few people around the school if they could tell me why it is used. Many said they didn't know. Anyway, here are a couple of explanations:

"The reason you put the *chííh* on the cradlebaord is that people live with red around here. There are many things that are red like the earth and the rocks. So they put it on the cradleboard, and the baby also lives with it too."

Another person said: "You can't put the baby in the cradleboard if you don't put *chííh* on the cradleboard, because a long time ago when the old people had one of their people die they just had to bury them right in the ground because they didn't have any coffins in those days. Maybe this way everyone is reminded that we all will end up the same way. That's why you have to put *chííh* on first."

Whatever the reason, after Peter had put the *chííh* on the cradleboard, his daughter placed a mattress and blanket on the back boards and then put her baby there. She took the 'sunbeam' and laced it through the 'lightning bolts,' and her baby was snuggly wrapped in the cradleboard. A cloth can also be tied on top of the rainbow to cover the face of the baby.

Directions to Do or Make Something

Explain step by step an activity that results in a product or has a specific end in mind—how to craft an item, repair a machine, build a henhouse, prepare for a long-distance bicycle race, or train a horse to jump fences.

Your reader should be able to gather from your instructions how to tackle the same project. Insert whatever background information may be necessary for both understanding and reader enjoyment. Use photos or sketches if they'll help readers understand what's going on. Discuss with a group of other writers the wording and organization. Ask others to try to follow your directions and tell you what happened so you can see what needs changing. Make copies for interested people. Include the piece in a how-to booklet.

The Production and Enjoyment of Paper Snowflakes

ERIC FOSS

The magic and enchantment of winter don't last all year long. Due to this unfortunate fact, people of years gone by would invent ways to allow winter magic to survive any time. One of the most creative of these ways was the production of paper snowflakes.

Just as in the case of real snowflakes, no two of the paper variety are alike. Any scientist will tell you that the intricate designs don't follow a pattern but are spontaneously produced.

The production of paper snowflakes does not necessitate gobs of creativity, and anyone can be successful at it. The only things that must be assembled are a few sheets of white paper (any size), a pair of trusty scissors, and a trash can for your scraps.

Step number one in this highly complex process is to fold your plain white piece of paper in half. Now fold it in half again in the other direction. When folding, be sure to make good, hard creases. Using the handle of your scissors is a nifty way to accomplish this.

The second step is the first requiring precision, albeit little. With your scissors, cut about a third of your paper away, leaving the middle corner, the one with the fewest single edges, intact. It should now resemble a triangle. Clutching the middle corner, bring the two outside of the three remaining corners together. Crease this new wedge-like creation as you now know how.

It is now decision time. There are different avenues you may choose to explore. If you fold your wedge together again, your finished product will be more intricate in design. If you are anxious to finish, begin your inner cutting.

When you are ready to begin cutting, things become a little more difficult. Your shape is now somewhat thick, and cutting into it is not an easy task. When starting out I don't suggest cutting too elaborately, for you could confuse yourself. Start out by snipping small shapes off the edge of your paper. The shapes can be triangular or like semi-circles. You can cut out more advanced shapes as you become better. Be sure to cut the middle corner off. Snowflakes with solid centers are generally considered (in the paper snowflake industry) to be ugly, probably because real snowflakes always have holes in the middle. Once in the first grade, making paper snowflakes was a class activity. After making several of the normal variety, I decided to leave mine with a solid center. It looked very stupid and everyone laughed at me. That day was one of the worst in my life. Now you know what can happen. Cut off your middle corner!

If you think it will make your task easier, you can draw the cuts on your wedge and then trace with your scissor. This is not something I would suggest, however; the finished product will have small lines on it. Another disadvantage to the tracing method (as it is referred to) is that it puts a stranglehold on your creative impulses. Planned-out snowflakes rarely surpass the beauty of spontaneously cut ones. Wouldn't you feel dumb if someone thought you had to pre-design your cuts?

When you have cut as much as adequately reflects your snowflake taste, set your scissors down. Take all your scraps and sweep them away into the trash receptacle you set aside earlier. We don't want trash in any way marring the ceremonial opening of the snowflake.

Take a deep breath and start unfolding. You might like to have some inspirational music playing in the background. Unfold with the utmost caution; you do not want to rip the delicate designs. Some pieces tend to stick together, so beware. If anything tears, the snowflake is ruined and you have to start over again. When you have unfolded it, gently smooth it out and admire what you have accomplished. If there are places that look awkward or unsmooth, remember what they look like so that you will not make similar cuts next time.

This exciting paper snowflake extravaganza does not end here, fortunately. Pasting your snowflake to a piece of colorful construction paper highlights your creativity. A rare bunch of paper snowflake manufacturers color their flakes at this point with magic markers or crayons. I do not care for this method, however. If you are in a festive mood, you can tape them to windows or hang them from the ceiling with string or wire.

You probably have noticed that your creation is kinky in shape. It does not lie flat. If you want a flat flake, place it in the pages of a thick book. After several days it will be more agreeable to you.

Some reputable psychologists believe that paper snowflakes are the truest way of judging a person's character. I do not know why this is, but it helps inspire one to do a good job.

How To Make Flat Hair Curl

AIMEE GROVE

Forget the self-help books rife with techniques to "improve one's self-image from the inside out," and disregard Linda Evans' claim that "Beauty comes from within." We all know that in reality we are cursed or blessed with the body components nature dictated. Most of us have at least one flaw over which we lament on a dateless Friday night in front of the mirror. In some cases, this flaw can dominate one's life. My flaw falls into the life-altering category. Technically defined, it is "fine-textured, straight hair." I call it a mane of limp locks, listless enough to make a sixties flowerchild green with envy.

Because true "thin-hairs," as I dub the unfortunate, are a rare breed in California, where the sunny seasons cultivate bronzed bodies and gold-streaked tresses, it is difficult to find others to sympathize with my plight. Here is a quiz to locate fellow victims:

1. Do you (passionately) hate the rain? Does a brief dash to class in a light drizzle mean a matted-to-the-forehead, slimy hairdo? Do you store an emergency umbrella under the car seat at all times?
2. Do you (secretly) hate convertibles? Do those essential California-mobiles spell disaster for your hair, even after a thorough dousing in creme rinse?
3. Do you (blatantly) hate your thick-maned friends? Have you ever watched enviously as your buddy bounces through wind, rain, and the Junior Prom—and wakes the next morning with the same curls as the night before? Are you stifling an urge to break out the nail scissors and do a little late night trimming?

A yes answer to any of the quiz questions indicates a "thin-hair," someone searching as desperately as I for a miracle cure. Although I cannot promise that, I can share my tested procedure for mastering flat hair, which demands only time, money, sincere effort, and a little luck.

Two advance preparations are necessary to the success of my procedure: a permanent and a quality haircut. Although it will inevitably look grotesque for a month, a tamer perm will inject artificial wave into lifeless locks. Hair length will also make a difference. Thin hair should not hang below or above the shoulder blades. Long hair will droop dejectedly in spaghetti strings, and a short style minus volume can create the "pin-head" effect.

A trip to Long's Drugs will provide a thin-hair with all the necessary tools:

1. *Mousse.* This is the number-one essential, so stock up.
2. *Hairspray.* Avoid the lacquer, bouffant variety.
3. *An airvent brush.*
4. *Thickening shampoo.*
5. *Curling iron.* Be sure to purchase the metal variety.
6. *Hot rollers.*
7. *Sponge curlers.*
8. *Ponytail holders, ribbons, and clips.*

Armed with these materials, you are ready to employ the procedures. Before tumbling into bed at night, shower and shampoo. Do not use conditioner! Weighing down potential curls is your worst enemy. Ignore your mother and your hairdresser or you will be doomed to a lifetime of lifeless tresses.

While hair is still damp, set it with sponge curlers (the same kind Alice wore on the *Brady Bunch* before a date with Sam). Now, lock your door, and unplug your telephone; you will not want any surprise visitors at this point.

I was a child with stringy hair and scuffed knees, and I hated taking baths. Nevertheless, my mother used to reprimand me, "Suffer to be beautiful," a trinket of stern advice still valuable today. Thin-hairs must sacrifice a few hours of sleep to resemble a normal person. Set your alarm for 5:00 a.m.

At dawn, remove your spongy curlers and dampen hair with a spray bottle. Squirt a handful of the mousse into your palm and massage into ends and scalp, fingers teasing the slick strands without mercy. Apply additional squirts for added lift wherever desired, but do not get carried away to the extent that your head is a wet mop of the sticky substance. Now you are ready to blowdry.

Okay, blowdrying is one area in which thin-hairs hold an advantage. Instead of struggling with round brushes and meticulous styling techniques, you can flip your hair, set the dryer on "High," and go crazy. Crunch, muss, and sculpt your hair, until, when you resume normal posture, you could pass for Tina Turner. Unfortunately, this wild, airy state is temporary, and hot rollers can only fight the force of gravity.

Your hot rollers should be plugged in and warm by now, assuming you are on top of things. Secure these strategically around your head, avoiding hot ones near your neck or ears. You are now allowed a ten-minute break while the rollers cool.

After removing the rollers, do not brush out the kinks. Instead, style bangs with the curling iron (stay away from that vulnerable patch of skin, the forehead—the burns aren't very pretty). Sometimes rollers will not suffice, and an entire manual recurling is necessary. If this should occur, do not throw brushes or scream profanities at the mirror; just remember the extra hour you gave yourself.

Finally, after one or two curlings, your head is ready for the short, flipping motion of the airvent brush, appropriately termed, "brushing out." Flip hair once for volume and spray lightly with hairspray, preferably an unscented brand that won't clash with your perfume. At this time (usually 7:15 and ticking) with a bit of luck, you will have achieved a full head of luscious homecoming queen curls.

So what do you do, then, if your curls only make it to 3rd period math analysis before they start to sag? In this case, you can excercise one of three options:

1. Utilize your stockpile of clips and rubber bands;
2. Comb it behind your ears for the studious look;
3. Go home. (I don't have five classes and a lifetime supply of yellow slips just because I'm a senior!)

Research Article

Survey

Select a subject about which you want to know other people's opinions. Write out a question or a set of questions. Then ask the people whose responses you seek—maybe a particular group, or a mixture of people for comparison. Record their answers.

Pull the answers together and write up the results. Part of your summary might be in the form of numbers and percentages, or charts or graphs. Some quotations might be good for illustration. Summarize also in your own words the gist of what people said. Weave this together with any figures or quotations. You might combine this information from your survey with what you find in books or articles.

Post this, or put it in a newspaper. Or make it part of a bigger project like consumer research on a product.

Sophomores Include Clans in Dating Decisions

RONA LEE SUEN

Rock Point [on the Navajo Reservation in Arizona] students learn some clan dating rules at home from their parents. Last month, three high school students answered questions on clanship and dating. Two sophomores stated that clan relationship plays an important part in choosing a date, but the other one stated that it doesn't.

Two of the sophomores said they would not go out with anyone who had the same clan as their mother or their father. One reason is their parents told them not to date anyone who is related to them by clan. The students explained that their parents followed the dating rules when they were young and expect their children to do the same. Their parents are now teaching those clan dating rules to all of their children.

Each of the three students interviewed had a different way to find out the clans of a person they were interested in dating. One said that she would ask the person she's interested in what his clans were before going out with him. Another said that the person she was dating told her about clans. The last person said he would ask around for the clans of the person that he was interested in before dating her.

When the interviewees were asked how they would feel if they went out with anyone who had the same clans as their mother or father, the interviewees said they would feel uncomfortable and embarrassed. Two said they would feel uncomfortable because they would know that the people they were dating were related to them by clan. The other one said that he would be embarrassed because people would say that he was dating his own relative.

Two of the three sophomores interviewed said they wouldn't let their parents know they were interested in dating a person related to them by clan. They said they would hide it from their parents because their parents would get angry. Their parents had told them not to date anyone who had the same clans as they. One person said she wouldn't hide the fact that she was going with a person who is related to her by clan because her parents want to know who she dates.

Two sophomores would consider clanship before deciding whom to date, but the other one wouldn't.

Cheating: Student Perspectives

KIM WEST

Cheating has always bothered me. A friend of mine was accused of cheating. The teacher snatched her paper up in front of the class and threw it away. Needless to say, she was embarrassed, humiliated, and innocent! Teachers handle cheating in different ways. A large number of them ignore it, while others watch you so closely that you feel like you're in cell block eight, San Quentin.

Of course, they have a justifiable reason to do that. A surprisingly large number of people cheat. Some of the top students in this school cheat. It infuriates me! People don't deserve what they get dishonestly. I like to know that I earned my grades by myself, on my own; therefore, I wanted to find out how many people really do cheat in school and how they can not feel guilty doing it.

I began my search in the school library. I found small blurbs about cheating in educational psychology books. All of these were outdated. For instance, *Educational Psychology in the Classroom* (Lindgren, 1972) said that if an honor system were imposed, cheating would be reduced because students would feel encouraged by teachers trusting them. I know this isn't true from my own experience. I have had many teachers who have trusted their students implicitly, yet cheating still occurred. This old theory is that cheating is caused by discouragement.

Looking in the periodicals I found some more up-to-date information. One article I read was an editorial someone had sent in based on ideas she had (*Seventeen*, 1983). In the past, it said, good grades were nice, but now they are required to get into college. Also, some people would rather cheat than be punished by their parents for rotten grades. These are good ideas, but they are not in the foreground, according to what I learned from my survey.

I used the survey to get some field data from my peers, the students. Through their responses, I acquired a better understanding of the cheating that goes on in our school. Trying to draw conclusions from the data was confusing, to say the least. I got many answers to many questions I did not ask. I found some to be more interesting than others, and I used the data accordingly. Given the choice of 'always,' 'sometimes,' or 'never,' seven of fifty people who responded checked that they never cheated; thirty-seven checked sometimes; one checked always; and five wrote in their own response such as "very rarely" or "a couple of times." From this, I concluded the hard fact that most of the students in our school cheat. Even some of the people who responded "never" said later that sometimes they did. As to why people cheat, people replied that they didn't study, that "the class isn't worth trying in," and "in order to get a better grade."

When asked, "What makes you cheat in some classes but not others?" people provided me with a wealth of input. A predominant answer was, "It's not a big thing, others do it too." Another student wrote, "I don't cheat that often and I know 99 percent of everyone else does it a lot more." Many other students say they could justify it because "The teacher deserves it for giving such a hard test," or "In an overall perspective I would say that I cheat as a last resort." Someone else added, "In some classes, you are almost forced to cheat. Teacher's gone, everyone is exchanging answers."

Finally, one student said, "I respect some teachers more than others, and I feel I can cheat in a class with a teacher I respect less." Students don't respect some teachers because they feel that these teachers just don't care.

In an interview that I had with one student, he added to this thought by saying, "Some teachers let them cheat!" Usually, he feels, because they don't care about their students, only about getting their report cards out on time. Something like trying to curb cheating is too much for them.

One former teacher of mine confirmed this by ignoring blatant cheating in her class. Students took tests with their books open on their desks, and she did nothing about it. I thought she cared though; I don't know why she let the cheating go on.

To find out why, I would have to survey the teachers also. Maybe that will be my next I-Search. Some of my conclusions are concrete, while others are pretty wishy-washy. Fact: 74–88 percent of the students in our school cheat, or have cheated. Since so many people do it, the guilt is nearly nil. Only about half of the people surveyed said that they felt guilty when they cheated. It doesn't seem as bad because it is such a common practice. A major reason for cheating is that it's so easy. Sometimes you have to try not to. For instance, the teacher stupidly leaves the room and the whole class compares answers. Or the room is arranged in such a casual way that you're staring at someone else's paper.

If teachers would do two things, I feel that they could reduce cheating drastically. First they need to obtain mutual respect between themselves and their students. Second, they need to take some preventive measures such as having the desks moved apart and giving a "DON'T CHEAT!" speech. This should not be done as a punishment; that would arouse resentment. It should be an encouraging, trusting, yet preventive atmosphere to take the test in. One thing that I've learned is that teachers have much to do with cheating. I wish they'd realize that!

References

"Cheating," *Seventeen Magazine* [December, 1983].
Lindgren, H. (1972). *Educational Psychology in the Classroom.* New York: John Wiley & Sons.

Local Research

Take some question that has come to your attention through local circumstances and that has aroused your curiosity. See if you can answer it by local research. Think of what people, places, records, or writings you might get access to that can help you satisfy your curiosity. Put this together as an informative article that might go in a local newspaper, newsletter, or other publication.

The Beach in Summer

MATT NICHOLSON

Upon visiting Goleta Beach Park after a recent storm, I was astounded by the transformation of the beach. I immediately realized what the change was: all the sand had vanished. I examined the beach more closely. Gone was what had formerly been a vast expanse of dry sand, untouched by wave and water. The green grass of the park, instead of sloping gently to the dry sand, dropped off abruptly about a foot. Twigs, rocks, branches, and shells littered the wet beach and even intruded upon the park grass, as far as two yards in some places. The large logs that had bordered the grass and the volleyball courts were gone. The pier stood several feet higher than I remembered. Clearly, a vast amount of sand had disappeared. I wondered how much, if any, would return by summer.

Shortly after my excursion, I read an article in the local paper. According to this article, the unusually heavy surf of the winter's storm had intruded upon the beach much farther than usual and had dragged a lot of sand out beyond the waterline. This fact explained why the waves I saw at the beach broke so far out and rolled for so long. In essence, the storms had leveled out the beach. Instead of a quick drop-off at the water, the sand sloped smoothly from the grass to the edge of the water and out under the surf, causing the long waves. Normally, stated the article, the gentle summer waves would gradually push sand back in; however, this year that might not happen. (2:B-9)

The article did not elaborate on that point, so I decided to check farther. I talked with Brian Ramirez, who has worked at the beach for several years. Brian said that every winter some sand gets dragged out, but he has never seen such a change as this year. In fact, during past years, more sand has come in during summer than has gone out; thus, the beaches were getting larger. Because so much sand got pulled out this year, Brian thought it might get caught in the southerly current and be gone forever. He was sure that the beach would be smaller this summer. He suggested that I check the UCSB Marine-Science Lab for more specific data. (4)

Paul Bach, a marine biology major at UCSB, gave me his opinion on what the beach would look like this summer. Some sand would, he thought, be caught in the current, but sand from northern beaches would replace most, though not all, of it. Thus the amount of sand would remain close to constant, but, because of the severe winter, it would require more than one summer to push it back in. This summer the beach would remain much lower and leveler than in the past, but it would retain some of its length, though tidal shifts would be more extreme because of the flatness. A series of severe winters, he reasoned, cause sand to be lost permanently, and thus shorten the beach dramatically over several years. (3)

Apparently, with milder winters and time, the sand will return. However, a pamphlet Paul gave me presents some intriguing possibilities for the long run. As sand moves down the California coast, it alternately comes ashore in summer and goes out and down the coast during the winter. Eventually, however, it reaches a canyon or rift in the continental shelf that comes close to shore. Sand drifts into the rift and flows out to sea. This lost sand is continually replaced by grit and rock washed down inland rivers. However, damming and cementing California rivers has curtailed this flow to the point where sand is not being replaced. Though beaches may regain most of their sand this time, over the years they may begin to shrink alarmingly as their supply is cut to the source (1:8). The beaches may be safe for now but in the future they may be doomed.

Sources

1 Crilliere, Jim, *Tidal and Current Action on the Californian Continental Shelf*, unpublished UCSB Marine-Science thesis.
2 Sims, Karl, "Winter Storms Demolish Beaches," *Santa Barbara News Press*, March 13, 1983.
3 Bach, Paul, UCSB Marine Biology student; interview, March 28, 1983.
4 Ramirez, Brian, Park ranger, Goleta Beach; interview, March 24, 1983.

The Esperanto Language

HUGH AGUILAR

Originally, I had no interest whatsoever in language, foreign or otherwise. I took French this year because it was necessary to enter the University of California system. Taking this class has since developed in me an interest in languages. Languages, I found, are very interesting but also very hard. When I read an article about Esperanto and other "planned languages" (1), I decided to look into it. A "planned language," I reasoned, would not have all the unnecessary complexities and ambiguities of natural languages.

I had some skepticism about the concept of invented languages. We already have too many languages as it is. Aren't planned languages just additions to the Tower of Babel? I knew of at least four planned languages: Esperanto, Langlo, Volapük, and Shavian (created by the playwright George Bernard Shaw).

International languages are supposed to create world communication and alleviate intercultural friction, but is this realistic? Will people learn a neutral language or continue to force their own native lingo on others? I knew that every written document of the Common

Market had to be translated into seven languages (soon to be nine) at a cost of $400 million in 1982. (1)

Aren't planned languages that borrow only from certain language families just generalizing the same problem? I knew that Langlo was similar to Chinese, and Esperanto was similar to romance languages. (1) Wouldn't an already established natural language like English, French, or even Latin (which is the root of many languages) make the best second language? Wouldn't a language as structured as a planned language must be, be too stilted and artificial to be suitable for literature and conversation?

With these thoughts in mind, I began my search. First, I interviewed all of the foreign language teachers at my school except one who was on sick leave. None spoke a planned language, but Mr. Osborne, my French teacher, did have some familiarity with Esperanto. He told me that Esperanto was the most popular of the planned languages and that the others weren't of much significance. (2) I decided to narrow my search to Esperanto. The next thing I did was call up every school in Santa Barbara County. Never before have I met so many who knew so little about so much. I looked in the phone book one last time. There, between "Erickson" and "Evans" was the answer. I called the number and got an interview with Mrs. Dorothy Holland, the head of the local Esperanto group.

She concurred with Mr. Osborne that Esperanto is the only planned language that enjoys a large following. "It has stood the test of time" (3), she stated, explaining that Esperanto was invented in 1887 by the Polish oculist Dr. Ludwig L. Zamenhof. The need for a language like Esperanto was especially apparent in Dr. Zamenhof's village, where six separate languages were spoken. Esperanto, I learned, was banned by both Stalin and Hitler but now enjoys government support behind the Iron Curtain. In fact, the Chinese are really "talking it up." (4) For many Chinese, Esperanto is a stepping-stone into Western languages. "If we could take Esperanto as the means, and internationalism and revolution as the ideal," the late chairman Mao Tse-tung said in 1939, "then Esperanto can be learned and should be learned." (4) "Although Esperanto has almost no Chinese in its vocabulary, the way its words are made by adding prefixes and suffixes to a root is similar to Chinese. An average of ten to fifteen words are made from each root," explained Mrs. Holland. This results in an Esperanto dictionary one-tenth the size of a natural language dictionary. (3) An example of this is the word "bona," which means "good" and the world "malbona," which means "bad." It is my opinion that Esperanto does this without the Newspeak effect of limiting thought, but you'll have to learn the language to see.

By pure chance, the next day was the second Saturday of the month, and hence the local Esperanto interest group's meeting. The only English spoken in the meeting was for my benefit. I concurred with Mr. Osborne that spoken Esperanto sounded like Spanish but disagreed that it was "stilted" and "ugly." In the meeting, several up-and-coming Esperanto courses were discussed, and the members talked about their correspondences with foreign Esperantists, including one from the Soviet Union. I looked at the pictures in several foreign magazines published in Esperanto, and we viewed one member's slide show from his native Holland. I learned of one of the big reasons for Esperanto's popularity in several African countries. The countries have been invaded by people of many languages, all of whom forced their language onto them. Esperanto has no political ties. Learning Esperanto has none of the implications of learning English or French as a second language. In many countries around the world students are not allowed to study English without also studying Russian. At the meeting, I met Arturo Eikenberry, whose class in Esperanto was to begin on the 22nd of March.

During the first class I learned more about Esperanto than I had learned about French during my first semester of it. This is not counting vocabulary, only about how the language is put together. A language, you see, has three parts: spelling and pronunciation, rules of grammar, and vocabulary and word-building. Concerning spelling and pronunciation, Esperanto is a phonetic language, like what Dewey failed to make English. It has a 28-letter alphabet which is like the English one except that it lacks the letters Q, W, X, and Z and has added the letters Ĉ, Ĝ, Ĥ, Ĵ, Ŝ, and Ŭ In addition to these, there are six diphthongs (aŭ for example), which have their own unique sound. Each letter has exactly one, and only one, pronunciation. There are no silent letters in words, and the accent always falls on the second to the last syllable.

Concerning the rules of grammar, there are sixteen. We've already covered two of them, concerning spelling and pronunciation. An example of another rule is that of the definite article. It is "la" and is used for all sexes, cases, and numbers. There is no indefinite article. An example of another rule is that nouns end in "o." For the plural, add "j" (which sounds like an English "y"), for the nominative case add "o," and for the accusative, add "on" (object). You are already one-fourth of the way through Esperanto grammar. As you probably surmised, there is nary an exception to any of the sixteen rules.

Concerning the vocabulary and word-building, we have already discussed the use of prefixes and suffixes. The greater majority of Esperanto words are of Latin origin, and hence are easily memorized because they are similar to many languages' words. The prefixes and suffixes are as constant in meaning as are the words. In English, for example, the suffix "ess" makes a noun feminine (lion/lioness) but not always (hero/heroess?). In Esperanto, adding the suffix "in" to any word at all makes that word feminine.

I am sold on Esperanto; all my skepticisms and doubts have been allayed. Esperanto does not extend the Tower of Babel but offers a viable alternative. The other 300 or so planned languages do not have large enough followings to create a "planned" Tower of Babel.

Whether people will learn a neutral second language or not remains to be seen. There are five billion people on Earth, who speak 3000 different languages. As intercontinental travel becomes more and more available to the common people, the need for an international language grows. There are three basic solutions to this need. As it stands, 20% of the people speak Chinese (5), 10% English, 7% Hindustani, and 6% Russian. One possible solution is that everyone pick one of these natural languages, probably English (1). This solution is fraught with political problems and learning difficulty. Another solution, one that will probably happen spontaneously, is that the languages will combine. As the cultures mix, words from one language become part of another. The increase of education is killing off tribal languages generation by generation. This solution will take until half past forever to complete. The third solution is Esperanto. It is easy to learn and has no political hang-ups. It is four to six times easier to learn (5) than a natural language. An experienced linguist can learn it in around 20 hours (4), and the ordinary student is qualified to teach it after one year of studying it.

The fact that Esperanto, which is derived mostly from Latin, can be learned by any culture is evidenced by the 120,000 Chinese that are learning it. (4)

Esperanto is going to become everyone's second language eventually, I think. It is suitable for literature (books are translated into it quite smoothly, and there is a growing amount of original Esperanto), as well as general conversation. Speaking of translations, Esperanto offers an interesting prospect. A computer will probably be able to translate into and out of Esperanto before it can go between two natural languages. Now consider this example: There are N different languages. Translating directly from one language to the others requires $N \times (N-1)$ translations. On the other hand, if every language is first translated into Esperanto, only N translations are required.

Notes

1   "Global Language: Easy to Learn but Seldom Used"; *Santa Barbara News Press*, February 18, 1984.
2   Interview with Mr. Barry Osborne.
3   Interview with Dorothy Holland.
4   "*Esperanto—Chinese Are Talking It Up*"; *Los Angeles Times*, January 27, 1984.
5   *About Esperanto*, booklet from Channing L. Bete., Inc.; no author given credit.

Feature Article

Research some local or topical issue and write up what you learn. Visit, interview, and consult print sources, according to the nature of the subject and where the information lies. This isn't a news story that will be immediately superceded tomorrow but an article whose information and ideas will not date for a while at least. It could go into a newspaper or magazine. Pull the material of your sources together by putting everything into your own words, except for a few well-chosen quotations, and by arranging facts into an order your readers can comfortably assimilate.

[The first of the following examples was printed in a town newspaper, the **News-Record** *of Maplewood-South Orange, New Jersey, the second in a high school newspaper,* **The Columbian***].*

Tragedy on the Tracks: Can It Be Avoided?

JOHN M. SHUE

i

Six young people have lost their lives on the railroad in South Orange and Maplewood [NJ] in the last 10 years. Three of the accidents occurred in Maplewood; one in South Orange.

One earlier accident occurred in 1959, claiming the life of Daniel Bolger, a resident of South Orange.

Daniel was walking along the Parker Avenue overpass in Maplewood, when a westbound express came speeding through an unfenced area. According to Danny's mother, Mary Bolger, her 8-year-old and a friend were playing at the Farrell Field recreational park. Upon seeing a fire across the tracks, the two children were lured to the sight.

In order to get to the fire, the boys had to cross the tracks. With no fence to stop him, Danny walked onto the tracks and was caught on the overpass. There was no time to get off. According to Maplewood Detective Lt. James DeCicco, this was the first accident of its kind in the South Orange-Maplewood area.

For 15 years no deaths were reported on the tracks in our communities. In 1975, it happened once again.

Three days after Christmas, John Collins, 13, finished his yard chores at home; he planned to meet his friends Craig Strutz, 13, and Kevin Konkowski, 13, to go to the South Orange village. The Strutz and Konkowski youths lived adjacent to the railroad.

With no fence to stop them, the three boys, along with a fourth, climbed onto the tracks and walked westbound towards the village. About 100 yards east of Mountain Station, an Erie Lackawanna westbound train struck and instantly killed Collins, Strutz and Konkowski. The engineer of the train, Jacob Yurgosh, said he did not see the boys because his lights were dimmed for an oncoming eastbound train. Just like cars, trains dim their lights as a courtesy to oncoming traffic.

It is probable that the boys saw the eastbound train approaching them but did not hear or see the westbound train coming up behind due to the noise of the oncoming train. Engineer Yurgosh learned that he had hit someone nearly an hour after he had finished his run to Gladstone.

Three years later, in February, 1978, tragedy struck once again. This victim was Ronald Caton of South Orange. Ronald was walking eastbound along the tracks toward South Orange village near the Jefferson Avenue overpass in Maplewood when an eastbound local came up behind him. At the same time a westbound express, which rides on the middle track, approached at full speed. Ronald, unfortunately, stepped to the left instead of the right, according to former Maplewood Police Chief Vincent Klebauer. Ronald was 13 and attended South Orange Junior High School.

Six years later, two Millburn youths were killed on Maplewood's Baker Street trestle in January 1984. They were Tina Sanzalone, 13, and Rosemarie Lepore, 13.

They were walking along the tracks westbound towards Millburn with four boys when a westbound express came around the bend through Maplewood Train Station at about 50 mph. The train could not stop in time. The two girls could not jump to safety. The four boys did.

Who is going to be the next person to lose his life on the railroad? As Mary Mooney, in a letter to the *News-Record* in 1978 said: Children have "an insatiable curiosity that goes far beyond good judgment and their usual good behavior. Trains have literally drawn children to them since their invention."

If this obsession with the railroad is so innocently natural, how can a youth be at fault when there are no continuous safety education programs, no signs saying "No Trespassing" or no harsh punishment for being found on the tracks? Improvements in these areas would help, but unfortunately, to a minor degree.

A fence, which would create a guaranteed deterrence, is the most sound solution.

Interviewed last week, Mary Bolger said, "I don't think Danny would have been able to negotiate a fence."

There is a solution.

ii

Last week I spoke with Maplewood resident Anthony Adams. Mr. Adams lives adjacent to the tracks on Mountain Avenue. When I asked him if he sees kids walking on the tracks, he replied, "All the time." He said that they are not all teen-agers but small children as well.

Mr. Adams spoke of one incident in which he saw a 5-or 6-year-old child playing on the middle track in an unfenced area. He immediately carried the child off the tracks to safety. Had there been a fence, such an incident would not have occurred.

There are various types of railroad hazards in our community. A few are: lack of fencing, lack of pedestrian walkovers, and the non-existence of "No Trespassing" signs.

My own personal experience exphasizes these dangers. In the fall of 1983, my friends and I continually crossed the tracks behing the A&P and Pathmark in order to get to the Old Waterlands field, where our freshman soccer practices were held. Because access to the tracks was so easy and our fear of trains so minimal, we never thought about the dangers involved. One time there was a near miss; if I had tripped, I wouldn't be here to tell the story. It was a short cut—a way of getting to our destination faster.

However, this inclination to save time is inherent in everybody, not just children. At the western end of Mountain Station in South Orange, the median fence on the tracks is not long enough. It is at this location that I have seen several commuters walk around the median in order to get on the eastbound platform. These adults are taking a short cut, which is a natural human tendency.

Another major problem that parallels fencing is the insufficient amount of pedestrian walkovers on the line. There is a remnant of a pedestrian walkover at the conjunction of Mountain House Road and the railroad. If this walkover were still existing, commuters as well as children would not be crossing the tracks in order to get to the eastbound platform.

One area where I feel walkovers would make a dramatic difference is at playing areas where children are most likely to be found. An example is the Waterlands Park, which lies between Third Street and Parker Avenue. Because there is no break in the tracks the chances that children will cross at the underpass are slim. The normal child will cross the tracks in between underpasses.

As a youth, I can say that just the symbol of a fence is a sound deterrent. Many children recognize a fence as a warning and do not dare attempt to scale it. But with no fence, how can one sense danger?

Because the railroad is private property and it is an obvious danger in our community one would think that at least "No Trespassing" signs would be installed.

I spoke with Anthony Grazioso, an official of NJ Transit's Public Information Bureau and I asked him if NJT installs "No Trespassing" signs along the railroad. His reply to me was "We try to put them up."

After viewing the tracks thoroughly in our community I have yet to find one "No Trespassing" sign.

A 1903 New Jersey state statute actually favors the existence of cattle over people. This statute, 48: 12–46, specifically states, "Every railroad company shall erect and maintain fences on the sides of its road of the height and strength of division fences by law . . . sufficient to prevent cattle and other animals from getting on the railroad. Until such fences . . . are erected the company shall be liable for damages done by trains to cattle or other animals straying on its railroad."

What we need now is a statute that will replace the word *cattle* with *people*.

If one were to compare the railroad to other forms of transportation as well as to other dangers in the community, he would notice that the railroads' attempt to improve safety conditions falls short of other efforts.

According to Jean Citrino, a specialist for the NJ Turnpike's Public Relations Bureau, "The NJ Turnpike is fenced from beginning to end on both sides." In addition, the areas that the Turnpike travels through are less dense than the areas that the railroad travels through.

Another comparison is that of a private or public swimming pool. By law, pools are required to be completely fenced in. Because a pool can be classified as a "dangerous instrumentality" in the community, one could be held liable if there were no fencing and an injury or death occurred.

Is the railroad any different from the NJ Turnpike? Is it a dangerous instrumentality in our community? Why isn't NJT required by law to fence off their property? On the railroad in our community, six lives have been lost in the last 10 years. It is time for NJ Transit to take action.

iii

In the early morning of March 31, I stood on the platform of the South Orange train station. I saw several South Orange and NJ Transit policemen. Two NJ Transit officials were wearing white hard hats. On the side of the hard hats, in black letters, it said: "Think Safety." Lying prostrate at their feet, covered by a white sheet, was Craig Vinelli, age 37.

Vinelli, a bank executive from South Orange, had been reading a neatly folded *Wall Street Journal,* while standing on or near the white safety line. An eastbound express train came through the station traveling between 50 and 60 mph. Vinelli was struck by the side of the first car and instantly killed.

The white "safety" line is 29 inches away from the edge of the platform. Would you feel "safe" 29 inches away from the edge of the platform? Would you feel "safe" 29 inches away from a train traveling 50-60 mph?

Earlier in March, accompanied by others, I measured, surveyed and mapped the railroad, the stations, and the fencing conditions between the Millburn-Maplewood border and the Orange-South Orange border. Here are some of the results:

Maplewood, Mountain, and South Orange stations are unsafe. Approximately half of the track through our two communities is completely unfenced.

There are almost three miles of railroad within the boundaries of South Orange and Maplewood; six miles to be fenced on both sides. Approximately 45 percent of this six-mile length is totally unfenced. Of the remaining 55 percent, 8 percent has inadequate and flimsy fencing, while 47 percent is sturdy. If six feet was to be considered the minimum height for safe fencing in our communities, we would have to fence almost 79 percent of the railroad within South Orange and Maplewood.

After investigating the cost to fence the local tracks, I have determined from quotations from several fencing contractors that it will cost roughly $10/linear foot installed for six-foot high chain link fencing. Considering the length of railroad unfenced or inadequately fenced (23,800 feet of the total 30,166 feet), the approximate price to fence off the tracks would be $238,000. With respect to NJ Transit's annual $500 million budget, $238,000 is a small price to pay to save lives.

There are three areas where officials should be commended for having installed adequate fencing. These are the Waterlands Park, Cameron Field, and an extensive portion on the eastbound side between Jefferson Avenue and the Maplewood train station.

Sections within all three of these areas have been fenced in with some kind of fencing that exceeds six feet in height. Someone felt quality fencing of this type was necessary. Someone was aware of the danger. But this is the exception.

Take a look at Lackawanna Place in South Orange. It is a dead-end street which lies adjacent to the track. Along the entire length of the street, there is no fencing. According to 48:12-48, adopted in 1903, the South Orange Trustees have the right to control the speeds of trains at Lackawanna Place. This statute says that if there is not an adequate four-foot fence or embankment where the railroad "adjoins a public highway" a municipality has the right to regulate "the speed of its trains along streets."

This statute was designed to prevent "children and horses" from getting on the track, but it only applied to areas where the street lies right up against the railroad. Why can't this statute include the entire length of the tracks? "Children and horses" don't only walk along streets.

Above, I pointed to another 1903 NJ statute which required the railroad to install a four-foot fence to protect cattle. People somehow were overlooked. Since 1903 there has been no improved legislation. However, the NJ Supreme Court, 78 years later, in 1981, finally gave the railroad a reason to erect fencing to protect people.

Due to a case called Renz vs. Penn. Central Corp., the railroad is no longer protected under the ancient Railroad Immunity Act. This act made the railroad immune to any prosecution. Anyone standing, playing, or walking along the tracks was to be considered "contributorily negligent" and therefore could recover nothing from the railroad./

This case introduced a new condition. If one is able to prove that the railroad was more negligent than they were, then they would be able to recover. This doctrine eradicated the Railroad Immunity Act by allowing for "comparative negligence."

There are several areas in our communities where immediate action is needed to prevent imminent tragedies. Fencing should be installed at the following areas: conjunction of Mountain House Road and the railroad, conjunction of Meadowbrook Place and the railroad, the northeast corner of Cameron Field, behind the South Orange Field, behind the South Orange Post Office, behind Pathmark and A&P, the Parker Avenue overpass, the Jefferson Avenue overpass, the walkway between Mountain Avenue and Carleton Court, the Maplewood Country Club; and the conjunction of Carleton Court and the railroad.

There is good news for new legislation. I have met with and urged NJ Assemblyman Harry McEnroe to help. He identifies with railroad safety problems and wants safe conditions.

He has agreed to introduce railroad safety legislation, which will primarily address fencing. In addition, he says he will seek bipartisan support.

In the last 10 years, seven people, six children and one adult, have lost their lives on the tracks in South Orange and Maplewood. As citizens of South Orange and Maplewood, we must unite and urge our State Legislature, public officials, and NJ Transit to ensure safety within our community.

The High Cost of Education

ANN PAO

More and more people are realizing the importance of having a college degree when job hunting. Yet, although the number of people attending college has steadily increased, it is becoming increasingly difficult to pay the high costs of higher education.

College costs have doubled over the past decade. According to an article in the April 8, 1985 *U.S. News and World Report,* while inflation is below 3 percent presently, the average price of a year's tuition will jump about 8 percent next fall. Currently, the average tuition at a public four-year college is $1,126. The average rate at a private college is $5,016, and it is not uncommon for total college cost figures at top universities to approximate between twelve and sixteen thousand dollars. Next fall, M.I.T. will raise its tuition to $11,000, thus becoming the most expensive university in the United States.

Why the high costs? Surprisingly, salaries of professors have not contributed greatly to the costs. In fact, faculty salaries have declined 19 percent in real dollars since 1970, perhaps one reason why so many top professors have left the academic ring for jobs in the private sector, which may offer salaries up to 20 percent higher. Rather, schools are trying to attract students by offering better facilities, such as renovated dorms and new buildings, modern equipment, and a prettier campus. The demand for high-tech computers and up-to-date research equipment is a costly one, but a necessary one if colleges wish to remain strong in their science departments. Some colleges may even be hiring more professors to increase teacher-student ratios. The cost of all these projects is then passed on to the students and parents.

Today, government-financed student loans are becoming scarcer and standards for receiving student loans are tougher. Under the Reagan Administration, new Secretary of Education William Bennett is trying to pass a proposal in which families with incomes over $32,000 would be ineligible for subsidized government student loans. Families with incomes over $25,000 would not be eligible for grants, subsidized jobs, and direct government loans. He would also like to see a $4,000 maximum per student per year of financial aid.

What can students do to defray the cost of a college education? The college itself may provide a solution. Not only have most colleges increased the portion of tuition dollars devoted to financial aid, but many offer a variety of financial aid packages which help contribute to paying for the cost of college. Many universities offer work-study programs in which students are paid good wages to work in the cafeteria, administration offices, etc. Students at Williams College in Williamstown, Massachusetts, pay a tuition of $9,273 a year in 10-

month installments. At the University of Pennsylvania, a loan program entitled the Penn-Plan allows students and parents to pay tuition plus interest in monthly installments for up to six years after graduation. Other colleges permit students to pay the full four years' college cost all at once, to avoid increasing college costs over the next four years.

Students are also more careful about what college in which to enroll. Some may decline their first-choice college in order to go to a college which offers them financial aid, a scholarship, and/or money grants. Second-rate colleges are offering full academic scholarships to first-rate students. Other universities are improving their curriculum in hopes of attracting better students. Rutgers University, for example, offers a General Honors Program which offers accelerated and higher level courses to those top-quality students who can't afford more expensive, prestigious colleges, yet don't want to sacrifice good education. Surprisingly, the armed forces have seen a noticeable increase in recruits, some joining to take advantage of a good college education with minimal costs. Others want to take advantage of the fact that Uncle Sam will contribute to the cost of college for its enlisted men after their time of service is up.

With the cost of college skyrocketing, students and parents are asking more questions when shopping for a college. Can we afford this college? What types of financial aid packages are available? Is there a less expensive, but comparable college to this one? Some people are even asking, "Is a college education worth it?"

State-of-Knowledge Article

Lay out the facts known so far regarding some topic about which knowledge is constantly accumulating or changing, such as certain social, technological, and scientific developments. Draw your information from interviews with specialists in the field, from recent articles in periodicals, and perhaps from background books as well. Consider as you write this up how general or specialized an audience you want to read this.

After you've gathered your information, organize your notes and decide which points about your subject should come before others and which should go after others. An outline might help to fix in your mind this sequence of topics and the ranking within a topic. Try your article as a talk to some group. Speak from your notes and outline. Ask for response from your audience to help do your next draft. If you tape your talk, you can revise that into your article, taking the audience commentary into account. Try this draft out on some readers to see if it needs further improvement. Look at a book or article that cites sources in footnotes and lists them in a bibliography. Follow that form for your own.

Print up copies to distribute and submit for publication. If there is a particular group, like a club, that deals with yur subject, you might read your talk to them as a lecture.

Acupuncture

KRISTINA YOUSO

"I saw more of acupuncture than I know how to believe. As you stand there watching these procedures, your scientific brain says, 'My God, this can't be true.' But you're still . . . watching it. I'm still not sure how it works, but I have to believe there is some margin of truth to it" (Duke, 1972:15). This quote from Dr. E. Gray Diamond, chairman of the health sciences department at the University of Missouri Medical School and a world renowned heart specialist, portrays the western world's astonishment concerning the many modern medical utilizations of acupuncture. An ancient Chinese healing method, acupuncture cures a tremendous variety of diseases and relieves pain by the insertion of needles into the patient's body. Not only is acupuncture widely used today, but in many cases it has succeeded where the Western world's advanced procedures have failed.

In old China, acupuncture and herb remedies were the only methods used to cure illness. They were prescribed for every affliction known to man, from simple colds to smallpox and malaria. "Acupuncture healed China's sick, whether they were peasants or emperors" (Duke, 1972:2). Acupuncture developed largely because doctors were formerly very rare and only for the rich. Before the Communist Revolution, there were fewer than one thousand hospital beds for 650,000,000 people. Western medicine was introduced to China in 1840; an unsuccessful attempt to abolish all traditional medicine followed in 1920. Following the revolution there still was a great lack of trained doctors, and so-called 'barefoot' doctors were introduced, who continued the traditional medical practices, including acupuncture. Mao Tse-Tung was a strong believer in the value of this ancient medical practice and encouraged its popularity (Cameron, 1974:102).

During the twentieth century while acupuncture was continuing to expand in the Orient, doctors in the West were only beginning to learn of its modern successes. Many were very skeptical and considered it a hoax or a type of brainwashing which worked only for psychological reasons. In 1971 there were two doctors practicing acupuncture in the United States. The World Acupuncture Congress, however, held at the University of Pennsylvania in 1974, involved practitioners from all parts of the world who reported their own successes and helped to expand the field.

The basic philosophy behind acupuncture, the explanation of disease and the approach of the acupuncturist, is simple. "Acupuncture sets out to correct any imbalance that is in the body or mind, and to restore harmony and equilibrium, thus eradicating the causative factors of sickness. If all of the functions and organs of the body are working properly and in harmony, then there cannot be sickness within the body or mind" (Worsley, 1973:8). This philosophy stems from traditional Chinese acupuncture laws, wherein the three aims of the acupuncturist are to treat the patient as a whole, the union of a body and mind; to find the cause of disease; and to attempt to remove the cause (Worsley, 1973:3). This philosophy seems to be a reflection of the Chinese culture in general—an emphasis on a simple way of life, moderate lifestyle, and refraining from thoughts and acts of excess worry, all of which are excellent for both physical and mental health (Worsley, 1973:61). Therefore, mental illness is treated by acupuncture because of the mind-body connection. Physical health is necessary for mental health, and the reverse is also true.

The methods of diagnosis and treatment of a doctor of acupuncture, in accordance with the traditional philosophy and laws of acupuncture, differ greatly from the procedures that are familiar in the West. Doctors of acupuncture are quite concerned with the prediction and prevention of disease. Along with a diagnosis, a check-up is made to sight imbalances in body energy that could lead to future disease. Acupuncture practitioners teach guidelines for living which stem from ancient Chinese practices. Western doctors have been greatly impressed by the ability of a practitioner of acupuncture to foretell the coming of disease before physical symptoms have appeared, by the method of a pulse reading, which often reveals more than advanced medical equipment, and by healing techniques that have succeeded where other, modern techniques have failed. (Worsley, 1973:170-71). "Acupuncturists treat their patients for hundreds of different ailments that cover the entire spectrum of illness and disease. Chinese doctors claim an average success rate of ninety percent in more than two hundred types of illnesses" (Duke, 1972:13). A difference between the Western and Eastern approaches to medicine and overall health is apparent. In the West, the main concern is usually treatment of a particular disorder or symptom rather than the cause; concern for the individual as a whole is not emphasized. Doctors of acupuncture view the mind and the body as a unit, their goal being the restoration of life force. A healthier approach to life seems evident in the dramatically lower rate of cancer, mental illness, and stress-related diseases in China.

The duration and type of treatment depend on the severity of the illness and how long the patient has suffered from it. Modern acupuncturists usually administer two treatments per week for two weeks, and then once a week treatment for as long as necessary.

Needles are usually left in the acupoint for fifteen to twenty minutes. The most frequently used acupoints fall on the legs, feet, forearms, and hands. In past centuries, acupuncture needles were made of a variety of metals, including gold and silver. Prior to the Bronze and Iron Ages, they were made of bones. Today stainless steel needles from one half inch to five inches in length are used. Nine basic types of needles are used, differing in length, shape, and function. Expert acupuncturists need only one needle to treat illnesses; however, in some instances up to a dozen may be used.

Besides the simple insertion of needles, various other methods of treatment are employed by acupuncture practitioners. Moxibustion involves the application of heat to an acupoint by the placement of moxa (the dried herb Artemisia ulgaris) on the needle handle and igniting it. Moxibustion is often used to treat rheumatism, bone disease, and cramps. Acupuncturists often advise their patients to apply pressure with their fingers to the acupoints utilized in treatment to alleviate pain.

As successfully utilized as acupuncture has been in the past centuries, it still has the capacity for a broad range of use in the modern world. Acupuncture can be applied successfully to all illnesses; the philosophy of treating the mind and body as a whole has an expansive application. It is excellent as an analgesic. The relief from pain acupuncture brings may often be the first desired step in the normalization and treatment of chronic illness. It is a good initial approach to such traumatic injuries as whiplash and sprains. It can be used to treat virtually all psychological problems. The only exceptions are made for pregnant women, with whom needles are not used in the abdominal area, emergency accidents, problems such as fractures and cataracts, and terminal cases beyond human help, although it can be used in these cases to ease pain and suffering.

Recent findings reveal a broad spectrum of acupuncture uses. Deficiency diseases respond well to acupuncture as it attempts to aid the body in restoring production of its own vitamins. One acupoint can correct low or high blood pressure, and another can slow down or speed up a heartbeat. Another has been shown to increase the number of white blood corpuscles. Two Danish physicians have reported success of treatment in facial pain, also known as astic douloureux or trieminal neuralgia, which involves severe pain and does not always respond to drugs and surgery. Acupuncture was found to be a very effective long-term pain reliever. The time of healing fractures may be shortened by the energy acupuncture needles bring to the area. Soviet findings report success in treatment of angina pectoris, a form of heart disease, as well as impotence. German physicians have treated Parkinson's disease with acupuncture. At the World Acupuncture Congress in Philadelphia, American doctors relayed their success in treating migraine headaches, tension headaches and cluster headaches (histamine cephalalgia) with a combination of acupuncture and point stimulation. Good results have been achieved in the treatment of "phantom limb" pain, often experienced by amputees to whom their missing limbs seem intensely painful. Even poliomyelitis has been successfully treated with acupuncture.

One startling use of acupuncture has gained popularity throughout China in the last decades. This is the use of acupuncture as anesthesia in all types of minor surgery, from pulling teeth to heart surgery and the removal of tumors. One of four needles is stimulated for fifteen to twenty minutes before the operation until a feeling of numbness is induced, and the needles are stimulated at various times during the operation. The anesthetic was first used in Shanghai in 1958, and since then 400,000 people have received it as anesthesia, including children and elderly persons, with a ninety percent success rate. In 1971, Audrey Toppin, one of the first reporters allowed in China since the Communist takeover, witnessed open heart surgery and an operation in which a throat tumor was removed with no anesthetic except acupuncture. James Reston of *The New York Times* saw acupuncture used as an anesthetic for a tuberculosis patient whose left lung and part of a rib were removed. He also witnessed the removal of a brain tumor. In all these instances, the patient was fully conscious and able to converse with the doctors and nurses, sip water and eat fruit during the operation. The patient felt no pain and was able to get off the operating table and walk to his room when surgery was completed.

Acupuncture is used by dentists for oral surgery and extractions, and has been very successful in brain and face tumor operations, Caesarean births, and many types of lung and heart surgery. There are many advantages to acupuncture as anesthetic. The patient is relaxed, and his or her blood pressure, breathing, and pulse remain normal throughout the operation. There are no side effets, and recovery is quicker. Persons for whom drug anesthesia would be impossible, due to their age and/or damage to the kidneys and cardiac system may undergo operations with this anestheic form.

Many Western theories have been formulated to explain these amazing usages, but the reason for acupuncture's success is still basically unknown.

References

Bloodworth, D. (1967). *The Chinese Looking Glass.* New York: Farrar, Straus, and Giroux.
Bonavia, D. (1980). *The Chinese.* New York: Lippincott and Crowell.

Bricklin, M. (1976). *The Practical Encyclopedia of Natural Healing*. Emmaus, PA: Rodale Press.

Bunge, F.M., and Shinn, R.-S. (eds.) (1981). *China: A Country Study*. (Foreign Area Studies: The American University.) Washington, DC: Government Printing Office.

Cameron, N. (1974). *China Today*. London: Collins.

Chaitow, L. (1977). *The Acupuncture Treatment of Pain*. New York: Arco.

Cohen, J. L. and Jerome, A. (1980). *China Today*. New York: Harry Abrams.

Duke, M. (1972). *Acupuncture*. New York: Pyramid House.

Worsley, J.R. (1973). *Is Acupuncture for You?* New York: Harper & Row.

Electro-Magnetic Pulse: The Unknown Danger of the Nuclear Age

DOUG KORNREICH

On Johnston Atoll, a small island in the Pacific, a small group of scientists are waiting to launch a nuclear-tipped missile, which will enable them to study, among other things, the chaos-producing effects of electro-magnetic pulse (EMP).

EMP was first discovered in 1962, after an exo-atmospheric burst (a nuclear burst outside of the atmosphere) over Johnston Atoll; in Honolulu, some 800 miles away, street lights went out, circuit break-ers popped, burglar alarms rang, and some power lines went out (Broad, 1981:1116, 1248). This was the last above-ground nuclear weapons test by the United States before the Partial Test Ban treaty of 1963. Many scientists and scholars say that the USSR discovered the effects of EMP and signed the treaty to prevent us from doing the same.

The scientists on Johnston Atoll may be shocked at what they find. Since 1962, the semiconductor "revolution" has occurred, and it has been determined through simulation that the new semiconductor technology is ten million times more vulnerable to EMP than old, reliable vacuum tube electronics. The new technology includes such things as solid state television, radios, and computers. Today in Hawaii televisions could blow up and computer memories could be erased by a single exo-atmospheric test burst. The scientists need an abrogation of the Partial Test Ban treaty in order to test for the effects of EMP. Until that happens, EMP will remain the uncertain certainty.

EMP is a highly charged electrical field which is caused by a large emission of X-rays and gamma rays, most probably from an atomic bomb. These high energy waves free electrons from the atoms in the air by a process known as Compton's effect. Compton's effect (also called Compton scattering) occurs when highly charged photons collide with electrons, which then become free. These free electrons are called Compton electrons.

When a nuclear weapon explodes within the atmosphere, the EMP efects are confined to a relatively small area immediately around the blast zone. These effects are quite large, perhaps approaching 500,000 volts/meter, but due to all of the atoms in the air, very little Compton scattering takes place. Of this slight scattering, many of the effects are hidden by the blast wave of the explosion.

In an exo-atmospheric nuclear burst, the gamma and X-rays can travel for long distances without encountering atoms. The first atoms that the rays come in contact with are the upper atmosphere atoms. Since the air is still very thin in the upper atmosphere, the Compton electrons swirl around the geomagnetic field and travel for great distances. The higher a burst occurs, the more territory it can cover. Of course, the amplitude of the waves when they strike the atoms would be less because of the added distance, but at an altitude of 500 km there would be a field of at least 25,000 volts/meter with peak fields of as much as 50,000 volts/meter.

The other major type of EMP is system-generated EMP (SGEMP). SGEMP is similar to the exo-atmospheric EMP in that Compton's effect is the reason for its generation. Also, like exo-atmospheric EMP, a very small yield is needed to wreak a great deal of havoc. The way that SGEMP happens is that when the gamma and X-rays hit the outer skin of the satellite, Compton electrons are generated inside the satellite, and all EMP sensitive equipment inside the satellite is affected. While satellites can be "hardened" against weak gamma and X-rays (hence a weak SGEMP) there is really no protection from SGEMP that can approach 1,000,000 volts/meter (Gladstone, 1977:521-22). When the SGEMP strikes a satellite, the delicate circuitry, which is at least one million times more sensitive to EMP than the old vacuum tubes, will just blow up.

EMP and SGEMP together pose difficult problems for our military in both peace and war. Recently, the Joint Chiefs of Staff requested $7 billion to harden our weapons systems against the effects of EMP (Broad, 1982:1228).

The space frontier is very important to the well-being of the nation. SGEMP is one of the most serious threats to our satellite communications and defenses. We are spending over $300 million on sophisticated equipment which could be rendered useless by a single, low-tonnage nuclear weapon.

The methods for defending against SGEMP are few and relatively inefficient. One method is to separate the outer skin of a satellite from the inner skin, thereby creating a barrier to high voltage.

The main factor in deciding whether a satellite will survive a burst is its distance from the burst point. The amount of radiation striking the satellite depends on the square of the distance from the burst point.

While there is concern for our space-based military equipment, our earth-based equipment is certainly susceptible to EMP effects. There is a grid of telephone lines beneath the US which collectively would be a giant collector of EMP. The Department of Defense rules state that there are 43 different ways for the President to send out the Emergency Action Message. Testimony has indicated that the EAM system is more vulnerable than previously thought (Broad,- 1981:1116).

The Pentagon has been slow to harden most systems against the effects of EMP because of the "unholy alliance" (Broad) of DOD with AT&T. AT&T has no satellites, but satellite communication is much safer from the effects of EMP.

Just as there is a telephone grid under the US, there is also a power grid. Unlike telephone lines, there is no real way to harden power lines from the effects of EMP. Voltage surges caused by the collection of EMP would come through and blow the computers' delicate circuitry up and would trip circuit breakers and blow fuses. This effect would cause a coast-to-coast blackout.

There is an increasing belief that EMP would induce nuclear meltdowns in the nation's nuclear power plants. With this extra concern about the nation's power supply, it is very unlikely that any public power would remain.

The EMP problem counters the concept of a limited nuclear war. EMP greatly reduces the chances of a survivable nuclear war because it will lead to panic, destruction, and a "use it or lose it" mentality. Due to the factors stated above, EMP, the uncertain certainty, highlights our nation's vulnerability to nuclear weaponry.

References

Broad, William J. "Military Grapples with Chaos Factor," *Science* (September 11, 1981).

Broad, William J. "A Fatal Flaw in the Concept of Space War," *Science* (March 12, 1982).

Broad, William J. "Nuclear Pulse," *Science* (May 29, June 5, June 12, 1982).

Glasstone, Samuel and Philip J. Dolan, *The Effects of Nuclear Weapons.* Washington: Government Printing Office, 1977.

Stein, Daniel L. "Electromagnetic Pulse—The Uncertain Certainty," *Bulletin of Atomic Scientists* (March, 1983).

"Would EMPs Induce Nuclear Meltdowns?" *Science News* (June 6, 1981).

Imagination
(Thinking Up)

Dreams

Jot down a dream soon afterwards so you'll remember it, or even better, keep a notebook of dreams regularly. Tell the dream to a partner or group until you have it well in mind, listen to what they have to say about it, then write it as a story and perhaps as a poem, feeling free to alter it to suit a particular form. If the dream features dialog, write it as a script and give it to others to perform.

Help!

EDNA NEIVERT

"Warning! There is an armed student roaming the halls here in Columbia High School. Teachers, please keep all students inside classrooms and . . ."

A wave of fear with shrieks and cries goes through the class in the art room, drowning out the rest of the announcement. The real art teacher that day is absent, so Mr. Sloane, a substitute, is teaching instead. Unfortunately, Mr. Sloane ignores the announcement and continues to confidently teach the useless theories of perspective. He seems to deliberately taunt the class by leaving the door open. Screams rise up from the class to close the door but Mr. Sloane, caught up in his own "intelligence," barely acknowledges them. Finally, he reluctantly leans over and taps the door closed since the class is in an uproar and hysterical with fear. The tap is insufficient, though, and the door, after slightly clicking, falls open again. All attention is focused on the open door with Mr. Sloane's voice a dull monotone in the background. The hallway is dark and eerie with a ghostly red light glowing from somewhere. The door inexorably closes and the room slowly fades out.

192

A different classroom with students sitting at desks in orderly rows. Heads are bowed and the quiet scratching of pencils can be heard. Tracy Szaboda is sitting next to a girl with brown hair whose gaze occasionally wanders from her work to rest on Tracy, diligently working on her math. Miss Wilson, a teacher from the school, walks in and discretely approaches Tracy. There is a rustling in the hallway and the girl sitting next to Tracy notices two policemen waiting there. The girl senses an almost embarrassed feeling from the policemen. They are ill at ease and look out of place. She watches as Miss Wilson leans toward Tracy, and she hears the word "cocaine" whispered. The classroom gets very quiet, and the little incident creates a charged atmosphere. Tracy looks scared, and everyone seems to be waiting for something. The something is Tracy breaking down and crying. She tries to explain, but it's a feeble attempt; she is caught. It all seems so sad. It was her first time, she hadn't meant it, etc. Miss Wilson sadly shakes her head, and Tracy is led away pathetically trying to control herself. The students are all very sympathetic, but there's nothing they, or anyone, can do.

Announcement. The school's on fire. There is no apparent escape from this room; the crowd is trapped. It's a large room and Dina and a couple of others are huddled by the back wall. What looks like an elevator appears, and it seems to be a secret escape route. There is a risk, though. Anyone who uses this elevator might end up an amputee. Dina's brother quietly walks into the elevator, along with some others, as if he's been ordered to and has accepted his fate. Despairingly, Dina watches him go. The doors close.

Dina and two teachers are in the next group. Surprisingly, the elevator does not go down, but sideways away from the building. Free from the restraining shaft, it streaks toward a set of tracks in the air which look like the monorail at Disneyworld. Something goes wrong, though, and it doesn't quite make it all the way. Abruptly, the tracks curve toward the escapees in the elevator; fate has intervened, and the group has one more chance, but they'll have to jump for it. Dina stares at one of the teacher's feet. Her sneakers are bright in contrast to the dark steel track. Suddenly the whole group is standing on the smooth grey rails; the elevator had accelerated straight for the rails and the crew just slid off.

Dina is worried about her brother. She searches for him in the dark, gloomy night, but that familiar white hat and beat-up sweatshirt refuse to show themselves. Her desperation mounts as she paces through the streets without a sign. Dina stops running and stands still for a moment, frantically calling his name. She turns suddenly when something white catches her eye. It's a hat bobbing in the distance! It's Robert!

Vision of the Past

LISA CRAWFORD

I sit here alone in the darkness of my room. My mind begins to wander; pictures float through my mind until one is trapped inside. A blurry shadow of the past begins to come into focus; it's a man. I close my eyes and concentrate hard. "Who is he?" I question myself.

Finally the picture is locked into place, and I can see him clearly. I recognize him immediately, even though my eyes have not seen him for some time. Then my mind reels back even farther, and I am lost in the span of time. I feel trapped. The flood of visions in my head comes to a stop at last. I see myself and my brother sitting on what appears to be a park lawn. We're watching something—baseball; we're at his baseball game!

I look up and see him in the position I know he belongs—the pitcher. I look at my brother sitting next to me and am amazed to see that he is so small. "Why he must be only 8 years old!" I exclaim under my breath. I look at myself and realize that I am reliving my 11th year. It feels so funny, so odd. It's like I'm really there, but I'm only dreaming, I know. My father looks very much like he did when I last saw him. he's about 5 ft. 8 in., of average build, with a mustache and beard in the same shade as his dark hair, with a few grey hairs scattered about his head.

I watch him closely for a moment, wondering if he's seen us yet. The game ends; my father's team has won. We run up to congratulate him, but he walks right by us! We run up to him, thinking that maybe he just hasn't seen us. I grab his arm—"Father," I plead. He doesn't see us! It's as though we're not even there! Now we are screaming at him wildly, in an attempt to get his attention, but it's no good; to him we're really not there.

"How can this be?" I question myself in bewilderment. "Why is it I feel so close to him now?" Inside I begin to panic. Surely he hasn't forgotten us—his own children!" I cry inside. "It's only been two years!" I must try one more time, I tell myself determinedly, but my voice chokes as if unable to form the words. Then at last I can speak, but the words are only whispers. "Father, Father, please . . . it's me." My heart sinks as I realize it's useless.

My mind slowly begins to return to the present, and before me I see my father. He's not wearing his baseball uniform. Confused, I ask, "What are you doing here?"

"I've come to visit you," he answers. His voice is emotionless. I jump to my feet elated, and run towards him to hug him, but he is not here, no one is. . . .

Goodbye for Now

EMILY KVASNIKOFF

I am going to tell you about a dream that I had which I was afraid to tell people because I thought they wouldn't believe me. I have told a couple of people and they said it was possible that it happened.

I was in Egypt with Prime Minister Anwar Sadat. We were riding in a black limo with his wife. She was wearing a black dress and a pearl necklace. He was wearing a grey-colored three-piece suit and black sunglasses. All of a sudden the limo blew up and I was at home with my mom in the kitchen.

I told mom, "I'd better go and see Paul before I go to heaven."

Mom said, "You better or he'll miss you if you don't visit him."

I was wearing a green plaid-like shirt and red corduroy pants.

I went into Paul's trailer, and he was eating fried chicken, mashed potatoes, and corn and drinking some orange juice. I tried to talk to him, but he wouldn't answer so I cried and thought he was ignoring me. I didn't realize that I had been dead and walking around as only a spirit.

The scenes changed again. I was wearing an off-colored dress with small pearls on the bib, and my hair was curled. Flying behind me there was a blue-laced scarf.

As I neared the mountain top I saw Paul there waving at me. He wore brown pants and a green shirt. After I said good-bye to Paul a cloud took me to heaven.

In heaven it was beautiful and very very bright. The colors were misty but bright. My deceased sister Tammy came to meet me at the opening of the clouds. She was six years older now and wearing a beautiful pink gown. I mean she was pretty. Everyone I saw there was so beautiful. When she came to me she put her hand on my shoulder and said, "You're not finished on earth. We're sending you back; that is why you can't see God yet."

She kissed me on the cheek and said, "I'll see you when it's time."

I started going down fast. It was dark when I opened my eyes. I found the light, which I turned on and found myself on my bed sweating.

To this day I still am confused about it. This is one dream I'll never forget.

A Strange Town

JENNY ENCINAS

You are in a strange town,
the houses all the same
but different colors.

Soldiers are after you.
You are alone,
running.
It feels
like you are running in water.

You finally make it
to a red house.
You go to the top bedroom.
They are still after you.

You have an idea,
you will hide
under the bed
and hold on to the slats
so you aren't touching the floor.

Soldiers are in the room
looking everywhere.
They look under the bed.

It works!
They didn't see you,
they don't find you.

You will do the same every time.
You dream this over,
and over,
five times.

Plays

Duolog

Make up a conversation between two people that runs for at least two to three minutes if actually spoken aloud. Write the name of a speaker in the left margin, put a colon after it, then write down what he or she says. Do the same thing each time one of them speaks. Give the duolog a title that catches the main action or relationship. If the place and physical action can't be made clear in their speech without awkwardness, state these briefly between parentheses at the appropriate points. (Looking at a play script will show you a standard form.)

Your dialog can make any point. It might emphasize personalities or relationships. Or it might develop serious ideas or be a funny give-and-take.

Direct two people in a rehearsal of your script so that they can do a good reading of it for the class or another group. Make changes if rehearsals show any need for improvement. Include it in a collection of plays that others can read or perform.

The Louse

MONSERRATE MELENDEZ

ADAM: Hi, Jenny. How are you?
JENNY: Don't talk to me!
ADAM: What?
JENNY: You heard me. Don't talk to me.
ADAM: What's with you?
JENNY: Do you know what day yesterday was?
ADAM: Yeah. Wednesday
JENNY: You fool! Just don't talk to me.
ADAM: Why?

JENNY: Because yesterday was Valentine's Day.

ADAM: So?

JENNY: So! "So," you say. Don't you know that on Valentine's Day a guy is supposed to give a girl a Valentine's present?

ADAM: Says who?

JENNY: I don't know who said it, but it's a tradition.

ADAM: Yeah. So it is.

JENNY: So, why didn't you get me a Valentine's present?

ADAM: Because I didn't have any money.

JENNY: No money? But you got paid on Tuesday.

ADAM: Yeah. But I spent all my money.

JENNY: On what?

ADAM: On a girl.

JENNY: On a girl! You louse! I was waiting for you all day yesterday, and you have the nerve to tell me you spent your money on a girl instead of coming here.

ADAM: Yes. For a present.

JENNY: A present!

ADAM: Yes. Happy Valentine's Day, Jenny.

Going Off Duty

LOUIS LARSON

KID: Sure is smoky in here . . . you been workin' in this crummy place all day?

STAN: Yeah . . . I came on at noon. The fryer's acting up . . . but that's Eeeeeola Inn for ya. I hate working with lousy equipment.

KID: Hey, you should check out this water pressure over here, Stan; I'd be better off washing these dishes in the river.

STAN: Yeah, and it'd be cooler too. Hey, did ya hear about that massacre over in El Salvador? If things continue, it could become another Vietnam.

KID: I guess. Were you in Vietnam?

STAN: Yeah. I was about your age too when I got my draft notice. Scared the hell out of me.

KID: I gotta register for the draft pretty soon or ol' Uncle Sam's gonna have a penalty for me.

STAN: At least ya don't have to worry about going into combat . . . at least not yet. I'll never forget those experiences over in 'Nam. The action started the first day I got there.

KID: Sounds like you got right into it.

STAN: After the plane landed we took helicopters to the place that would be our home for three months. I was a gunner. Anyway, we were flying to our base when we got an emergency call to give our support over by Danang. Just as my chopper was about to land and pick up some really messed up guys, some gook opened fire on us. The pilot's head blew up like the Fourth of July and our chopper hit the ground sideways. I ran off into the bush with my M-16 and the chopper exploded.

KID: That must of been pretty sick to see someone's head get blown off like that.

STAN: Yea, it was gross, but it didn't compare to the horror my friend went through. We were on a patrol through the jungle when my friend stepped on a Bouncing Bettie.

KID: What's that?

STAN: It's a mine that shoots the explosive waist high, then blows up. Anyway, when my buddy stepped on that thing, all you could see was blood, bones and pieces of his uniform.

KID: Sick. What did you do?

STAN: What everyone did. Made my way back to base and smoked some joints of opium laced with pot and watched the sun set. It was really beautiful.

KID: God . . . I guess you were glad to get home.

STAN: Well, coming home wasn't exactly what I expected either. When my plane landed, all I could see was a bunch of screaming hippies, calling us baby killers and a bunch of stuff. The whole attitude of the country was like, let's forget about Vietnam. Not exactly like when my dad came home from World War II and got parades and kisses, ya know?

KID: Well, at least it's all behind you now, right?

STAN: Yeah, sure kid. It's all behind me now. Hey, it's time for me to get outa this place.

KID: Sure, Stan. I can take over now. You gonna check out?

STAN: I'm gonna check out all right. Think I'll check out right over here in the bar with some J.D. Take care, kid.

KID: Yeah, later Stan.

Two Students

ALEXANDRA D'ITALIA

(The lunch bell has just rung. Johnny, a popular jock, slips into the bathroom for a short smoke and meets a small boy who looks a little like a freshman.)

JOHNNY: Hey! What are you doing here?

BOY: *(Uneasily.)* I'm in here because *(Pause.)* I am kinda confused.

JOHNNY: Yeah? Maybe I can help. *(Takes out a pack.)* What's ya name?

BOY: Herman . . . Herman Lustom . . . What's yours?

JOHNNY: Johnny. *(Takes a drag.)* Ya new here?

HERMAN: Yes, I am. I just came here last week. Everybody seems so . . .

JOHNNY: *(Blows out smoke.)* The kids are cool. But some are pretty mean. Ya have to watch out sometimes.

HERMAN: *(Losing his shyness.)* For what?

JOHNNY: For some kids who aren't as nice as I am. *(Starting to laugh, then calming down.)* No, really, some of the kids here get kinda rowdy with new kids. I'll give ya some advice, Herman. *(Putting out his cigarette.)* Stay away from Peter Schiff. He hates little kids and he *is* mean.

HERMAN: *(Nervous again.)* I . . . I will. What are the teachers like?

JOHNNY: *(Combing his hair.)* They're all right. Most of 'em teach ya somethin' by the end of the year. *(Pausing to think.)* Hey! Do you have Mrs. Red?

HERMAN: *(Looking at his schedule.)* Yeah, I have her.

JOHNNY: You are so lucky. She's the best. Everybody likes her. Hey! Let me see that. *(Grabs the schedule from his hands.)* Ya gotta pretty good schedule but *(Breaking into a smile.)* ya have band? That's hilarious!

HERMAN: *(Turning towards the sink.)* What do you mean?

JOHNNY: Man! Band is so . . . ah, forget it. I'm on the football team *(Lighting up again.)*, with Quigley as coach. We had a pretty good season this year. We'll be even better next year. *(Giving Herman a cocky smile.)*

HERMAN: Are any of the other teams any good? I heard they stink! Especially the freshman teams! *(Starts to feel some confidence.)* What's wrong with band anyway?

JOHNNY: Don't make fun of our teams! *(Now shaking his cigarette butt into the toilet bowl.)* Honestly . . . *(Coming closer to Herman.)* they're pretty good once they get on the field, but they just walk on the field like jerks. I think Smith is a pretty cool guy even though he's strict!

HERMAN: Have you ever been in the computer lab? *(Smiling snobbily.)*

JOHNNY: I took a "Basic" course in my sophomore year. It was good, but the computer was always down! It was boring as hell! Why? *(Making faces in the mirror.)* You don't gotta home computer, do you?

HERMAN: Yes, I have Fortran A! *(Looking very snobbily at Johnny.)*

JOHNNY: Oh! *(Looking at him.)* So you're a smarty? All level 4 classes, right?

HERMAN: No *(Grinning with his braces showing.)*, I'm in two level 5 classes!

JOHNNY: Two level 5 classes. *(Mimicking Herman in a high voice.)* Ohhh! An extra brain! I bet you have biology, too?

HERMAN: Yes! *(His face lighting up.)* I've just dissected a sheep's heart! It was great! The chambers of the. . . .

JOHNNY: Please! *(Holding his stomach.)* My lunch! Speaking of lunch . . . . *(Looking at his watch.)* Ya made me miss lunch! *(Looking at Herman's face fall.)* It doesn't matter, I wasn't that hungry. *(Turns around and walks to the door, pauses, then turns to Herman.)* Herman, you'll have a good year. *(Johnny smiles and walks out, leaving Herman alone in the bathroom.)*

Dialog for Three or More

Set down in script form what three or more characters say to each other during one continuous scene running for 6-20 minutes that develops to some sort of climax. It's better to try this after doing Duolog at least once. If your script is for film, look at a film script for terms and directions indicating camera angles and actions. If for radio or audiotape, where visuals are missing, you might use "stage directions" to indicate how lines should be read. But rely for this mainly on the way lines are written and punctuated. If possible, have your script performed, filmed, or taped. A Reader's Theater presentation is often a simple and appropriate way to perform a script, for it depends essentially on voice and requires no memorization, costumes, or staging.

The Barbershop

SUSANNE WEISS

(A wall divided by a large sink. To one side is a rack of white towels. The bottom half of the wall is shelves of lotions, sprays, and lotions. The top half is a huge panel-type mirror.

In the middle stage there is one old barber chair. On left stage there are four regular chairs and 2 tables with magazines and newspapers.

There is no one on stage. Everything is dark.

Off right stage a sound of a door unlocking is heard, lights go on. Hank, a plump old man, balding, walks on stage. He is whistling "Dixie" to himself. He slowly takes off his coat and hat and puts on a white apron.

Jingling bells signal another person entering the building. The second person is another elderly man, Bill.)

BILL: Hi, Hank.

HANK: Mornin, Bill. In kinda early, ain't ya?

BILL: Yah, guess so. Had trouble sleeping again. (*Bill steps up into barber chair.*)

HANK: Rheumatitus?

BILL: Nah, Martha's curlers. I never see how that woman sleeps with them things. They bug the heck out of me.

(*Another man comes in, younger than the first two, but still retired.*)

HANK & BILL: Hey, Dave.

DAVE: Howdy, boys. Beaut of a morning, ain't it? Boy, I'll tell ya. I love Mondays. Used to hate 'em. But love 'em now. Don't have to go into that post office no more. I love it.

(*Dave walks over to one of the chairs and sits down, burying himself in a magazine.*)

DAVE: Hank, I hear you are only staying open half a day now. What are you going to do the rest of the day? Are you going back to the bank?

HANK: Nope. I think I'll take up fishing. I'm going to really be semi-retired. I'm tired of working all day. My bones are getting tired of standing around all the time.

BILL: Did you two see the old mystery column last night?

DAVE: No, anyone we know?

BILL: They said old Kirt Dugle got his number called. Heart attack.

HANK: Real shame. Kirt is . . . was . . . good boy.

DAVE: He was only 52 or so, wasn't he?

BILL: Yeah. Poor guy.

HANK: Why do you say that? At least his waiting is over.

BILL: Because, that new doc didn't let him go. He had to play hero and try all that new fangled equipment to keep Kirt going for a while.

(*Silence for a few minutes.*)

HANK: (*Quietly.*) Why don't they just let a man go?

DAVE: (*Looking at audience.*) Dag burn it. That rain is back! I knew it. I told my boy he'd better get his last load of hay in, but he said the TV man said it weren't going to rain again. Just 'cause I spent my time in a post office that kid doesn't think I know nothing.

BILL: Yeah, kids are always like that. Never listen.

(*The sound of the door bursting open is heard. A young man of about 20 walks in, drenched.*)

MAN: Uh, hi.

(*All three look at him really impressed.*)

HANK: Mornin, son. Take a seat. I'll get to you in a minute.

MAN: (*Nervously.*) Okay, I'll sit over here.

(Man walks over to a chair and sits down. He acts very fidgety.)

DAVE: Hank, how's that granddaughter of yours?

HANK: Sally's fine. Had herself a baby boy. Just what I need, another boy. Another boy to join in some city street gang, or shoot a cop or go to prison like James and Elroy. I'd like another pretty little girl once more.

BILL: Sally's a fine girl, real fine. I remember bouncing her on my knee.

(The man jumps up so fast that his chair falls.)

MAN: Look, I can't wait all day!

HANK: *(Gives man a withering look.)* Patience is a virtue, boy.

MAN: I don't have time for virtue, old man, I'm in a hurry. *(Man whips out a pistol.)*

MAN: I don't want a haircut, I want money.

HANK: *(Unimpressed.)* We all do, son.

MAN: *(Waving gun around.)* I ain't standing here all day waiting for you to finish that cut. Open the register and give me all the money.

BILL: What do you need money for? I hear it's easy for kids like you to get a loan at the bank.

MAN: It's none of your business about the money, just get it.

HANK: *(Still working on Bill.)* That gun loaded?

MAN: *(Yelling.)* Of course it's loaded, fool!

HANK: Well, I suppose you're right. But I remember once—at the bank I was a guard there—well, a man came in with a gun and he waved that piece around a bit also. Only the poor guy forgot to load it. Another time a young woman—disgraceful—came in with a sawed off shot gun. . . .

MAN: *(Interrupting.)* I don't care!

DAVE: Who taught you manners?

MAN: *(Obviously trying to keep control over himself.)* Look! This is a real gun with real bullets! If I don't get some action soon, I'm going to blow this place apart!

HANK: Well *(Looking around the stage.)*, it wouldn't take much to make this place come apart, it's even over half-way there now.

MAN: *(All control gone.)* I give up! You're all crazy old fools!
(Man runs out off stage. Door slams.)

BILL: No respect! I tell ya, kids just don't have any respect for their elders.

(Dave begins to read the paper again.)

BILL: That's the problem with this country. If more people had respect, the world would be a better place.

DAVE: Hank, think that young 'un would've used that pop-gun?

HANK: Oh, I dunno. Maybe. But I once learned, a long time ago, that it helps to shoot when the safety is off.

BILL: *(Laughing.)* And that kid called us fools?
DAVE: What about that woman?
HANK: What woman?
DAVE: The woman you said came into the bank.
HANK: Oh, her.
BILL: I don't remember that one.
HANK: Well, this real pretty young woman came in with a sawed-off
     shotgun and wearing a bikini swim suit.
DAVE: You're kidding?
HANK: Nope, she really did.
BILL: Did you talk with Jonathan the other day?

(Lights fade off gradually, with voices.)

Exterior Monolog

Create a character whose way of speaking you feel confident you can reproduce on paper. Imagine him or her telling something to another person in a certain place. Write down exactly what she or he says and nothing more except minimal stage directions to indicate setting and action. To be performed in a playing time of 2-5 minutes. Such a monolog calls for a situation in which one person is realistically holding forth for so long while the other or others merely listen and react without words. What you want to accomplish by this depends on how you see such a situation being used. Consider different media too. For a more challenging version of this task, write your script for pure voice—no visuals, no sound effects.

Now Hear This

JEANNETTE FLORES

Good Morning.
My name is Miss Applebee. I am your general biology teacher for this term. The topics we will be learning this term are reproduction, ecology, photosynthesis, etc. For notebooks, I would like a section in a looseleaf or spiral with only the work I'll distribute. I'll be checking notebooks at the end of every three months.

As soon as you come in, there will be a "Do Now" for you to do everyday. Now let's talk about your marks and how I'll be grading you: 1/3 tests, 1/3 participation, and 1/3 homework, which means if you miss six homework assignments, you'll fail automatically.

I don't like rude people. When I talk, you'll listen, but when you talk, we all will listen. But don't call out. You have a hand, so raise it. Monitors will be chosen tomorrow. I'll be assigning seats tomorrow also.

Absence, lateness, and cuts are your problem. If you're absent, bring a note to excuse yourself, but don't make it a habit. If you're late more than five times, you'll fail. If you cut, I will find out; you will get a cut card and be sent to Mr. Korn about that.

For now, we will be filling out these delaney cards. It will take me a week or two to remember your names. I hope we will get along very well so there won't be any problems this term.

Listen! My temper is as fast as a speeding bullet. So don't pull my trigger. See you tomorrow.

Lullaby

ANNE GETIS

Come on, Allen, your parents have left, it's time for you and me to have some great fun! *(Sitter goes over to child, takes the child's hand, which the child suddenly jerks away.)* What's bothering you? Didn't you kiss your Mommy goodnight? *(Stoops down to child.)* Well, its all right, you'll see her tomorrow when you wake up. Now, Allen, what would you like to do? *(Allen begins to cry again.)* What's wrong, Allen? Why are you crying again? Oh, please, Allen, stop crying. Don't you want to have fun tonight? *(Sitter goes over to bookshelf.)* Look Allen, here's *Big Bird* and look, oh wow, here's your favorite. *Cookey Monster!* *(Sitter goes back over to Allen.)* Allen, couldn't you stop that silly crying? If you don't I'll go and watch T.V. and leave you here. *(Sitter pretends to leave but then changes mood.)* Allen, if you stop crying you can have your dinner *and* watch T.V. You'd like that wouldn't you? Why don't you tell me what the matter is. *(To audience and kind of nervous.)* What will your parents say if you don't eat your supper? Why does this always happen to me? What will your parents think of me when they discover you've cried all night? They probably won't pay that much. . . . (Looks back at Allen.) Won't you at least say something, Allen? Oh, please, please stop crying! Most good kids don't cry all night and give their babysitter a rotten time. Don't you want to be a good kid? Well, I guess you don't care, huh? *(Goes over to Allen, who is now huddled on the bed.)* Now, please, dear sweet Allen, don't worry about Mommy and Daddy. They went out just for tonight. Don't worry. They'll be back very soon. In fact, as soon as you open those blue eyes of yours and those tears disappear, they will be back. *(Sitter stands up and looks at Allen's body on the bed.)* Did you hear me? Well, *(to audience)* believe it or not the kid is asleep! Now, only 6 more hours until your parents arrive. *(Covers Allen up.)* Sleep well, Allen.

Just Another Day

JESSICA WOLFF

Oh Sam, hello. (*She throws her arms around him.*) It's so nice to have someone waiting when I get home.

It has been the absolute worst day. As soon as I got to work I discovered a run in my stocking. The meeting with the boss turned out to be a reprimand rather than a raise, and Mabel stood me up for lunch. I feel like I don't have a friend in the world, except you, of course. Let's go into the kitchen so I can start dinner.

Anyway, to continue the story of my wonderful day, I brought the car in the morning for a 15,000 mile check-up, and when I went to pick it up they told me it needs about $600.00 of body work. Somehow the bottom of the car got all dented and rusted, and if it's not fixed soon the pieces will start falling out. I thought that was quite interesting. Hansel and Gretel left a trail of breadcrumbs and I'll end up leaving a trail of car parts! Oh, while this is cooking, follow me upstairs so I can change.

Where the hell am I going to find an extra $600.00? The rent is due next week, and I'm still making payments on that damn car! Don't give me that happy-go-lucky look. You've been no help in paying the bills!

Oh, Sam, I'm sorry. I am really truly sorry. It's been an awful day, and I'm a bundle of nerves. I have no right to vent my anger on you. You've been so patient, listening to all my problems. You're always there for me. You're the only one I can always count on. Sam, you mean the world to me. I love you so much.

(*Sam looks up with mournful eyes, licks her face, and slowly wags his tail.*)

Solid Quiet

KARL M. LARSEN

(*Enter a single man in dirty but not ragged clothes. He wears no shoes. The stage is brightly lit to simulate heat. The man carries a portable tape recorder. He walks to center stage, grips the tape recorder in both hands and presses the "on" button. He then speaks.*)

I am the only man to ever know the feeling of being truly alone. There must be some sort of built-in mechanism that tells a creature when it is the last of its kind. It's a kind of emptiness that opens up in the stomach and swallows the heart. Now I walk . . . alone. The silence roars in my ears. The incessant quiet is *too loud*! I wish for a noise, anything. *(Looks at the ground.)* But there is none, no wind, animals, water . . . nothing.

I can almost hear the sun. Hear the crackle of its flame and the splash of the heat released as its light pounds into the ground. I can almost hear it, almost *(Voice trembles with stress.)*. . . . But not quite. *(Kicks the earth, making no sound.)*

I can't even tell if I'm speaking or thinking. Either way, I'm making no sound. There is no one to hear me. If nothing hears me, then I must not be making any sound. Besides, if I made sound, there would be no silence *(Sits quietly.)*, but all I hear is silence, that constantly pounding silence echoing in my ears.

Do I even exist? The waves of quiet have submerged me from existence. I am in the realm of quiet where I may be a figment of my own imagination, or just a bit of sound smothered by stillness.

I have one hope. *(Begins to rewind tape while muttering.)* My last hope. . . *(Pushes play button and gets only silence.)*

Noooo, *(sobbing)* no, I am doomed. *(Leaves quietly whispering.)* I am doomed!

Maggie's Lesson

MICHELLE SULLIVAN-McDERMID

(The setting is a college dorm room; Maggie is talking with her roommate.)

I remember. . . . Daddy would come home at six o'clock sharp each day after work. He was a doctor, ya know. I used to wait and listen for him. I'd hear the latch on our gate click and then he'd tramp up the driveway, and the gravel would crunch under his squeaky leather loafers. *(She smiles.)* I'd run out in my nightgown, and he'd gather me up and squeeze me real tight. Then we'd race to the kitchen and wolf up Momma's supper. After, Daddy would sit back in his scratchy green chair and perch me on his knee and tell me stories about being a doctor—how he stitched up some boy's chin and fixed some old lady's broken leg. *(Maggie sighs.)* Oh, how I envied him. He seemed so. . . so stable and strong. I used to tell him that I was gonna grow up to be like him. He'd grin at me all proud—and then roll back in his green chair and let out a real hard belly laugh. . . *(Maggie smiles, remembering.)* He said I could be *anything* if I wanted it bad enough. . . .

Once Momma got real annoyed at the way me and Daddy were talkin'—she had a funny habit of twitching her eyes when she was worried about something. She whispered low and harsh to Daddy, *(Maggie imitates her mother.)* "Don't be placing ideas in Maggie's head." Then she reached out her warm broad hands and wrapped them in mine—I'll never forget what she said. "Rosebud," she whispered.

(Rosebud was her special nick-name for me.) *(Maggie acts like her mother.)* Rosebud, you must learn that you aren't ever gonna be a doctor like your Daddy. Nice girls don't need to worry their heads about fancy jobs or money 'cause there will always be a man who will do it for them." *(Maggie sighs.)* Well, Daddy didn't say nothing, but he winked at me and I knew. *(She shakes her head sadly.)* I'll sure tell you one thing: she was DEAD wrong! *(Maggie pauses, then sinks slowly into her chair.)*

Five years later, I graduated from North Hampton High, and they divorced. Daddy went away, and Momma—she couldn't bear it. She had nothing. No friends, no job, no money. She was so afraid—like a frightened little girl who has lost her parents at the circus. *(Maggie begins to cry softly.)* Later, Daddy called me—he said he would pay for me to go to Wellington College. I couldn't wait to get away from my mother. I wanted to help her—I really did—but I was scared, too. *(She lowers her head, ashamed.)*

I had always thought I'd marry a strong, ambitious man like Daddy—but not after watching Momma struggle like that. She went from a mother and wife in a decent, comfortable home to working as a waitress and living in one of those small, musty apartments on the east side. Oh . . . she survived all right—but it changed her. She became bitter. Momma was like a living dead person. *(Maggie shudders, then shakes her head as if to rid the thought from her head.)*

I vowed that I'd do everything possible to live my life differently from mother. I made a firm decision that I was never gonna depend on anyone—not for love or money. I learned a lot from Momma—not what she meant to teach me, though. I guess that's why I'm here.

Interior Monolog

Make up a character whose way of thinking and speaking you feel confident of reproducing. Imagine him or her some-where in particular doing something in particular. Write down what this person is thinking and feeling during this time in the exact words the character would be thinking in. Use interior monolog for what you think it can best do. To be performed in a playing time of 3-5 minutes. What medium would be best for your script? Write directions accordingly. Or write the script totally without any directions at all.

First Day

KELLY CARRAHER

I can't go through with this. It's bad enough going to a new school but having to explain about my cancer all over again is going to be terrible. I think I'm going to be sick. Maybe I'll just go home. Oh no! Here comes that lady from the attendance office with her "I'm so sorry" type of smile. A crowd full of inquisitive teenagers is better than her. Well, here goes.

Oh boy! There's more people in here than I thought. Where's the teacher? There she is. Another one with that smile. Please God! Don't make her introduce me in front of all these people. No! Just let me sit down before I barf. Thank God!

Oh great! Wouldn't you know she'd sit me by the class clown. If he touches my hat I'll just die! Wait, where'd the teacher go? Hey leave my hat alone. God no!

You First

KAREN ROGGE

In his eyes I can see him closing the pathways to his feelings. "What's wrong?" Should I tell him I like and care for him and want to talk over things? yes. . . No. . . .I should . . . . but I can't. Like him, I don't want to expose my feelings too much; that's how people get the upper hand on you. If someone sees too much, you're at their mercy. Take a chance . . . but remember last time? No! Don't dwell on the past; that's how you withdraw into yourself, turning into one of society's zombies!

"Talk to me, or at least meet me halfway. Look, I'll tell you how I feel, then you say how you feel!" That's what I'll say. No . . . I can't, what if he just laughs and says, "You gotta be kidding!" No, he won't, he's a good friend. Oh, why couldn't he be a girl, it would make things a lot easier. There are things you just don't say to a boy, even though you're great friends. I can change things. O.K. just say what you want and if he laughs, well hey, maybe he wasn't as good a friend as you thought. But he's nice, and I really like him, I just don't want to say something that could end our friendship. Then, I guess I'm back to where I started, the pathways to our feelings are slowly being closed.

The Portrait

FRANCINE DOLINS

I shall sit here quietly. Why does this man have to stare so? I did not want my portrait painted. Especially by such a scandalous person as Goya. I told Señor Garcia that I would pose for Goya, but I did not wish to. Garcia just laughed (or at his age it was more like cackling) and bid me do as he pleased. And because I am a good wife, and I was brought up properly, I must do as he says.

Well, I will ignore Señor Goya as much as possible. I will never care for this stupid portrait.

When I get home today I will be as cold as I can to my husband. He will see what happens when he ignores his wife's wishes. Why Mama wanted me to marry this old goat I'll never know! He is so old; he falls asleep at the table. When the Queen's nephew dined with us, Garcia fell snoring into his fruitbowl! Ah, to be attached to such a man!

Before I was married, I had many suitors. Some of them were well-to-do, but Mama would have me marry the richest—and the oldest! Ah, well. Maybe he will die soon.

If he should die within the year (I could probably see to that), I can mourn for a few months and then get married again. This time to someone of my own choice.

Could I really kill him? I wonder what kind of picture Goya would paint of me if he knew what I was thinking. Probably something with horns! Ha! I could no more kill Garcia than I could kill a spider!

Anna is coming to tea later on. She should put me in a good mood; she always does. After she leaves I will go out to the garden (that is if Señor Garcia doesn't see me. He always wants to discuss his stupid business. What do I care about banking!) and sketch the sunset. I can never make it quite as beautiful as I see it.

We are having company for dinner tonight. Who is it again?

What a waste of time it is to sit here for this Señor Goya. Such a funny-looking man. His fat face all puffy and pink. Rather more like a bottom than a face! Oh, I must tell Anna that one.

"What? . . . Oh yes, I'll keep my hands folded. Very sorry, Señor Goya."

Silly man. Now where was I? Oh yes, my brother and his wife are coming to dinner tonight. I shall wear my red dress. I hope that Garcia doesn't dribble food into his beard. It is so revolting to eat with him. Such an old goat he is!

Yes. I shall definitely sketch the sunset tonight. I imagine this strange painter here could do a wonderful sunset.

"Señor Goya, do you do sunsets? . . . What? . . . Oh, you're finished? . . . Yes, I like it. It's very nice. Good day, señor."

Monday Night Blues

DEAN CHISIN

It's freezing out here! Why couldn't they have an indoor spa? Who's going to come out here on a night like this? I had to come tonight of all nights. I'm missing Monday Night Football. Well, if no one shows up I can catch the fourth quarter. I might not even have to get wet. I can't stand out here forever though. I'll step inside onto the soft, warm carpet of the hallway. Oops! Someone's heading this way. . . . Back onto the cold cement of the pool area. One leap and I'm standing on the wooden deck of the hot tub. A little better. . . . Whoa! What are they trying to do here, kill people? Maybe I'll report the capital neglect of the club's maintenance men who left this deck so slippery. How does this cover come off? Oh darn, I've torn it! Him . . . it doesn't look torn. Ah! It's in two halves. O.K.

Phew! These people are criminals. Why did they make the water so hot? Now . . . it's either exposure or be boiled to death. Put your right foot in . . . ouch! Take your right foot out. Do the hokey pokey and turn yourself about. . . . That's a silly song. All right. Slowly, slowly. What was it that I read about medieval torturing devices based on hot water? They must have been really effective. But this isn't even that hot. No bubbles! What's wrong with this dump? No matter. I'll make myself comfortable. There. This will be my vantage point. And now one last thing—the invisibility potion. Aahh!

Ta-ta! The door bursts open and a man walks through with a can of Gatorade in his hand. The guy must have swallowed a tire. Yeah, that's it. There are radial tracks on his abdomen. A second guy follows the first, and a third brings up the rear. Estimated ages: mid-twenties. The last two have two bottles of Coors light apiece.

Number two is speaking: "That was one hell of a workout. Benched two-fifty."

Number three, with a deep sigh: "Yeah."

"What's the matter?" Number one is climbing into the tub. "Come on in, guys."

"How's the water, Mark?"

"Nice, really nice. Feels good."

Number two: "Come on, what's wrong with you? Are you in love or something?"

"Did you see her, Jay? Those eyes. . . ."

"That ass! Forget about her. She's divorced with two kids, Butch."

"I don't care."

"Little brother, you're a fool!" Jay steps in, then lowers himself into a squatting position. He sets a beer on the rim, opens the other, cocks his head and guzzles. Five seconds later he sets the empty bottle on the rim and lets out a loud burp. "Haven't lost the touch yet," he exclaims. "Why are you drinking Gatorade, Mark?"

"Why shouldn't I? I'm thirsty."

"Yeah, you're just a lightweight."

"You're the one with the beerbelly?" Butch slips in without a splash. He's the only one with a relatively flat stomach. It's getting crowded in here. I wonder what time it is. It would be so nice and peaceful if these imbeciles weren't here. I feel relaxed, the stars are out—perfect! O.K., so my butt's a little sore. I guess this is as lively as it's going to get on a Monday night. Listen to their stimulating conversation. . . . Weight gained, weight lost, weight lifted. How exciting! I'm so impressed. Oh, they're alumni of my high school. They've stayed in town this whole time? Funny, I can't picture myself living in Fairfield after graduating from high school. I want to go on to bigger and better things. Why don't they? Maybe this is good enough, big enough for them. Maybe they like it here. Maybe this is their idea of a good life. Or maybe, just maybe they haven't gotten over the high-school student stage yet.

What will I be doing eight years after graduation? Where will I be? Maybe I'll be right here with a beer in my hand and a potbelly to boot. Who knows what the future holds in store?

One-Act Play

Write a script of several scenes that would take 20-30 minutes to perform and that would place several characters in different combinations. If this is to be a stage or film script, keep the number of scenes and characters low and the staging feasible so that it might actually be performed or filmed locally. Imagine some characters and events at least somewhat like the kind of people you have had chances to observe in real life. What you want to show, or what you want to do to the audience, is up to you. This script might be an occasion to combine Duolog, Exterior Monolog, and Interior Monolog with the dynamics of more crowded scenes. This might also lend itself to a radio play or a film script for animation.

Making Adjustments
(A Film Script)

PAT HOPKINS

Scott Billings	Tom Sandford
Scott's Mother	Mainerd Thompson
Tim Hauser	Students
History teacher	Pat Schmidt
Tom Anderson	Loraine Schmidt (Pat's daughter)

(At rise of curtain a room of students is listening to a history lecture. Note Scott Billings, sitting at the front left corner of the first row, not a very graceful kid, has pimples, a prominent nose, and short-cropped hair.)

TEACHER: Okay, Class, listen up. *(A touch exasperated.)* I'm trying to review tomorrow's test. What was one of the leading causes of America entering WW II against Germany?

(The class sits bored, except for Scott, who raises his hand.)

TEACHER: Scott?

SCOTT: Some people think it was the sinking of the Lusitania, but it was really the economic interests that U.S. businessmen and the government had in Europe.

TEACHER: Very good.

TEACHER: *(Talking in dead silence except for the noise of a fly buzzing in the room and the hum of traffic floating through an open window.)* True or false. Japan signed a nonaggression pact with Germany.

(Waits for an answer; Scott raises his hand.)

TEACHER: Yes, Scott?

SCOTT: True.

TEACHER: Very good. One last question, and then I'll let you go. True or false: Von Braun defected from Germany. . . . *(In the middle of his question the bell rings, and everyone gets up and walks out.)* Don't forget the test! It's a double grade! *(Calling out the door at his disappearing students.)*

Scene changes to a two-story house painted white and set back off the road with well cared for rose bushes lining both sides of the driveway. A school bus is stopped out front. Scott steps off the bus and walks to the mail box. Tim Hauser sticks his head out the window.)

TIM: Don't study too hard, Tubbs. *(Spits a stream of brown tobacco juice juice at Scott. It hits the top of the mail box. Scott stares at the beaded tobacco juice on the top of the white mailbox, then turns and walks slowly up the driveway, carrying the mail and an armload of books. The family dog comes out and nips at his feet, following him up the driveway, but Scott pays no attention.)*

(The inside of the house. He tosses the mail down on a writing desk.)

SCOTT: *(In a flat voice.)* I'm home, Mom.

MOM: *(Calling out from the kitchen where she is kneading bread dough.)* Pat called today. She wanted to know if you were going on that backpacking trip with the class at church this weekend.

SCOTT: *(A bit irritated.)* Did she call you or did you call her? *(When his mother doesn't answer Scott continues.)* I wish you'd stop messing around in my personal life. I don't want to go.

(He runs up the stairs and slams the door to his room. At the sound of the door slamming, the scene changes to the kitchen, where his mother sighs and stands with a troubled look on her face, her hands still buried in bread dough.)

(Scott in his bedroom. On the walls hang posters of the space shuttle, and other craft like Voyager; also drawings of different planets. Beneath a window sits a desk with an Apple IIe home computer. He drops his books down on his bed and sits at the desk and turns the computer on. He sits staring for a moment at the green blinking cursor in the upper left of the screen, then he slowly turns it off and opens his desk drawer and takes out a photo album and starts flipping through it. He stops and looks at one page; the camera comes in for a close up; and it turns out to be a picture of two identical twins dressed in little suits blowing out the candles of a birthday cake. His mother's voice interrupts his thoughts.)

MOM: Scott! Supper's ready!

SCOTT: *(Loudly.)* All right.

(He closes the album, puts it in his desk drawer, and exits the room.)

(At the dinner table in the dining room, Scott sits eating his supper moodily. His mother also sits eating quietly.)

MOM: Scott?

SCOTT: Yeah, what?

MOM: *(A note of sadness in her voice.)* Scott, why don't you go?

SCOTT: *(Voice full of tension.)* You know why.

MOM: What you and your brother did was common for identical twins to do. You can't lock yourself away from people because of it. *(She pauses, her voice grows softer.)* Remember how much fun you and your brother and your father used to have when you went out on those weeklong hikes? *(Her voice grows brighter.)* I remember the time you came home covered from head to foot with bee stings because you found a nest in an old tree and wanted some honey.

SCOTT: *(Smiling faintly.)* Yeah, I remember.

MOM: *(Reaching across the table, she rests her hand on his arm.)* Won't you go? It'll do you good. Even if they are no longer here they would want you to go on living life to it's fullest.

(At the mention of the word "others" Scott's face drops back into a mask of blankness; he hurriedly rises from the table and rushes upstairs. His mother sits quietly for a moment, her face flushed and pained.)

MOM: *(Turns her head to a portrait on the wall and starts speaking softly.)* Andy, what am I to do? You thought you were going with Scott, but it was Bill, Andy. *(Her voice starts to break.)* Andy, what happened? Where are you? *(She sits, tears rolling down her face. After what seems like hours she gets up and clears the table. The quiet of the big house makes everything feel sad and alone. Her face is still screwed up as if crying, but no tears flow. Her steps seem heavy. In the light streaming through the kitchen door she looks very old.)*

(Scott's mom is now in bed. She lies still on her side of the bed, not disturbing the covers on the other side. She stares at a wedding picture and waits quietly for the morning.)

(The hall outside Scott's room. Light pours from beneath the door; inside muted sounds can be heard. Camera slowly fades out with the light at the bottom of the door being the last thing to disappear.)

(Hallway scene at school, which is replaced abruptly by a bunch of students crowding through the history room as the tardy bell rings.)

TEACHER: *(Loud.)* Quiet down, quiet down. *(This has no effect, so he takes a yard stick and cracks it down on his desk sharply. Voice now controlled, he holds in his hands a stack of paper.)* You have until the end of the period. If anyone talks or looks around during the test his paper will be torn up, it will be a double grade. Good luck. *(Passes out papers.)*

(Same room but later. Scott has finished his test and sits reading a book. Tim Hauser gets up carrying a broken pen and his test and walks by Scott's desk. He reaches and wipes the pen across the page of Scott's book, leaving a thick trail of ink.)

(A crowded hall between classes. Lorainne Schmidt walks up to Scott at his locker).

LORAINNE: I saw what Tim did.

SCOTT: *(Voice expressionless.)* So?

LORAINNE: *(Nervously.)* I—I just—I just wanted to say that I don't care for what Tim does either. *(Lapses into a nervous silence.)*

SCOTT: *(Still in the same even tone.)* I really don't much care what anyone does any more.

LORAINNE: *(Switching the subject, her voice more controlled.)* We're having a backpacking trip this weekend. We'd like to have you; all you have to bring is yourself and a change of clothes and a sleeping bag. *(The last sentence was more like a question.)*

SCOTT: I'll think about it. *(He turns at a door to enter but before he does does he turns back and calls after Lorainne.)* Thanks for the invitation.

LORAINNE: *(Cheerfully.)* Sure.

(Scott turns and enters the room of his Computer Programming class. He walks up and sits down in the front row with his lab partner Mainerd Thompson.)

MAINERD: *(Relaxed tone.)* Get Program #7 done?

SCOTT: *(Also relaxed.)* Yeah, here it is. *(Hands a print-out to Mainerd.)*

MAINERD: *(A bit enviously.)* How can you do these so easily?

SCOTT: *(A touch of pride.)* I got plenty of time, that's all.

(Changes to Scott's home. Scott is still at school. Scott's mom sits in an easy chair talking on the phone.)

MOM: It's been two years since Andy and Bill left. Scott blames himself for it. *(After a pause.)* I've told him that many a time. *(Voice grows heavy.)* I'm worried about him. Would you call him and talk to him, please? *(After a pause.)* Thank you.

(Scott is walking home from school. A car pulls up beside him and stops. In it are Tim Hauser, Tom Anderson, and (in the driver's seat) Tom Sanford.)

TIM: *(With a smile on his face.)* Hop in, we'll take you home. *(Scott looks looks doubtful.)* I was just kidding in history. *(Scott says nothing but climbs in. The car drives away; music from the car stereo grows fainter.)*

(Inside the car Scott sits between Anderson and Hauser. Anderson slowly slips open Scott's computer class notebook and removes a sheet with some coding on it.)

(The car with Scott in it pulls up in front of Scott's house. Scott climbs out of the car but turns around to talk to Anderson.)

SCOTT: They changed the code words on the computer files with the history test scores in them. Those code words you took are useless. *(Turns and walks up the driveway. Tom Sanford tears down the road, angrily accelerating the car.)*

(Inside the house. Scott drops his books down on the table in the living room.)

SCOTT: *(Loudly.)* Mom, I'm home.

SCOTT: *(Starts heading up the stairs to his room. The telephone jingles. Scott stops and walks to the phone and answers it.)* Hello. *(Pause.)* Oh, Pat. *(Another pause in which the scene changes to Pat's house; she is sitting at the kitchen table. When Scott next speaks the scene will change to his house then to Pat then to him, and so on.)*

PAT: (*Cheerfully.*) Just called to get a definite answer about that trip. (*Pause.*) You won't? Why not? (*Pause.*) I can probably guess. You used to go on every outing we had (*Her voice grows uneasy, hesitant.*) until that happened.

SCOTT: (*Voice is hard.*) It's really none of your business, you know.

PAT: (*Voice is calm, even soft.*) Yes it is, because I hate to see a person throw their life away. If it had been your brother that stayed home what would you say if he were doing what you are? (*Voice is calm.*) Call me if you decide to go, Scott. Bye.

(*Scott slowly puts down the receiver and walks upstairs to his room. Again he has out the photo album, but he looks at a different picture this time. It is a picture of Scott sitting in a marsh boat. By the boat a duck and some babies can be seen. There is also another picture of Bill and Scott sitting in an old eagle's nest.*)

SCOTT: (*Whispers.*) That was some fun, wasn't it, Bill? (*He sits for some time looking out the window, lost in thought. Outside the window the sun has dropped low; it looks like a giant red bubble with the dark shapes of houses and telephone wires etched on it. He has a half smile on his face as he sits thinking. After a while he gets up and lies down on the bed, still looking out the window. Eventually he falls asleep and dreams about rivers and eagles, as we see.*)

(*Scott's dream: he stands at the top of a high cliff and looks down through binoculars at an eagle's nest. In it are two babies. One is near the edge of the nest when the mother comes back with a mutilated jackrabbit, but the other baby rushes to the edge and falls out. The mother screeches for a bit, then settles down to feeding her baby. Scott now finds himself laying on a bank by the river. It is early afternoon and Scott is looking at two bugs. One disappears, and the other continues swimming. Scott awakes abruptly; it is night out. His window is open, and a cool night breeze blows through it, carrying the sound of insects and frogs. He lies and listens, deep in thought. He finally gets up and slowly turns off the light, opens the door, and closes it behind him, leaving the room completely black. The night sounds slowly fade out.*)

(*Scott is walking through the front room towards the door.*)

MOM: Scott, where are you going?

SCOTT: (*Door open, he stands just outside.*) Out to the garage to dig out my back pack. (*He closes the door and stands, savoring the cool night air. He looks up at the star-filled sky and smiles. He then walks around the corner of the house. Lights slowly fade, but the night sounds linger on past the visual.*)

Connections

SONYA SOBIESKI

Scene 1

(Present time. The house of Sharon Green. The front door of the house is centered in the back of the set. A sofa and assorted chairs and tables denote a living room center stage. There is an open kitchen downstage right and a door leading to a hall stage left.

Through the front door enter Sharon and her two children, Keith and Emilie, and her best friend, Christine. Sharon and Chris are both in their thirties and attractive. Keith is fifteen or sixteen, and Emilie is around eight years old. They are all laughing as they come in.)

SHARON: That was so much fun! Here, hang up your coat, Emilie.

CHRIS: The best part was on the way home when we saw that—

KEITH: No, no *(To Chris.)*—the funniest thing was the waiter tripping over your coat and asking you to please not throw your clothes on the floor. And you said, "Why not? I always do at home." *(He starts laughing again and the others follow; it is their own joke.)*

CHRIS: Wasn't the look on his face incredible?

SHARON: Actually, Chris, I wish you hadn't done that, because he didn't serve us one right dish the entire night! Do you realize that we got nothing we ordered? He was definitely out to get us.

CHRIS: I did feel pretty bad about being rude to him, especially after I got my food. Blueberry-cucumber chicken—can you believe it?

EMILIE: It wasn't all that awful. I kind of liked it. *(They laugh again and Sharon hugs her. Keith begins to exit stage left, still with his coat.)*

CHRIS: Ahem, Keith. You forgot to hang up your coat. *(With a great flourish, Keith tosses his coat onto the floor.)*

KEITH: But why should I? I always throw it on the floor! *(Sharon and Emilie laugh.)*

CHRIS: I asked for it, didn't I? Sharon, why did I even say anything? Will I ever learn?

SHARON: Don't worry, Chris—you've got a while to.

KEITH: Oh, Mom, I told Josh I'd call him when I got home, so I'll be in my room.

SHARON: All right.

CHRIS: Isn't it a bit late?

KEITH: Not for Josh. *(Exits stage left.)*

SHARON: Looks like the party's breaking up. *(To Emilie)* And it's getting late for *you*. How about going and getting ready for bed?

EMILIE: Wish there was somebody *I* could call. *(Exits left.)*

SHARON: Let's have something to drink. *(They cross to kitchen.)* Chocolate milk?

CHRIS: Sharon, when haven't I come home with you and had chocolate milk? Just name a time.

SHARON: I seem to recall one particular evening when we were in high school when we got home at—was it 3:30?—and I don't remember that we were thinking much of food.

CHRIS: You mean—? Oh, no, don't bring that back again! I—*(Keith enters. Sharon and Chris adopt "adult" expressions but have a difficult time trying to stop laughing.)*

KEITH: Mom, I'm going over to Josh's. Mike and Andrew are down there, too. *(Begins to get coat.)*

SHARON: Wait a minute. You can't just waltz off like that. How about asking?

KEITH: We're not going to do anything! It's Saturday and it isn't even eleven!

SHARON: I'd appreciate some planning, Keith. You are part of a family of which I am the head. Check with me before agreeing to go out with your buddies, all right?

KEITH: *(A little annoyed.)* Are you letting me go or not?

SHARON: I don't suppose there's any way I could keep you from going without a huge fight, is there? Go on—you know when to be back.

KEITH: *(Gets coat, heads to the door.)* Thanks, Mom! See ya, Chris! *(Exits center.)*

SHARON: *(Pause.)* Sometimes he gets so—oh, I don't know.

CHRIS: Teenagers are like that, I guess.

SHARON: It's not only the age—it's other things too.

CHRIS: Other things? Like what?

SHARON: You know he's not doing as well in school as I think he'd like to. That upsets him, but he tries not to show it. None of his friends are really great achievers. They're smart, but they don't try. I don't want him to become like that, but there isn't a lot I can do, besides encourage him.

CHRIS: Lots of peer pressure?

SHARON: Goes with the territory. Thank God he isn't into drugs, and, well, I don't think he'll ever smoke. *(Silence.)* He was old enough when his father died to know what caused it. That probably has a little to do with it—no father and everything.

CHRIS: There's nothing wrong with the way you raised him, Sharon, even if it was by yourself. Neither of them has missed anything in life.

SHARON: Except a father. That means so much.

CHRIS: But you've been both a mother *and* a father to them.

SHARON: No. You can't ever be both. *(Emilie enters.)* You ready to go to sleep, hon?

EMILIE: Yeah. But I wanted to say goodbye to Christine first.

CHRIS: *(Crosses to hug her.)* Great! Let's see, I think I'll see you all—oh, sometimes this week, isn't it, Sharon?

SHARON: Probably. Although you and I are having lunch on Tuesday for sure.

CHRIS: Terrific! Then I'll see you soon, Emilie.

SHARON: *(Has crossed to Emilie.)* Come on, let's go, Em! *(They exit left.)*

CHRIS: Goodnight!

EMILIE: *(From backstage.)* 'Night! *(Chris crosses back to kitchen counter; Sharon returns and comes up next to her.)*

CHRIS: Emilie seems to be doing pretty well.

SHARON: Oh, she is.

CHRIS: And Keith is too! Sharon, they're doing great! They've got you. They don't need anyone else!

SHARON: Thanks, Chris. But what if something happens to me?

CHRIS: It *won't.*

SHARON: It might. I can't overlook possibilities, Chris. And what then? Did you know the kids' closest relatives are third or fourth cousins, removed or something, on Jim's family's side? They're strangers. Without me, who would they have?

CHRIS: Me. You know that! What did you ask for?

SHARON: I wanted to make sure.

CHRIS: Hell. What's the matter?

SHARON: I've been making my will out. Christine—the kids' legal guardians—I don't want to leave them with people I don't know.

CHRIS: You were thinking of me? Oh my god, I'd love to! I would have offered, only I wasn't family—.

SHARON: Don't be ridiculous! I had to say something to you about it, even though it wasn't in terribly good taste. I mean, these are my children we're dealing with!

CHRIS: Oh my god, you're right. Your children. I can't do this. I'm not a mother. Here we are talking about how hard it is to raise children with only one parent, and I haven't got a husband either!

SHARON: Oh, I don't think it'll always be that way.

CHRIS: I think it just might, Sharon.

SHARON: Just because it didn't work out with Brian—.

CHRIS: That's not just it. I am the way I am and that happens to be single. And there's nothing wrong with it. *(Not defensive, just matter-of-fact.)*

SHARON: I know that. I am too, you know. And if I can be a single parent, so can you.

CHRIS: Oh, no. You always were more patient than I was.

SHARON: Christine—.

CHRIS: Yes, yes! Are you kidding? I'd be honored to be your kids' godmother. Godmother—weird term, isn't it? Sounds like something out of a fairy tale. It is—but I'm not. It's a lot of responsibility, but I want to take it. You know I'd do anything for you.

SHARON: This is a big anything.

CHRIS: I realize that. But I want to do it. For you, for them. It's hard for me to say exactly what I feel. But I love them. You know that.

SHARON: I know. That's why I asked you.

CHRIS: You knew what I'd say.

CHRIS: I knew what you'd say. *(They hug and toast with their glasses.)* Hey, there's a horror movie on television tonight. Vincent Price. Let's watch it!

CHRIS: That would be wonderful! *(Looks at her friend.)* Really.

Scene 2

(A few months later. The Greens' house, as before. The scene is darker now, in spite of the many bunches of flowers in different places in the rooms. It is strangely quiet.

Christine is sitting on the couch. Keith is in a chair with Emilie beside him.)

KEITH: They're all gone. Finally. Why did they have to come here anyway? *(He is talking to no one in particular.)* Why couldn't they have left us alone?

CHRIS: *(She is also talking without looking at anyone.)* They were doing doing what they thought they were supposed to do. They didn't even like it any better than we did. After a while, you get used to everyone saying how sorry they are. You learn to just nod and not even bother hearing what they say.

KEITH: I heard what they said, but I didn't care. I wish they had just gone home after it—after the funeral. I don't see why we had it anyway. That big ceremony. Funerals are a big waste of time.

EMILIE: They're so you can say goodbye—.

KEITH: The person's dead. He can't hear you. She can't hear you. She's dead. *(He gets up and walks across the room. Emilie follows.)*

CHRIS: They're a way of accepting that the person's gone. Getting used to never seeing them again—.

EMILIE: I'll never get used to it.

CHRIS: —paying your respects.

KEITH: But she can't hear! She's dead. Mom's dead.

EMILIE: She can't be.

KEITH: She is.

EMILIE: *(Holds onto him.)* But I don't want her to be!

KEITH: *(Hugs her.)* Nobody does, Em. *(Stands up straight.)* That doesn't seems to matter much, though. *(Looks around.)* All these flowers. I've got to get out of here. I'm going to my room. *(Exits left, Emilie begins to follow him but realizes she isn't welcome and stops.)*

CHRIS: Come here, Emilie. Sit down. *(Emilie crosses to couch, sits at other end.)* You okay?

EMILIE: *(Shrugs, then a pause.)* I'll never get used to it.

CHRIS: I don't know if I will either.

EMILIE: I keep thinking she's going to walk right in that door.

CHRIS: I do too.

EMILIE: But she won't, will she?

CHRIS: No, she won't.

EMILIE: It doesn't seem real.

CHRIS: Maybe because it happened so suddenly—*(She stops.)*

EMILIE: We had a cat that got hit by a car. It was a long time ago. I was a little girl. Mom told me that the same thing could happen to me and that I should always be careful of the street, of cars. *(Tearful.)* Then—why wasn't she careful?

CHRIS: Oh, she was, Emilie! Or, maybe she wasn't. I don't know. We can't think about it forever. As they say, you have to go on.

EMILIE: Go on? But how? I haven't got a family any more. You can't have a family without a mother. Can you?

CHRIS: It's a different family. That's all. It's you, Keith, and me. We'll make it.

EMILIE: You're going to stay with us from now on?

CHRIS: Well, we're going to have to move to my apartment later, but yes, I'm your guardian now.

EMILIE: Is that like a mother?

CHRIS: Yes, it is like that. But you know I can never take your mother's place.

EMILIE: You're going to be our—guardian—for how long? Until I grow up?

CHRIS: That's what I'm hoping.

EMILIE: Hoping?

CHRIS: *(Seems to change the subject.)* You met a lot of people today. There were two of your cousins from out west. Do you remember meeting them? Jenny and Robert Thomas?

EMILIE: Yeah, I guess I remember them.

CHRIS: What did you think of them?

EMILIE: *(Shrugs.)* I don't know. They were okay, I guess. Pretty nice. But everyone was trying to be nice. Why?

CHRIS: As far as I know, they're your closest relatives. I think they were here to check me out. They might feel that because they are related to you, and I'm not, they should be your guardians and I shouldn't.

EMILIE: But we don't even know them!

CHRIS: Sometimes that doesn't matter. Maybe they feel they were slighted in some way. They might go into some sort of legal battle. I think they're going to try and prove me an unfit guardian.

EMILIE: Unfit? Why?

CHRIS: Well, I'm not home a lot of the time. And I suppose some of it has to do with the fact that I'm single—that I haven't got a husband.

EMILIE: Why not?

CHRIS: Why haven't I got a husband? *(Puzzled chuckle.)* That's just the way it's turned out.

EMILIE: A little while ago, there was some guy you came here with a lot.

CHRIS: Yes. That was Brian.

EMILIE: How come he's never here any more?

CHRIS: Because I don't see him any more.

EMILIE: Why don't you?

CHRIS: I decided that we weren't—right for each other.

EMILIE: Were you going to get married?

CHRIS: Yes, we were.

EMILIE: Why didn't you?

CHRIS: I decided that I really didn't want to get married at all right then. I don't need a husband to live my life—I do fine the way I am. And I came to the conclusion that if I *were* to get married, I certainly wouldn't marry Brian.

EMILIE: What was wrong with him?

CHRIS: *(Humorless chuckle.)* Wrong? His attitude—his condescending attitude. He thought that I couldn't live without him, but I could. He refused to see that. He said that no woman could live without a man. I had to prove him wrong.

EMILIE: So you didn't marry him?

CHRIS: No. *(From offstage left, loud music is heard. Chris is annoyed; this is more than she can take.)* Keith, do you mind? Turn that down! Or better yet, off! *(The music stops, a door slams.)*

KEITH: *(Comes out in a rush. He is concerned about everything kids his age age are supposed to be concerned about, but also more, which is sometimes difficult for him to deal with.)* Listen, I'll just leave, all right?

CHRIS: Hey, I only asked you to turn your music down—.

KEITH: No, no. I'm not upset about that, really. I just need some air. I suppose you're staying the night again?

CHRIS: Yes, Keith. Keith, you knew I was going to be your guardian.

KEITH: I knew. But I never thought I would have to worry about it. When are you going to bring all of your stuff here?

CHRIS: We have to move to my apartment soon.

KEITH: What?

CHRIS: We can't stay here. You know that. You have to come live with me. The lawyers say—.

KEITH: You can't just transplant us! This is *our* house!

CHRIS: You'll still be in the same neighborhood!

KEITH: I don't want to think about it right now. *(Gets coat.)*

CHRIS: Where are you going?

KEITH: I'm just going to take a walk. I don't know where. Just around.

EMILIE: *(Stands up.)* Can I go with you, Keith?

KEITH: No, Emilie. I think I want to be by myself. *(Exits center.)*

Scene 3

(Some weeks later. Christine's apartment. The door of her apartment is in the back of the set, slightly stage right. The stage is Christine's living room. The furnishings are slightly more modern than the Greens'. An entrance to a hallway is stage left.

Emilie is sitting, reading. Christine is looking through some papers when Keith enters through the door.)

CHRIS: Hi, Keith. Nice of you to show this morning. How are you?

KEITH: Fine.

CHRIS: Your timing's perfect. Now you can stay with Emilie while I go down and talk to the building manager for a few minutes. I'll be back soon, okay? *(Exits door.)*

KEITH: Hi, Em. How are ya?

EMILIE: I'm all right. I don't see much of you any more.

KEITH: I know. I'll make it up to you soon, I promise. I'm just trying to work things out for myself. You been feeling okay?

EMILIE: I don't know how I've been feeling. Kind of lonely.

KEITH: Me too. And I'm sorry. I really should stick around here. It's been difficult for me.

EMILIE: It's hard for me too, Keith. And for Christine.

KEITH: Yeah. I'm sure it is. How are things at school?

EMILIE: *(Shrugs.)* I don't know. *(Brightens.)* Timmy Hoffman keeps getting in trouble for standing in front of Mrs. Ryan's desk and turning his eyelids inside out.

KEITH: Really? That's one weird kid. Have *you* been getting into any trouble, huh? *(Teasing and tickling her.)*

EMILIE: *(Smiling.)* No!

KEITH: Well, you'd better not! Or who knows what I'd have to do with you! *(Heads to the door.)*

EMILIE: Where are you going?

KEITH: Oh, I'm not leaving. I'll just be out in the hall for a minute.

EMILIE: Oh, okay. Because the last time you left me alone Christine got really mad.

KEITH: I know. I remember. But I'm not leaving you alone, okay?

EMILIE: Okay. *(Keith exits. Emilie walks offstage left after a glance at the door. Then Keith stalks back in and slams the door. It opens again and Christine comes in yelling.)*

CHRIS: I can't believe you were doing that! You were actually smoking —right out in the hall! Weren't expecting me back so soon, huh? Sorry I had to come back and spoil everything.

KEITH: *You're* sorry.

CHRIS: Yes, I am. *(Softer.)* I really am. *(Louder.)* How could you do that? After what happened to—.

KEITH: My father? He got lung cancer and he died. What does that have to do with anything? The same happens to millions of people every year.

CHRIS: What are you saying? What are you thinking? This is your father we're talking about. Smoking killed him. The doctors know it, you know it—.

KEITH: So I'm not supposed to smoke because cigarettes killed my father? Does that mean I can't drive either, because a car killed my mother?

CHRIS: *(Mention of this hurts.)* I don't know. Maybe it does. Maybe it should. Maybe it should mean *something. (Keith attempts to leave the room.)* No, don't you dare leave! Come back here! (He stops.) Maybe you should start thinking about your own life. What you're doing to it—.

KEITH: *(Whirls around.)* I'm ruining it, I suppose?

CHRIS: You're working on it. But I'm not going to let you.

KEITH: You don't let me do anything.

CHRIS: Hell. You never listen to me. It doesn't matter if I know what's better for you or not. You still don't listen.

KEITH: Why should I?

CHRIS: The simple fact is that I've been around for longer than you have. I really do know more than you do.

KEITH: I don't doubt that. I really don't! Adults are always saying that we think we know it all. They're always pointing out how much smarter they are. I believe it—you're smarter. You're right—it doesn't matter. I'm just trying to live my life, okay?

CHRIS: Well, that's a really selfish way to go about things, isn't it? *Your* life. Your life affects more than just one person. It affects everyone around you. Can't you see that?

KEITH: Would you just stop bothering me?

CHRIS: No, I won't stop bothering you!

KEITH: Every time I come in here, I do something wrong. Well, I'm sorry. But that's the way it is. I'm not perfect.

CHRIS: No one said you had to be! But a little more effort would be nice!

KEITH: I don't know what you want! And do you know what? I don't care! *(Emilie has appeared from offstage. She stands in the hall silent and scared, watching the two argue.)*

CHRIS: Keith, you do care.

KEITH: I don't! It just doesn't matter any more! You don't belong here, or I don't. I don't know. But you're trying to control my life, and I need some air. I can take care of myself. I don't need you, or anybody.

EMILIE: Keith. . . .

KEITH: I'm tired of my life not being how it was! Tired of not having a house of my own, a real mother, or—.

CHRIS: You think this has all been wonderful for me? Well, I'm tired of having to wait up until you come in late because I don't know where you are. I'm tired of you never picking up any of your things. *(Phone begins to ring.)* I'm tired of you always talking to your friends! And being with them when you should be doing other things, like just being with your sister, or—.

KEITH: My friends are the only ones that understand me!

CHRIS: If you think that, then you are seriously mistaken, young man.

KEITH: I don't think I'm mistaken at all. You don't know how things are for me and you don't bother trying to find out. At least I feel in place when I'm with my friends. *(Phone keeps ringing.)*

CHRIS: You are so immature—.

KEITH: That's it! I'm leaving!

EMILIE: *(Gets in his way.)* Keith, don't! *(She is a problem Keith isn't prepared to deal with.)*

KEITH: Be quiet, Emilie. *(He goes past her. Emilie is frozen. The phone is still ringing.)*

CHRIS: Stop right there! *(He doesn't.)* Keith! *(Shouts.)* Emilie, would you go in there and answer that phone! *(Emilie, scared, runs offstage left, and the ringing stops in a few seconds. Keith has reached the door.)* We haven't finished this. You can't go!

KEITH: Oh, yes I can. And I'm not coming back either.

CHRIS: What? That's ridiculous! You can't run away!

KEITH: Watch me. *(Exists through front door.)*

CHRIS: I can't just watch you—*(Slam, softer.)*—run away. Don't leave. *(Whisper.)* Please don't leave. I can't handle this—not alone. *(Emilie enters.)*

EMILIE: *(Alarmed.)* Where's Keith?

CHRIS: *(Every word is difficult.)* He left—he went out for a while. *(Pause, then asks, but doesn't really care.)* Who was on the phone?

EMILIE: It's a man. He says he's Brian Mi— something. He wants to talk to you. Or, he said he wants to talk to you if you're ready to talk to him. *(Is slightly puzzled. Since mention of name, Chris has been looking past Emilie's head, continues to do so.)* Are you going to talk to him?

CHRIS: *(Long pause, no emotion in face or tone.)* Hang up. *(Emilie puzzled.)* Just hang up, Emilie.

Scene 4

(Later that day. Christine's apartment.
Emilie is sitting alone, playing quietly, but not very involved in what she is doing. She keeps looking toward the door. She drops something with a clatter. Christine runs in, sees it isn't Keith and looks away.)

EMILIE: He's not back yet.

CHRIS: No, he isn't.

EMILIE: *(Pause.)* Are we having dinner soon?

CHRIS: Oh, I thought we would wait a little longer.

EMILIE: It's getting awfully late, Christine.

CHRIS: I know.

EMILIE: He's coming back tonight, isn't he?

CHRIS: I don't know. I hope so. Yes, he will.

EMILIE: He has to. *(Door opens. Keith walks slowly in looking somewhat defensive. Emilie runs over to hug him.)* He did! *(He hugs her back.)*

CHRIS: Where were you?

KEITH: It doesn't matter.

CHRIS: It matters that you didn't tell me!

KEITH: You're not my mother!

CHRIS: That's not a secret I've been keeping!

KEITH: You're not even anybody's mother!

CHRIS: Believe me, no one knows that better than I do!

KEITH: *(Pause. He almost regrets what he said, but chooses not to.)* I want to tell you to get out, but I can't, because this is *your* home!

CHRIS: No! It's yours, too!

KEITH: It sure doesn't feel like it.

CHRIS: Well, I wish I knew some way to make it feel like it was. I've been trying, but I guess I just can't. I'm sorry. But I can only be so sorry! *(Silence. Emilie is confused over whose side she is on.)*

KEITH: *(Doesn't really mean what he says, but does not know what else to do.)* I guess I'll be leaving now. I just came back to get—.

EMILIE: No!

CHRIS: You're doing no such thing!

KEITH: Why shouldn't I?

CHRIS: Because you're not a child any more! You can't just run away from conflicts—you know that. You have to try to work them out.

KEITH: And what if they can't be worked out?

CHRIS: You wouldn't know if they can or not because you haven't tried!

KEITH: Oh, I haven't tried, have I? What have I been doing here, then? I wouldn't have stayed as long as I did if I hadn't been trying to make things work.

CHRIS: And now you've decided that they won't, so you're just going to leave it all behind, right? Leave your sister behind. . . .

KEITH: Don't bring Emilie into this!

CHRIS: And why not? She's as much a part of this as anything and you've been leaving her out, ignoring her.

KEITH: I—I didn't want to hurt her.

CHRIS: By running away, you wouldn't hurt her?

EMILIE: Stop! Wait. *(To Chris.)* You've been forgetting about me too! You're using me as something to fight about and I don't like it! *I am* part of this, even if I don't want to be. I wish you wouldn't fight. I wish that we all got along like we did before. I wish that—that—I wish that everyone could be happy. But they can't. Why can't they? Why can't we? *(Crying, she sits on the floor, Pause as Keith reaches down to her.)*

KEITH: We can. *(Looks to Chris.)*

EMILIE: Can we? Will we?

CHRIS: In a way, I suppose that's all up to your brother.

EMILIE: Keith?

KEITH: It's up to all of us. I'm willing to go at it again. *(To Chris.)* And you?

CHRIS: *(Smiling.)* That's a stupid question. You know I am. *(Crosses to the two, takes Emilie's hands.)* You know I love you both, don't you? I care a lot about you; and I hate to see everything this way. But I don't think there was any other way it could have been at the beginning. It won't be that way any more?

EMILIE: No, it won't. Will it, Keith? *(He shakes his head.)*

CHRIS: It's later now. We can—turn over a new leaf, so to say.

EMILIE: And be happy.

CHRIS and KEITH: And be happy.

Scene 5:

(A week later. Christine's apartment.

There is no one on stage, and then Christine enters through the door carrying an assortment of bags and papers. She is dressed as though she has just come from an executive office. She is looking very cheerful as she puts everything down and looks around.)

CHRIS: Emilie! Keith! Where are you two? Hey, I've got some news about some new neighbors we might have! *(Pause.)* Don't you want to hear? *(There is silence as Emilie walks slowly in from left.)* Hi, Emilie! Where's Keith? He left you alone, didn't he? *(Is becoming angry.)*

EMILIE: *(In a small voice.)* I'm okay.

CHRIS: I told him to make sure that someone was always with you, but no—he just deserts you.

EMILIE: Christine—.

CHRIS: He's with Josh again, isn't he? Doesn't he realize it's dangerous to leave you here all alone? I don't know what I'm going to do about this. . . . Where did he go? *(Isn't even looking at Emilie.)*

EMILIE: He's gone, Christine.

CHRIS: *(Glances at Emilie and realizes what has happened but does not want to accept it.)* Well, do you know when he's coming back?

EMILIE: I don't think he is.

CHRIS: You don't—? *(Slowly sits in large chair.)* It all seemed to be working out, but it wasn't. Life always seems to be that way. *(Emilie crosses to her side.)* I knew it was going to be difficult for me but I didn't think about you two. I knew it was going to be very hard to be a mother, but it was a lot harder than I thought it would be. I was thinking of it under only a normal family's circumstances. I forgot that you would need to adapt also. And that takes a long time. In a way, I'm glad that Sharon isn't here—to see me. I make a terrible mother.

EMILIE: Mom only had more practice than you. That's all.

CHRIS: You learn from mistakes. I know that. But when you're dealing with human lives, you simply can't afford to be this inexperienced!

EMILIE: *(Begins to cry.)* Why are you doing this to yourself?

CHRIS: *(Takes her hand.)* Because I don't have anyone to do it for me. *(The phone rings and Chris picks it up from a table next to her chair.)* Hello?. . . Yes. . . . Yes, I'll fight. . . . I know. I understand. . . . *(Very gently she sets the receiver back down.)* That was my lawyer. Your cousins have decided to fight for custody. They say that I'm not good enough for you. That you need a stable home and that I can't provide one for you. I said I wanted to keep you, but maybe— maybe they're right.

EMILIE: They're not right. I think you're great.

CHRIS: And I know you are. *(Hugs her.)*

EMILIE: What happens now?

CHRIS: Hard to say. They'll probably win. *(Emilie gets onto chair with Christine.)*

EMILIE: I miss Mom.

CHRIS: So do I. And wherever Keith is, I know he does, too.

EMILIE: Why did it have to happen?

CHRIS: I can't answer that. Sometimes I wish I could. So do millions of other people. But none of them can.

EMILIE: When I grow up, I'll find out the answer.

CHRIS: You can try. But I'm not sure that you really want to.

Full-Length Play

Alone or with others write a play of any number of scenes meant to take an hour or more to perform. If it is aimed at theater, plan for it to be tried out, then rehearsed and fully produced, making changes freely along the way. If it is aimed at cinema, try to get help from school and community to actually film it and show it.

A full-length play would best be tried after doing most of the other script-writing assignments preceding this one, so that you have gained some skill in working with monologs and shorter dramas.

The Sun Will Rise Again

TOM CHEN

Preface

The story of Wu Fong has intrigued me from the day that my parents first told it to me. I have always wanted to write a play about this great man. Although most of the play is fiction, Wu Fong and the Ali-Shan Mountain are a very real part of Taiwanese culture today. Wu Fong was a Taiwanese philosopher who lived in the 1700's. The exact date of his birth is unknown. However, he died in 1769 in an attempt to prevent the inhabitants of the Ali-Shan Mountain from sacrificing human lives again. Mt. Ali has an altitude of 2,869 meters and is famous for its beautiful scenery. The Sea of Clouds and the three-generation-old tree are famous landmarks. At this mountain, a shrine built to Wu Fong can still be seen. Although most of the natives originally living there have been driven away, the temple has remained. Ali-Shan Mountain is now a tourist attraction. Here, visitors from all over the world can still pay homage to one of Taiwan's greatest men.

Dramatis Personae

WU FONG, Taiwanese philosopher.
MAY LIN, Wu Fong's lover and daughter of Wang.
WANG, Chief of the village.
HWANG, Wu Fong's rival and usurper of Wang's position as chief.

CHEN
HO   } friends of Wu Fong
TSE

1st NATIVE
2nd NATIVE
3rd NATIVE
4th NATIVE

LEE, the village sage

FAY MAY } attendants of May Lin
SUE ING

Act I

Scene I

(Enter natives with captive.)

CHEN: O, Wang, we have been successful tonight. While we were climbing down our mother mountain, we spotted a group of pilgrims going to worship. This man became separated from his party in the darkness of the night.

HO: We crept down and hid behind the bushes. He was completely unarmed. We surrounded him. We took him. He gave us no trouble.

WANG: Good, my brothers and subjects. You have indeed done well. May Tuti-Kong bless you and give you a good harvest this year. Commence with the sacrifice!

(A statue is brought in.)

O, Tuti-Kong, most mighty god! You have given us a most bountiful harvest last year. Now, the time for planting the sweet, life-giving rice approaches again. Help us, Tuti-Kong! Give us bountiful rain and a constant supply of your warm light. Bring in the victim!

(Captive is led in.)

Tuti-Kong, this victim is yours. You gave us life. We return it to you. You can create life and destroy it. O, most mighty god, we are aware of this awesome fact. Now, we give this man to you.

(Cuts off the captive's head. A cheer rises from the masses that have gathered around. Enter Wu Fong.)

WU FONG: What is this commotion about? I heard a yell. I ran as hard as I could.

1st NATIVE: A victim has been sacrificed, reverent teacher. This year will surely be a time of plenty.

WU FONG: Another sacrifice? Where is Wang?

2nd NATIVE: He is at the altar. Up front.

WU FONG: What is the meaning of this sacrifice, Wang? Did I not tell you to stop killing people? Why do you constantly ignore me? It was my love for your people that made me leave my own people in the rolling hills of the low country. I came to help your inhabitants of the Ali-Shan Mountain. I gave up the easy life that I had. Yet you still do not appreciate my sacrifices and continue to murder people upon this dirty altar.

WANG: Wu Fong, I have always appreciated your help for my people. But can you come here and expect me to change our whole civilization to fit your ideals? My ancestors were chieftains before me, and they have always sacrificed to the god Tuti-Kong. Yes, I know what you will call it. It is "primitive," "barbaric," "fit only for savages." But have you ever considered the fact that we "savages" consider many of your ways barbaric also? You will go to war against your neighbor because he has stolen some of your land or harvest. We do not do that. Here, all the land is Tuti-Kong's. We do not divide up the land among ourselves. We share everything. We are all brothers. You cannot judge a man according to your own set of ideals, Wu Fong. You must step into that person's soul and experience life as *he* feels it, not what you think he should feel.

WU FONG: Wang, you wrong me. I love your people and your customs. I respect you as human beings. But, as human beings, we must control our own destinies. We cannot expect the rice to grow, the rain to fall, the sun to shine, because of worship to some dirty idol!

CROWD: Oh, blasphemy! Kill him! Appease Tuti-Kong quickly, Wang! We must have a good harvest this year!

WU FONG: My friends. Peace! I did not mean to offend you. All that I am saying is that we do not have to depend upon Tuti-Kong for our supply of food any longer. We can control our own supply of water.

HWANG: That is idle talk! Only Tuti-Kong is capable of providing rain.

(He spits contemptuously and leaves. Crowd murmurs.)

WU FONG: No, stop! Listen to me! Beginning tomorrow, I will show you how to dig reservoirs and ditches so that you can store your water. Have you ever had years when you worshipped Tuti-Kong but still received no rain?

WANG: That is true. However, we had always assumed that it was because we had sinned against Tuti-Kong and angered him.

WU FONG: No, that is not true. Give me your support, Wang, and I will teach the people. If I fail, I personally guarantee you a head for your sacrifices.

WANG: We will do as you say, Wu Fong. May you succeed.

Scene II

(Enter May Lin, a beautiful girl of sixteen, and friends.)

MAY LIN: Here, my friends, let us stop here. The river god must be especially jolly today. Look how the water sparkles and laughs in the sunlight. Oh, look! Fishes. Oh, they *are* so beautiful.

FAY MAY: Yes, indeed, my lady. It *is* a shame that we have to work on our clothes today. Washing is so dreary and boring! I wish we could just sit here and dream away.

SUE ING: Fay May, you are so lazy! Let us start working. You see this old river every day. It looks the same to me. It is just a stream of water. I do not have time to sit here and dream my life away.

MAY LIN: Friends, friends, we will start our wash right now. But after we are finished, you may either leave or stay with me to enjoy the scenery. But wait, I hear voices approaching.

(Enter Wu Fong, Ho, Tse, and Chen.)

WU FONG: You have done good work, my friends. We have planned out a site for our reservoir already. I think it will work. Now, let us devise a method so that we will not have to depend on Tuti-Kong for our rain.

CHEN: Reverent teacher, you know I have always respected you. Since your arrival to our poor village in this great mountain, I have been a faithful adherent of your teachings. However, you are tempting Tuti-Kong to destroy us completely by words such as these.

WU FONG: *(Laughing.)* My friends, ease your fears! All I intend to do is to carry water from this stream and direct it toward our reservoir.

HO: But you will destroy the beauty of our country. Look at the stream bubbling with joy. Will you destroy it? Look at this land. It is beautiful. Yet, you intend to destroy it by digging holes through it. You are a great teacher, Wu Fong. I respect you for your beliefs. But this land is not your country. I grew up here. I have roamed, hunted, fished, and rested in this mountain. I love my country. Will you destroy it by your new ideas?

WU FONG: Do not mistake me, my friend. It is true that I came from a different country. Yet, I love your land. Its freshness and beauty will always remain first in my heart. I intend to build our reservoir and turn it into a lake. I want to raise plants so that the land will remain green and beautiful forever.

CHEN AND TSE: We believe you, Wu Fong. We are yours to command. Teach us. We will obey.

WU FONG: Thanks, my friends. Your support warms my heart. Who have we here? Who are those maidens on the other side of this river?

CHEN: Why, that is Wang's daughter and her friends. Her name is May Lin.

WU FONG: *(Aside.)* May Lin. That is a sweet name. It is sweet and free like this stream. They tell me that people sometimes experience love at first sight. I myself do not believe such a thing. Yet, I do feel something in this heart of mine. Yes, she is wild and beautiful. A river nymph indeed.

May Lin, I greet you. May your day be as beautiful as these wild roses that grow so bountifully here.

(May Lin is at first startled, then embarrassed. She acknowledges his compliment and retires with her attendants.)

Scene III

(Enter May Lin.)

MAY LIN: I have dismissed my attendants. I thought they guessed my feelings. I must be careful or they will tell my father. But that stranger! He seems so noble, so full of energy and strength. He is not shy like my people. All the other boys hang their heads and turn red when they see a girl come up to them. But this man, Wu Fong, he greeted me and acted as if it were the most natural thing in the world. His expression seems so intelligent. He is young. However, he is old in his wisdom. My mother tells me that youth is a time of infatuations. I am only sixteen! But I did think I felt something special and warm within me when I saw him. Can it be? *(Goes to her basket-weaving.)*

Perhaps work will still this wild heart of mine. Mother always cleans up our house when she becomes angry. It's no use! I cannot stop thinking of him!

(Sings—voice gradually fades away.)

"Ali-shan's girls are pretty as the clear water.
Ali-shan's boys are strong as the mountains. . . ."

Act II

Scene I

(Enter natives working on reservoir.)

NATIVES: *(Singing.)* "This is a song of high, green mountains—
Mountains high and green.
The stream is long and sparkling, clear blue.

Ali-Shan's girls are pretty as the clear water.
Ali-shan's boys are strong as the mountains.

Ah, Ah, Ah, Ah, Ah,
Ah, Ah, Ah, Ah, Ah.

Ali-shan's girls are pretty as the clear water.
Ali-shan's boys are strong as the mountains.

Mountains are always green.
The stream is forever blue.

Boys and girls are always together.
Like the beautiful, clear water circling round the strong
mountain."

(Singing continues in background.)
(Enter Wu Fong and Wang.)

WU FONG: The work is going well, Wang. I have divided your people into four groups. The first body is working near the stream.
They will divert the water into the reservoir. This way we
will always have some water even if Tuti-Kong chooses not to
give us any rain. The second party is working at the reservoir.
This group is the biggest team of all. I have chosen a level tract of
land so that the digging will be much easier. My men have
already cleared away the bushes and shrubs. The third squad is
working near the reservoir. They are digging the ditches that will
direct the water toward the fields.

WANG: What about the fourth group, my friend?

WU FONG: The fourth group? They are leveling the land so that
the water will be able to flow smoothly and evenly across it.

WANG: Your technology and your skill are all beyond me, Wu Fong.
I feel like a small child who must be explained everything. Yet,
the people call me their chief. My friend, I have something to
confide in you.

WU FONG: What it it? I am listening.

WANG: It is hard for me to admit this. But even though I am
credited to be wise, I am not really wise at all. All I have is a
deceiving front that proclaims my intelligence. Inside, I know my
own weaknesses and insecurities.

WU FONG: Why are you telling me all this?

WANG: I will be frank with you, Wu Fong. I am troubled. I do not
know if what I am doing is right. I have let you proceed with this
construction that I have never heard of before. I have ordered my
people to labor in the sun. I have agreed to let my motherland be
cut up in her very bosom. You tell me that is progress. It will help
my people in the end. What if it doesn't? I will be the only one to
blame. I will have failed my people.

WU FONG: My friend, ever since I came here you have listened to
my words. Have I ever failed you?

WANG: Never. But that is not the point. Yesterday, I had a dream.
I thought I saw my ancestors dancing in a circle. They were
singing a song of death. Their faces were not angry. Yet they
seemed to be very sad. I just cannot stop wondering if they are
disappointed in me. Perhaps I have failed them by letting you

proceed with your plans. My ancestors have always lived the ways of their fathers before them. Our lives have always been in harmony with Tuti-Kong and our surroundings. We plant only enough to eat. We hunt only if we are hungry. We drink only if we are thirsty. This pattern has always been our life—a life of tranquillity and peace. But now I am letting this life slip away. Is it worth it?

WU FONG: You are indeed a good leader, Wang. You care for your people. I talked with Ho and Chen about the same thing yesterday. They were as troubled as you are. But don't you see, there will always be risks in everything we do. You plant your rice every year. But are you not risking starvation if the rice fails to grow? You hunt for your meat. But what happens if you are killed by some animal? Progress is not much different from everything else we do. There will always be the risks. However, we must weigh out the advantages and disadvantages. if we see that the scales tip in favor of change, then it is foolish not to change. In your case, I believe that the odds are in favor of change.

(Enter Chen.)

Hello, my friend. How is the work at the stream coming along?

CHEN: We are almost finished. The stream has been diverted and will soon be flowing toward the reservoir. But, Wu Fong, I did discern a certain air of dissatisfaction among the men when I told them what they had to do.

(Enter Ho and Tse.)

HO: We received the same impression, Wu Fong. The men seem to be unhappy and talked about Tuti-Kong's anger.

TSE: Hwang certainly was not helping any. He tried to stir the men against you, Wu Fong. But we were there. He dared not go all the way to incite rebellion.

WU FONG: It does not matter. Did they finish their work?

HO: Yes, the reservoir and the ditches are all dug. We will soon be able to fill it with water.

TSE: The land has also been cleared. We will soon be able to plant some rice.

WU FONG: Good. When the reservoir fills up and the rice begins to grow, there will be no more unhappy murmurings among the people. I'll show them that they can control their own lives!

Scene II

(Enter May Lin and Wu Fong.)

WU FONG: I'm glad you decided to come along, May Lin. Tse tells me that the sunrise is beautiful in your mountains.

MAY LIN: It is wonderful. I have been up here several times. But, it's so dreadfully cold! The last time I was up here I caught a chill.

WU FONG: *(Hestitatingly.)* Does anybody know that you are up here?

MAY LIN: I don't think so. I pretended to be sound asleep. When everybody was snoring peacefully, I sneaked out.

WU FONG: That's terrible. Why didn't you tell your father?

MAY LIN: Oh, no. I would not dare to tell him. He admires and reveres you, Wu Fong. But you are still a foreigner. I am not allowed to associate with you.

WU FONG: Why, that. . . . ! I'll go up and tell him of our relationship myself.

MAY LIN: No! Don't! You musn't tell him. Can't you just savor what little we have together?

WU FONG: No, I cannot. I must tell him. Every time I'm out with you, I feel like some kind of thief.

MAY LIN: If you tell my father, Wu Fong, I will just have to leave you. Don't you think I have a sense of honor too? My father brought me up to be respectable and to marry an important man from my tribe.

WU FONG: What important man? Who?

MAY LIN: *(Unhappily.)* I am to marry Hwang. My father made an agreement with Hwang's mother that we were to be married. I guess he felt responsible for Hwang's father's death. I was only two at that time. If my father or Hwang discovers our love, I'll be disgraced forever.

WU FONG: *(Sighing.)* All right. All right. You win. But, look! The sun is coming up. Is it not beautiful? Look at the clouds! I never realized they were there. Why, they form a very sea around us. I think I'll call it the Sea of Clouds. Look, May Lin, doesn't that cloud look just like a dragon?

MAY LIN: I never really thought of it that way. Yes, it does look like a dragon.

WU FONG: And now the sun's rays are just beginning to warm up the land. Look how it penetrates even the sturdiest rocks in the mountain. Look at the sky. It's turning to a beautiful gold shade. This sunrise *is* beautiful.

MAY LIN: I am glad you like it. Although I've been here before, I have really learned a lot from you. Your way of looking at things—they are so different and original.

WU FONG: You know, May Lin, looking at this beautiful sunrise makes me feel that there should be some kind of divine force in the world.

MAY LIN: But of course, Wu Fong. Tuti-Kong created all of this mountain, the earth, the grass, everything!

WU FONG: Did he create you?

MAY LIN: *(Hesitatingly.)* I think so. But father never told me that.

WU FONG: Have you ever seen Tuti-Kong?

MAY LIN: Yes, I see him everyday.

WU FONG: *(Surprised.)* You do?

MAY LIN: Yes, I see him in the grass, in the birds, in my people, and in the mountains.

WU FONG: May Lin, sometimes I wish I had as strong a faith as you do It would make life a lot simpler. But no matter how hard I try, I just cannot believe. I cannot see Tuti-Kong in the grass and in the trees. I have to see him with my own eyes. I guess he will just have to appear to me and tell me that he exists. May Lin, why doesn't Tuti-Kong reveal himself and tell us that he exists? Why does he hide himself but still expect us to worship him?

MAY LIN: There are many things that Tuti-Kong does not reveal to us. It only takes faith. Why don't you just let him come into your life and work in you? I'm sure you won't regret it.

WU FONG: Perhaps I should. But I just can't stop thinking that we are something special. We are a cut above the grass and the animals. They are not able to think. We are able to. If we do not use our ability to reason, we will simply revert to the same level as the common animal. We will be simply beasts. May Lin, I have seen this trait all too many times in people. If we depend on Tuti-Kong for everything, we will not be able to think for ourselves. All we will be doing is praying and making those dreadful sacrifices in the hopes of a miracle. We will be something like the grass. We are unable to control our own lives. Instead, we sway back and forth, swept by a wind of circumstances.

MAY LIN: Wu Fong, you are somebody special. Ever since our first meeting, I have always felt that you are a cut above the normal village boys. I cannot agree with your philosophy of life. But I can still respect you for your ideas.

WU FONG: Thank you, May Lin. I have seen many people who are so stuck to their own ways and ideas that they will not listen to anybody else. Instead, they condemn people who think different-ly from them. These pig-headed idiots make me ashamed to call myself a human being!

(Silence.)

Well, I guess I've given you enough of my philosophy to last you a lifetime. We better head back. Your father will soon be wonder-ing where you are.

Act III

Scene I

(Enter group of natives.)

HWANG: Brothers! We have labored under the sun for many days now. We have endured and suffered much during this time. Finally this large dung-hole which Wu Fong calls a reservoir has been completed. But, friends, what is the use of this dung-hole without water? Do you think that Tuti-Kong will give us any water after what we have done? We have made a mockery of him by following this foreigner. Do you remember what he called Tuti-Kong? He called him a dirty idol!

(Crowd murmurs.)

Not only did he insult most mighty Tuti-Kong, but he also said that we did not need him any longer. If your son, whom you have reared and protected all these years, said these words to you, would you still love and care for him?

1st NATIVE: No, I would not. Nobody would.

CROWD: Of course not!

HWANG: But don't you see, my brothers, *we* are the disobedient son. We have agreed to turn our backs on Tuti-Kong and follow Wu Fong. By agreeing to his plans, we have made ourselves accomplices of his evil plans.

2nd NATIVE: Hwang, I will never forsake Tuti-Kong. I cherish and love him as much as ever. However, Wu Fong is a good man. He has many strong beliefs. He does not mean ill. He wants to help us.

HWANG: Fool! Do you still think that Wu Fong is a good man? What has this foreigner done for us since he got here? He has ordered us to labor in the fields for some illusory plan that he has. How many of you know why you are digging and slaving in the fields?

(Silence.)

Has Wu Fong ever told you?

1st NATIVE: He mentioned something about controlling our own destinies from now on and not having to depend on Tuti-Kong any longer. But in truth, I do not even know what he means by "controlling our own destinies."

HWANG: There's an honest man. Who else knows why we are digging and slaving every day?

(Crowd is again silent.)

Lee, you are deemed the wisest man in the village. Even Wang reveres you. We all bow to your judgment. Do you think that

Wu Fong knows what he is doing?

LEE: I am not sure. It is hard to say.

HWANG: Wang always consults you before he makes a large decision. Did Wu Fong ever consult you in this matter?

LEE: No, he did not.

HWANG: Are you admitting that Wu Fong is smarter than you are?

LEE: I am not admitting anything. But who says that Wu Fong is smarter than I am?

HWANG: Well, you are. You let yourself be kicked around by Wu Fong. Nobody listens to you any more. Everybody ignores you. Wang doesn't ask you anything now. It is always Wu Fong. Wu Fong knows everything. Wu Fong is the reverent teacher now. You are only a second-class philosopher!

LEE: Yes! Yes! You are right. That Wu Fong is a good-for-nothing foreigner! Friends, is my reputation still worth anything? I have always cherished my special position as the village teacher. You have always listened to me. Now lend me your ears again. Listen to Hwang. He is right. This Wu Fong is a menace. He will destroy us by his foolish ideas.

3rd NATIVE: Do you hear that? Even Lee agrees with Hwang.

4th NATIVE: Yes, yes. Wu Fong is a dangerous man. Let us get rid of Wu Fong!

CROWD: Yes, yes! Let us get rid of him!

HWANG: But wait a bit, friends. What abut Wang? Do you not remember that he is still chief? Wang reveres Wu Fong. He will not let anything happen to him.

1st NATIVE: Then Wang should not be chief if he persists in this foolishness.

HWANG: But patience, brother. It is true that Wang has committed many mistakes. He has let Wu Fong make a puppet out of him by always listening to him. He has ordered the sacrifices to Tuti-Kong stopped. He has ordered us to toil in the fields for something we do not understand ourselves. But he has also done some good things for our village. Remember he is still chief.

4th NATIVE: Perhaps he should not be chief. Let us have Hwang as our new leader. Down with Wang and Wu Fong!

HWANG: Friends, I dare not accept. I am a peaceful man. I will not be the cause of any bloodshed if Wang should resist. Therefore, pardon me, I cannot. It is against my principles.

CROWD: Please accept our offer, Hwang. We need your leadership and help.

3rd NATIVE: We want Hwang. Hwang for chief!

HWANG: You overwhelm me friends. I have no choice. I bow to your demands. My love for you and our country force me to accept. But, remember I accept only with the greatest reluctance.

CROWD: We know. We know! Hail, Hwang!

2nd NATIVE: What do you think we should do, Hwang?

HWANG: Well, friends, I say that we march bravely up to Wang's house and demand that he give up Wu Fong. We will banish Wu Fong from our country forever. In addition, you will tell Wang that I am the new chief. My modesty forbids me to declare so brazenly my newly acquired honors. We will let Wang remain in our village. Our love and generosity will not let us forget his past services. Do you agree reverent teacher? *(Indicating Lee.)*

LEE: Certainly. Hwang is right. This Wu Fong is dangerous. He will destroy us.

HWANG: But wait, friends. Have we forgotten Tuti-Kong? Has our love for him diminished so much already? Has Wu Fong caused such a change in our character? I say that we continue with our sacrifices tomorrow. We must appease Tuti-Kong quickly. He has been most kind and generous with us so far. Remember the bountiful harvest we had last year?

CROWD: Yes, yes!

HWANG: Do you think we'll have another good year again? Why, I won't be surprised if he destroys us completely. He probably won't send any more rain to us anymore. What about his life-giving light? Do you think that after what we have done Tuti-Kong will let us share it with him any more? Why, he'll probably cause such a huge storm that we will all be destroyed and drowned in that very hole we dug so hard at.

CROWD: Oh, no! Oh, no! You are right, Hwang. Tomorrow we must sacrifice to Tuti-Kong again. He must be appeased. Tuti-Kong must be appeased!

1st NATIVE: Let us get to Wang's house now. Every second counts.

CROWD: Away. Away! Down with Wu Fong! Down with Wang! Hurry, friends!

Scene II

HWANG: Fools! You can be swayed more easily than the trees. Yet, you call yourself better than the common animal. What is man? Why, he is only a beast. He cannot think. He cannot reason. He has to be guided around like sheep. Like the good shepherd, I have led them toward my pen. With the right care and the proper amount of nourishment from my deceiving words, my neighbors will soon be totally under my control. Wang, I have waited long for this moment. Did you think I could forgive you for ruining my father? O, father, you unhappy ambassador! Chided for a failed mission in front of the whole village. You poor man. You took Wang's rebuke so hard that suicide seemed better than life. Now,

Wang, the time for repayment has come. What you did to my father will soon be repaid! But, wait, am I losing my senses? What about Wu Fong? He is my archenemy. He came into this village with his vague ideas of human dignity and pride. Soon he had everybody under his control. Everybody loved him. Everybody adored him. But I didn't. I hated him. Now this hatred burns even hotter in this breast of mine. He had the gall to order *me* out to the fields to work on his dung-hole. Why, he's acting as if he were Tuti-Kong himself! And May Lin, that wench! Did you think you were so clever sneaking off in the mornings to meet your precious Wu Fong? I don't give a damn about you. But you *are* Wang's daugher—Wang's only heir. Who could be a better chief than Wang's son-in-law? If these plans of mine fail, I'll have to marry you for sure. Those fools must be nearing Wang's house by now. I must hurry. If they succeed, I want to be there at the right time. If not, I will be ready to deny their whole story. Wang is too sentimental. He will forgive me.

Act IV
Scene I

(Enter natives.)

1st NATIVE: Wang, come out. We want to talk with you.

2nd NATIVE: Wu Fong too, brother. We must not forget him. Remember Hwang's words.

3rd NATIVE: That's right! Bring that foreigner out!

LEE: He's a dangerous man. Hwang is right.

4th NATIVE: Come out, Wang! We know you are in there. Look, even Lee condemns you.

LEE: Quiet, you fool! I only said Wu Fong.

(Wang and Wu Fong step out of the house.)

WANG: Friends. Brothers. Why this racket? Why are you disturbing the peaceful night with such angry words? In all my years as your chief I have never seen you so angry. What is the matter? Tell me. I am ready to listen.

1st NATIVE: It is you and Wu Fong. You have let this foreigner take over our whole village. You have ordered us to labor in the hot sun on something that we do not understand ourselves. We demand that you banish Wu Fong from our country. He is not to return again on the penalty of death.

2nd NATIVE: We will also like you to resign, Wang. You have served us for many years. We will not forget that. But you have failed us by letting Wu Fong dominate your thinking. You are not a good chief. We demand a new leader. Hwang for chief!

CROWD: Hwang! Hwang! Hwang for chief!

2nd NATIVE: Have I forgotten anything friend? I think I said just about everything Hwang told us. Lee, did I miss anything?

LEE: No, I don't think so. But I will just like to emphasize the point that Wu Fong is a dangerous man and must be banished.

3rd NATIVE: But, wait. We have forgotten Tuti-Kong again. Hwang says that we must commence with our sacrifices the day after tomorrow if we are to appease him.

4th NATIVE: No, you are wrong. It is tomorrow that we must begin our sacrifices.

3rd NATIVE: How could it be? I am right. It is the day after tomorrow. What day is it, Lee?

LEE: I am not sure. I was not listening at the time. But using all my years of experience and logic, I would say the day after tomorrow.

2nd NATIVE: No, Lee. It is tomorrow.

1st NATIVE: It must be the day after tomorrow if Lee says so.

2nd NATIVE: No, it is tomorrow. Listen! Were you asleep during the whole time? Your honesty certainly does not help your intelligence.

(Punches 2nd Native. General scuffle takes place as natives take sides.)

1st NATIVE: Am I to be insulted like this in front of my friends?

(Punches 2nd Native. General scuffle takes place as natives take sides.)

WANG: Friends, I beg of you. Peace. Silence. Stop! Stop!

(Crowd quiets down. Resentful looks cast at Wang.)

A while ago I said that in all my years as your chief I have never seen you so angry. Now I would like to change that statement. In all my years as chief, I have never been so ashamed of my people! You come here declaring a grievous wrong that you want corrected. You disturbed us and woke us up when we were just savoring the delights of sleep and rest. I was ready to listen to you. Instead, you started bickering among yourselves over some trivial detail. Looking at your stupidity just makes me sick! Through the years, I have always tried to serve you faithfully. Has anyone ever said "thank you" to me? No! All I hear every day is complaints. Such ingratitude. Such baseness. Do you want a new chief? Do you want Hwang to be your new leader? Then i quit! You can have Hwang!

(Crowd murmurs.)

But Wu Fong? How has he ever wronged you? Wu Fong is a good man. He loves you. Why should he be forced to leave? He—.

WU FONG: Enough, friend. Let me speak for myself. Friends. What is the matter? What are you so angry at? If I were you, this night should be a time of celebration. You have completed the reservoir and cleared the fields for planting the rice. Everything is ready for a good harvest. Now you are free men. You can control your destinies. You do not have to depend on anybody. Not even Tuti-Kong!

(Hwang appears from behind a nearby hut.)

HWANG: You go too far, Wu Fong! Listening to your words of nonsense just makes my blood boil. Do you think that this dung-hole of yours is anything to Tuti-Kong? He can flood it and dry it up at will. It is nothing compared to his power. You pride yourself as an intelligent man. You think you can control your own life. Well, we are more modest. We believe in Tuti-Kong. We want him to control our lives. He is the only true god. We have worshipped him for years. Why should we switch because of you? Are you a god? Are you a chief? No, you are just a foreigner!

CROWD: Tuti-Kong, Tuti-Kong! Down with Wu Fong! Down with the foreigner!

HWANG: Wu Fong, we demand that you leave us at once. We do not want you. We do not need you! Take your ideas somewhere else. As for us, we will continue to worship Tuti-Kong. Tomorrow, we will commence with the sacrifices!

(Crowd cheers.)

WU FONG: You fools! I thought that I could make you into better men. I was wrong. I'm sorry that I ever met you. Do you still want a head for your disgusting sacrifices tomorrow?

1st NATIVE: Yes, we will begin tomorrow, Wu Fong. You cannot stop us now.

WU FONG: You will get your head, you disgusting savages! At the peak of your mountain, you will find a man dressed in black. Do not ask him any questions. Take him by surprise. Cut off his head before he can reply. However, do not look at his face until you return back to the village. This is my last wish. Follow it.

(Wu Fong leaves.)

Scene II

(Enter Wu Fong and May Lin.)

MAY LIN: What are you doing? Why are you taking those black clothes?

WU FONG: It is cold, May Lin.

MAY LIN: Why not your other clothes? You intend to be the man at the mountain, don't you? You are going to die. I know it!

WU FONG: No, May Lin. Of course not. Why should I?

MAY LIN: Because I know you. You still hope to convert my people. Why don't you just give up. They hate you. They said they did not need you. Why sacrifice yourself like this?

WU FONG: I don't intend to do anything like that. But what if I did? It's my life. I can still control a little part of my world, can't I?

MAY LIN: Now I know for sure. You do intend to go through with it. But what about me, Wu Fong? You can say that you are going to sacrifice yourself and be a martyr. I cannot. I do not want to. I am still young. I have a whole life in front of me. I don't want to lose you. You still have some kind of conception that what you do will not affect others. But you are wrong. We are all tied together in one long chain. If you break away from this chain, the continuity is lost. For my sake, don't do a foolish thing like sacrificing yourself.

WU FONG: I am not asking you to be a martyr, May Lin. You do have your whole future in front of you. You can marry Hwang just like your father wanted. You said you did not want to be disgraced. Now here's your chance to redeem yourself.

MAY LIN: Don't talk like that, Wu Fong. You sound like you don't care anymore. Let's get away. We will take my father with us. We can go back to your people. My father is in disgrace here. He will not mind leaving. We'll be happy together. O Wu Fong, I love you and I don't want us to be separated. Can't you understand that? Do you have to analyze our relationship and find a rational explanation behind that too? I'm living and I'm breathing. I can feel love and I can experience happiness. Is there some kind of formula that can explain my emotions and feelings?

WU FONG: I am not analyzing our relationship. But don't you understand, love is not the answer to everything. Just because we love each other does not mean that there can be no problems in this world. We cannot form a little magical bubble in which we'll be happy and ignore everybody else. You said yourself that we have to be aware of other people. I am aware of my world. Now I have to go.

MAY LIN: Where are you going? Don't leave me like this. You can't do this to me! Make peace with Tuti-Kong, Wu Fong!

(May Lin cries. There is no answer from Wu Fong, who has left the house.)

You think you can toss me off like a piece of bad cloth, don't you Wu Fong? Well, I'll teach you something. I am not going to do anything to get you back. I'm stronger than you think I am. If you can play your part, so can I. I'll live! I'll marry Hwang. I'll become the wife of the chief in my village. I don't need you, Wu Fong. I have a whole future in front of me!

Scene III

(At the peak of Ali-Shan Mountain.)

WU FONG: O man, you ungrateful wretch! I tried to help you, but you refused my help. You did not need me. You cast me away like an old blanket. Your people were my whole life, Wang. I tried to do what I thought was best for you. You were the meaning of my existence. Through helping you, I began to feel a new purpose in living again. I would get up in my father's house every day and just wonder about the meaning of life. Before I came here, my life was an endless, dreary cycle. I would get up in the morning and study. Then I went to school. When I came back home again, it was chores and more studying. Father, forgive me, you tried your best to give me an education. But you did not give me a purpose in my life. Yes, I remember. My one great dream was to be the smartest student in the class. How futile and puny that dream seems now! If I stand back and just look at that goal of mine from the top of the world, I just can't stop thinking that life is made up of petty goals and dreams. Kings who are renowned throughout the world, they die too. Shih Huang Ti was a great emperor. He must have been a vain and proud man when he lived. He ruled the whole world! But now isn't he just a name in the history books? His whole life is open and left free to be scrutinized by the lowliest scholar. Even a king does not really have a purpose in living. For after he dies, he just returns to the earth that he was created from. But then what is the purpose of life? Is it simply a monstrous joke? Is life just a ludicrous and dreary cycle? Oh, how silly life seems!

But if life is so worthless, is death the only alternative? Yet most men will tremble at the sight of death. The man who is suffering from the most incurable and hopeless disease will still cling to life. Why are we so scared of death? Is it because of the fear of the unknown? What will follow after we die? The priests who have given up their lives for their gods say that they will go to heaven after they die. They look upon life as a transition between death and eternity. But foolish men, what if there are no gods? What if life is simply life? You will just be wasting your life away on some illusory dream. And you mighty warriors! Dying for your country is a great honor to you. You think that the war god will reward you for your faithfulness. But what if there is no war god? You will just have sacrificed yourself for nothing. Nothing. Nothing. Nothing!

But, then, is life not simply one great compensation after another? The warriors, the priests, are they not simply compensating their lives for others? They die. Others live. Do they think that they will help humanity by playing their roles in life? Or are they really doing it for themselves? Perhaps the warrior, when he sets out to die for his country, secretly hopes to gain fame and reputation. He hopes that all the glory of the battle will be heaped upon him. Perhaps he hopes to become the greatest general in the world. Winning battles, killing men, and impressing the people, these goals might be his purpose in setting out to do battle.

But why am I dying? I have no country to die for. I have no religion that I care for. Perhaps I am sacrificing myself because I hope to help Wang's people. Or am I dying because I am proud? That must be it! I am dying because I hope to become famous throughout the world. People will mourn for me and call me a great man. Yes, I can see it now. Wang's people will be tearing their clothes in agony as they see the great loss they have suffered. And May Lin! I do love her. I can see her too. She will stand there crying yet proud of me. She will proclaim her love for me to her people. And Wang will regret that he ever made that agreement with Hwang's mother. Ha, ha! I can see Hwang now. Just turning over in his sleep as he groans in envy of me!

But wait! What if May Lin is right? What if the people really hate me? They will probably cut off my head and then hold one great celebration. "Good riddance!" they will probably exclaim. "Who needs that troublemonger?" they will ask. Perhaps May Lin will forget about me. She'll just marry Hwang and live happily ever after as the wife of the new chief in the village. Hwang, that rascal! That scum! He'll probably laugh and say, "Thank you, Wu Fong, for being such a fool. You handed me everything on one gold platter. May Lin, the title of a chief, fame, reputation, and the love of Tuti-Kong." Oh, how wretched!

But what about the principle of the matter? Am I not dying on a matter of principle? I promised Wang that I will *personally* provide a head for the sacrifices if I fail. I have failed. The people reject my beliefs. I must be true to my promise. Perhaps that is the meaning of life. Principles and virtues! How a man lives in his lifetime is the only surviving part of him. His virtures and his goodness will live on in the world. He will become a light in this evil world. Therefore, the unscrupulous man will have no purpose in life. He does not believe in principles. Is life not simply a principle in itself? If a man does not follow his beliefs, he will simply lead a senseless existence. I have followed my beliefs. I am ready to die. May Lin told me to be reconciled with Tuti-Kong. I cannot. To me, Tuti-Kong is simply a principle in himself. He represents a divine being. I am the principle and representation of a man. We are both principles. I am on the same level as he is. I do not need him.

But wait, the natives approach. The sun rises. May Lin,

farewell. May I always remain somebody special in your life. Live for me!

Act V

Scene I

(Enter natives.)

1st NATIVE: We did as Wu Fong instructed. Before the sun's mighty rays had a chance to dispel the night's dark cloak, we set out for our mountain top. The going was rough and dangerous.

2nd NATIVE: But the thought of pleasing mighty Tuti-Kong kept us going. Eventually, we labored up the peak of their mountain. There we found a man dressed in black just as Wu Fong had promised. We formed into two groups of six. We were ready to ambush him.

3rd NATIVE: But to our surprise, this victim gave us no resistance whatsoever. In fact, he seemed to be expecting us. We immediately cut off his head. It was easy. Because of the dense fog and our promise to Wu Fong, we did not see who our victim was. Therefore, here is the head. It is ready for worship. Let us bring out Tuti-Kong.

(A statue is again brought out.)

4th NATIVE: O Tuti-Kong, you mighty god. We have sinned. We forsook you and followed the ways of a stranger. Now we would like to come back to you. Please forgive us. We are only men. We cannot be perfect like you, mighty Tuti-Kong. Forgive us. We have a head today that we would like you to accept as a token of your mercy. Here is the head, mighty earth god!

(Takes out the head.)

1st NATIVE: O gods, can it be? It is Wu Fong! He was the man at the mountain!

(General commotion results. Enter Hwang and Wang.)

HWANG: What is all this excitement about, friends? Did you return already? We were not expecting you until later. But it is as well that you have returned early. Let us proceed with our sacrifices. But what is the matter? You all look shocked. You seem as if you have seen a ghost.

1st NATIVE: The man at the mountain—.

HWANG: Yes, yes. What about him? Wu Fong told us he would be there. Didn't you get him? Have you failed? I told you to be careful. Or has Wu Fong lied to us again?

2nd NATIVE: He was there, Hwang. We did our mission. We did not fail. He was there.

(Holds up Wu Fong's head.)

HWANG: Gods, the man at the mountain was Wu Fong! Why did he want to kill himself? Perhaps he felt that dying was better than leaving our village in disgrace.

(Enter May Lin.)

MAY LIN: Leaders of my people. Although I am only a woman and not allowed to speak in public, I have something to say regarding Wu Fong.

HWANG: We are not interested in what you have to say.

WANG: Speak on, child.

NATIVES: Yes, tell us!

MAY LIN: First of all, on this altar before Tuti-Kong and Wu Fong's head, I have a confession to make. Although I was betrothed from my childhood to Hwang, I was in love with Wu Fong. He loved us. I tried to stop him before he left to die for our people.

1st NATIVE: For us? Why? We told him we did not need him.

MAY LIN: Will you not understand? Wu Fong loved us.

HWANG: Enough to die for us? You must be crazy. Why didn't you tell us he was going to die?

MAY LIN: I loved him too much to try to stop him. I would have disgraced him even more than you did. Besides, you still don't know what loyalty and love mean, Hwang. To Wu Fong, these two qualities were the same. He promised us that he would convert us from our use of human sacrifices for Tuti-Kong.

3rd NATIVE: And if he failed, he said that he would personally promise us a head for our worship. Yes, I remember. Everything is becoming clear to me.

MAY LIN: That's right. He felt that he had failed us and himself. He wanted to make good his promises to us.

CHEN: But he did not fail us, May Lin. We failed him. Friends, it was because of our lack of trust for him that made him eventually kill himself.

HO: He had everything all planned out. If we had waited longer, he would have a chance to prove whether his plans were correct. We did not even give him a chance.

WANG: May Lin, was he bitter when he left?

MAY LIN: He tried not to show it. But I knew that he was bitter and angry at our people. O father, I did love him! Now, he is gone! He died to save us from the sin of killing innocent people.

(Sobs.)

WANG: *(To natives.)* Did I not tell you that Wu Fong was an honorable man? Did I not tell you that he loved us? You did not believe me. Now here is the proof of his love!

(He holds up Wu Fong's head.)

1st NATIVE: Oh, woeful day!

2nd NATIVE: What have we done? We have killed a man who loved and cared for us.

3rd NATIVE: I am not responsible for his death. Hwang is the one who told us not to trust Wu Fong. He told us that he did not love us.

4th NATIVE: That's right! It's all Hwang's fault. He stirred us up against him. We have lost a good man and friend.

CROWD: Down with Hwang! Hwang, you have lied to us!

HWANG: No, no! I only told you the truth. I honestly felt that Wu Fong was a bad man.

WANG: Bad man! You are the evil one, Hwang. You stirred up the people against me. You caused Wu Fong to be disgraced in public. You wanted us to continue in our cruelty. Now I will give you until tomorrow to pack your clothes and leave this village. On the penalty of death, you are not to return again.

CROWD: That's right! We don't need you, Hwang. Get out! You are a nuisance.

(Exit Hwang with some natives.)

1st NATIVE: Wang, will you remain as our chief? We were wrong about you. Hwang is evil. He stirred us to do evil. We were not responsible.

WANG: I will remain as your chief only on one condition.

2nd NATIVE: Name it, Wang. We will listen.

WANG: I order that Wu Fong's work be continued. We will carry out his plans just as he wanted. When the rain falls, the reservior will be full. We will use this water to plant our crops. I also want the human sacrifices to be stopped.

3rd NATIVE: Are you asking us to stop believing in Tuti-Kong?

MAY LIN: Of course, not. Wu Fong always wanted to believe in the gods. But he could not. It is good to have a strong belief. I am as faithful an adherent of Tuti-Kong as you are. But we do not have to appease him with human heads. We will use the heads of our animals to worship Tuti-Kong.

WANG: We will also build a temple to Wu Fong. It will stand forever as a token of our belated love for him.

CROWD: Yes, yes! Let us do that. Wu Fong will live forever in our temple. We will set it by the reservoir that he worked so hard at.

(Natives leave.)

MAY LIN: I was wrong, Wu Fong. A man can control his destiny. What he does can change other people. Although you have died, your virtues and your high principles will live on forever. We lived our lives in darkness. Now the sun will rise again. You will live in this high mountain that you love so much. Farewell, love.

Stories

Stories from the News

Make up a story based on a true news item. Take the main events and fill them out with details you invent. Feel free, of course, to add events or people not in the original and to change things around to develop what seems most interesting to you. What conclusion or significance do you see in the story that may not have been dealt with in the news item?

It can be very interesting to your reader to read the news item along with the story you based on it. Which one do you want to be read first?

Escape

JIM BLAU

July 26

We leave today: Chappo, Carlos, Juan and I. We pray that the celebration will aid our flight. Carlos has hidden the inner tubes and supplies down by the beach. Chappo was angry and said that all would be lost if they were found and they should have been brought to Chappo's house. But Carlos said it was better this way because the police would find nothing if the house was searched, and anyway all the police and soldiers would be patrolling the carnivals. Juan asked Carlos if he really thought that Castro's boys would just go away and let us through. Carlos called Juan a little fool and told him to stay home and continue to live like a pig if he was afraid. I think Juan would have hit him, even though Carlos is twice his size, if I hadn't stepped in. After all, they are both my friends. I think they hate each other.

Later:

We are crazy. We are trying to get to Florida on an inner tube raft. Crazy. But we are desperate. We have heard a lot about the United States and we know we will have it better there. All we have is a compass, knives, and fishing poles. It took forever to get out of sight of land, but no one saw us. An hour ago, a wave washed all our food and precious water overboard. No one says anything, but I think we might die. We watch for sharks. The raft is so small we cannot move.

Carlos asks me what I am writing. I tell him I am writing a journal, that I have kept one since I was in the seminary. "That's pretty fancy for a bartender, Humberto," he says. "Do you plan to earn a living in the United States by writing?" Carlos is hard to get along with in such close quarters. He is especially nasty to Juan. I wish Juan would stand up for himself more; he never stands up for anything. He is like my small brother sometimes, who was a sullen brat until he died of the flu.

27-

We are cramped and thirsty, and hungry too; although we have caught some fish it doesn't taste good raw. Carlos dozes and I whisper to Juan to stand up to Carlos and stop being such a fool. Juan says he knows more about it than I do. He weeps and says, "Humberto, I stole money from Carlos once." I didn't know Juan was a thief. He broke a commandment. My brother used to steal too; I hated him; no, I loved my brother; it was not my fault we had no parents and he died. We are thirsty; we cannot move.

28-

Cannot write, weak, no more fish. It's hot, sun from sky, sun from water. We are weak.

30-

Weak, have seen strange things, lights in the sky. Carlos called Juan a damn thief it is so hot. Juan said he is an atheist so doesn't matter. I looked down in the water straight down dark down, down. Juan stood up knife in his hand the sun so hot behind his head, face black. The Devil, said Carlos, I saw, the Antichrist so thirsy little brat my knife in my hand I don't know Juan's leg bled he fell down, down straight down into wet darkness he belongs
    Now we walk on the water says Carlos
    Angels of God

Later:

The angels of God were the U.S. Coast Guard. They gave us water; oh it tasted good. We slept. When we woke we acted as though Juan never existed. The Americans do not know. But sometimes Chappo and Carlos look at me, especially Carlos; he looks at me; I can't stand it; I didn't. . . . I won't write any more.

Cubans Flee Communism by Inner Tube

BY MARY BETH SHERIDAN
ASSOCIATED PRESS

MIAMI - Three exhausted Cubans who lashed three inner tubes together and paddled 230 miles to freedom said they spent five days without fresh water, survived on raw fish and began hallucinating two days before they were plucked from the ocean.

"We saw visions," said Luis Alloma Chappottin Marin, 31, a secondary school teacher. "We even wanted to walk on the water."

Chappottin, bartender Humberto Rodriguez Valdes, 28, and Carlos

Enriques Quintana Orosco, 23, a student, were rescued off Fort Lauderdale on Wednesday by a Coast Guard patrol boat, said spokesman Dave Anderton.

"They looked like they had been in the weather," said Coast Guard Petty Officer Ron Feldman. "One guy could hardly walk."

The men, wearing orange Immigration and Naturalization Service-issued jumpsuits, said during a news conference that they fled Cuba the night of July 26 as the nation celebrated the anniversary of Fidel Castro's 1953 revolution.

"We knew all the armed forces were with Fidel . . . and we knew the local police would be patrolling the carnivals," said Rodriguez.

"I was not happy with the rule," Quintana said. "I don't like communism. I never did."

"When you get your check, it is already spent," said Chappottin.

The Cubans said a wave washed their food and compass overboard their first morning at sea. Each lost 15 to 20 pounds.

The Cubans said they worried about sharks for the first two days, but when none appeared, they became more confident. The biggest problem, aside from a lack of food and water, was a storm that whipped up six-foot waves.

Fictional Additions

Make up a new part for some novel, play, or short story that you have read. Write something the author didn't but that is in keeping with the plot, characterizations, and theme. This might be a scene that you add to the action or a retelling of some of the original action from a different point of view. Consider various techniques exemplified elsewhere in Imagination.

Since other readers of the same work will get the most out of your contribution, think of the best way to share this with them, in or out of class.

Postscript (from Charlie in Flowers for Algernon)

ASTRID SOTO

Dear Miss Kinnian,

I am ritin to you from Warren. I stil no how to rite good. Im so happy that I havent forgoten how to rite good.

I dont lik it hear Miss Kinnian. I wich I wuz there with you. I miss you and my freinds down at Donners bakery. I red my old progris riports and I cant beleeve I rote them. I dont understand them but Im happy that at one time I wuz smart like you.

In one of my progris riports I sayed that I luved you and that I maid luv to you. I dont no what the last part meens to good but I no what the first part meens. I stil luv you Miss Kinnian and I wich I wuz back at the Beekmin School so I coold lern how to reed and rite better. I still remember when I held you in my arms but now I no that you dont luv me anymor becuz im dum. At won time I wuz smarter than you and now Im dummer then you. Why cant we ever be the same?

Say hello to Prof Nemur and Dr Straus for me and wood you pleese go to Algernons grav and say helo for me. I beter stop ritin becuz my hand and my head herts and the papers getin sogy with my teers. Please remember me Miss Kinnian and cum visit me son.

Luv,
Charlie

The Old Man and the Sea

MICHELLE MOWRER

I am happy I am going out so far. The fish will be big. Bigger than the ones closer in. Today is the eighty-fifth day I have gone without taking a fish. Last time it was eighty-seven. But today I feel that eighty-five is a lucky number. Today should be a good one. La Mar looks promising. She is not cruel today. She is happy, like me. I wish I had the boy with me. He is good company. He can help me fish. Today, I know, I will be lucky. I can feel it in the air. A big one out there will come and take my bait. I know he will take it and eat it well. Then, after he has eaten it well enough, I will take him. It will be easy, just like DiMaggio plays ball, I will fish with no fear and all my confidence.

I will take one and he will be one like me. Strong, calm and fearless. He will be my brother. But I will kill him anyway. The people at home need him. They need my brother. He will feed many and his meat will bring much money for me so that I may survive. So that I may eat and keep warm during cold seasons. I may even have enough to buy the boy and me a cast net. I wish I had the boy. I wish he was here, then he could share the joy of taking the big fish.

Some of the other fisherman think that I am crazy. They know I was strong once. I still am, but my body is old. They respect me, but they think I have weakened. I will show them I am still strong. I will prove to them I am still strong. I will take a big fish, bigger than ever! And I will show them I can still endure so many risks and so much suffering!

Yes, there are a lot of risks out here. I am old and alone. I should have the boy. A man my age should not be alone. But I am and I am going out far. So far to where I cannot see land. I can always trust the sun and the glare of Havana to lead me, but I may run out of water. That is always a risk but the flesh of any fish will help that. Not solve it, but help it. But what if I do not hook any fish? No! I must not think that way! I am a fisherman. Like my father and the father of my father. I will hook a fish. I will hook a big fish!

I will show the fishermen who think I am too old. I will show the ones who think that I am going crazy. I will show them all that I can still hook a big fish. My brothers will help me. They will not let me down.

The Forgotten Scene

JACQUELINE JENNINGS

I was looking through my old Salinger files, reading over my notes about **The Catcher in the Rye** *and reminiscing about my editing days. Mixed in with a batch of other papers was the following scene, not published in the novel, although a note reads, "To be inserted between the chapters where Holden sneaks home and visits his sister Phoebe (Chapters 21-23) and the chapter where he visits with the Antolinis (Chapter 24)." I have no recollection of ever having seen it before. I present it to you without further comment.*

Salinger's Editor

Outside, the wind was really kicking up from the river, and after being cooped up with old Phoebe all that time, it felt good to be out in the air. With only eight bucks to my name, I decided to walk to the Antolinis' rather than grab a cab. A hundred of them went by before I walked a block, but you could bet if I were lookin' for one there wouldn't be a yellow light in sight.

I crossed Lexington Avenue heading across 56th street toward Sutton Place. The streets were quiet, but the coffee shops were crowded with people spilling out of the bars for a quick sober up before they staggered home to face the music. An old guy stumbled from the shadows near a newsstand and tried to hit me up for some change to get a cup of coffee. He was real scruffy, and Jeez, did he scare the hell out of me. I brushed him off, but afterwards I felt kind of bad and I thought I might go back and give him a quarter. When I looked back he had faded into the darkness of the buildings, and I thought better of doing a good deed that might get me a whack over the head.

A block later, near Third Avenue, I spotted an empty table in a greasy spoon plastered with chintzy Christmas decorations; rolls of thin green and silver tinsel were wrapped around the sugar canisters, soiled red Santas with butter-grease stains on their coats sat stupidly against the windows. It was lousy, and I got real depressed.

There was only one waitress serving on tables, a colored woman about forty, and she looked tired and kinda mean, but when she finally got around to taking my order she was really nice.

"I'll have a cheeseburger and a coffee."

"How ya' want that burger?" she asked. She gave a little smile that took away the tired look that hung around her half-closed eyes. "Don't take it too well," she said. "There isn't much left after all the grease gets burned off."

"Medium," I said. "With some pickles."

"How about the coffee?"

"Cream and sugar, O.K.?" I didn't know why I was asking permission and apparently she didn't either.

"It's fine with me," she said, and she shuffled off behind the counter shouting the order to a little Spanish guy who was cracking eggs on a grill shiny with oil.

I was only in the joint about three minutes and a lady with a paper shopping bag and cloth pocketbook tucked under one arm came in. She was dressed in a black coat with two buttons missing near the top. She looked about fifty or so, and tired. It seems everyone in this town looks tired at night. She seemed to be soaking up the warmth because she stood for a minute without moving, just inside the door. I tried not to look at her because I knew the seat across the table from me was the only vacant one in the place. I kept staring out the window, but I could see her edging toward me in the window's reflection.

"Would you mind very much if I sat here, young man?"

I pretended to be taken by surprise, but I was getting pissed. I mean damn, it's really tough in this town. When you want someone, you couldn't get them to give you a peep, but when you want to hide, you got a million buddies.

"No, not at all," I said.

She put her shopping bag near the window. It had a newspaper sticking out of it along with a blue sweater and a grey scarf. Her pocketbook she kept next to her, as if everything she owned in the world was in it.

"It's cold out there," she said, and I started to feel very uncomfortable.

Before I could say something, and I really had nothing to add, the waitress came with my coffee.

"What you gonna have, honey?" she asked the new occupant of the booth. My guest looked at the steaming cup before me.

"I'll have a coffee," she said. "Regular."

"Anything else?"

There was a pause before a response came.

"No, not right now, thank you."

Again the waitress shuffled off to take new orders from the stove.

I took a sip of the coffee, and it was pretty crummy, but it was hot. Again I looked out the window, hoping to avoid conversation, but I knew it was coming because I could see her staring at me in the window.

"It's really turning cold," she repeated.

"Yes it is," I said. I turned back to the window, but before I did I noticed that she had a nice face, sort of pretty, or at least a face that was once that way. In the window I could see that she got the hint that I didn't want to gab because she looked down at the table kind of sad-like.

The waitress came back with my cheeseburger and my lady friend's coffee. The burger smelled good, and I was about to take a real huge chunk of it when I noticed that old lady friend was really quite thin.

"Do you work around here, m'am?" I asked. "If you don't mind me asking, that is."

"No, that's all right. I work in the office building a block away, on Lexington. I clean the first three floors."

I took another bite of my burger. It didn't taste as good as the first one, and I was pretty sure the way this conversation was goin' the next bite wasn't goin' to be any better.

"It sounds like pretty hard work."

"It gets tiring," she said sipping her coffee, "but I need the money, although it doesn't pay very much. But it's something." She looked at my ratty burger. "That looks good," she said. "Finish it all."

Damned if she didn't sound just like my old lady. But she didn't look like her, although I bet she could have if she had a better coat or was a little heavier. I'll bet she was a pretty good lookin' broad in her time.

"How long have you been working?" I asked.

"Ever since my husband died, seven years ago."

"Do you have any children?" I was really getting into it.

"Just a daughter. But she's married and lives out in Hawaii. I haven't seen her in over four years. She's got a family of her own now."

I hadn't even half finished my first cheeseburger, but I called the waitress over and ordered another and another coffee. "Can I get you anything?" I asked my old lady friend.

"No thank you," she said. "That's very kind, but I'm fine."

I knew she was going to refuse, but I wish she hadn't. I waited for about three minutes, glancing at the waitress every so often as I chewed the fat with my old lady friend.

Suddenly, I looked at my watch. "Oh, my God, I'm dead late." My old lady friend looked startled. "Listen," I said, faking panic all the way, "could you do me a big favor?"

"Well, I don't know if I can," she said.

I got up from the booth as I pulled the bunched up eight bucks from my pants pocket. "The bill is no more than three bucks. Would you be able to pay the waitress for me?" I put a five dollar bill on the table.

"Of course," she said, "but what about your cheeseburger and coffee?"

"I guess they'll just have to throw them out. That is unless you'd like them."

"Well, I do hate to see them go to waste," she said. "It's a sin to waste food."

"Yes, it is," I said. I was also going to say it's a sin for a dumb broad to be sunning herself in Hawaii while her mother has to work her butt off without even so much as a "how are you." But I didn't. Instead I told her I had to run and that it was nice meeting her.

Outside, the warmth from the restaurant stayed with me for about a block. But then the cold crept in and I thought, "I should have taken a cab."

A Memo to God from Eve's Psychiatrist
(à la Mark Twain)

ROBIN RITTER

To God:

In reply to your recent inquiry as to the mental health of the woman Eve:

Eve is progressing satisfactorily in her therapy and seems to be adjusting well to the move from Eden. In her last session we discussed the events that led up to the "original sin" and her feelings at the time. It is my opinion that Eve was and is suffering various neuroses. It was temporary insanity that pushed her to the deed. At the time of temptation Eve was so out of touch with herself and the world that it is a wonder she didn't listen to the fruit and eat the snake. She had extreme anxiety caused by fears of rejection. Doubts plagued her mind. She had no "mother" figure to form a role for her to follow. She was susceptible to outward influences and easily persuaded due to her lack of security. She felt that things were being withheld from her, and her vision was clouded. Adam offered no sympathy or explanations. When she ate the forbidden fruit it was an act of searching for better understanding rather than an act of defiance.

I would urge you to work with her and try to patch things up. Continue open communication—*listen* as well as speak.

Fictional Correspondence
Write a short story told by one or more of the characters in the form of a correspondence; that is, a series of letters from one only or an exchange among two or several.

A Dying Man's Honor

FRANK TRINITY

To: Jonathan Eferding
From: Bureau of the Registry of Austria
Re: Address Request
Date: October 3, 1939

Sir:

In regard to your request that the Austrian Government release into your hands the address of one Greta Vordenberg, we unfortunately are not authorized under existing laws to oblige you. It is the policy of the Austrian government to protect the interests of her citizens, and your request is not in compliance with this policy.

If you wish to pursue this matter further, an inquiry placed with the Office of Records of Austria may be helpful.

It has been our privilege to be of service to you.

Johann Vladik
Assistant Clerk

To: Jonathan Eferding
From: Office of Records
Re: Address Request
Date: November 28, 1939

Sir:

The function of the Office of Records is almost exclusively to provide officials with important information concerning the population of Austria. It is not a policy of this office to provide private citizens, let alone foreign citizens, any access to our records.

However, in light of your situation, we have waived the restrictions and are willing to supply some details.

We have thoroughly checked our resources on the present address of one Greta Vordenberg. Regrettably, there is no known address of the person in question.

We do have our records that indicate that Greta Vordenberg was born between 1875-1882 in the Alps, in the southwest corner of Austria. We have no records which indicate that this person now lives in Austria or even if this person is alive.

That is the extent of our existing file on the above-named person. It is our hope that we have been of service to you.

If you wish to continue to investigate this matter, it would be advisable to contact the local provincial governments.

Karl Muldenschmitt

To: Jonathan Eferding
From: Office of Public Affairs—Tyrol Province
Re: Address Request
Date: January 16, 1940

Sir:

We have received your urgent inquiry concerning one of our loyal subjects of Tyrol Province.

We have expediently researched the records of Greta Vordenberg and are pleased to report her last known address. In our 1920 census, Greta Vordenberg was recorded in our files as living in the village of Lienz.

We wish you luck in your search for Greta Vordenberg.

Wolfgang Fraugher
Head Clerk

The Honorable Martin Dirkinbeer

Sir:

It is my fervent hope that your influential position as Mayor of Lienz will aid me in my urgent quest for my sister Greta Vordenberg. It is of the utmost importance that I reach her as soon as possible.

My declining health leaves me with precious little time for the most valuable things in my life. My wish to reach my sister is my only desire to fulfill in my remaining time.

You can ensure my eternal happiness by making every effort possible in forwarding the enclosed letter to Greta Vordenberg or anyone who might expect to contact with her.

I am forever in your debt.

In gratitude,
Jonathan Eferding

My Dearest Greta,

It has been two generations since I last saw your face. Two generations is too much a price to pay.

Time is a cruel thing; it has no heart. Time has made me a bitter man. One mistake 42 years past has haunted me like an apparition.

If I had power over time, I would go back 42 years and begin anew my life.

As a stubborn young man, I put my ideals ahead of my family and my family's honor. You cannot imagine the silent agony that I have suffered because of my hard-headedness. It is hard for a man to face the fact that he attached an eternal mark of disgrace on his beloved family. That is why I fled to America.

I deeply regret the grief that I have caused you and the rest of our family to suffer.

I do not expect you to forgive me. I only ask that you do not hate me. If you can find it in your heart to dispel the hatred of me, it will make me a happy man.

Your loving brother,
Jonathan Eferding

My beloved Jonathan,

Upon receiving your letter yesterday, my heart leapt with joy. It was beyond my wildest dreams. It warmed my heart to learn that my treasured brother, Jonathan, was alive.

I was so filled with excitement and wonder that I could not sleep at all last night. As soon as the sun rose today, I decided to waste not another moment and I began to write.

Your guilt and grief have been for naught. Alas, I pity your aching heart. Suffer no more forever, my dearest brother, for all has been forgotten in these parts.

To think that you have been burdened with guilt since those days of 1897 is overwhelming. Shortly after the successful revolution of 1905, your name was vindicated. In fact, many look upon your name with reverence.

Our two sisters have long since died, as well as my cherished husband, Andre.

It was my conviction that you were still alive, but so many years went by before yesterday that I had some doubts. That is why I am such a picture of happiness on this beautiful day.

You must bury any bad feelings about 1897 once and forever.

Your affectionate sister,
Greta

March 22, 1940

My dearest Greta,

It was a stroke of good fortune that you should receive my letter. I have been trying for months to contact you.

In all honesty, I received your surprising reply with reservations. It is hard to believe that the furor aroused over my dismissal dissipated in just eight years.

But it is not my nature to mistrust the only family I have left. Therefore, I thank you for the news of my vindication and I accept it.

Although my self-imposed exile was not necessary, I felt it was the only way to salvage any remaining respect for the Eferding family name. Now that I am no longer considered a traitor, I am enormously relieved.

Honor was the only virtue I ever strived for, and I hope that I have adhered to that ideal.

It was with a heavy heart that I learned of the deaths of Ruta and Lisa. You are the only family I have, and I should thank God that I was able to reach you.

I am sorry that your husband died. Even though I never met him, I am sure that he was a good and just man.

Have you any word of Isabel? I would appreciate hearing anything about her.

> Your loving brother,
> *Jonathan Eferding*

April 20, 1940

My beloved Jonathan,

Be satisfied that you have attained a place of honor in our history. No matter what bitter memories you have, erase them completely.

You must return to your native country. It would put your mind at ease forever if you were to visit here for but one day, and the people would receive you with open arms. Please arrange a way to come to Austria as soon as possible.

In response to your question about Isabel—she married an affluent merchant in 1911 and died in 1936 during a bad winter. This must sadden you deeply, for I know how special she was to you.

Please send me any word on the possibility of your return.

> Lovingly,
> *Greta*

June 14, 1940

My dearest Greta,

Thank you for the word on Isabel. Upon learning her fate, I wept. We were especially close during those days of turmoil.

The remarks on my standing in Austria were appreciated.

I would like to share these first-hand. However, I am not able to travel at the present time. I have been ill for some time now and am too weak to risk an ocean journey.

You might consider the possibility of your coming to America. It would do me some good to see you with my own eyes.

> Your loving brother,
> *Jonathan Eferding*

July 4, 1940

My beloved Jonathan,

I was disturbed and worried to hear of your ill health. I am sure you will get well soon, God willing.

I am putting all my energy into finding a way to come to America. The effiency of the Austrian government is not very good. I should know soon when to expect a passage across the Atlantic.

Until then, stay in good health.

Lovingly,
Greta

August 9, 1940

My dearest Greta,

It gives me strength to learn that you are going to visit me. That thought sustains me through the most difficult times.

My doctors tell me to save my strength, but I tell them that I must write to you because you are my only living family.

Please send word on your expected arrival.

Jonathan

September 29, 1940

My beloved Jonathan,

Please be rest assured that I am making every effort to obtain the necessary papers for a foreign trip. It is very difficult to make progress through the government channels, but I am trying.

I should have all the details worked out soon.

When I receive the go-ahead to leave the country, I will contact you immediately. Stay in good health until then.

Greta

October 25, 1940

Dearest Greta,

I have waited for so long to see you Greta, my sister.

They say the sun is shining outside, but my body grows colder every day. I can feel my life slipping away.

But I must not give in—it is my one wish that I should see my sister. How could I be deprived of that?

Send word quickly.

Time is a cruel thing.

Jonathan

Either Side of the Law
KATHY PROFETA

Oct 15, 1972

I HAVE A GUN. DO NOT MAKE ANY UNNECESSARY MOVES. PUT $50,000 IN UNMARKED BILLS INTO THIS BAG. ANYTHING SUSPICIOUS AND I WILL SHOOT.

Oct 16, 1972

Dear Ma,

Yesterday was the most awful day in my whole life! A man came and held up First Securities! I was so terrified. He held up *my* window! The note said not to do anything suspicious so I didn't, I just gave him the money. Mr. Jacobsen said I should have pushed the secret alarm system, but I was just so nervous I forgot. He's taking it to the bank head, and I may lose my job. Fifty thousand is a lot to lose, even for a bank. What will I do if I lose my job? Please call me when you get this, I need to talk to someone about it.

Love,
Margie

Oct 22, 1972

Dear Vera,

Thinking of you. Boy, would you love it here! The beach is great. I'm having the time of my life. Don't worry about last week, that was my last adventure. Stay sweet, sis, and see you when the statute of limitations runs out!

xoxo *Paul*

Oct 30, 1972

Dear Ma,

I lost my job. Mr. Carooney told Mr. Jacobsen that I had just been briefed on the new system, so I should have remembered. Mr. Jacobsen said Mr. Carooney's very upset because the new video system took fuzzy pictures and so we didn't get any good shots of the man. I told Mr. Jacobsen that wasn't my fault, and if he wanted I'd try to help him draw a picture of the man, but Mr. Jacobsen said sorry, hon, it won't get your job back. So starting tomorrow I'm out looking again. Mrs. Carruthers said one more week for the rent and that's all. If I don't get a job in the next week I'll have to drop night school and ask for my tuition back, at least part. But I don't want to do that, I know you want me to get my degree. And don't think I'm asking for money from you, Ma, I know you couldn't scrape it up right now. I'm trying hard, Ma, but things are falling apart all at once.

Love,
Margie

Nov 6, 1972

Dear Ms. Tanare,

I'm really sorry but any longer and no room. I already got the Joneses in 3c with the noise problem, and Mrs. Thompson with her complaints, last thing I need is late rent payment from you. It's gotta be in three days, honey, or else.

Mrs. C.

Nov 11, 1972

Dear Miss Tanare,

We are extremely sorry at your decision to leave Hilltown Night College. We hope you were aware of our policy of refunding only one-third of tuition once the year has begun. Enclosed please find a check for that amount.

Regrettably Yours,
Dana Winters
Admissions Dean

Jan 3, 1973

Dear Vera,

Sorry to bother you with my existence again, but just thought you'd like to know my status. I'm having a great time here. I met this classy girl here, her name is Juanita. Not marriage material like I know you're thinking, but she'll pass the time! Also got me a job, sis. Don't faint now. I need some kind of job to justify my money, you know, so people don't wonder what I'm living off of. And anyway, I don't want to use too much of the fifty grand in case it's marked. So I'm a waiter at the Mexico City Sheraton (don't laugh) but not for long. I'll find me a better job. See, I told you I'd go straight, sis, as soon as I got rich enough!

xoxo *Paul*

Dear Marg,

Meet me in front of Delany's at 2:00 with anything you want to bring with you. I'll have the car and then we'll be finally getting out of this Iowa hicktown and going to where the action is. Maybe Las Vegas. See you then.

Herb

Jan 20, 1973

Dear Ma,

My job is gone and I lost my room at Carruthers' too. I quit school and they only gave me 1/3 of the tuition back. There was nothing else for me to do, Ma. So I'm out of this town. You know that guy Herb I told you I met? He's going southwest in his car and he said he'd take me with him. I'll write next time I have a permanent place to stay. Don't worry, Ma, I'll be fine. I just need a break from this kinda life before I settle down and start trying to make something of myself again. Hilltown Night College wasn't such a good school anyway. Next time I'll go someplace better.

Love,
Margie

Feb 17, 1973

Dear Vera,

Well, you were right again. When your brother decides to settle down, he goes all the way. Juanita and I got married this morning, by a judge in Mexico City. She's the greatest, sis! She's made me want to turn my life around even more. She gets greater every day! It looks like I'll be here for a while, even after the statute of limitations runs out. Raise myself some little niños and niñas. I'm even starting to learn the language, see? I've moved up to maitre-d at the hotel restaurant, but I'm still out looking for a job with more opportunity to move up. Please try to come down and visit me one of these years! Bring the kids too, I feel like an uncle now.

xoxox *Paul*

News clipping - 2/19/73
Las Vegas Press

DYNAMIC DUO HOLD UP 5 DRUG STORES IN ONE WEEK

Yesterday at 5:00 a curly-haired male about 25 years old held up Fitzhugh's Drug and Deli, getting away with over $1000 dollars in cash. He was seen escaping into a green Vega with a sandy haired girl at the wheel. What makes this incident unusual is that this same pair has held up 4 other stores in a similar fashion in one week, and still managed to avoid the police.

Feb 21, 1973

Dear Ma,

Hi. I'm not in Las Vegas any more. Herb and I decided to leave, after we'd made a little money. It was getting a little too boring there anyway. Right now I'm mailing this from Arizona but who knows where I'll be in a week. I'll write you then.

Love,
Margie

March 4, 1973

Dear Vera,

Well, I finally am setting up in life. Juanita and I bought a two-family house in a Mexico City suburb. Only twenty minutes from the beach! And I have a new job: it's really ironic, I work in a bank! Don't laugh, sis. It's a really small branch of the Mexico City bank and I think pretty soon I'll be able to move up from a teller to an officer. This is so much fun, sis! Why didn't you tell me sooner what fun straight living was? I'm serious about you visiting me, sis. Come soon!

Hasta Luego,
Paul xoxox

March 20, 1973

Dear Ma,

Right now I'm in Mexico. Herb and I just got here last night. We won't be here long, we just want to work enough to get money to charter a boat to the Virgin Islands. That's probably where we'll end up for good, but I'll write again to tell you. Don't worry about me, I'm fine.

Love,
Margie

March 22, 1973

THIS IS A STICKUP. I HAVE A GUN. DO NOT MAKE ANY UNNECCESARY MOVES. PUT $50,000 IN UNMARKED BILLS IN A BAG. ANYTHING SUSPICIOUS AND MY PARTNER AND I WILL SHOOT YOU (AND THE REST OF THE PEOPLE IN THE BANK).

P.S. HAVEN'T I SEEN YOU SOMEWHERE BEFORE?

Fictional Journal

Tell a story through a journal you make up as if one of the characters in your story is keeping it. All the reader sees is this character's journal, so that everything has to come through it. Indicate where the entries begin and end. Write in the style your character would use. What series of events is this person writing about from day to day or time to time in his or her journal?

Present this to others as you might any other story. Reading aloud might be especially good if you or someone else wants to act the voice of such a character.

Diary of a Sixth-Grader

PATTY DOYLE

January 6

Why are some of the girls getting so boy crazy? We're only in 6th grade. You don't have boyfriends when you're this young, or do you? Mom said that you just like boys 'cause they're cute or handsome or are the fastest runner in the class. Cathy and Maria keep following Michael wherever he goes. Don't they remember when they used to think that he had the cooties? They are being so air-headed.

January 8

Cathy said that I'm a prude 'cause I wear shorts under my dress at school. I said to her, "Don't you know that when you play kickball in gym that all the boys look at you when you run so they can see your dress fly up?" All she said was, "I know." She is still following Michael. Maria is following David now. She said that she loves his blue eyes. What is so great about blue eyes? I have blue eyes and I don't see anyone following me around.

January 15

Some of the other girls have gone boy crazy. We had to do square dancing in gym, and my best friend Alicia, who I always am partners with in square dancing, asked Tommy to be her partner. She has lots of nerve. Tommy always picks his nose when he thinks that nobody is looking. GROSS! I asked Mom if she thought Tommy was good looking. She said, "Beauty is in the eye of the beholder, and can you empty the dishwasher before dinner?" So much for talking to Mom. She is so old-fashioned.

January 25

Cathy wore perfume to school yesterday. It smelled up the whole room, and the art teacher said, "Did someone drop one of the turpentine bottles?" Everyone knew that it was Cathy's perfume so we all laughed. Ha-Ha! What a burn. She'll never wear that again.

February 2

David keeps sitting next to me and following me. He is like Maria and Cathy. Maria is mad at me 'cause she likes David. I say she can have him. I hate having David around. Maria really hates me. She said that I made him like me. Now how would I do that? She is a pain.

February 18

David called me the other night. Thank God I wasn't home. Mom thinks that I like him. I told her that he probably called to get the math homework. He never does his math homework.

February 25

Today when I was in the girls room cleaning the paint that I spilled in art off of my dress, Cathy and Maria came in. Maria gave me a snotty look 'cause David still likes me, and Cathy came right up to me and said, "Guess what I got?" I ignored her 'cause she is real snotty to me and I'm not her friend. But she went right on and said, "My mother got me a bra." I was so surprised she even said the word. She doesn't need one. She thinks that she is so hotsy-totsy. (My grandma always says that word.)

February 28

Yesterday I asked my mother if she could get me a bra. My father was in the other room, and he overheard and came and said, "What do you need a bra for?" Well, I kinda mumbled that I had to go to the bathroom, and then the subject was dropped.

March 15

School has been BLAH! David stopped following me after I told him that I thought that he was a pain in the butt. Maria is back to following him. My mother says that Maria is fickle. I don't know what that means, but since it rhymes with pickle it has to be something dumb.

March 29

Now Mark is bugging me. But I don't mind it so much. He's not like David. Mark is nice. Maybe I'm going boy crazy! I don't feel any different.

March 31

Mark called me and asked me for the math homework. Then he asked me if I wanted to go to see a movie with him. Before I said yes my heart went Blump and landed right in my stomach. I could feel myself turning red. Luckily I was using the phone. It would have been even more embarrassing if he saw me turn red.

April 14

The movie was real neat. Mark held my hand through the whole movie, and he even bought me a Jumbo Popcorn with melted butter. I like Mark.

April 18

My birthday is coming up next week, and I'm going to have a family party, but Mom said that I could invite one friend over. Guess who I'm inviting? I hope he can come.

April 26

Today is my birthday and I had a great time all day. In the morning my mother took me shopping for a dress to wear at dinner. We also went out to brunch. When I got home my father brought me out back and showed me my birthday present. It was a small puppy. I love him so much. I still have to think of a name for him. Mark gave me a corsage and a bottle of perfume. He said that his mother picked it out. The dinner was great.

May 1

Mark and I went to another movie. I really like him. He is so nice to me. He walks me home from school every day. He also gives me a candy bar every day. My mother likes him too.

May 8

I thought of a name for my new puppy. I'm going to call him B.C. And that stands for Boy Crazy!

Love Thy Neighbor... PLEASE!

JAMES SIE

December 17

Well, we finally did it. We made that long, perilous journey from one state to another. Ah, the dangers of moving! Actually, the trip was only three hours, but it seemed like an eternity. Life on *The Waltons* is a piece of cake compared to what I went through.

At first, things went rather smoothly. We packed our last few items, we cried with our neighbors, and left. Then, after fifteen minutes, the savages in the back seat began to get restless. There was more punching, scratching, and kicking than a clearance sale at Bloomingdale's. I threw them a bag of Fritos and prayed for peace.

The peace was as short-lived as a Mid-East treaty. Within ten minutes the riot started up again. I searched desperately in my purse for that all-time pacifier, food, but all I came up with was a stick of stale gum and a Lifesaver covered with lint. What to do? My husband and I tried ignoring them, but as they began nibbling on our arms I knew something had to be done. Drastic measures had to be taken. George reluctantly pulled into a Dairy Queen, where we bought ice cream cones to go. This was a big mistake. Our back seat now comes in three flavors.

Next it was time to worry about the dog. Besides trying to escape out the window at each light, he needed to be walked every ten minutes. This proved tricky in those long stretches of tree-less highways. We found out that he had an inclination to relieve himself on cars waiting for the light to change. Embarrassing, but effective.

And, of course, what drive would be complete without little, sweet Allison's carsickness? Whenever Prince was taken care of, she was in danger of throwing up. We spent several exasperating moments at the side of the road, waiting for the refund of her ice cream. Nothing. Finally, though, as we pulled into a gas station, the jolt was too much for her. We cleaned up the best we could and drove off. I noticed the gas attendant didn't say thanks for stopping by. More lovely colors on the seat.

We finally made it to our new home. Unfortunately, the moving van didn't. George suggested sleeping in a hotel, but I refused to take another trip, so we settled down with what we had. We huddled on the floor that night, while Prince breathed on us for warmth. I had forgotten how cold a house tends to be in mid-December, when there is no heat in it. I spent a troubled night, dreaming that the moving van driver had taken a wrong turn and was now somewhere in Alaska with my furniture.

This morning, after unthawing, we drove to Pancake House for some (you guessed it) pancakes. Right now I'm waiting for the van, while the children are looking for rats and George is cursing the plumbing because it doesn't work and he's getting dysentery from all those pancakes. More later.

Helen

December 24

A week has passed since I last wrote, but I've been very busy. Unpacking is like playing Treasure Hunt. So far I've discovered the summer clothes and the plate, but not the winter stuff and the silverware. As a result, my kids are now sitting around the table in their bathing suits eating a tuna casserole with their fingers. Messy.

Christmas is tomorrow, and though it's sad that we can't have our decorations up in time, we're improvising. I strung parsley up for mistletoe, eggshells for tree ornaments, and my pantyhose for stockings. The children are lucky; I wear Queen size.

I can't wait to see what I get for Christmas this year. Last year I received a rubber band guitar, a painted box "dekration," and a toilet paper roll mobile. The kids gave me wonderful things, too.

Well, no one has come to visit yet, but I suppose it's all the snow and the holiday season. Burr, it's cold (I tell my kids to pretend they're in Miami). I expect the neighbors will be flocking to the front door once Christmas is over. That's all for now.

Helen

January 10

Christmas is over, a new year has begun. I have made a resolution with myself never to stuff turkey with Captain Crunch when I run out of bread again. The kids have promised never to lie, cheat, or yell again, and George promises to talk to us at least twice a week once the football season begins again. What liars we all are.

Still no sign of neighbors. This is getting depressing. The fruit-cake on my brightly polished formica counter that I have been waiting to serve to the first lucky doorknocker has long since decomposed. There seems to be no sign of life in the houses around us. What's the good of cleaning the house if you don't have neighbors to tell how much you hate cleaning the house? Still, there must be people around because my kids, now going to school (Ah, yes, the pleasure of the eight-to-five vacation once again!), are complaining of overcrowding in their classes. Maybe orphans are being bussed in from other towns.

I went into the town today, to get the local color, so to speak. The color seems to be a pale gray to black, the color of shrouds. The supermarket looked like it was Senior Citizen's Day! There are two whole shelves devoted to laxatives and denture creams. The daily sale in fruits is always prunes. Sometimes I think I must be in the Land that Time Retired In. How can you have an everlasting friendship with someone who has two months left?

I'm tempted to go and introduce myself next door, but I think that is a little forward. Let them make the first move. (I hope they can still walk.)

Helen

January 18

I don't know what to do. Right now I'm watching Julia Child prepare a soufflé au chocolat while eating my diet salad with no dressing (God knows why I diet, there's no one I want to impress. I guess it's just out of habit). This is not my idea of fun.

I don't know what's wrong. I've checked the kids for leprosy, but they all seem clean. What's wrong with our family? Sure, sometimes we don't floss regularly and I forget to put napkins in the kids' lunchboxes once in a while (Michelle has one with John Travolta on it that I am spellbound by), but does that count against us? Are vicious old women huddled in small groups at this very moment, whispering about "Those awful Kennedys?" Do they know I don't always choose the softest bathroom tissue for my family?

I really miss my old neighbors these days. On our left was Mrs. Burrows, who tried to get our dog arrested for trespassing on her lawn and in her garbage (Prince hid out in the cellar and we denied ever having a dog). Then there were the Pendergrasts, who borrowed everything we had, but never seemed to be able to return the Tupperware containers they were in. And who can forget the Johnsons, whose fighting kept George and me up every night that we weren't fighting. Oh, how I miss all those good neighbors.

Helen

January 30

A NEIGHBOR HAS BEEN SPOTTED!!!! We were outside doing our lawn work. I had gone to the garage to get a rake when I spied, across the street, a door beginning to open. I could hardly refrain from screaming. "Keep cool," I whispered to myself. I didn't want to scare off whatever was coming out. I noticed out of the corner of my eye that a figure was stepping out of the doorway. My heart beat faster.

I walked slowly to the end of the driveway and started raking up the mown grass, trying to appear as cool as possible. I stole a quick glance. It was a lady, and she was coming toward me! I looked down again.

She had reached our side of the road and was coming toward the driveway. When she was about ten feet away, I looked up. My throat was dry. "Hi!" I managed to croak out weakly. I think I sounded like a dying cow. Would she answer? I waited with bated breath (I always picture myself with a worm in my mouth) for her response.

"It's good to see you're finally doing something with that lawn of

yours," she said finally, and disappeared into the shadows.
Not a great beginning, but a beginning.

Helen

February 16

Well, diary, things have picked up. I found out the neighbors
across the street are the Rydells. We invited them over for coffee, and
they gave us the number of their two gardeners, their interior decor-
ator, and their maid. Last week we met the Petersons, who came
calling on us and dropped their kids off to get acquainted with our kids
(I'm hoping that they'll take them back in the near future), and
yesterday the Jenners came over with their trained parakeet, which
got loose, which is why Prince ate it, which is why they aren't talking
to us any more.

I feel at home at last. Who could ask for nicer neighbors? I'm
surrounded with people I love. Finally, I feel content and happy.

Helen

February 17

Oh, my God, George's got a transfer. We're moving!

Fictional Autobiography

*If your story material and intentions are of a certain kind
you may want to pretend that your main character is telling the
story. Your story would then be told in the first person by an
"I" as if a real person were telling a true story of something in
his or her life. Reminiscence that features oneself is autobiography. So whoever you have telling the story is the one
whom the events befall or who initiates the events, the one
whose experience is most important.*

Yes. Yes. You?

LISA RAMOS

I was tired and bored, wishing I were somewhere else. Mr. Carlyle was droning on about some ancient war, while half the kids were asleep with their eyes open. In front of me, Alex Anderson was continuing his quest to make the perfect airplane. To my right, Carol Rains was hysterically attempting to complete three weeks of algebra assignments before next period. To my left, Mary Munich was painting her fingernails a chilling, metallic blue, while simulating note-taking. Behind me, the incomparable Sheila Gardner was passing a note to the equally unattainable Alice Adams, using the old crumpled-paper technique. Pretending to have made some grievous error, Sheila would sigh, crumple the offending page into a ball and toss it casually in Alice's direction. Alice would wait for Mr. Carlyle to look away for a moment, then lean down to pick it up.

I found myself staring at the formica surface on my desk, wishing fervently that six months would pass in a flash, and I would be done with high school forever. I would make a new life for myself in college. I would become what I was never able to become at Harperview High School.

In the meantime, I had six months left to serve, six months to live out the last days of Joey Campbell, average athlete, average student, average-looking guy. This is the role that had been assigned to me four years before, and which I had accepted without complaint because it was how I perceived myself then. During my junior year, I began to change dramatically, but no one at Harperview High seemed to be aware that I was getting better looking, becoming a great basketball player, excelling in my classes, and turning into an all-around exciting kind of person.

I had to fight my way onto the basketball team, my teachers suspected me of cheating on my exams, and I could suddenly get dates with beautiful girls from *other* schools, but not from Harperview. College, I saw, would be a clean slate for me, a new start. I would be perceived for what I was, not what people thought I should be.

So there I was, staring at my desk top, when, without thinking, I began to write on the glassy surface with my pencil. Everyone doodled on the desks, although it was against the rules. I had done it a thousand times before. But I had never, until that moment, sent a message. I wrote simply:

"Help, I'm going crazy!"

Class ended. We all moved from the room, sleepwalkers in search of our next resting place. I entered my English class and finished my algebra while pretending, YAWN, to take notes on *The Scarlet Letter*.

Algebra came, then lunch, then P.E., then music, then basketball practice, then home, dinner, the dishes, two hours of piano playing, and then to bed.

The next day I collapsed into my seat in Mr. Carlyle's class, feeling more forlorn than I had the day before. I let myself drift into a fantasy of life after high school. Mr. C. began to drone and I began, without thinking again, to doodle on my desk top, when suddenly I saw it—a reply to my message! Someone had written in the neatest, tiniest letters:

"Who are you? How can I help?"

How can I explain the effect this simple response had on me? I was instantly filled with hope. Someone who had no idea who I was wanted to get to know me. Me, not good old average Joey Campbell, but me, my true self. Or so I hoped. I would have loved to write a whole desk top in reply, but I felt it would be wiser to hold back. I didn't want to reveal too much, too soon. I didn't want to scare my new friend away.

My initial cry for help had been erased, which showed good judgment on the part of the respondent. It was essential that we keep our replies brief and nearly invisible, lest others discover them and ruin the privacy of our exchange. The janitor, too, was a potential enemy, as he would note any lengthy correspondence and dissolve it with his wet rag.

I was poised to write my reply when Mr. Carlyle called my name. "I'm sorry, sir," I said smiling at him. "Could you repeat the question?"

"The pincer attack of Hannibal against the Romans. Would you describe it, please?"

I did this with ease, having recently read a description of the tactic in a science-fiction novel, wherein a desperately outnumbered force of Dravidian warriors used the trick to defeat an entire squadron of Freks in a deep space megabattle. Mr. Carlyle was impressed, as were several members of the class. They looked with disbelieving smirks, and I wanted to shout, "You don't know the half of it, you jerks! This is one exceptional person sitting here!"

I then wrote:

"J: Keep talking. Who are you?"

And so it began. My mornings at school revolved around receiving and sending a message for the day. My initial desire to tell all leveled off into an addict's delight at the slowly growing pile of information I was accumulating about A., and that A. was accumulating about me. Not wanting to forget any of our communications, I kept a record of everything we said to each other. The first five days went like this:

"J: Help, I'm going crazy!

A: Who are you? How can I help?

J: J. Keep talking. Who are you?

A: A. This helps. Write smaller.

J: How's this? Glad to meet you.

A: Mutual. I was lonely.

J: I am lonely. Six months to go.

A: College? Like to dance?

J: Yes. Yes. You?

A: Yes. Yes. Now what?"

The next question was the hardest for me to ask, because you see I was hoping A. was a girl. We were on the verge of revealing more intimate details of ourselves, and I felt the question of gender was unavoidable. I wracked my brain for a clever yet sensitive way to ask the question, but ultimately I resorted to simplicity.

"J: Now what? I am male. You?"

Having asked, I spent the rest of the day feeling anxious, wishing I hadn't been so blunt about it. A friend of either sex would be nice. I couldn't expect to find true love through my desk top. The answer from A. though got me off the hook.

"A: Does it matter?"

I responded:

"J: No. A friend is a friend."

Nevertheless, I was delighted the next day.

"A: Good. I am female. What else?

J: Perhaps we should meet.

A: No. Fantasy surpasses reality."

I agreed with her, but my curiosity was pushing me to the limits of my patience. I wanted to ask her if she was beautiful and charming, but I knew that would change our unique and mysterious relationship into a mundane boy-meets-girl affair that very probably wouldn't surpass the fantasies I was having, and I was having them aplenty. Furthermore, and this was the real crux of the matter, I probably knew her, and she probably knew me, casually, of course, and I could just see the disappointment of her face, *hear* the uncomfortable tone in her voice as she said, "Oh, it's you, Joey Campbell. (Sigh.) Just my luck."

And yet I had to know. I was, to put it mildly, becoming obsessed with the question of her identity. It wasn't just that I was lonely and love-hungry; it was that with every message she sent, she became more wonderful, more appealing to me.

"J: Does fantasy surpass reality?

A: No, but I'm afraid to disappoint.

J: Then this is fine. Birthday?

A: August 11. Crazy Leo. You?

J: October 5. Lazy Libra. Music?

A: Jazz! To dance.

J: The best."

It was just too good to be true. A big part of my transformation from an average person to an exciting kind of guy was a breakthrough I'd made in my music. Having slogged through seven years of classical piano for my mother's sake, I had discovered one night that I could play jazz. It was a revelation. And I had, since that night, been practicing two or three hours a day for almost two years and I was getting *hot*! But more than that, the music had given me a sense of myself that I'd never before had. It was mine, all me. The better I got, the better I felt about myself and everything else I did. And here was this sensitive, intelligent, crazy Leo woman who loved to dance, who loved jazz. It was too much.

"A: You play? Instrument?

J: Piano. You?"

But she never answered that question. Her next message came as a total surprise to me.

"A: Don't try to find out who I am."

I replied:

"J: Trust me. I will not."

But even as I wrote those words I knew the sanctity of our relationship, the unspoken trust was gone. It was time to end the communication. I needed a real friend, not just a fantasy. But A. provided the way out.

"A: Let's take a break. I'm sorry.

J: No problem. Thanks. Good-bye."

By the end of the basketball season I had advanced to the starting team and in our final game I went all out and scored twenty-five points. We won the game, and I was named Athlete-of-the-Week, complete with a big picture of me in the paper. Hot on the heels of that came an article in the paper about my jazz group (The Young Punks) and how popular we were. No more Joey; it was Joe Campbell, superman-on-campus. Girls started asking *me* out. I was somebody. Or was I?

I was sitting in Carlyle's class on the verge of dozing off, thinking how unfair it was that young superstars had to sit through the same lectures as everyone else, when I happened to glance down at the corner of my desk. I hadn't done that in a long time. I had forgotten all about A. But there was a message. My heart began to pound.

"A: Don't let it go to your head."

The implication of this statement was staggering. This meant she knew who I was. How unfair. But she was right. I was letting it go to my head. I needed a good friend to point it out.

Instead of writing back I set out to find out who she was. I looked through Carlyle's seating charts, but there were no girls who sat at my desk and no "A"s either. What a fool I'd been. She hadn't needed to look for me. She'd known who I was from the very moment I wrote my initial plea. She had given herself away with the last message. It had to be someone who saw me every day, someone who could study me; only she would know I was letting it, success, go to my head. It had to be, you see, Sheila Gardner, who sat behind me in Carlyle's class.

I came to class the next day dizzy with anticipation. I hadn't slept a wink, wondering how it would be when I finally spoke to her.

I turned in my seat and looked at her, waiting for her to look up at me. After a moment, she did, a slight blush in her cheeks. She met my gaze and waited for me to speak.

"We should meet," I said quietly.

"Yes. Yes. You?" she said, nodding.

"If only I'd known."

"We both needed time," she said, smiling at me.

Mr. Carlyle called for quiet and I turned to face him. He began to drone about the Spanish Armada, but I didn't mind so much because I knew I wasn't alone any more. I picked up my pencil and waited for just the right words to come.

Raimen

LINDE LYNCH

I did not often take a left at the crossroad, because I was unfamiliar with the path. I usually turned right. Having only been in the area for a short time, I still had to feel my way around the twisting paths that surrounded great Uncle Chester's mansion.

I felt very uncomfortable in a mansion. It was too rich for my blood, but I had figured that it would not hurt to try and butter up old Uncle Chester before he died. So I'd made the sacrifice and had left my three-room apartment and my unemployment check behind in the city and had paid Uncle Chester a visit. He was my last chance.

The long walks I took everyday were my salvation, because staying in that house listening to Uncle Chester babble on about everything under the sun for more than half an hour was enough to drive any sane man straight to Bellevue. At least he was not like my parents. They were always harping at me all the time to find another job and move back home, because my apartment was too expensive anyway, and to think about finding a nice girl and settling down, because I was twenty-six and wasting precious time. Those were the main issues. The list is miles longer. My parents' nagging drove me to Uncle Chester just as much as his large, rather attractive-looking fortune did. Fortunately, Uncle Chester was more concerned with talking about his lifelong accomplishments than me, so every day I received a new bit of history about his life.

I guess you could say he liked me. At least, more than he liked anyone else in our family. He always said how he admired the way I stood up for what I wanted. That was how he had gotten to where he was. Just from things he had said the last few years, I knew he was undecided about his will, so I had nominated myself as the best candidate for his heir. My only job was to convince him of that.

Anyway, getting back to the path I was first talking about. I was in the mood for something new that day. I followed the path as it swung around to the right and then down a steep incline through a grove of pine trees. As soon as I came to the clearing, I saw that the path did not pick up again. I started to walk to my left and eventually came upon a stream which ran alongside a small glen. I found myself a rock and sat down to rest. The air was still and everything was strangely silent. I could not even detect the sound of a bird, so that when I heard a small voice behind me, I was startled.

"What do you think you're doing here?" the voice asked.

I swung around. Before me stood a child who could not have been more than eight years old. He had shaggy brown hair, brown eyes, a slender build and a slight look of annoyance on his face.

"Well," he said, "I asked you a question."

"What does it look like I'm doing? I'm sitting here resting."

"And who told you you could sit here?" he shot back, his large, doe-like eyes boring through me.

"I did, kid. Would you like to join me?"

"I certainly would. After all, this is *my* place. You'll have to excuse me. I don't mean to be nasty, but you took me by surprise. No one ever takes that path."

"That's O.K.," was my reply, "but how did you know what path I took?"

"There happens to be only one path that leads here. By the way, my name is Raimen."

"I'm Ronnie," I said. "Do you live around here?"

"Well," he hesitated, "you could say that."

"Oh, then you must know my Uncle Chester."

"Yes," he said with a strange calmness, "And you must be his nephew from New York."

"Yeah, I am."

"Good old Uncle Chester isn't doing so good, huh? I bet you can't wait to get your hands on his dough, with you being out of a job and all," Raimen said, with a slight smile.

I looked at him in shocked silence. Who was this kid anyway that he knew so much? He had to be related to someone who worked for Uncle Chester.

"Listen, kid," I said, "how old are you anyway?"

"The name is Raimen, Ron, not 'kid' and I'm seven and a half."

"You don't sound seven and a half."

"Not only looks are deceiving," he replied, and then, changing the subject, "Have you ever seen any place so peaceful?"

"No, I haven't," I agreed, suddenly caught up in his mood. "You must come here often."

"Always," he said. "Do you like it here, Ronnie? Not like New York, right? You don't like New York much, do you? Although, I guess it really isn't the city, it's your parents. Always expecting too much." He went on, "Well, you were right to come here. Uncle Chester trusts you."

"What is going on? How do you know anything about my parents or how much Uncle Chester trusts me?" I demanded.

"Now, Ron," he soothed, "don't get all upset."

"I can't believe this?" I yelled. "A seven year old kid telling me not to get upset."

"Seven and a half, Ronnie," he insisted, "seven and a half."

"Oh, whatever," I threw at him with annoyance.

"Now, just calm down, Ron. You may surprise yourself, you know."

"Surprise myself?" I asked, puzzled.

"Yes, you have the power to do whatever you wish, just as Uncle Chester did. Whatever you want."

"Oh, right, kid. Tell me about it. Listen, you better get your nose out of the storybooks and read a daily newspaper, so you can get the cold, hard facts. I mean, I have no job, no apartment and a family I can't stand, but I suppose I can still do whatever I wish, right? Wake up, Raimen."

"No, Ronnie, you've been the one sleeping. Now just sit and relax for a while. You're shattering the placid quality that I love about this place. The quiet is divine."

"Well, excuse me. Where did you ever learn to talk so fancily?" I asked. "Are you sure you're not a forty-five year old midget?"

"Far from it," was his reply.

"You sure don't sound seven and a half."

"I'm seven and a half *here*," he said simply.

"Well, then you can stay *here* as long as you want," I said, "I'm going back to the house."

"Remember, Ronnie, life is too short to bother letting petty things slow you down," was his last remark to me.

I looked at him once more, and he flashed me a knowing smile. I just shook my head and left. I went back to that glen for the following three days, because Raimen had really intrigued me, but he was never there. As much as I thought he was a smart-mouthed brat, I still wanted to talk to him again.

I asked around the house, but no one seemed to know him. When I mentioned him to Uncle Chester, he just gave me a really strange look and mumbled something about the "inevitable."

The whole thing was beginning to give me the creeps, and I even considered leaving, but decided instead to wait it out a few more days.

It was a good thing I did, too, because two days later, Uncle Chester had his lawyer in and it was not long after that that he fell very ill. I guess he knew his time was coming. I had to call the family and tell them about his death, so everyone would be able to make it for the funeral. It was funny, but as much as Uncle Chester got on my nerves, I kind of missed the old guy.

It took several weeks to settle the estate, but the lawyer finally called a meeting for the reading of the will in Uncle Chester's study.

I was sitting there gazing out the window when I heard the lawyer read the part that said ninety percent of Uncle Chester's stocks, bonds and actual fortune was left to me, not to mention the house and its surrounding grounds. I thought of how I would be able to tell that brat that the glen was mine now and he could not boss me around as he had tried to do, when I suddenly saw him pop up in the window. He smiled, waved and flashed me a victory sign, the first two fingers on his little hand forming a prominent "V."

I looked quickly around the room, but no one had seemed to notice him. When I turned toward the window again, he was gone. To everyone's amazement, I bolted out of the room and ran out the front door.

I looked around. "Raimen!" I yelled, "Raimen, where'd you go?"

I ran all around the house, but he was nowhere to be seen. I headed for the woods and made my way directly to the glen, but no one was there. I was suddenly struck by the true beauty of it and I assured myself that it was really mine.

"It always was," a voice said.

This time I did not feel startled. Instead I let my eyes roam across the trees, searching the figure I thought would follow the voice. Then I noticed a bird chirping and I could hear the stream gurgling and splashing. I had never really noticed it that much before. The glen was no longer far removed from the world. It had lost that placid quality that Raimen had mused about. Maybe that was what Uncle Chester had meant by "inevitable." It was as though neither Raimen nor I had ever been there that day.

Maybe we had not.

Fictional Memoir

For a certain kind of story material you may want a character other than the main one to tell the story. The "I," in other words, might be a friend or acquaintance of the main character or even just a witness or outsider. Reminiscence that features someone other than the author is a memoir. This gives the reader an as-seen-by point of view that can be very useful

when you want a personal narrator, such as the cowboy in
The Ox-Bow Incident, *who is present at the main events but
is not a principal participant. This is one possibility, at any
rate, that you will want to consider in deciding how best to tell
your story.*

Bystander

WILL ROBERTSON

Gunshots sounded off the walls in East Los Angeles as a terrorist
executed his victims on a primetime television show, their actions
caught forever on thirty inches of celluloid film. I barely even noticed
as I tied my shoes and put on my jacket to go to the store. I had to pick
up some groceries for my mom before I went to the movies with my
friends. I knew that Vons would be crowded so I decided to go to a
mini-mart that was nearby.

The small store was empty. The girl behind the counter smiled at
me. She had a cute smile and dark brown eyes that reflected everything she saw. I smiled back and walked over to the bread aisle. As I
went to the back to pick up a carton of milk, I heard the door open
again. When I turned around, a young man was standing in front of
the counter talking to the girl.

I heard the cash register ring as she opened it. When I turned
around again, he had a gun on her and was backing toward the door.
Suddenly for no apparent reason he stopped, raised the gun, and shot
her. As he ran out the door, I stood there with a loaf of bread in one
hand and a carton of milk in the other. I dropped them and ran to the
counter and stopped.

Her face was just as before except for a single drop of blood on
her cheek, like an obscene beauty mark placed there by a deranged
makeup artist. Her eyes were like silent movie cameras frozen on the
last frame of a film she couldn't bear to see. And the terrible thing was
that I couldn't change the channel for either of us.

Jason

AMY PHILLIPS

Allow me to introduce myself; I'm Amy Phillips, and I'm going to
tell you a true story about something that happened a little over four
years ago. I was at Magic Mountain with my two friends, Jenny and
Terri. Magic Mountain was to open a new rollercoaster, the Colossus,

advertised to be the most spectacular of its kind in the world. Being the curious person I am, I somehow talked the apprehensive Jenny and Terri into accompanying me on that dreadfully hot day.

Even though the ride had not been officially opened yet, many people had been standing in line all day; they wanted to be among the first to ride this spectacular coaster. We weren't as interested in it as we were in the excitement and entertainment. After four hours of walking around, they were eager to get on some interesting rides, while I was just fascinated by looking around at the sights and people. I told them to go on, and I'd meet them later. I decided to head over to the Colossus; I couldn't go home without a button that said "I survived the Colossus." The hordes of tourists continued to gather, snapping pictures and watching the magnificent ride. Finally getting into the mile-long line, I inched up very slowly, laughing and talking to a few kids in front of me. I took out my comb several times, and ran it through my damp, entangled hair; the heat was intense; it didn't seem to get any cooler. I spent the spare time imagining myself going ninety miles an hour down the mountain-steep drops, screaming with joy as the wind brushed against my face and through my hair. While I was in the middle of my daydream, I heard a faint whimpering close by. I was the only one to notice, for everyone else continued laughing and screaming. I looked around but saw no one crying; the faint cries sounded closer. A small boy appeared out of nowhere; he was about five or six years old with brown hair and eyes and a small birthmark on the side of his cheek. I glanced at him for a second; and when he looked up at me, I quickly turned my head, not wanting him to think I was staring. He continued crying, but no one else noticed him. I leaned down close to him and quietly asked him what was wrong. His bottom lip quivered as he took a deep breath.

"I—I—"

"It's OK, just relax," I comforted him.

"I—I—can't find my brother," he sobbed.

"Well, what's his name?" I asked. "Maybe I can help you find him."

"Michael Fitzpatrick," he replied, a little calmer now, looking intensely with total faith in me. "Could you help me find him?"

By this time, I was near the head of the line, only a few steps from my turn. The cars took off, and only one more time around and I'd be on the rollercoaster screaming like all the rest, but I decided I would help him.

"By the way, what's your name?" I asked him.

"My name's Jason," he said, clutching my hand tightly.

We weaved out of the line, eventually, and began to walk toward a snack bar; I wanted to buy him a soda. As I looked back, I saw the Colossus take off without me. We were some distance away when we heard the terrible crash: the Colossus had derailed. The confusion, noise, and panic was unbelievable as we ran to get away from the flying pieces. In the commotion I lost Jason in the crowd; I was worried but I hoped he had found his brother. After forty-five minutes scanning the area for Jason with no success, I went to the nearest snack bar. As I was standing near a table trying to figure out how to find Terri and Jenny, I started talking to a boy a few years older than I. We talked about the accident and he said he was visiting from Philadelphia. I told him the whole story about Jason in detail, describing what he looked like, what he said and the fact that he was looking for his brother, Michael Fitzpatrick. The boy turned pale as I finished my last sentence.

"My God," he said. "This is impossible; I'm Michael Fitzpatrick. Jason is my brother."

"Well, did you find him?" I asked.

The boy was shaken as he said, "Jason drowned last summer."

A Fine Line

ANDY SHELFFO

He was a writer, and a damn good one. I was a writer, too, and I was jealous of him because he was better than I; but as I got to know him I realized that he was truly great. The things I read of his were stunning. When I found out that he was going to be my roommate for my sophomore year in college, my first reaction was to find a new roommate. Then I decided to stay with him in hope that some of his talent would rub off on me.

The things that Dan Cunningham wrote about were very depressing; death and drugs mostly. I pictured him as a small, sort of sad-looking kid who funneled all of his time into writing. I found out that I was wrong the moment I met him.

I waited for Dan in our room, but he never showed up, so I went down to the pub on campus, because I'm not one to pass up a beer. I was sitting at the bar by myself, when a guy about 6'2", weighing close to two hundred pounds, came and sat down next to me. He was good-looking, quick with a smile, and, I found out, easy to talk to. After a while, when his beer was gone, he said to me, "I'll bet you a beer that you can't tie your shoes all by yourself." Well, I had been drinking, but not that much. I leaned over and untied my shoes while he just sat there calmly. Then, as I began to tie them again, he quickly leaned over and began tying his own. When I realized what had happened, I laughed while he quickly ordered two beers on me. This was Dan Cunningham. He was fun to be around, and took me for at least five more beers before I stopped taking his bets. We ended up getting very drunk together and stumbling back to our room. I was looking forward to a fun year.

As weeks passed, however, I found that Dan wasn't always fun to be around. I was spending a lot of time in our room because I had a lot of work. When I wasn't spending time on my school work, I would spend time writing. Dan, on the other hand, didn't seem to do any work, at least none that I saw. I also never saw him do any writing, which struck me as being odd. Whenever Dan was around he would either take a nap, read, or listen to the stereo. He was also very moody.

One day I remember that I was getting ready for my Friday morning class. I was a little late, and in a hurry. In my rush, I made a little too much noise, and felt a shoe hit my back. "Quiet," Dan commanded, his voice muffled by a pillow.

"Sorry," I said, "I'm running—"

"Quiet," he repeated in a more menacing tone. Now, I was late, so I didn't pursue the matter any further.

After my class Dan wasn't around, so I just sat and wrote. Then Dan came in. I hadn't been looking forward to his coming back. I didn't even look up from my work.

"Hey," he said, "What's up?"

"Nothing," I said.

"Look, uh, I'm really sorry about this morning. I, uh, had kind of a rough night last night."

I smiled and told him not to worry about it.

"No, no," he said. "Let me make it up to you. Let's go out to eat."

I went out with him and had a great time.

It was all very strange. One minute he would be warm and friendly, and the next he would snap at me, or not talk at all. The only time we ever really talked was when I found him in the pub. There, he was always friendly.

On Thursday afternoon I got back to our room after my last class and found Dan at his desk, writing. The desk was covered with papers, notebooks, a dictionary, and all around him were papers crumpled into little balls.

"What's up?" I asked. He just grunted. I figured that he was in one of his moods, so I just started my homework.

I finished a couple of hours later, but Dan was still hard at work. I asked him if he wanted to go and get something to eat, but he didn't answer, so I went out by myself. When I came back, he wasn't writing, but was reviewing his work. By now, I wasn't going to say anything to him and was just planning to go down to the pub by myself. He stopped me.

"Have you ever," he said to me, "had a story that you just had to write? I mean, one that you felt compelled to write?" I nodded. I had felt something like that before.

"I'm obsessed with this story right now. I've been at it for almost six hours straight. And you know, I don't like it."

I knew how he felt. Many times I had worked on one story for so long that I became sick of it. I told him this and suggested he take a break.

"No, it's not that," he replied. "I've been sick of stories before, but I've never felt like this. Maybe I should go down to the pub, though."

We went to the pub together, but we didn't leave together. He stayed much later and got much drunker than I did. He was asleep when I woke up and asleep when I got back from my one and only class. His desk was just as he had left it the night before, with his story right on top, in plain view. I tried to get it out of my mind, but I was curious. What kind of story could possess him like that? I gave in to my temptation.

I only intended to glance at what he had written, but after reading the opening paragraph, I was mesmerized.

The story was about a young man in college who had a drinking problem that was ruining his life. When I finished the story, I was overwhelmed and drained. I had never read a story with such emotion. This was obviously Dan's best. Then I realized why it was so good; because it was true. I read the story again, and Dan himself was clearly the main character. There were a few differences, but it was Dan.

Dan was still asleep when I finished the story, and I went and got something to eat. When I came back, both Dan and the story were gone. The next day, Dan was back, but I never saw the story again, and I never saw him write anything else. Instead he would spend all of his time at the pub. Eventually, he dropped out and I never saw him again.

Some time later, after I'd graduated, I was waiting in a doctor's office, leafing through a copy of the *New Yorker* to pass the time. First, I looked at the cartoons, but as time dragged on, I turned to the short stories.

It was an excellent story, smooth and well-crafted, but there was something missing. It was an historical piece set during the Depression and the painstaking research was obvious, but there was no emotion. I didn't get the feeling that the author had experienced any of the story. Not that it was really necessary, after all, it was in the *New Yorker*, but it would have made the piece, already excellent, that much better.

I finished the story, and then glanced at the author's name. It was Dan Cunningham. It didn't hit me right away, though, that it could be the same person. After all, it was a pretty common name, but when I re-read the story, I knew that it was the same one.

I was a bit disappointed when I realized this. He had been so great before, but now he was only good. This story was good, excellent, but it wasn't in the same league with his others. His other stories made one think and feel, they were alive. This one seemed artificial.

As I was finally called in to see the doctor, I was saddened by the fact that no one would ever get to see what Dan Cunningham was really capable of. But then I realized that I was one of the lucky ones. I had seen the greatness that Dan Cunningham possessed.

Third-Person Fiction—
Single-Character Viewpoint

When you plan a story, it's necessary to determine who will tell it—whose voice the reader will hear. Not all stories lend themselves to first-person narration, where a character in the story relates what's going on. The alternative is some kind of third-person narration, where you tell the story by referring to your characters as "he," "she," and "they."

This decision still leaves you with several choices. One is to enter the mind of only one character, whose thoughts and feelings are central to the story. Consider this along with the other options to follow.

The Toy

LOREN NOVECK

Seth was happy. Mommy wasn't happy any more, but Seth was. Mommy hadn't been happy since Daddy went away. Seth didn't care. He didn't like Daddy very much anyway. Daddy didn't play with him. Mommy didn't play much any more, though. Now Mommy went out, dressed in funny clothes with hard buttons that hurt Seth's face when he hugged her. She wasn't home when Seth got out of playschool, either. Seth had to go home with his neighbor, who was fat and had a son with red hair. The son was in Seth's playschool, but Seth didn't like him. He smelled funny.

Mommy would come and pick him up at the end of the day, and Seth would want to play. But Mommy always said she was too tired to play now, just like Daddy used to. Seth got mad at Mommy when she said this. Once he even hit Mommy on the leg. Mommy didn't even get mad like she used to. She just told Seth to go play by himself. Seth knew Mommy was worried about money—he heard her say that she needed to find a better job, and thank God she had her grandmother's jewelry to sell if she was desperate. She said that on the telephone. Seth wasn't quite sure what any of that meant, except grandmother, but it didn't sound like something good.

Seth didn't get mad at Mommy any more, though. Now he had a new toy to play with. Mommy had said he couldn't have any new toys for a while. That was when he hit her. But Seth was very proud of himself, because he had found his own new toy. He found it in Mommy's room. It was a pretty toy—it was round, to go on his finger, and it had a big sparkly thing on the top. It was a rainbow-maker toy. Seth had fun making rainbows.

Mommy called Seth for dinner. Seth was going to tell Mommy about his new toy, but then he found out they were having fish for dinner. Seth didn't like fish at all. This made him angry at Mommy. He decided not to tell her about his sparkly thing. It made him feel grown-up to have a secret.

Later, Seth came downstairs to get some ice cream. There was chocolate ice cream. Mommy was on the telephone. She was crying. Seth was scared to see Mommy crying. Maybe if he told her his secret, she would feel better. Seth listened to what Mommy was saying. She was talking about something called a "diamondring." Seth wondered what a diamondring was. It sounded nasty.

Seth went to the freezer to get his ice cream. He was going to be a big boy and get it for himself. Then he dropped a bowl on the floor. Mommy came running over and yelled at him. She even hit him on the arm. Now Seth was crying. He wasn't going to tell Mommy his secret now. He went into his room and played with his pretty sparkly thing. This made him feel better, but he was still mad at Mommy.

Mommy came in to see Seth, to put him to bed. She was being nice to him now. Seth was still mad anyway. Mommy asked him if he had seen her diamondring. She was crying again. There was that word again—*diamondring*. Seth was sure it was something lucky now, because Mommy had been crying both times she talked about it. Seth wasn't crying now. A diamondring must be something that made you cry, then. No, Seth didn't have that. Mommy cried even more when Seth told her that. Then Seth went to sleep.

The next day, Mommy told Seth that she had gone to the bank and found out that they didn't have much money left. Seth understood about banks. He had one shaped like an elephant that he kept his pennies in. Pennies were money. Mommy also said that her job didn't make enough money for them to live in a big house anymore. Seth didn't understand jobs—how did you make money?—but he didn't tell Mommy that. Mommy said that she was going to sell their house and they would move to an apartment. Seth thought that was okay. His friend Dennis lived in an apartment. Seth wasn't mad at Mommy any more. He was going to tell her about his rainbow toy, but Mommy didn't have time to talk about toys. She had to go talk to a man about their house.

The new apartment was small, but it was nice. There was a girl named Susan across the hall. She came and played with Seth after his school was over, so he didn't have to play with the smelly boy anymore. Susan was a big girl. She knew how to read. Mommy was working more now, so Seth went to school more and then he played with Susan. Seth forgot all about his sparkly toy. Susan was teaching him how to read.

Mommy looked different now. She had grey stripes in her hair, and lines on her face, and she wasn't soft to hug. Seth liked the old Mommy better. Susan said his Mommy was working very hard, and Seth should be very nice to her. Seth wanted to do something nice for Mommy, to make her laugh. He hadn't seen her laugh in a long time.

On a Saturday in the winter, Seth got up early. It was cold in the apartment. He went to get his slippers. He found his sparkly rainbow toy in a slipper. He played with it a little. Then he had a good idea. Maybe he could use his toy to make Mommy laugh.

Seth went into Mommy's room. Mommy was still sleeping. He kneeled on Mommy's bed. He held the sparkly thing in his hands over Mommy's head. He opened up his hands, and the sun in the room made the toy sparkle. The toy made rainbows on the bed. Seth had forgotten about the rainbows. They were so pretty. Maybe he should keep his toy. He put it into his pajama pocket. He could tickle Mommy to make her laugh.

Making the News

MICHAEL FERRARO

The man with the silver hair walked down the street. Maple was the name of it, and it was only a couple of blocks from where he and his wife lived for over thirty years. He fit right in with the impeccably manicured homes lining the area. Part of the scenery in his tailored grey-flannel suit. This would help him immeasurably and make today's busy schedule move along much faster.

He looked around. As he grew older he appreciated everything so much more: his wife, children, and the job he loved. As his mind drifted to this neighborhood, which meant so much to him, a little girl came over and said "Hi" in the biggest voice she could muster.

"Hello, Kimberly. How are you today?"

"Oh, I'm just fine. What are ya doing?"

"I'm taking my morning constitutional."

"Your morning consti—what?"

He smiled. "That's just another name for my morning walk. I guess you've never been up so early. You've seen me around."

"Yeah, I guess." Kimberly was now quite fed up with all the niceties adults called conversation. She finally blurted her purpose. She lifted the pad and pen she was holding. "Wanna buy some Daisy Scout cookies?"

"Of course. I was just saying to my wife: 'Miriam, no year would be complete without some of Kimberly Weslen's Daisy Scout cookies.'"

Kimberly giggled with delight. Three boxes away from the surprise grand prize for the best Daisy Scout salesperson. "O.K., then all ya have to do is sign your name and address here, and . . . Oh, do you want Mocha Minties, Peanut-Butter Bubblegums, or Banana Chipsters?"

"Gee, Kimberly, that *is* a difficult decision, I'll tell you what, why don't you order me a box of each." Though those Peanut-Butter Bubblegums sounded even more menacing than what came the way of the Daisy Scouts in past years.

Kimberly was ecstatic. "Wow, thanks a lot. Let's see, that'll be three-seventy five. Of course," she read from the order form, "with every order the customer gets a comp- compli-. Free." She looked up. "Ya get a free calendar."

He tried not to laugh. "What would I do without it?"

Kimberly's mother, who had waved from the lawn, walked over and joined the pair. She looked at the man with an apologetic expression.

"Hi, Joan," he said. They joined hands and kissed.

"I hope she hasn't bothered you."

"Not at all."

"It seems Daisy Scout is synonymous with sales-shark these days."

"Believe me," he chuckled, "they've been doing it since my daughters belonged, and I'm not even going to tell you how long that's been."

Kimberly had somehow managed to slip out and tell her friend, Sue, about the sale.

"By the way," said Mrs. Weslen, "remind Miriam about the cocktail party I'm having Saturday. It'll start at about seven-thirty. I forgot to tell her what time when I called. You can come?"

"We'd love to."

"Great. We're just inviting a few neighbors. Cal likes to keep these things small."

"I agree. There's nothing worse than two-hundred lost souls wandering around with cocktails and little napkins."

When Mrs. Weslen left, he checked his appointment book, just to make sure about Saturday evening. Fine. He wrote it in. It would be a busy day, but he was sure he could work in a little gathering. Anyway, he promised himself he'd take Miriam out more and spend a little more time just enjoying himself.

Now, for the day's business.

As Joan Weslen walked back to her house, she thought about

him. He was a handsome man and he had a great speaking voice.
A lot of people liked his looks and voice.

The man continued on his way down the street until he finally
reached his destination: a large, grey, clapboard house that stood out
sorely among the others. Its grounds were very poorly kept, and had
been since Mrs. Thatcher was widowed. People said that her stinginess
would not even allow her to pay a neighborhood child a few dollars to
trim the lawn. He knew her, though, and at this point she was quite
senile. If he had been a few years younger, he would have helped with
the yard, but his back strained easily now.

He walked to the rear lawn. The day was beautiful, and he
breathed in deeply. Then, he pulled gloves and electrical tape from his
pocket, put on the gloves, and spread the tape over a pane of glass in
the back door. He found a stone and hit the glass. Not a sound. He felt
for the inner knob and undid the latch. He went in and found himself
in the kitchen. There were several drawers near the sink, and he went
through them until he found a good, sharp carving knife.

He went upstairs and found her bedroom. She was sleeping as he
took a handkerchief from his pocket and put it on her chest. He
stabbed the handkerchief. Dead. Not a sound. And not a drop of blood
on his grey suit either.

As he left, he thought of what a nice day it would be. His work
had finally taken him closer to home for a while. It was still very early,
so he could have breakfast with Miriam for a change, relax and read
the *Times*. He wouldn't have to work again until later, when he'd be the
first on the spot where she was found. Old lady is latest victim in
Westchester Handkerchief Murders.

He went on his way and, upon arriving home, saw an unfamiliar
car in his driveway. He went through the kitchen door, where he
found a pleasant surprise.

"Daddy!" called a very familiar voice. She ran to him from the
butler's pantry and they hugged.

"Ruth! You didn't tell us you were coming."

"Well, actually I didn't know either. Ben was called East on a
sudden business trip. We can only stay a short while, then we have to
drive into Manhattan."

Miriam and Ben entered the kitchen.

"How are you, Ben?" he asked, shaking his son-in-law's hand.

"Just fine, Dad, and you?"

"Well, I must tell you I'm feeling great."

"I'm glad, Daddy," said Ruth, "I was just telling Mom how
worried I get with you two here in New York. The winters are so
violent and when I hear about all the accidents . . . "

"Yes, you really must move to our part of the world," said Ben.

"Never," said he, "I prefer snow and ice to your mud-slides or
whatever you get out there in California."

"Dear," said Miriam to her daughter, "I think you'd better give up on your father. We both love it here. I was born here," she reminded Ben.

"But I've been reading that you've had some terrific offers from the West Coast, and—"

He interrupted Ruth, "Gossip, that's all it is, dear girl."

"I don't believe you, Daddy."

"Believe what you like." He smiled. "So how are the children?"

"All right, I give up. They're just fine. They're staying with Ben's mother."

Ben pulled out his wallet. "You've got to see these photos."

"Oh, they are nice," he beamed, looking proudly at the pictures.

"Ben," urged Miriam, "You have to tell him what little David said."

Ben laughed. "He looked up at me and said, 'I want to report the news just like grandpa when I grow up. Nice and easy.' Hey you know, I wouldn't half mind having your job either, Gramps."

"Wait a minute," the man in the grey suit chuckled. "It's not as easy as it looks."

Third-Person Fiction—
Dual- Or Multi-Character Viewpoint

Write a short story in which the point of view alternates between two or more characters because comparing their thoughts and feelings is important to the story.

Monday

DEREK CAPLINGER

"Francis, are you awake?"

Francis was vaguely aware of his mother's voice drifting up from downstairs.

Ever since he could remember, he'd hated the name Francis. He didn't even look like a Francis, and that made it worse.

"Honey, if you don't get up you'll be late for school."

Francis' mother was known for her profound statements.

Francis Kenneth Muldoon wasn't a particularly conspicuous name. He could easily picture himself as one of a million other Francis K. Muldoons. Francis Muldoon, Typical American Boy. Thomas, now there was a successful name. Tom for around school and Thomas for special occasions.

Francis rolled out of bed just as his mother called for the third time. "I'm up, I'm up!" he yelled down the stairs. He pushed open the drapes and found a bleak, sunless morning. He let the drapes fall shut.

"I really dislike Mondays," he said, pulling on a sock.

"We don't have any bacon or eggs yet, so you'll have to run on Cheerios today," said Ginny's mother.

"Ugh. Going to the store today?"

"Yep. Need anything?"

"Uh huh, bacon and eggs." Ginny paused, "Mom, do I have to go to school today?"

Ginny's mother frowned.

"I didn't make you go on Friday because it was the end of the week. But this is a new week and as good a time as any to start a new school." She looked at Ginny for a moment. "I know it's hard to go to a new school and find new friends. I went through it myself. And look at how well I turned out. Ginny, it won't be that bad, honest."

"All right. I'm taking your word on this."

"Good girl. Are you nervous?"

"Nah. I'm not really hungry though. S'pose I could pass on the cheerios?"

Ginny's mother gave her a worried look, then smiled.

"I never ate much on my first day either."

Francis twirled the dial on his locker to the right numbers and gave the handle a tug. Nothing. He ran his hand through his dark hair, took a breath, and repeated the process. Same result. He kicked the locker a couple of times and tried the combination again. Bingo!

"Hey, Francis!"

Francis had spoken with Doug Johnson once at the beginning of the year. Apparently he'd been the only one to do so because from periods one through eight he was under Doug's constant surveillance.

"Hey Francis," Doug called again. "Did you study for that history test?"

History test! Francis was quite prepared to give up on Monday. He turned away from his locker. "No."

Francis already knew what Doug was going to say next.

"Oh," said Doug casually, "I did."

Ginny worked her way thrugh the halls, desperately trying to find the counselor's office. She spotted a teacher and managed to get close enough to ask directions.

Three minutes and one wrong turn later, Ginny stood at the door to the counselor's office. She took a deep breath and plunged in. By the time she'd finished getting her schedule, the tardy bell had rung. Aside from a few stragglers, the halls were empty. Ginny looked at her schedule card and headed in the direction of room 407. A minute and a half later she was standing outside the door, listening to a teacher explaining dangling modifiers. Not wanting to make a big production of her entrance, she waited by the door until the teacher finished speaking. She straightened her hair, smoothed her dress, and stepped in.

Francis was doodling on his paper, thinking about the history test, when a girl walked into the classroom. She was average height, had light brown hair, and looked as if she were about to have a nervous breakdown.

She walked over to Mr. Matthew's desk and got her book. He wrote her name down in his book and told her to find a seat. She looked around the classroom and picked one by the wall, which was where Francis sat. She asked him what page they were on.

"One twenty-eight," he said, not looking at her.

The rest of English passed slowly. Francis kept thinking about his history test, his doodles, the new girl in front of him, his name and, subconsciously, about dangling modifiers.

After lunch, Francis walked into the library. He saw the new girl walk over to the magazine rack and pick up a month-old issue of *Time*. She walked back to sit at her table.

Francis went over to the librarian's desk, picked up the current issue, and meandered toward the new girl's table. "Hi," he said, forcing himself to be casual. "I thought you might want to look at a more current issue." He waved the magazine a little.

"Oh, I didn't know there was one. Not on the shelves, I mean."

Francis smiled slightly. "You have to know how our librarian thinks. He won't put a magazine on the shelves unless he's sure that it's too old to get snatched. All the good ones are at the desk." He paused, "By the way, I'm . . . Francis."

Well, that's that.

The new girl smiled. "Pleased to meet you, Francis. I'm Ginny. Would you like to sit down?"

Francis said that he would. For the next twenty minutes they talked about which teachers she should avoid, how to get an "A" in

Mrs. Detweiler's class, and all the other things which were of use in surviving the rigors of Thompson High.

"Well," said Francis, looking at his watch. "The next bell's going to ring any second now. What do you have next?"

Ginny looked at her card. "Art, room 203."

"My locker's that way. I'll walk with you."

As they stood up, Ginny brushed her schedule card off the table. Francis bent down to pick it up. He glanced at the card as he handed it to her, then stopped and looked again. A smile creased his face.

Something about Ginette Rhibaldi and Francis K. Muldoon appealed to Francis' sense of humor. He grinned. Monday might not be so bad after all.

The Paper Route

MIKE MEUNIER

The sound of his feet shuffling through the loose gravel caused Doug to yawn sleepily despite the fresh, crisp pre-dawn air that was biting at his face. He stuck his right hand deeper into the warmth of his coat pocket and readjusted his grip on the paper bag strapped across his back. Behind him dust from the gravel lifted and slowly sifted back to the ground.

He was walking with his head down, and his feet could not seem to pick up, only shuffle along. He could have kicked himself for wearing dark pants, not only because they would show the dust when the sun came out, but a car might not see him with dark clothing.

He relaxed though, as he could not recall ever hearing of a paper boy being hit by a car, and it would be growing light within a half hour. Besides, his paper bag had a reflective red stripe across it, something the *Daily Tribune* required for safety precautions. He thought this was a good idea since most of the distributers had to start their delivery routes in the darkness of early morning. If a car came up on him, its lights would surely shine on the stripe.

He was walking with his head up now, and he was slowly awakening as he approached the part of his route that he always dreaded. He hated this part of his route more than he hated anything. The half mile ahead of him was enclosed by woods on both sides, and he had no deliveries on it. The fact that there weren't any deliveries didn't bother Doug in any significant degree compared to the woods. The darkness the trees produced always made his heart speed up. "There should be lights on this road," he mumbled to himself as he plodded along.

As he entered the forest-enclosed part of the road, the darkness that had now fallen made it impossible to see more than 15 yards in any direction. The smell of the woods seemed particularly strong on this night. The pine trees towering overhead gave off a sharp distinct smell that reminded him of the fragrance of the air freshener in his Aunt Opel's car. Flowers grew plentifully on both sides of the road, and he could detect their presence with his nose, although the deep shadows the trees cast made it impossible to see them. But there was another smell too, the smell of decay, Doug thought. He always imagined that if you cut the bark off a dying tree the bug-infested core would smell like the decay on the inside.

He involuntarily began walking in the center of the road. He noticed the noise he made shuffling his feet and began lifting them unusually high to prevent waking up Bigfoot. He always thought about Bigfoot on this road, but not as much as he used to. When he was nine years old and had just begun the route he had seen a T.V. special on Bigfoot.

After that he always brought his dad's big silver flashlight with him. The flashlight was 18 inches long and was quite heavy when it had batteries in it. He didn't bring it with him for light as much as for protection. If Bigfoot were to attack him he always thought he would knock him unconscious with it.

This was two years ago, and Doug didn't even bring the flashlight with him any more. Any time he thought about it he laughed at his immature foolishness, and after all, he was older now.

He laughed at himself now and moved over to the side of the road again. The laugh was intended to reassure himself, and he had moved over to the side mostly to prove to himself that he wasn't scared. He even hung his head again, trying to slow down the pounding of his heart and be drowsy. He was, however, happy that the side of the road was dirt instead of gravel and he wouldn't awaken Bigfoot.

When he was about half way through the woods the atmosphere changed suddenly. The smell of flowers was replaced by the smell of stagnant water and the decay odor was stronger. And there was something else too; something he couldn't pinpoint.

Suddenly he stopped in his tracks to listen to the silence. He stood listening for a full minute without moving. Not a cricket chirped. Not a bullfrog burped. He didn't hear anything. On most nights the forest was alive with the sounds of the night animals, but tonight not a single sound echoed from the woods.

He strained his ears, trying to pick up any bit of noise. To him the minute seemed like a hour. He then re-adjusted the strap on his paper bag because it had begun to dig into the skin on his neck. He again began to walk, his pace noticeably faster than before. He had only gone a few feet when he heard a voice off to his left that caused him to jump with a start.

"Help me, please, I'm hurt" came in a man's voice from a clump of bushes off to the side of the road.

Doug's heart was pounding on the inside of his chest like a jackhammer. He withdrew his hand from his pocket and advanced a few feet. He was walking laterally and facing the other side of the road.

A rustling in the brush caused him to stop again. He strained his eyes in the direction he thought it was coming from. The voice had barely been audible to him, and now he was hoping to hear it again. The rustling stopped, and he heard a gasp for air.

His mind was racing through pictures. Flashes of someone lying in the foliage badly injured. He had seen some movement from the bushes and had now advanced towards it. The clump of bushes was about 30 yards from the road. The road itself dropped off about four feet, and an irrigation ditch ran below that. Dry grass covered the ground, and the clump of bushes was surrounded by trees on both sides and behind.

Doug now stopped as he was getting ready to jump the ledge; he began to get an eerie feeling he was being watched. He spun his head around, and his eyes were shifting from side to side.

He slowly backed out towards the center of a road. A cold sweat broke out on his forehead. He noticed his hands were shaking involuntarily. He was turning clockwise and scanning the surroundings while he tried to decide what to do.

The rustling in the bushes began again, and he looked over in their direction. A short gasp emerged, and then there was silence.

Doug once again felt he was being watched and looked over his shoulder. A dim ring of light was beginning to outline the silhouette of the mountains to the east and fill the sky with a blue tint that foreshadowed a nice day to come. The stars were still set in the dark sky, and Doug noticed that a slight wind was blowing from the north.

The bushes rustled again and Doug jumped another step away from that side of the road. He began to consider the possibility that something might be trying to trap him. The feeling that he was being watched from behind was stronger than ever now.

Suddenly Doug knew if someone was hurt in the bushes that Bigfoot must have attacked. By now all thoughts of going off the road to help someone was out of the question. If Bigfoot was here, Doug didn't want to be.

He spun around and began to run. His paper bag had been gradually working it's way down his shoulder, and now it was barely hanging in position. When he began to run he lost hold with his left hand and the bag slipped down his arm, causing him to break stride as he turned to let the strap escape his arm. The bag landed and rolled over. Half of the papers slid out and spilled on the road.

The man who lay sprawled out among the bushes couldn't tell what the boy had dropped in the road. He thought it might be a backpack, because he saw an orange reflective strip on it. He wished he could crawl out and use it to stop the worst part of his bleeding, but he hadn't even been able to call out to the boy as he ran off, so he was much too weak to crawl up the ledge. If only the boy hadn't been scared, then he might have had a chance to make it.

"Looks like a bear attack, sheriff," yelled the deputy.

"A what?" questioned the sheriff.

"Bear, sir, big bear," he replied. "Real big bear."

The deputy raised up from his kneeling position and started back towards the ledge where the sheriff stood.

"Had to be a bear, sheriff. I heard from a couple of buddies on the State Patrol that a bear had been tearing up garbage cans over by the river." The deputy now stood next to the time-hardened veteran and stood surveying the hills.

"Our bears don't attack people, Len," the sheriff stated as he rolled the tobacco from one side of his mouth to the other. "They're scared of people. Hell, this is too close to the city for any bear."

"I know, sheriff."

"What was it you said he was doin', Len?"

"He was doing some research for some college somewhere."

"Research, what the hell on?"

"Well, when he interviewed me and the others he asked about bear sightings."

"Bear sightings?" He spit out his plug. "Well, I guess he found his bear."

"Yeah, a mighty big one too. A big mean one."

"Why a bear research so close to a city like this? We only get a dozen or so a year, and besides none of them are even this close to the city."

"He wasn't doing it on bears, he was doing it on Bigfoot."

"Bigfoot, no such thing," the sheriff said as he looked inquisitively at the deputy. "Are you sure?"

"Yup."

"Well, you go pick up that paper bag and I'll radio the city boys to get up here. They won't believe this mess."

The deputy walked to where the bag lay on the road. He felt his breakfast begin to crawl up his throat. "One hell of a big, mean bear to do that to a man," he muttered as he bent over to put the spilled papers back in the bag.

Third-Person Fiction— No-Character Viewpoint

Write a short story in which you avoid going into the minds of any of the characters because you want the story to stand entirely on what the reader can see from the outside. Such a story will be very much like a play script in that visible action and dialog convey most of what the story is about.

A Memorial Day Story

BETSY BRUBAKER

The red Chevrolet rolled along the highway. Mr. and Mrs. Richardson sat stiffly in the front seat, while Burt and Julie remained silent in the back. They turned off at exit 217 and eased up the off-ramp. Buildings and signs crowded the horizon as the car inched through the heavy Memorial Day traffic. Burt was the first to speak.

"Mom, I hope coming here wasn't too difficult. You know Julie and I couldn't get a leave from the base any other time."

Mrs. Richardson smiled weakly at him. "Oh, don't worry abut it, Burt. Getting up early wasn't that difficult."

The car passed through the cemetery gates, and Mr. Richardson drove steadily down the tree-lined avenue. He stopped in front of the caretaker's shed and herded people out. "Let's make this quick," he said. "We want to beat the breakfast crowds."

The group trod over the soft green lawn to the gravesite. It was one of the plain, flat stones requested by the cemetery because it speeds up the lawnmowing. Mrs. Richardson and Julie dropped their bouquets into the flower pots and backed away. Burt slowly stepped up to the grave and read aloud, "Daniel Richardson, born March 12, 1950, died June 30 1967." He bent down and gently positioned a flower garland on the grave. "Only 17 years old."

"For God's sake, Burt, let's hurry. It's 8:30 already," growled his father.

"You and Mom go ahead. Julie and I'll meet you at the pancake house downtown."

"All right. Come on, Pat." The two of them turned and started back to the car. "Will that place be okay for breakfast?" he asked.

"Troy, something's wrong with you, I can tell. What is it?" questioned his wife, her face suddenly looking tired and very old.

"Nothing's wrong. Just getting hungry, I guess," he replied. He turned away and stared at the ground as they reached the car, but his wife remained facing him.

"Is it something between you and Burt?" He shook his head sullenly. "Is it a problem at work?"

"I said *no*, Pat! Now let's just forget the whole subject!" She got into the car obediently without another word and leaned wearily against the car door as they backed down the avenue and merged into the traffic. Her husband spoke again after a few moments.

"I'm glad we're going to the pancake house; they have fast service there."

"I guess," she said.

Julie led Burt over to a moss-covered bench and spread out her coat. They sat down gingerly and stared at the family car until it started up and drove away. Other mourners began to enter the cemetery, talking in subdued tones.

"Burt, I didn't even know you had a brother until you told me this weekend. Were you and your family close at all?"

"Oh, we were, Julie, but it goes back a little," he replied quietly.

"Well, I want to know," demanded Julie. "We're engaged, aren't we?"

Burt grimaced. "Don't open up old wounds, Julie. You don't know what you're getting into."

"But I need to know. I don't want anything interfering with our life together."

"Well, then, you asked for it," sighed Burt.

He shifted his seating a bit so that he faced toward the grave. "Dan and I were close in high school, and we understood each other; or at least I thought so. When I wasn't strutting around being Mr. Achiever, we did a lot together. We built and flew model planes. I guess that's where I got my interest in flying. In fact, he's the one who told me about civil air patrol." Burt frowned suddenly and shrugged his shoulders as if shaking off some unwanted memory. Julie touched his arm.

"What's wrong?"

"This is where it gets hard."

"Please go on," said Julie warmly. "I really want to know about you and Dan."

"Okay," sighed Burt, "but let's start walking towards town. Dad's probably sitting in the pancake house right now, checking his watch."

By this time, the dew was gone and the grass had been trampled by countless pairs of shoes. Flowers and crushed cigarette butts had been scattered near the roadside by visitors who neglected to use the gravel paths.

"As I said," continued Burt, "Dan and I were close. We got along great until I turned 18, and then something just snapped inside of him. I hadn't gotten my draft notice yet, but still I decided to join the Air Force. That one move severed our friendship completely. During the spring of my senior year Dan got real hooked on this conscientious-objector thing. Later he got into drugs and started cutting classes." The two stopped at the street corner.

"I can tell just by your face that it was hard on you," said Julie.

"It *was* hard seeing my brother drift away like that, but at the time I refused to care. I didn't do anything to help him." Grief and frustration, long bottled up, now flashed across Burt's face.

"The night before I left for training school Dan and I had a huge fight. I came fumbling in, late at night, in a drunken stupor. I found Dan in my room hunched over, staring at one of my trophies. I didn't realize until later that he had been crying."

"What happened next?" asked Julie.

"I entered the room and mumbled something obscene; then I insulted Dan and called him a coward."

"The next morning I tried to apologize, but he wouldn't talk to me. I was running late and I thought I would miss my plane, so I hurried off."

"About two weeks later I got an urgent telegram from my father. Dan had been found in his room, dead, apparently the victim of an accidental drug overdose. I don't think it was so accidental." Burt leaned against a lamp post. A few passersby stared curiously. "All these years," whispered Burt, "I've blamed myself for his death, and so has my father. I loved going into battle! I kept hoping I'd die, that I'd get shot down, but then Nixon decided to pull out the American troops and ours was one of the first to return."

Julie embraced him. "I had no idea, Burt, no idea at all. I'm sorry."

A lump formed in Burt's throat. Quietly, he pointed to the pancake house and led Julie by the hand across the street. Through the smoky latticed window they could see Mr. and Mrs. Richardson being seated.

"Should we go in?" asked Julie.

"I think I have to," replied Burt. "I have to clear this thing up with Dad."

"Then I'll come, too." They entered the restaurant and headed straight over to the Richardson's table, ignoring a distressed hostess and a "Please wait to be seated" sign.

"Oh, there you are, Burt. That didn't take too long!" said Mr. Richardson. He was obviously feeling better after his first cup of coffee. "You two look like you've just been through a hurricane. Why don't you sit down?"

"Thanks, Dad, I feel like I've been through one," replied Burt. He and Julie sat down, looking rather nervously at the two faces across the table.

"We haven't ordered yet," said Mrs. Richardson. "Why don't you look at the menu?"

Julie said thank you, but Burt waved it away; instead he fixed his eyes on his father.

"Dad, I need to ask you something—" said Burt, his voice fading away.

"Well, what is it, Burt?"

"It's something I've been thinking about for a long, long time and—"

"Just get to the point," interrupted Mr. Richardson sharply.

"—and I want an honest answer," finished Burt weakly.

What little warmth had been there now faded from Mr. Richardson's face as he anticipated the upcoming confrontation. "Well, I'll do my best, Burt, but it's hard to predict anything when I don't know the nature of your question."

"I think you know what I'm going to ask you; maybe you don't reflect on it very often, but it's nothing new."

Even Mrs. Richardson was becoming intent on the conversation. "Now you've gotten *my* curiosity up, Burt. What *are* you going to ask your father?"

Burt surveyed the three surrounding faces in a quick glance. The sullen, tense line of his father's mouth and the stony expression in his gray eyes contrasted sharply with his mother's prim caricature and Julie's empathetically knit brow. He took a deep breath and then quickly plunged into his question. "Dad, I've always had the feeling that—that you've blamed *me* for Daniel's death."

Mr. Richardson dribbled some coffee down his shirt front. "What?" he sputtered.

"I said, do you blame me for Daniel's death?" Burt's words seemed like shouts across the silence of a vast canyon. No one spoke. In the background, an argument between a frazzled waitress and a fry-cook was boiling. The couple in the adjacent booth began to chain smoke, and the suffocating cigarette fumes drifted over the Richardson's table, assisted by the breeze of a vent.

Mr. Richardson toyed with the half-empty coffee cup in front of him and stared at his grease-spotted placemat as the minutes ticked by. Finally his sad eyes looked up.

"Do you really want an answer, Burt?" he asked quietly.

"Yes," said Burt.

Mr. Richardson looked down again. "I did blame you, Burt. Up until five minutes ago, I blamed you for Daniel's death and everything it did to our family."

"I thought so," mumbled Burt.

"But I can see that something has changed inside of you. The hardness that I've always noticed in your eyes is softened now." I can't blame you any more, Burt; I've got to learn to accept this thing now."

The two men clasped hands firmly across the table top. It was the first warm gesture they had made toward each other in five years, and it seemed to charge them both with a new, powerful, joyful energy that glowed and radiated from their faces. Mrs. Richardson sniffled daintily and mumbled something about how touching it was.

"You know, Dad," said Burt, "I hope Dan is watching us now; we're together like a whole family again."

"He does see us," said Mr. Richardson, "and in spirit, he's with us too."

Involuntarily, the group glanced around. No one would've been surprised to see Daniel approach and pull up a chair.

Slowly, a silence fell over the group as each person drifted away with his own thoughts and contemplations. Only rhythmic breathing and the drone of the thickening traffic outside filled their ears. An aggressive waiter interrupted their trance-like state.

"May I take your orders, sir?" he asked.

"Uh—yes," stammered Mr. Richardson. "What do you want, Pat?"

"I'd like the morning special, please."

"I'd like the blueberry pancakes," added Julie.

"All right," said the waiter, "One morning special . . . one order of blueberry pancakes . . . and what would you like, sir?" he asked, pointing to Burt.

"I'd like the Denver omelette," said Burt, after a pause.

His father smiled. "I'll have the same."

Science Fiction

Imagine that some physical condition of life as we know it was suddenly altered somewhat—the temperature of the earth or chemistry of the brain. What would follow? Invent some such change and imagine the consequences. Think of some characters who might react to the change in interestingly different ways. Or imagine a world that has already changed in some significant ways, that simply operates by different natural laws than ours today. Make up a story and characters that fit such a world. Try your story out on local science fiction fans, then with some magazine.

Strange and Dangerous Beings

JENNIFER BARTEL

"Last night, around 8:30, while I was still doing my homework, that creature I found a couple of days ago started talking," said Mark to his sister. "It's voice was small and shrill. It kept repeating things like, 'Let me out; I don't belong here. . . . You've got to believe me. . . . I'm from another planet. Let me out.'"

"What kind of creature is it?" Julie asked.

Mark said, "I'm not sure. I've never seen one before. I'll have to look him up in the Intergalactic Book of Beings."

When Mark finally found the description, he read, "Violent by nature and naturally curious, this species is not to be trusted. They may for an instant be kind and warm, but in the next instant this species can be harsh and dangerous. They cannot be contained;they can travel under any condition under water, on land, in the air, and across vast distances of space. They populate an area for the sole purpose of destroying it. This species originated on the third planet of our solar system many years ago. They are called HUMANS."

"He sounds terrible," winced Julie. "I think you should give him to the Creature Control Center before he has the chance to hurt something or someone."

"Yeah, I guess so, but he's kind of cute," Mark replied.

With that Mark and Julie wrapped their long, furry tails around their cat-like bodies and curled up for an afternoon nap, while in the distance one could hear the creature, "Please, you've got to believe me. I'm not a bad person. I can prove it. Just let me out. . . ."

Subchild #3

JUNE RANDRUP

The sun rose early, sharp and clear on the morning of the third month of the year 2021. It cast its warm, grey light on the earth, waking the three children at 7:00 sharp. They hopped out of their cubicles at exactly 7:09.

Entering the main hall of their housing unit, each said in a monotone, "Good morning." They walked into the kitchen and punched buttons for their breakfast selections. Their parents had already eaten and gone off for their four-hour work day.

They ate in silence until Subchild #3 found a voice to speak. "Teacher #0124 told us something yesterday."

"What is it?" asked Subchild #2 uninterestedly.

"Well, it told us about colors."

"Colors? That term is never used any more. Why did #0124 mention such an archaic word?"

"It said you might be able to see color, if you tried hard enough."

The others laughed at #3. "Don't be silly. The only colors are what we call hues that range from pure white to shades of grey and finally to black."

"But I believe in colors," cried the little girl. "And #0124 said that if you believe in them enough, you might see them."

"But you wouldn't even know what to look for! Nobody can grasp the concept of color. How did #0124 explain it to you?"

"Well, I . . . it . . . " faltered the little girl, as she burst into tears.

"#0124 needs to be dismantled, putting such nonsense into your head."

They finished their breakfast in silence, the start to another grey day in the lives of three children.

The next morning at 6:40, #3 excitedly raced outside from a dream to the freshly rained-on surface of the earth. She drew in her breath. No one needed to tell her what to look for. The colors were suspended in the sky like great ornaments, rarer than perfect diamonds. Although she couldn't identify the colors, she did know they composed what used to be called a rainbow; she gave each stripe a name. "Blue, red, orange, yellow, green, purple." She savored the words in her mouth, as if they were the finest chocolates imaginable.

The rainbow only lasted fifteen minutes in the morning sky. She realized that she had not gotten her brother and sister out of bed to see the beautiful thing, and for this she felt guilty.

The next morning, not once did #3 mentioned the colors. She would share her experience later, but for now, the vision was for her to savor.

That These Things Never End

JASON EISNER

Eili, eili, shelo yiganeir l'olan, hachol vehayan, rish-rush shel hanayin, berak, hashanayin, tefilat ha'adaz.

Oh, Lord, my God, I pray that these things never end: the sand and the sea, the rush of waters, the crash of the heavens, the prayer of man.

—*Chanah Senesh*

And now the sea is dying.

The water, dark and dull now, is all but still; the sand is black and soft, bringing up an occasional sluggish bubble as it slowly slides itself down into the somber waters.

It is very quiet.

From above I watch through a window, alone. Very alone. No one else is left to watch with me.

Julie! Where are you? I need you here, sister. Come, sit with me, watch the waves still themselves. You loved the sea.

So did I. I had hoped that the sea might endure, the sea that was near me all my life, the sea that kept its tossing wildness even when the sky and the trees had gone. I was wrong. It too is dying, leaving only me, a tired old woman gazing through sad eyes and a grimy window at what she does not understand, knowing only that she must stay until the end; me and the lonely cottage and the sun piercing a black sky with its too-bright rays.

I remember when I saw my first tree die, two weeks ago. I was young then, and happy.

It was early summer, the gentlest time of year, and I was standing under a sky that was still blue and a sun that was still kind. As I admired a maple, a leaf near the top slowly reddened, then leaves near it, not only red now but orange and yellow and brown and violet and gold that were flowing faster and faster round the branches and up the twigs and through the leaves. All autumn passed in minutes. When the tree was drenched in color, the leaves dropped quietly to the ground and decayed; after a few moments the trunk and branches darkened, rotted, and crumbled. That was all.

The entire process had taken perhaps ten minutes. It had been one of the first to die; within three days, not a tree was left in the world.

Another world, another time might have seen countries around the globe unite to fight the problem. But it seemed to be a new kind of chemical warfare; by the time that all nations had discovered that their enemies had been similarly affected, it was too late to do anything. The grass and green plants were following the trees. The billion-year tradition of photosynthesis was ending, the air irrevocably yielding all its oxygen to countless pairs of greedy lungs.

That alone would have killed us, in time. But first came the storms: immense typhoons, tempests and tornados raging over land and water like an angry child smashing his toys. Then three days ago (can that have been all?) the storms died away to a mere whisper of wind. Those few people who were still alive began to hope again.

That night, the atmosphere quietly dissolved into space, and there were no longer people to hope, or wind to whisper.

I have not yet written how I escaped bursting in the vacuum, how I come to be here, wearing a makeshift pressure suit and an oxygen tank in what I like to think of as an old-fashioned cottage by the sea. I suppose there is no need to explain; although I am writing as if for an audience, no one will ever read this. I am trying only to satisfy that aesthetic something inside me that asks for completeness and order, that same force that binds me here to watch, to fulfill the position destiny has given me. Trying to satisfy that, and to put down something, anything, to relieve the pain and the fear and the uncertainty that I feel inside.

And the loneliness.

Where are you now Julie? Are you somewhere up in that black, black sky, watching from a star, pitying me? Did you know, years ago, that it would be like this? Did you choose not to wait for it?

Outside, the last of the sand has moved itself down into the dark, silent sea. The surface of the water is very still under the glaring sun.

I never thought it would be like this.

With all our fears of a world-ending nuclear war, solar nova, collision with an asteroid, or invasion from outer space, it never occurred to us that the earth might simply die. We took it for granted that the planet would be here for us until something happened to it from the outside. Yet everything dies eventually, even that which is taken for granted. Even the earth.

Why is it dying, I wonder? Old age, probably, or illness. Signs were there for those who cared to look, I imagine; symptoms, the Ice Ages perhaps. Could we have done something, had we noticed? I hope not.

It may be that it chose to die, to succumb to illness and abuse. It has had many billions of years, though I knew it for but a few decades. Perhaps it felt that it had lived enough. Perhaps it felt ready.

Is that what happened with you, Julie? Did you want to choose your own time, when you were still young and full of life? Is that why you left the cancer to worm away inside you, knowing from the beginning that it was there, yet letting it do its work, not fighting it? Did you forget that there were others who loved you and needed you?

What do I do now?

The blinding sun is low now, unattended by any pastel in the sky or reflection in the water. And the moon, much higher, is nearly full. Odd; I had nearly forgotten about the moon.

I forgive you, Julie. I cannot decide your life for you, or its end; and I cannot call you selfish for having been true to your feelings. It is neither my right nor my place.

Nor am I so sure, now, that you chose wrongly.

Outside, a boulder cracks into several pieces, then crumbles into dust and lies still. The rocks, it seems, must die too.

I have decided what I must do.

Tonight, before I go to bed, I shall take the tube connected to my oxygen tank and loosen it, very slightly. Sometime during the night, I shall die, very quietly, in my sleep; die sleeping in a cottage by the sea.

I wonder what I shall be dreaming of when I go.

Yes, I will do it. For I, like the trees and the sky and the sea, am part of the earth, and I have no reason to try to outlive it any longer. It is not that I am giving up. It is not that all my spare tanks of oxygen will not last me forever. Only that the trees are gone; the grass is gone; the people and the animals; the rocks; the sky; the sea. I am part of the earth, it is part of me, we have lived together, and we shall die together; and there is a comforting sense of order in that. Like my sister, and perhaps like my home, I am choosing my own time to close my affairs and my eyes.

Besides, I have watched all that I need to watch, and forgiven all that I need to forgive, and written all that needs to be written. I am done here. There is nothing left for me to do. Oh, I could pray, I suppose, but what is there left to pray for?

Circles

KATHY PROFETA

I

The sun is setting over s small Arizona town as two ten-year-old boys walk through the dusty alleys. As they walk, the dust swirls up and suspends itself in the rays of yellow-orange light. They wear nearly identical faded denim overalls, and one has a slingshot sticking out of his back pocket. They take their time, dawdling and talking as if their supper will be warm for them no matter when they get home.

"Tom," one says to the other, "Do you ever get an extreme case of déjà vu?"

"What?"

"You know, déjà vu." The boy pronounces this word in a slurred fashion, sounding it like "dayshvoo." "That's when you think you've been somewhere before. I got that right now."

"Sure you did. We've been here lots of times."

"No—that's not what I mean. See, you don't know exactly why you think it, but you feel like—well, forget it. You won't understand anyway."

"Mark!" The other boy is clearly annoyed. "That's all you ever say." He mocks Mark's voice, "You won't understand anyway."

"No I don't!"

"Yes you do! You say I don't understand how to roof your doghouse. I don't understand how to make a good peanut butter sandwich. And I don't understand how to use your chemistry set! Why do you think I'm so stupid?"

"Tom, stop it! Of course you understand. Remember, you and I are going to grow up to be great scientists together! You understand the chemistry set, don't you?"

"Yeah, I guess so," says Tom, not sounding like he means it.

"Sure you do. Tell you what. Come over after dinner and we'll work on the new experiment together. We're going to learn how to turn copper into brass!"

"Oh, Ok."

II

A skinny but musclar young man runs up a stairwell, skipping every other step. He bursts into a grey painted door marked 4D.

"Tom, look what I just did!"

A scrawnier, dark-haired kid glances up from a scratched old desk nearly smothered in papers.

"What now?" he groans.

"Look!" The first boy thrusts a tattered composition book in front of his friend's face and directs his attention to a few hastily scrawled numbers in red ink.

"I figured out the equation! Now my midterm will be a snap! Look, now I can do this whole series of equations in just one step!"

The other kid rises from his chair, caught up in the excitement.

"Oh my gosh! How did you do it?"

"Look, right here. This is the step."

"I don't see—"

"Tom, you won't understand right now. I'll show you later. It's just important that I did it!"

"Oh—Well, God, Mark, what are you waiting for? Go show Professor Delaroix!"

"Yeah, I was on my way! Just wanted to stop and show my pal first—"

And with that the young man burst out the door again, leaving his friend to shake his head in wonder over his pal's intelligence.

III

A cold white corridor stretches far into the distance, and a fluorescent light buzzes. A dark-haired man in his early thirties in a white lab coat walks down the hall. His wing-tip shoes thud against the blue-white linoleum. He walks purposefully over to a door marked "For Authorized Personnel Only."

As he swings open the door, a large warehouse-type room is revealed. As he takes his first few steps into the room, a taller man of the same age accosts him.

"Tom, I'm so glad you're here! We're on the verge of the greatest discovery! And I said to Brad—didn't I Brad?—I couldn't complete it without the aid of my good friend, Tom." He gestures at a short, curly-haired man on his right. "Brad here is taking care of the mechanics aspects." Brad nods a cautious greeting. "If we can just get a few more specific figures, we'll be operational."

"Geez, I had no idea you were so far along, Mark. Did you work on all the Alpha series calculations? I've been working on something of that sort at home and I think I could help you there—"

"Oh, thanks for the offer, Tom, but we've completed those. Right now I need help over here, with the final adjustments." The taller man leads his friend over towards a humming mass of metal. "Imagine the implications of this discovery. Time travel has never before been plausible to man! What types of things can mankind achieve with this discovery? It boggles the mind."

"In fact," adds the third man, who has been hovering on the sidelines until now, "I'm already in the process of developing a way in which, in case of nuclear war, the whole of mankind could be projected back into the past to avoid its destruction."

"Wow," says the newcomer, "this does boggle the mind. Do you think it's possible?"

"Who knows now? If it is, then this is the first step."

Continuing their discussion, the three men slowly walk towards the humming machine and begin to work on the complicated wires and circuits.

IV

The sun rises over a misty green lake as two old men, hunched over their fishing lures, glide out into the center of the lake. The only noise is the smooth watery hum of the outboard motor. Suddenly one man lifts his snow-colored head and speaks:

"Well Tom—what do you think is going to happen?"

"Mark, I don't know. I'm too old to be worried. Whatever happens will happen."

"Right now I hear we're in a stalemate. I hear both of us are waiting with itchy trigger fingers. One nervous move and those missiles will be out."

"I don't think we've ever been this close to nuclear war, do you?"

"No, we definitely haven't. It seems inevitable."

There is a pause. "Do you think Brad ever completed his time machine project?"

"Gee Tom, I don't know." The other man looks up, as if he is intrigued by the idea. "When we abandoned that project, I put it out of my head. But Brad stuck with it. Do you suppose. . . ."

"Yeah, I've been thinking about it for a while now. If he completed the project, that means that when the earth starts to explode, it will suddenly be projected back into time about sixty years."

"But the problem is—when we go back in time, who says that everything will not have to be exactly the same? We'll just be going around in circles eternally. . . ."

The other man glances out across the water. "I guess there's no way we'll ever know, even if it does happen."

There is a pause as the men stare over the glassy water at the concentric ripples formed by the two fishing lines. Suddenly two white streaks shoot across the pale blue sunrise sky, followed by a hot rosy glow that covers the entire scope of the heavens.

V

The sun is setting over a small Arizona town as two ten-year-old boys walk through the dusty alleys. . . .

Myth

Invent a supernatural story that pretends to explain some
real phenomenon in nature or in human nature. This could be
set in our world of today or in an invented or previous time and
place. Mythic figures stand for forces and aspects of life; plots,
for relationships among these forces and aspects; objects and
places, for other factors and circumstances. So make your story,
characters, and settings symbolize things you want to deal with.
A series of such stories could generate a whole mythology. Use
these for discussion after some others have heard or read them.

How the Stars Were Made

KEVIN HEADLEY

A long, long time ago, before the golden age of mankind, there
was a great problem among the gods. They had run out of things to
do, and they were bored! Of course, Zeus was distressed by this, so he
decided to call a meeting among the gods to figure out what to do.
After much discussion, the decision was made. Zeus would create all
kinds of creatures who would worship the gods and play with them.

First he created the animals—big and small, strong and weak. In
fact, some of these animals are still around today. Then he created
man with a tail just like the animals. However, it looked very funny
and kept getting in the way, so he decided to cut it off.

The gods loved the new creations very much and gave them
anything that they wanted. These new creatures lived a life of ease!
They had sunlight 24 hours a day and as much food and water as they
wanted.

The humans called a meeting to decide upon a name for themselves. They thought it appropriate that their name should be the
Cawanies. Some years later, a group of mischievous Cawanies children
killed hundreds of little animals just for the fun of it and left them in
the forest to rot. The gods were furious! After calling a meeting, they
decided that the correct punishment would be to cover up the sun with
a black sheet so that there would be darkness on earth forever.

The Cawanies prayed in darkness for nights and nights, but still
there was no light. They ordered their greatest warriors to throw
spears and try to poke holes in the black sheet, but to no avail. No one
was strong enough to reach it. Just when there seemed to be no hope
left, a little hummingbird appeared and asked if he could help to poke
holes in the black sheet. Their reply was, "Surely you are too small and

weak to fly that high, but it cannot hurt to try. Go ahead if you must, and fly swiftly."

The hummingbird flew up and up, and finally when he thought that the was going to collapse, he reached the top. The little bird poked thousands and thousands of little holes in the black sheet to produce tiny rays of light that the Cawanies called stars.

There was forgiveness in Zeus's heart as he watched the brave bird and the grateful Cawanies. Since they had gone to so much trouble to get light back, he decided to give them sunlight again, but for only half of each day. The other half would be dark, except for the stars. To remind the Cawanies that Zeus and the gods still loved them, Zeus sent a great round light (later called the moon) to guide the stars across the sky and make way for the new dawn of daylight.

How the Leopard Got His Spots

JAY DeYOE

As we know, leopards have many spots to help camouflage them from their prey when they hunt.

There have been many stories told of how the leopard came about his spots, but this is the only one you should believe.

Many years ago, coyote was walking around his home in the great mountains of the West, now known as the Rocky Mountains. Coyote had many great adventures in his lifetime, but this one would top them all, because this time he was going to help one of the animal people.

As the coyote walked down one of his many trails, he saw a great glare about a quarter mile up the path. Coyote, being wise and all, approached with caution.

As coyote grew nearer, he saw leopard crying, kneeling over a rock. When coyote went to help leopard, without knowing, he walked through a tar puddle.

When coyote finally reached leopard, he asked, "Why are you crying?"

Leopard in return said, "Whenever I go to hunt my prey, they always see me coming."

While coyote was thinking of an idea, he scratched his belly with his paw. When he removed it, he saw a black spot from the tar.

"I have it," said coyote; "Come here and place your back in front of me." The coyote busily touched his front paws on the back of leopard. When he was complete, the leopard had many small spots on him resembling a small paw. And that is how the leopard came about his spots.

Mermaid of the Underworld

BARBARA FOSTER

There was once a young mermaid who lived with her grandfather far beneath the ocean. She had a garden where she kept valuable things very dear to her. Among these things was a statue of a handsome prince of some kind that had floated from a ship that sank. She fell deeply in love with this prince, yet she had never seen him before.

One night there was a terrible storm. Arielle, not being allowed to leave except with a group of many girls, stole quietly away from the safety of her home to venture towards the dark surface. As she neared the surface, big waves covered her in dark mists unknown to her. She saw a gigantic ship in distress. She watched as many men jumped from the sides of the sinking ship.

She drew nearer, and the closer she got the more she could see the men's faces. Very near to her, she noticed an almost drowned man barely hanging on to a piece of wood. It was her love! She carried him gently on the thrashing waves in her strong, yet tender arms. When she reached the shore, she dragged him carefully to a small cove. She couldn't stay out of the water for very long. She kissed him and returned to the water.

She waited for him until daylight to wake up, but he didn't. Arielle returned to the shore and gently touched him. She was startled by the laughter of three girls coming down to the beach. One of them breathed into his mouth and then left him. He awoke only to see a glimpse of the beautiful girl's face, then drifted back to sleep. Arielle came to shore again and touched him, and he awoke. He was surprised at her uncommon beauty. She knew she had to return to the water, or else she would die. Arielle made her journey towards home. She was very sad to leave her handsome prince, whom she so dearly loved. She talked to the underworld plants and fishes in her sweet, ringing voice. Arielle thought of an idea. If she could only become as a human, she could stay on shore and be with her prince. She would have to pay a visit to Poseidon, god of the sea.

Arielle started on the strange and dangerous course to lead to the temperamental God of the Underworld. She whirled and spun in the dark waters of the Underworld. When she arrived, Poseidon told her that he would grant her the wish she longed for if she would give up her beautiful voice. Arielle did this and woke up on the shore of the small cove. She searched everywhere for her prince, but he could not be found. This went on for many months and Arielle longed for her home.

One day, Arielle sighted two people on the beach having a picnic. As she drew closer, she discovered it was her prince and the woman

who brought him back to consciousness. The prince walked off for a
moment and Arielle followed him. She explained to him that she had
rescued him from the sea many months ago. He remembered her and
told her he had searched for her everywhere. Then he gave up and fell
in love with this other girl.

Arielle was very hurt and didn't know what to say. She ran from
him, and he called after her. Arielle spoke to Poseidon again by way of
a small fish. She asked if she could return to being a mermaid again.
Poseidon's reply was that if she killed the one she loved so dearly, she
could return to being a mermaid. The small fish relayed this message
to her and brought a sharp dagger in its mouth. Arielle waited for the
prince to return to the beach, and soon he did. He walked off again
from his love, secretly seeking Arielle. Arielle had no knowledge of
this. She almost killed him, but couldn't. He walked back to his love,
and they stood hand in hand at the ocean's waters. Arielle walked out
to the ocean, longing so deeply for home. She looked back at the
couple. She was so sad she plunged the dagger into her own breast,
instead of her love. Her body turned to foam, forever lapping at the
shore. Her soul went up, and other girls surrounded her, comforting
her. For the first time ever, a tear fell from her eye and fell to the
waters of the ocean. From that time on, the ocean has always foamed
when it reaches the shore. It has always been salty, because of the
salty tears that fall from Arielle's eyes when she sees her love at the
shore. Little does she know that when his eyes look out over the
waters, he secretly longs for Arielle to be with him, forever.

Parable

*Read some parables, and then create one—a short story
that makes a general point about people without stating the
point. Draw material from either our current world or remote
or imaginary times. Entertain while instructing. The point may
be moral or psychological and is embodied in the story. Try
your parable on others to see if your point is clear. You might
read it to a group and discuss it afterwards—an especially good
idea if the members of the group are taking turns, all reading
and writing parables.*

The Line

MILES INADA

Justin Henry hated lines. If pressed to give a reason, he would
probably explain that this hatred stemmed from the fact that he had
been standing in them for so long. In fact, Justin Henry had been

standing in long lines for as long as he could remember. The one that he stood in now was also exceptionally long as it stretched and twisted for as far as one could see in either direction. To the rear of Justin the single-file progression of people extended into an indistinguishable grey haze while to the front the line continued over a mildly sloping hill.

The area in which Justin stood could be called desert. It was dry and composed of yellow sand which rolled gently into dunes all across the horizon. The area, however, was not overly hot but a mild, slightly humid 70 or so degrees. Also odd was the fact that there was no wind. Thus the landscape never changed and the temperature never differed.

There was day and night here but no sun, moon or stars, just a dull, inoffensive glow for a period of some ten hours which then faded to a somewhat duller light. Justin never slept nor did anyone else in the line. At night things did stop moving so no progress was made. Justin didn't like the night. He liked to go forward. He had a bag in which he kept his marbles. For in this line if he moved forward he was rewarded. At various points along the line were stationed wooden podiums behind which were positioned men who would issue to each passing person a marble of an assorted size and color.

Justin hated lines, yes, but he didn't leave. This was probably because of one thing: he liked marbles.

Justin passed a lot of his time looking at his marbles. He had many different colors and sizes, and all were very pretty. There were red ones, green ones, swirled ones, steel ones, wood ones . . . and all quite beautiful. He would take them out and hold them. They gave him a nice feeling.

He tried to remember all of the days that he had spent standing in the line, moving but an occasional step forward every now and then. Through all of the identical humid days, past the same unchanging landscape, staring at the silent backside of the person who occupied the space in front of him. The marbles were what gave him his drive to continue.

This day was just like all the rest. The line of white-clad people stretched out over the horizon. People were either looking forward over the desert or into their bags.

Justin had decided he too would like to look into his bag today, and he pulled a green marble from within.

Justin examined the marble very carefully and felt its smooth surface. It was odd how something so perfect and so symmetrical existed in his world. It was dull and gave no reflection. This didn't really bother him, however, as he did not know of the concept of reflection. Justin had never seen his face and really had no reason to believe that he had one at all. But this did not upset or alarm him. He had his marbles, and he was happy.

So engrossed was he in his collection that he had failed to notice the podium which he was slowly approaching.

"Hello, Citizen." It was the checker. He was dressed, as Justin was, all in white. He stood behind a dark, wooden podium and looked down upon the line. Behind him stood two other men dressed in black, whose purpose was not revealed. A large, red-painted smile accented his garish white face and added a sardonic tone to his cheerful voice. Upon his podium was a large tome to which he now referred.

"Hmmm . . . number 562, Henry, Justin. Right?"

Justin nodded in affirmation.

"Take this in good will, Citizen. Go happily." The checker handed him a yellow marble. "Oh, excuse me. May I examine your bag?"

Justin gave him the sack. The checker grasped it and emptied its contents onto his podium. Upon doing this he began to count the marbles, assigning differents values to each one. After getting a sum, he cross-indexed the result with a table taped to the book. After doing so, he returned the marbles to the bag, which he in turn returned to Justin.

"Congratulations, Citizen. You have accumulated enough points to qualify for advancement." The checker smiled down on Justin with his emotionless grin.

Justin was escorted silently by the black-clad figures in the direction of the hill. He wondered what would await him over the enigmatic horizon. As they crossed the crest of the hill, Justin saw another figure, remarkably similar to the last checker behind an identical podium. There was no line here, however, just flat, expanding sand.

"Hello, Citizen," the checker greeted him politely.

"Hello," Justin managed.

"You are number 562—Justin Henry?"

"Yes."

"Step this way, please." The checker gestured for Justin to step from in front of the podium. Justin did so, wondering what the significance of this event was. In all his life he had never been called from the line.

"Thank you, Citizen," said the checker, his painted face grinning all the while. He pulled a revolver from inside of his podium and shot Justin in the face.

The black-garbed men picked up the warm corpse and started off towards a hill. The checker bent over to take Justin's marble sack, which he emptied into his own jar.

"A sad but necessary action," reflected the checker. "We couldn't run out of marbles now, could we?"

Fable

After reading a number of fables, write one of your own by telling a brief story that makes a moral point or observation about life. State the moral in a separate sentence after the story. Give the story a modern or remote setting. Test your fable by temporarily leaving off the moral until your listeners can supply their own ideas about what it is.

Variants:

- *Write a new fable for an old moral, perhaps with partners who are doing the same for the same moral.*
- *Write a modernization of an old fable.*
- *Retell a news story as a fable with a moral.*
- *Have a fable fest: post them; do readings of them.*

The Owl and the Weasel

SHELLY IMEL

One evening early in the fall the weasel made his way to his favorite chicken coop. He was unaware of two big eyes following his actions.

The owl figured if the weasel could get his dinner there, he would give it a try too. He swooped down and snagged a young chicken. The noise and confusion scared the weasel half out of his wits and sent him running for the cover of the woods.

He was very upset about the owl's intrusion on his territory. The next night the weasel would wait and teach that owl a thing or two.

That night the owl sensed the danger and sat in a tree over the coop, just watching.

The weasel got tired of waiting and slowly showed himself in the moonlight.

In a flash the owl had the weasel in his strong grip. In seconds the weasel lay limp.

Moral: If you're going to raid a chicken coop make sure you don't become one of the chickens.

Beware

JON TRESAN

One day in Sheepland, a rock came flying over the electrified fence. A sheep who happened to be strolling along just inside the fence was almost hit. When the sheep picked up the rock, he saw a note attached to it. He unfolded the note and eagerly read it. The note said: "Sheep, listen! We of Wolfland are tired of the struggle. We want peace and the freedom to mingle with joy among the sheep. We of Wolfland wish to coexist with you of Sheepland!" The astonished sheep quickly ran and assembled all the sheep in the town council. After reading the note, all the sheep agreed to take down the fence separating Wolfland and Sheepland. As soon as this was completed, the wolves rushed in and had a lifetime's supply of roast mutton.

Moral: When wolves use words like "peace," "freedom," and "coexistence," sheep had better use double voltage on their fence.

Color Alone Can Sway the Mind

DAVID JACOBS

Not very long ago, there was a huge herd of white wild horses. It was agreed by the horses that a mayor should be elected so that only one worthy horse could make the laws and rules of the herd. There were only two candidates for this position, one being a white horse and the other being a very intelligent black horse—the only horse in the herd that was not white. When the horses of the herd came to the polls to vote and realized that one of the candidates was black, they immediately signed their ballots for the white horse; hence the black horse lost the election. But the newly elected white mayor began to exercise her powers poorly. She always made the black horse run at the back of the pack. She kept an unreasonably huge portion of the annual crops for herself. She also passed laws which denied to certain horses in the tribe of their freedoms. The horses realized that they had made a grave mistake in choosing the white horse as their leader, so they asked the black horse if she would take over the position, but she only replied:

"If you judge a mare by her color, you get the mayor you deserve."

The Eagle and the Bear

JED NICHOLSON

There once ws a huge bald eagle who lived peacefully in a large tree. She was proud and spent her time hunting small animals and fixing her nest. One day she laid an egg and was even prouder than before, sitting and warming the egg all day long. About that time a mean brown bear moved into the area looking for food. The fish and berries he ate did not satisfy his hunger, and several times the mother eagle caught the bear trying to climb her tree. The eagle grew frightened and started adding more and more twigs and sharp sticks to her nest. She spent so much time building an impenetrable fortress to protect her chick that when the eaglet finally hatched she had no time left for him. She failed to answer his cries for food and water because she had to collect sticks to fortify the nest. The next time the mother eagle looked inside to admire her offspring, she found him dead, and she cried out in great sorrow. A dove who lived in the neighboring tree and saw the whole sad episode cooed:

"A strong defense is only important if there is something to defend."

Poems

Memory Poems

Take some memory that came up when you were writing notes for Memories and write it as a poem, transforming facts freely to develop some feeling or imagery or climax. Or change into a poem something you wrote for Autobiography or Memoir. Let your imagination play with the original facts, not necessarily to alter them but to underlay or overlay them with similar actions from other times and places and domains of thought. Rehearse and read it aloud to others, or include it in a collection of other memories or of general poems.

Schoolboy

CHRIS L. BOLLWEG

She punched me
In the hall.
Oh! Oh!
I punched her back
But not too hard.
Oh! Oh!
I like her so.

While the Grease Popped

JOHN KLEIN

Red, green and blue beautiful
   I love the ocean and a summer sky.
the popping of grease in a skillet
    the strong smell of meat cooking in a small room
          with a bed and a dresser
  a window on one wall with stained white curtains
   the door directly across
     with a loose doorknob and a lock to keep it shut
a bed neatly made with an old army blanket and a faded sheet
   the pillow leaned up against the bed and wall
         stained from the years of use
  the two-burner stove with the hot skillet on it
   the sink with a drippy faucet
   the white refrigerator with a towel hanging from the
    handle
On the floor a man who was tired of living
         lies in his own blood.

The Grip of My Father

DAVID SCHWARZBACH

He claps my collar
in hands whose skin seems
pinned up to air; they
move massive, pulling me back
within the doorway; dust
fills bowls of hanged light which

etch the fingernails, blurring his
hands; only my words rap upon his
brain, and his mouth, the spotlight,
burns my cheeks; I try to turn them away, he
won't turn, he has a mountain to wear, yet sand
fills the air, and
I won't cry upon those hands.

Moon Song

PAUL GRAF

His shouting mother. His shouting father.
The boy awakened and stared through the cracked window,
His thoughts adrift. Like molten lava within a violent
Earth they twisted and wound within him, yielding to the
Cool calm beauty of the lighted moon, and he saw a man.
Was this the man in the moon? So this is the person we
See in the cartoons. This man, this face. Why? The boy
Asked himself. So many faces, why the one in the
Moon? "It is peace" said a lady. "It is God" said
A man. Whether peace or God the boy continued to stare,
As the last cloud of a heavenly parade passed away,
Exposing the child to the full brilliance of this
Hypnotic medallion. He sat still like an iron
Tower, and there was no sign of the screaming
Prisoner within him. "See me, God."
"Find me peace, man." "Make it stop, this
Habit, the pain, the tears, and the screams."
So the boy thought but the man did not
Wink. A whiskey glass shattered.
"Maybe tomorrow night." With bruised
Hopes the boy fell to sleep upon his wooden cot.
Hoping to awake in the arms of that hopeful man
In the moon. His eyes closed and the moon turned
Its head.
"Shut up, Bitch,"
His father said.

Kite

GARY CHAVEZ

Beautiful, shiny, and black
Wanting to join the birds
But how?
Nobody here to tell me.

Place it on the ground.
Step back.
Now, run like heck.
I was still too young to say hell.

Don't drag on the ground!
Take-off and soar
Into the blue
But it won't.

Can it fly at all?
Nobody to answer
No mom
No dad
No friends
Just the laughing eyes of neighbors
Watching me
From the security of their curtains.

Meeting the Family

BRIAN FITZGERALD

I met her and her folks
    at their house,
On one of the nicest days
    of the year.
Her father shifted his weight
    from leg to leg,
His eyes darted around
    averting eye contact.
Her mother began dusting and
    cleaning—
She didn't feel like talking.
The daughter, my friend, stood
    confident,

Her chest swelled but her
  voice trembled.
  I mimicked her father
  for ten or twenty minutes . . .
  or hours.
After a while, mother broke
  the silence;
She asked me some basic questions
  I could've answered by giving
  her my license.
The silence being broken
  her father spoke . . .
  I answered.
  The room was again silent.
Her father, mother, and she
  all looked down.
Her father said his daughter
  had too much homework;
  mother agreed.
My friend appealed but
  to no avail.
  I said, "I can change;
  I can be anything you would
  want."
They looked up, catching my glare.
  "But I'm not going to. It is
  not the way I am, but it's
  the way I want to be."
Her father showed me to the door.
  I left feeling content
  and strangely happy with
  myself.

Immersion

SYLVIA MYERS

"Let's go wading!" I cried.
And you followed me into sun-dappled shallows,
Which suddenly became deep and cold,
As I knew they would,
And you suspected they might.

Together we watched the sparkling bubbles
Of your surprised gasp soar sunward
As we silently sank into moon-ruled depths.
I sighed.

Then we touched bottom—and pushed up,
Breaking back into warm, safe waters,
And struggled over slippery rocks to shore,
Where we lay in hot sands,
Listening to each other breathe.

Looking Back Home

JIM ANDERSON

The hearth and home are behind me now
Leaving our photos on the mantle with
   candles, plants, and a lantern
I see
Mom quilting on the couch
Dad deep in science magazines
Maynard sprawled out in the living room
   under the rocking chair
The late-night creaks of the old house frame
   settling down for the night
   snap in my brain
As loud as the graveyard mill whistle
Or the lonesome muffled rattle of the midnight
   freight train
The hot smell of the onion fields hangs dark
   under the eaves of my old bedroom
   window
Rolling down and sifting through the screen
   like sweat
The sweet scent lingers until autumn
But those night noises that once rang out
   like clockwork are absorbed
By the new sounds of a growing city
That turns them into a low hum
Like the neon lights that buzz yellow
Above store windows.

Storms

MICHAEL FERRARO

We were little then
And we stood in the sand
Just outside our house,
Rolled-up pants, bare feet, tanned skin

That felt especially warm
On cool, windy days,
And the clouds moved in
As the porch radio said they would.
The radio made its whining outerspace sound
And the porch door creaked a little.
I put myself in charge
Giving each of the others a side of the house.
It was all very earnest and militant and
Exciting—
Taking down the hanging plants
And I, secretly enjoying, anticipating;
Then, inside, Dad securing the windows
The radiator going to work for us, hissing,
And I, hoping for power failure and lighted candles.
The wind picking up the ocean and then stopping,
Passing—
No one understanding my sadness.

Later, on the sand
The dried-out man under the pier
grabbed my arm:
"The real ones come without warning—
In walled-in rooms, alone
And you'll beg for their passing,
To come back to a warm place
Where you light candles for now."

Sensory Poems

Take notes at some locale of your choice, as for **Writing
Up Sensory Notes,** and look for a motif or moment in your
observations and reactions that might make a good poem. You
might build up a mood or set of images or story or reflection
that would benefit from richer language or less common phrasing
or more compact expression than one usually expects in prose.
Also, what things not at all present in the scene you observed does
your imagination connect to what you did observe? Post or print
up and hand out. Or collect your sensory poems into a booklet.

Low Riders

CYNTHIA RUBIO

Sparkles up the street
Look like falling stars
But it's all the hometown
Low-riders
In their shining custom cars
Chrome
    And perfect paint jobs. . . .
Metal flaked
    And custom grills
Lifted first
    Then lowered fast
Looking for more thrills
Sitting low, driving slow,
    And feeling
Oh so free!

Coastal

DOUG ARBOGAST

There is a fern-covered
cliff where
flowers bloom in the
open. Nearby
there is a silver spring
falling from the side
of a high rock
with some
birds eating their
early morning meal
in a coastal city dump.

Lawn Party

AYLENE RHIGER

Elegant ladies
in white chat
among men of wealth

As bright croquet balls
bumping and rolling on,
and on, journey
driven by conservative taps.

A group of appointed
musicians play
Mozart.
    Women babble on,
and occasionally sip weak tea.

And as the music plays,
they waltz,
later,
by paper lanterns.

Beach

SAMANTHA YATES

Mirrored glasses reflect
The scene; he sits above them all
Like a god to his people
Zinc oxide rubbed across his nose
A symbol of his power.
Oiled bodies clump together—
Coconut vapor.
A few feet from the shore
The warm water ripples over
Cherry-red toenails.
Children cluster around, plastic
Pails gripped in their hands.
Their eyes follow the wave
Like boys following the swing
Of a woman's hips down the street
Watching their sculpture
Etched in sand complete
Its short life.
Elderly women sit under a
Striped umbrella
Their wide-brim straw hats
Sheltering their lined faces
From the sun.
Girls in french-cut bikinis
Surround him;
Their eyes search

His bronzed body
But it seems
To hold no flaw.
They giggle, smile, talk
In unison
Lacking the courage
To be themselves.
He smiles
Secure.

The Wind

CARLA WILLETTO

The wind whispers, then whistles through the cedar that I sit under. Small shivers run through me; my numb hands hold my blanket close to me. The sky is bright blue with clouds as white as the snow on the ground. The sun shines brightly. I can touch the mountains that sit on the horizon to the north. It is quiet.

Steam hovers with my horse's breath as he stands patiently, nuzzling the snow with his furry muzzle. I can hear the black lamb bleating, and the old ewe answers. A bell clanks as the lead goat paws through the snow. Every detail is sharply clear on the side of the beautiful mesa. A crow's rough call floats into my consciousness. A rabbit scurries from a sage brush, leaving his footprints on the sparkling blanket covering the silent earth. A hawk is suspended in the air, not a feather moving. And the wind cuts through my blanket and sighs in the silence.

Picture Poems

Focus on some image that sticks with you and begs to be put into words. It may be a rarity you glimpsed once, or something you see every day, an actual thing or a picture— whatever vividly recalls itself to you. Put it into words, a few well chosen ones. Make use of comparison (what is it like?), word sounds, rhythm, the breaks of line endings, the tone of words, perhaps rhyme, division into stanzas, and other resources you find in poetry. Try your poem out until you are satisfied that people see the image the way you want and feel what you're trying to arouse in them. Then read it aloud, post it up, print it and hand it out, include in a collection, or send it to a publication.

The Siamese Cat (The Awakening)

KEANE ROBERTS

The Siamese yawns
opens his jaws
stretches his legs
and shows his claws.

Then he gets up
and stands on all four
long stiff legs
and yawns some more.

He shows his sharp teeth;
he stretches his lip;
his slice of a tongue
turns up at the tip.

Lifting himself
on his delicate toes
he arches his back
as high as it goes.

He lets himself down
with particular care
and wanders away
with his tail in the air.

Scenes

LISA CHRISTIAN

Land
seemingly endless
small
against the clouded sky.

Water
rippled by the wind
flows through the marsh grass
photographed
by the old man's eyes.

Apples
strewn on the ground
like balloons in the sky
wasted.

Durango to Silverton

HEATHER REID

Show me
Steam
Cinders and smoke
Rattling
Down narrow-gauge track,

Chasing
A river
Under white-lace foam,
The cool
Definition
of Aqua.

Cradle
The Scene
In dominant cliffs,
Carefully
Sculptured granite.

Adorn it
With thousands
of rapier pines
And white
Whispering waterfalls.

Paint
The grass green
And paint
The sky cloudy
And somehow,
Paint the divinity.

Wardrobe

AYLENE RHIGER

A knitted green scarf
Of great magnitude
Is thrown out on the valley floor.
Little curious colored earrings
Burst and bud from tiny holes
In the growing scarf
As spring opens her closet.

Pieces of Eight

GREG HUNT

The sun is doused
Beneath the Pacific.
Sand-covered children
Are folded up like lawn chairs
And stowed
In the back seats
Of station wagons.
Little pirates,
They carry off their
Seashell plunder
In plastic pails.
The ocean is left to itself
And while no one is looking
It weeps
Mourning its stolen treasure.

Half-Antler on the Mantlepiece

NEIL TALBOT

The skeletal claw
with talons curling
the withered wooden hand
with palms of bone white
the many forked lizard tail
of petrified flesh

poised as the waiting
mantis
stark as the earth's deep
cracks
sharp as the rusted, twisted
hook

from what beast has this trophy
been cut so clean?

Borrow-a-Line Poems

Just to prime the pump, borrow a line you like from some published poem and use it as a stimulus for a poem of your own. An opening or a closing line is often the best—something that resounds in your mind and seems likely to generate ideas and lines of your own. You might start your poem with this line and write a new sequel, or you might write toward that line, building a new context for it. Think of this as inspiration, not imitation. Your poem will, after all, probably be about something very different.

This Is Just to Say

ROBERT SAVIA

This is just to say

I have hit
your car
that was
parked outside

and you
were going
to be out in
a minute

forgive me
it was so sleek
so bright
and so double-parked

Looking Through a Painting

CARMEN MENDES DA COSTA

The good gray guardians of art
  in the museums of Italy and France.
I visited the paintings, sculptures,
  and artifacts, once.
The brilliant marble shone and moved
  the statues to life.
Lights shone on the Adonis of love,
  while Venus stood her ground.

People came bustling in, from every
white, hollow tube and stepped
around the corners to look for
themselves through the pictures
of the past.
I have found myself in the midst
of a Greek painting.
At last I can see the people:
Caesar, Cleopatra, and Antony.
The aroma of olive oil strikes
a sense of place and being.
Now I stand in the painting
of centuries old, protected
by the varnish and paint,
by a painter's hand.

In Consistency

RANDALL POTTS

I don't give a damn
For the pain and inconsistency,
The scribbled notes
The Latin quotes and endless paper race,
The fading flowers
Laid on some dusty valentines,
A paled profile
To cover a cluttered mind,
A weary face
That hides the icy heart.
Why? What for?
Have I played it all quite wrong?
Read the books
But not yet lived the life?
The painful mornings
And artificial afternoons,
A busied evening
Amid a flash of colored light,
A blurry morning
Scattered round the living room.
I don't give a damn
For the pain in such consistency.

Poems on Pictures

Use a photo or painting as a muse to prompt a poem.
Choose one that takes hold of you and seems to ask for words to
bring out things in it. Interpret the picture this way.

Say things about it that can't be seen but are implied.
React to the realism of photos, the abstract quality of paintings,
or the mixture often found in either. Look at your picture a
long, long time, and keep track of what goes through your mind
as you do.

[Suggestion: Consider a photo of yourself as a child, a
possibility illustrated in the first two poems that follow.]

When...

J.S.

When bow ties and bare shoulders were in,
I wasn't.
When mini skirts and sweaters were in,
I didn't care.
When low v-necks and high heels were in,
Mom said I couldn't.
Now that bow ties and bare shoulders,
mini skirts and sweaters,
low v-necks and high heels are back,
I am too,
But sweatshirts and jeans suit me
just fine.

Possessions

A.R.

A new pair of pants,
A bright red hat,
How could I want more than that?

Trikes are for babies;
I need a bike;
I'm no longer a little tyke.

Gotta have a tape deck,
Need tunes to be cool,
Can't live without it, can't be a fool.

Now I've got a car
And a custom surfboard,
But how can I be so—bored?

A new pair of pants,
A bright red hat—
How could I want more than that?

Photo of Grandparents

KRIS URISTA

They stand stiffly as if at attention.
They smile but no sparkle lights
  their eyes.
The collars are tight.
Their breath comes laboriously.

The hot lights are burning.
They smile still, coldly, at the
passage of time
  Yet they think warm thoughts;
  they think of their children
  in far off places
Children who will welcome all
the trouble
of posing for a picture
that will last forever.

The Night Café
by Van Gogh

SCOTT YOUNG

A dimly lit galaxy
Where four worlds spin.
Silence prevails
Where shadows falter.
Muffled voices
Slide
Through a mist
Of old cigar smoke
And loneliness
Fills
The empty liquor glasses.

"The Bowl of Goldfish" by Harunobu

KIM CAMPBELL

The boy's imagination is shadowed
by the two attendants who entertain him.
A maid leashes him by the sleeve
as his hands swim about a bowl of water
bewildering the goldfish.
A second girl hollows a wild cherry pit
into an instrument.
She will blow through the seed-ball
Creating cautious tones
meant to please the pampered child.

Poems of Address

Write out some feeling or idea by directing it toward a person, place, or thing with which it is connected. Address directly in the poem whoever or whatever caused, inspired, or was otherwise involved in what you have to express. Make use of this address to focus and organize what you have to say and to muster a distinct tone of voice or dramatize a relationship.

Letter to My Grandfather

DEVIN SHELDON

As I write to you
The clouds outside my window speed by.
The large, strong seagull soars
As though he is going a long distance.

I hear the voice of an elderly neighbor
calling to his grandson.
The young boy reaches out
And smiles to the old man.

I live in the city
And my parents do not allow me to have a BB gun.
Do you still have the cardboard box
That we used as a target four summers ago
When I visited you in Mississippi?
Last summer I drove the riding lawnmower

And put twigs and branches in the wagon.
The next day my wallet was not empty.
The oak in your backyard has lost its leaves now.
The football games are played.
My wallet may get fatter yet from our bets.
You keep the postman heavily burdened
During the winter months,
But just the witty letters
Make our cold house seem warm.

The Flower in My Life

COOPER LEWIS

Was it you who threw my plant away
Unaware that its life was to last another day?
And if it is to be left unreplaced,
then I'll demand allowance for its space.

For that flower was the shadow of my life,
trapped, yet surviving until your knife. . . .
You rolled the spirit from its root,
shattering its hopes, leaving it mute.

I sit in silence, now and forever,
for you were quick to think, and all too clever.
Like the flower in the pot which strived,
You've separated me from you and ruined our lives.

Watchdog

MATTHEW NAGLER

That ain't no way to live,
With a watchdog.

He'll bark at your guests,
And he'll bark at you.
He'd bite them, too,
If you told him to.
You know it's true.

That ain't no way to live,
With a watchdog.

So you got a dog
'Cause you want him to chew up thieves.
But the thieves got a dog, too,
And he'll chew up your dog
And then chew up you.
So you get two dogs,
Think you've got the thieves beat,
But they get another dog, too.
They'll always have one more dog than you.

That ain't no way to live,
With a watchdog.

So you got a dog
'Cause everyone else on your block got one, too,
And you were afraid
That they'd all sic their dogs on you.
You were so undefended
So you got a dog.
You know it's true.

That ain't no way to live,
With a watchdog.

If all the dogs on the block got loose,
There'd be a big dogfight in the street
And on your lawn
And in your house
And in everyone's house,
And all the dogs would be chewed up
And all the people, too,
And all the houses would be wrecked,
If all the dogs on the block got loose.
You know it's true.

That ain't no way to live,
With a watchdog.

To a Little Brother
Who Watches the Moon

ALISON SEEVAK

You press your palms
up to the sky
finding her

not much greater
    than your thumbnail.
Watching you
I remember
    other August nights
when she was to me
a small, milky pet
    trailing behind
    captured and obedient
but
  I can't remember the feel
  of the thread that I held
or
    the sound of the final snap
    it must have made.
Funny,
    the way that
    childhood wanes away
leaving newly bloated moons above us.

Grandfather

LOUIS BEGAY

You have gone with the wind.
    You used to build the fire.
You made the light
    to light up the hogan.
You brought food
    to make us strong.
You woke us up
    before the sun.
You made us run
    to be healthy all the time.
You told us stories
    to make us think.
You were up before the sun.
    Now that you're gone,
we sleep till the sun comes up.

Be-a-Thing Poems

Pretend you are some object, plant, or animal and speak as that other being. How would it perceive some things? Get inside it and look at something you want to get a fresh perspective on. Use this imaginary displacement as a way of coming upon and expressing feelings or ideas you have about something—or discover that you have about something.

Television

JENNY ENCINAS

I am watched
every day.

I am powerful.
I can change your mood,
make you sad, laugh, scared.

I give out information
I give out entertainment.

Many different faces
turn around
and around.

Late at night
I am black.
I can't wait
till you turn me on again
and see my colors.

And let me watch your moods change.

Dive

KAREN SIME

And then, the halibut said,
I saw a most odd sea creature.
It burst into the water from
Nowhere at all. It
Emerged from a shroud of bubbles,
Then swam awkwardly
as if it hardly knew the currents.

It was long and black
With two small fins on the tail
Split, where one should be—
Two long thin fins in front
Moving even when and where the body was not.
Its back was humped and yellow and shiny.
Snakes connected its back to
Its head (it had no mouth)
And bubbles streamed from its head.
It had one big eye, flat and shiny.
Its front fins turned over rocks
And scraped up coral and sand.
It swam a short while, not very
Deep or far, and in a stream
Of bubbles disappeared into
The shiny sky.

The Perfect Beast

HEATHER HANDY

You do not understand me.
You do not know how my mind works.
　　But you think you do.
You mistake my actions.
　　Good ones for bad.
You misassume my intelligence.
You only think you have a superior brain.

Can you survive in the wild?
Can you be invisible in day or night?
　　Beware my twitching ear.
Can you get what you will?
　　I have you trained.
Can you solve your problems by prevention?
You only think you can answer these true.

I have no foolish morals.
I have my pride and use it well.
But no vanity.
My muteness is strategy.
You took it for ignorance.
　　I am wholly free!
You only wish you, too, were a cat.

Story Poems

Use a poem as a way to tell a story. Your story could be in first person or third person and could be realistic or fanciful. Think of how you may use the special resources of poetry for narrating—including "poetic license."

A Party at the Duke's

JAMES SIE

A ball was held at my lordship's today,
A pretty fine sight to see.
The punch was aplenty and the music was gay,
And the Duke danced on.

My lady arrived in her ruffles and lace,
Pausing to see her spouse frolic.
My Duchess then sat in her usual place,
As the Duke danced on.

What beautiful clothes all the gentlefolk wore,
And the Duke roared for more drink.
The punch bowl was empty so I hastened for more,
And the Duke drank on.

He passed by her way and she made herself heard,
She turned deaf and would not stay still.
So she sat down again and said not a word,
And the Duke danced on.

He danced with any young girl he could get,
The ladies, the damsels, the wenches.
His wife hadn't been asked to join him yet,
But the Duke danced on.

The Duchess, she watched, as the merriment grew,
Her fan tightly clenched in her lap.
Her face took on a deathly white hue,
And the Duke drank on.

We servants were frightened at the Duke's ball,
As tension was thrown in the air.
Milady's lips would say naught but her eyes would
    say all,
As the Duke danced on.

The Duchess could stand no more of our sire,
As he threw each young lass a kiss.
She walked up the stairs with her face all afire,
But the Duke danced on.

She came down as I was fetching master a drink,
Something clenched tight in her hand.
She took it from me and I heard a small "plink,"
As the Duke danced on.

The parlor room clock struck quarter to nine,
As she gave him that venomous cup.
She smiled, for she knew there was not much more time,
And the Duke danced on.

Home Remedy

SONYA SOBIESKI

I applied for a nervous breakdown
Last week
But they said my sanity papers
Were all in order
I told them to look again
There must be some mistake
But they said that
With all the applications
That they had
For nervous breakdowns
They simply couldn't administer one
To someone who
Just "wasn't qualified"
I told them that I was
That if I didn't get
A nervous breakdown
Something terrible
Was going to happen to me
But they turned me down

So I'm having one done
Backstreet
Sometimes the risk
Is worth
The result.

Reflective Poems

*Look over notes from a session done for **Dialog of Ideas** or **Stream of Consciousness** or **Writer's Journal** and pick out a thought, thought train, or constellation of thoughts and fashion this as a poem. Keeping some of the concrete context in which the thoughts occurred may be very helpful. Or try to bring out feelings, perhaps less well noted, that were underriding the thoughts. Look for unexpected connections among thoughts or feelings that at first seem unrelated. Do some of your thoughts focus on an object, person, place, or event that might provide a concrete center for the physical level of your poem?*

I See Poems

FRANCISCO HERNANDEZ

I see poems in my grandmother's kitchen,
the sun filtered through yellow drapes,
the old oak chairs creaking under my grandparents' weight,
tiny dust creatures floating endlessly on the highways
    of light,
(they moved out of my grandmother's path in mock respect)
the smell of flour tortillas and beans,
dust and cigar smoke mingled in my nostrils,
a small wooden cross hanging over the door,
a needle point saying "God Bless Our Home."

I see poems in construction workers,
high-beam walkers, and gorillas who run the hammers,
living in a world of concrete and dust,
forging works of art out of a steel mass,
building shrines out of stone.
They wear the American flag on their hard hats,
chain their wallets to their belts,
drink their beer out of cans,
and have three things that are sacred: the union,
The U.S. and God.

I see poems in corner bars.
I see poems in Willie and Joe.
I see poems in dusty libraries, Norman Rockwell prints,
file cabinets, the Four Horsemen, my dreams.
I see poems in the crows-feet around my grandma's eyes,
and poems in her burial clothes.

Things I've Lost

JOHN SCOTT

Money,
at a fair.

My comb,
from my pants pocket.

Parts of a car,
to our car.

My balance,
on a log.

A ring,
off my finger.

My way home,
in the woods.

Today

JEANNE PERRIN

Today
   Gas crunch
   Tomorrow's lunch
   Iran and Reagan
   Menachem Begin
   Inflation
   Starvation
   Lennon killed
   Oil spilled
   Someone shot
   Dope and pot
   Deaths and strikes
   From cars to bikes
   People waiting
   For a way
   To change things back
   To yesterday.

She Is like the Wind

SHANTRIN LININGER

The air, giving life and motivation.
The breeze, blowing through
    tousling my hair.
A hurricane, blasting through
    solid objects, letting nothing
    stand in her way.
The stillness, waiting for
    something to happen.
A whirlwind, tossing wind into
    a continuous circle, confused
    and light.

Lost

ALLISON WARREN

Dig beyond the obvious
Discover the retarded child.
Delicate like a warm wandering
        breath
The retarded child must be found.
She wanders in a world of simplicity
Guided by only a hand,
And
Followed by only her heart.
The retarded child must be found.

Boy from Minnesota

HIEP NGUYEN

Snow is white,
But not as white as water.
I strive for the sea,
    My last wish,
    My last chance.
I will not lie down until my eyes
        see the sea,
My lips taste the mist
    above the diamond water,

My ears listen to the silver waves,
My hands feel the thrust
    of splashing water,
My nose smells the atmosphere around.
I—I must live until time dissolves—
    For the dream of my life
        is waiting.

Cherry Trees

KRISTY KISER

I sit among the
cherry trees
watching aimlessly
as the
cherries
become
supper
to the hordes
of birds.

The river, like a vein,
feeds the grove of
cherry trees,
till cherries
burst ripe.

The house that I nurture
where I eat
my supper
sits nestled
among the cherry trees.

A roof
that is ripe red,
And window
facing the
ever-running river.

First Rain at Jenner

JASON DEWEES

When the sun fades but doesn't set
When the light dims, diffuses gray;
The ions sprinkle down from the clean
cream storeys.

Serpentine soils, parched,
Stand coolly, in anticipation
Of the
First, soft drops.
Humid winds
Rustle coolness through the cypress.

Slowly falls the dark.
From the Gulf of Alaska, from the
featureless
Subtropical Pacific, massed vapor
Awaits, dives fast, rafts south on
a river of air.

Convergence: suspended condensation
Throws its wash over the gold-grey hills,
Into the green groves,
Onto the white city, cleansing.

The sweep of the polar winds
Drags up and freezes mass moisture.
It flakes and cries on surprised peaks,
Whitening with its crumbled chalk,
Chilling the madrone, the digger pine,
The basalt, the rabbit.

Hours pass, last leaves pluck themselves
Wet from twigs, fall to green fur.
Watercourses glisten, roar, carry back
To the ocean, which, in rhythmic
Waves, washes a shore.

Today I'm a Mean Old Witch

BARBARA RHOADS

Today I'm a mean old witch, today . . .
Today I'm a mean old witch.

This I despise when I look through my eyes and see me
    out to terrorize
and cuss,
and fuss,
and fluster,
and bluster,
and muster all the strength to become a
madman like Custer.

Today I'm a mean old witch, today . . .
Today I'm a mean old witch.

What I Am

JUSTIN JONES

I consider myself a Bald Eagle,
    strong, bold and wise.
I hunt for rewarding things
    and fight for them too.
But sometimes I retreat and just sit
    on an old dead tree and dream.
When I think about what I am
    I fly again.

I Know Where Yesterday Has Gone

CINDY A. BOOTH

Yesterday stopped at the traffic light.

As it sat, Today tore by in front of it,
At a life-threatening speed.

And Tomorrow turned the corner, following
Slowly behind Today. It would reach its
Destination all too soon for anyone's liking.

Yesterday sat, its engine idling slower and
Slower.
The light, never to be green again,
Stared at Yesterday with a baleful
Red eye.

The traffic light of the mind realized,
It had the power to hold Yesterday
On the corner of Memory Avenue...forever....

It grinned, strangely pleased with itself.

The Park

JOHN MORALES

I sit in their world, and they watch.
It is what they do best
On these old smooth benches.
Many have come
To think, to be comforted,
To be engulfed by the silence
And look at the ground,
The cobblestones held together with snail tracks.
And the watchers sit and understand me.

There are those who come and play tag
To jump or stomp or squeal.
I am invisible to them.
As I write, they run
Past my cave of feelings
And I hate them.

The watchers are still above.
I am glad to be noticed
As I quietly break into their world
And stay.
Silent and soft the watchers see me

They will always see me.

Indian's Arrow

ELLEN WILL

Geese gliding through the damp winter air
   in a protective pattern
Like an Indian's arrow piercing the heavens,
Shooting through the sky in a point,
Unwary of the limits of speed.
Me, I have often marvelled at the sleekness
   of those who are able to
Take to their wings.

Truckin' Down the Highway

CARLA WILLETTO

Truckin' down the highway,
Get outta mah way.
I'm not in a hurry,
Just drivin' down the road.

Wave to all the cowboys.
See them tip their hats.
People look at each other
and see who has a CB.

"Breaker one-nine calling the black hat in the blue-and-
    white pickup."
"What's your handle, baby?"
"Sundance. What's yours, bull rider?"
"Midnight Cowboy."

Go to 7-11 and get some pop.
Go to Jack and Jill and get ice cream.
Read the posters:
    Rodeo at Round Rock
    Western Dance—The Thunders
    Voc. Training at Chinle Civic Center
    Movie—Kung Fu—Many Farms H.S.
    Dance at Chinle with the Takers.

Look for people you know.
Go say hi or wave and smile or look the other way.
She's sitting by him.

Wish it would rain.
The crops grow too short.
The livestock grows skinny,
searching for grass by the road and getting run over.

An old man walking alone
A breeze whispers in the evening
An eagle glides 'neath the clouds
The world is red-orange in the sunset.

I drive home. . . .

Shyness

JODY GEBERT

Shyness is a transparent color that blends so well it
    goes unnoticed.
It feels inside like a project that you once started and
    never finished.
Shyness tastes like delicious homemade bread,
    but very plain and mild.
It sounds like a gym hours before the game.
Shyness shows in big, dark eyes that observe all
    goings-on but never blink.

Confusion

JANELLE SANCHEZ

Confusion is all colors.
It sounds like music with no rhythm.
Confusion tastes bitter.
And feels paper thin.
Confusion looks like smog.
And smells of all seasons.
It makes me feel like I'm so
Far away in my own little world.

Lover

MIKE McQUILLEN

No wind blows as silky as my lover moves
In the idle rise of summer breezes.

No love grows any warmer than her fireside eyes,
Midnight winter lover when the season freezes.

Like a clear mountain stream pouring all the way down
To the soft green meadow clover
Floating on a river bed—a love that will never go under
Because it will never be over.

Poetry

STACEY YOUNG

Just this once
I'd like to begin
Without the traditional metaphor
That the sun was a ball of fire,
Because the sun was only shining yellow,
And the sky was not a sea of blue,
It was just blue.
Period.

And I'd like to say
That clouds were smiling down upon me
Without meaning that
God was with me,
And without meaning that
God was ever there,
For clouds are just
Clouds.

And I'd like to express myself
Without whispering
That I am enthralled by your pale beauty
And your pure white skin,
For a loud "I love you" will simply do,
Even though it may not
Rhyme.

And just this once
I'd like to end
Without having a last line,
So that poetic minds
Can be forever baffled
By my
Poem.

The Meditation

RANDALL POTTS

Caught here in conflicts of fire and clay,
Held here in wonder by winter and day,
Trying by movement of mind and of will,
To see the world when it's perfectly still.

Cogitation

(Thinking Over and Thinking Through)

Dialog of Ideas

Let two or three voices discuss some issue of real concern to you. Set this down in dialog form without stage directions. Make up this dialog straight off for about 30 minutes. Have the voices speak all the thoughts that come to you from all points of view. Revise first by reading it aloud, perhaps with a partner, and making changes where ideas or expressions seem weak, or add new ideas if they occur at this point. Use this dialog as a way to get out a lot of good ideas on an issue without having to conclude in favor of one viewpoint.

This can be performed by others, printed up, or used as a basis for further writing.

Now or Then?

JANE COLLINS

MITZY: I can't believe it. I've called seven of my friends, and I can't find one person who wants to see a movie with me.

SARAH: It's not that they don't want to, Mitzy. It just happens that they all have more important things to do.

MITZY: What's more important than having fun?

SARAH: "Having fun" can't be compared to planning for the future. Your friends are worried about scholarships, school, money, grades . . . . They're making decisions now that will affect them for the rest of their lives.

MITZY: I know that. I'm worried about the same things, and I'm faced with the same decisions. But there has to be more to life than worrying and decision-making.

SARAH: Of course there is. There's a time and a place for everything.

MITZY: No way, Sarah. You can't plan for a spontaneous moment or schedule a fresh idea. You have to snatch at care-free fun whenever you get the chance.

SARAH: Even if it will hurt your future?

MITZY: My future isn't just ten years from now. It starts right now, at this moment.

SARAH: So you're saying that what happens in the next ten minutes means more to you than what happens in the next ten years?

MITZY: Of course not.

SARAH: Well, everyone has a different plan for his life, you know—different priorities, different motives....But ten minutes of happiness is usually sacrificed for ten years, instead of vice versa.

MITZY: Why does anything have to be sacrificed? If I do exactly as I want to do every day, won't I be happy? And isn't that what counts? Whether I want to do my homework or watch TV, spend my money or save it, go to church or sleep in—it's my decision. I want to do whatever will bring me more happiness, regardless of *when* that happiness is. Do you understand?

SARAH: It seems to me that you do think ten minutes is more important than ten years.

MITZY: Let me put it this way. Ten minutes of happiness right now is just as important to me as ten minutes of happiness ten years from now is. Are you beginning to see my priority? My motive?

SARAH: You want to be happy.

MITZY: That's my reason for being alive. I want to be happy. But I don't want my happiness to be restricted by time. Thinking about how happy I'll be at some distant point in the future doesn't compensate for not being happy right now. If I strive to be happy at all times, then I will be happy at all times.

SARAH: When you think about it, being happy is everyone's reason for living, isn't it?

MITZY: That's true.

SARAH: The problem is that everyone has a different idea of what happiness is. So you might think that your friends are stuck in a rut, when really they're striving for happiness. On the other hand, your friends might believe you to be careless or undisciplined, even though you're as happy as they are.

MITZY: You think I should be more tolerant, don't you?

SARAH: Well, you can't blame your friends for wanting happiness, can you? Everyone has to have a reason for living. You must remember how personal happiness can be. Don't try to compare your happiness with the happiness of others.

MITZY: You're absolutely right. My happiness is personal.

SARAH: Yes.

MITZY: And I can only measure my happiness by my own personal standards.

SARAH: Right. Where are you going?
MITZY: To the movies! I'm going to see *Educating Rita.*
SARAH: You're going alone?
MITZY: Yes, just me. Alone, but happy.

Where Do You Put Your Faith?

KEN MEYERING

I'm sorry, but I just can't understand all this existentialism stuff. I mean—why would a person want to believe something that is so morbid?

No, no! You've got it all wrong! Existentialism isn't morbid, it's quite the opposite. You see, if you come to accept the idea that our life on earth is our only life, then you've taken the first step towards happiness.

That doesn't make sense. I don't see how a such a fatalistic view can be a step towards happiness. As far as I'm concerned, there's a utopia waiting for me after I die, and, come Judgment Day, I can bet that with all I've done, I'm gonna go to heaven.

That's just the problem. You are so busy trying to "qualify" for this utopian afterlife that you can't even look around and enjoy the life you have! That, my friend, is morbid.

Well, maybe I'm happy just having faith, and knowing that when this great struggle is over, mine will be a life of spiritual ecstasy.

Good for you. While you struggle with what you call faith, I'll live my life to the fullest. I really don't care whether or not I'm so great in the eyes of some fictitious god. What matters to me is that I qualify to myself!

I've never heard anything so selfish in my life. You're so wrapped up in you that you can't even accept the idea of a supreme being!

I can see how you'd say that, but I disagree. You see, I have come to accept the fact that I am going to die, entirely. This was extremely difficult, but I did it. Yet millions of people are so hooked on themselves that they refuse to acknowledge the simple certainty of death. Instead, they create grand illusions of an eternal life. But they don't stop here. To please themselves, they split the afterlife into two possibilities: Heaven and Hell. If you're good, you will enjoy the euphoria of Heaven. But—if you're bad, you shall burn forever in the torturous flames of Hell!

Wait a minute, you're using some pretty powerful language there, but I'm not gonna be trapped in your web. In theory, what you say is fine, but it has some very big flaws! Sure, it cures religious questions as to "where we're going," but what does it say about "why we're here" and "where we came from."

I'm sorry, but existentialism does not venture to offer such answers. Man can create whatever answers he sees fit. In one way, that's why religion is where it is today. Man, when confronted with such bewildering questions, can always refer the responsibility of answering them to God. God being the product of faith, man has rid himself of the burdening question by referring it to an imaginary source. Now, he is free to apply an answer that will fit most easily into the religious puzzle that he has created. The result: an ever-strengthening religion, and an ever-weakening man.

I have a feeling that you have never experienced the power of faith. You yourself have implied that man doesn't have all the answers. Perhaps you're the one without all the answers, and not mankind in general. Perhaps this is because you lack faith.

My faith is in mankind. I have found that when one begins to understand self-reliance, there is little he cannot do. People are the innate proprietors of the ability to think and solve real problems on their own. It is a terrible waste to see people losing this ability as they "grow towards God." Humans are in my eyes the most incredible machines around. Our capacity for growth is phenomenal—limited only by our own inhibitions. Most people are introduced to (and overwhelmed by) the idea of God by their parents when they are quite young and impressionable. The idea of God is like no other that the child has experienced. In short, he is hardly ready for such terrific concepts. Yet, the idea takes hold and distortions (as in the minds of all youngsters) are allowed to grow, until a very intimidating beast lives in the child's mind. This "beast" sometimes remains until the dying day. So like a kind of deep-rooted idea that must replicate itself, the idea of God lives on through indoctrination of the young.

Are you trying to say that religion is negative, like some kind of intellectual disease?

No, I'm not. For some, religion provides one very crucial element to life, meaning. Many religions have evolved to be quite mature and organized. This structured approach requires of its members an equally structured life. Some people have had difficulty finding structure and meaning in their own lives without turning to religion. For these people, religion is quite beneficial. It is, though, too bad that they must turn to external sources for salvation instead of finding enlightenment from within.

Sometimes I do question my faith. My church tells me that if one questions faith, then he does not have it. In their words, it's an "all or nothing" situation. I feel that faith comes from questioning, not without it. Perhaps some organized religions are more interested in the religion itself than they are in people?

That is all too often true. Most agree that the intention of religion is towards the ultimate goodness of everything. Yet these intentions have been blurred by those who are the victims of distortion. For them, religion is a tool to serve themselves. In these cases, the impressionability of people is being turned even more against them, further hastening an eventual decline in the human condition.

I must say that if your motives are also towards good, then I wish you luck in your quest for truth, but I refuse to believe that there is nothing more. Along the lines of what you said earlier, there are many things that man cannot understand, and in the end it just depends on which questions a man is satisfied leaving unanswered.

Dialog Converted to Essay

Rewrite your **Dialog of Ideas** *as an essay by merging its voices into one but without sacrificing any good ideas. Feel free to add new ideas, get rid of weak ones, change wording, and reorganize. You may regard this as a speech, editorial, or essay and follow up accordingly. Where viewpoints conflict, incorporate both into a broader framework accommodating both, and discover ways in which the language may allow you to contain discrepant ideas in the same sentence.*

[The following example includes the dialog on which it is based.]

Handguns (Dialog)

TED HOELTER

TIM: Hey John, did you hear what happened to Mr. Gates—you know, the guy who owns the liquor store on the corner?

JOHN: No, what happened?

TIM: Two guys came into the store last night at ten; one of them pulled a knife on him and told him to empty out the cash register. Instead, Mr. Gates pulled out a pistol and wasted them. Isn't that great!

JOHN: He's pretty lucky he didn't get killed or kill the wrong person.

T: What do you mean?

J: Most of the time when a handgun is used, a neighbor, relative, or other innocent person is killed or wounded. Handguns actually prevent very few burglaries or robberies, and personally I think that all handguns should be made illegal.

T: That's just probably due to improper training on the part of the owner. It doesn't mean that all handguns should be outlawed.

J: As long as there are people being accidentally killed it's reason enough, and that's not even considering all the crimes committed with handguns. What if the person who tried to rob Mr. Gates' store had had a gun and not a knife.

T: That's ridiculous; more people are killed each year in car accidents. Do you think that cars should be outlawed too?

T: The analogy you're making just doesn't work. A car can kill, that's true, but the only purpose for owning a handgun is to have a small, concealable weapon that's capable of killing. And don't tell me that handguns are the only way to protect yourself either. Mr. Gates could just as easily have stopped those two guys with a can of tear gas spray.

J: Tear gas spray? That's weak!

T: But there are still other ways to protect yourself.

J: All right, I won't argue that point, but if handguns are banned and law-abiding citizens comply, you can be sure criminals will have handguns. It's like a bumper sticker I saw once: Outlaw guns and only outlaws will have guns.

T: What you're saying is mostly true, but I don't see why it's bad. If its illegal to possess a handgun then possession of one is one more way to prosecute a criminal. Besides, do you really think that having a handgun is going to protect you from someone else with one? In the home a gun isn't going to help you anyway unless it is loaded and in an easily accessible place; and then its more of a danger to your kids than it is a crime preventer. Another problem with a loaded, easily accessible gun is that it is too easy to just pull the trigger in a moment of passion or accidentally shoot your neighbor because he's in your backyard at night and you mistake him for a criminal.

J: Everything you're saying is real nice, but don't you know that it's every person's right to bear arms. It's right in the Constitution. You don't propose that we change the Constitution too, do you?

T: That's one of the most misunderstood and misinterpreted sections of the Constitution. What is guaranteed is the right of the states and local governments to have militias or police forces. Private gun ownership is a long-standing tradition and privilege, but it is not a right.

J: I don't know about that one, but I'll let it pass for now. But I'd also like to point out that for most of our history as a nation we were a frontier people with a tradition of self-sufficiency, and guns have always been a part of that tradition. Besides, some people still depend on their guns as a means of getting food.

T: To your first statement I would say that America also is characterized by an ability to change. If something doesn't work, we don't keep it—we chuck it for something that does work. To your second statement I would remind you that I only propose that *handguns* be made illegal, not rifles or shotguns. How many people have you seen who hunt with a pistol?

J: What about all the sportmen who enjoy recreational pistol shooting?

T: Air pistols are generally non-lethal and offer all the same fun of shooting!

J: One of your big arguments for banning handguns is to prevent people, especially in the home, from using a gun on impulse. But what you don't seem to see is that anyone can pick up a knife or attack someone with a heavy object!

T: Other weapons just aren't as lethal as a gun.

J: All right, assuming all your other arguments are right (and I don't think they are), how do you propose to enforce such a law? After all if you can't enforce it what good is it?

T: Turning in handguns would have to be for the most part voluntary —but most citizens would comply. This was the case in several communities where such a law was tested.

J: Yeah, that will work for most people, but the main thing it will do is create a black market for handguns like what happened with alcohol during Prohibition, and I'm sure that some people *won't* turn in their guns.

T: Another bad analogy; guns are not alcohol, and the situations would be completely different. If a black market did develop it would be a problem, but there are problems to any law. Besides, guns still would offer an additional way of prosecuting; you can flush your cocaine down the toilet but not your gun.

J: What about gun shop owners or people with large and very expensive gun collections?

T: I'm not proposing the law go into effect immediately. There would be several years warning and gun shop owners would still be able to sell their handguns out of the country. As to people with large collections they would have the option of making all of their handguns inoperative or of moving their collections out of the country. Not very fair—but then very few people have gun collections.

J: All right, after they take my gun away what other freedom will be taken away?

T: It's still a free country where the majority rules and any law can be repealed.

J: All right, the bottom line is, will the people go for the law? I doubt it.

T: You're probably right, but the law has been passed locally already in some places, and I think that most people would favor tougher gun control laws even if it wasn't the total ban of handguns.

Handguns (Essay)

TED HOELTER

Imagine a corner liquor store lit with an overabundance of flourescent and neon lights. The time, 11:45 p.m. on a Tuesday night, when business is slow. A car pulls into the parking lot, and two men get out. They walk in, and one of them looks around while the other brings a purchase to the counter. The latter then pulls out a knife and tells the owner to empty the register. The owner opens the register, but instead of cash he pulls out a pistol. He shoots, severely wounding one of the men, while the other gets away.

Next, imagine a quiet residential neighborhood. The time is 2:00 a.m., and the occupants of the house are a couple with a teenage son and young daughter. A noise in the basement is heard by the father, who decides to investigate. He reaches into his nightstand, pulls out a .357 magnum, walks to the basement door in time to find a burglar entering the house. He shoots and kills the burglar with ease.

The situations described are typical examples of the way personal firearms, especially handguns, are used to protect lives and property, right? Wrong. One of the strongest arguments for the restriction or even banning of handguns is that they are largely ineffective in preventing crime. Often the "criminal" shot by a handgun in the second example is a family member or a neighbor. In the first scenario the store owner could have easily been forced away from the register, in which case he runs the risk of getting shot with his own gun. Even if he could get to his gun; the possibility exists that the store owner's shot could hit an innocent bystander.

The opposition to gun control argues that most accidents are due to a lack of proper training of gun owners and that the better solution is increased training in the safe use and operation of a handgun, not a ban. However, it should be pointed out that many of the people who buy guns for protection aren't interested in safety, only in blowing away a criminal. Also, accidents aside, many people are killed or seriously injured by handguns used in crimes. A ban is ridiculous, say some. More people are killed each year in car accidents than by handguns. Why not then propose a ban on cars as well? That analogy is a good argument for tougher driving laws but doesn't apply to handguns. True, a car can kill, but its primary purpose is transportationhe primary purpose of a handgun is killing.

Another argument brought up in opposition to handgun restrictions is that when handguns are outlawed and law-abiding citizens comply, only "outlaws" will have handguns. So in reality a ban would not prevent criminals from having and using handguns; it would just make it illegal for the rest of society to try to protect itself in the same way. But if it is illegal to possess a hangun then possession of one is one more way to prosecute people who belong in jail anyway. Also, in most cases owning a handgun won't protect you from someone else with one unless your gun is always loaded and easily accessible, in which case the gun is more of a danger to your family than it is a crime preventer.

The most famous argument used by pro-gun groups is that the Constitution guarantees them right to bear arms. In fact, what is actually guaranteed in the Constitution is the right for state and local governments to have militias and police forces. The use of this as a sole argument against gun control also is an indication that no legitimate arguments really exist.

Private gun ownership, while not a right, is a long-standing tradition. Along with this tradition of private gun ownership is the acceptance by all but a very small minority of people that certain weapons such as machine guns are not needed by the public. Handguns, because of all the needless deaths caused by them each year, should be put into the same category with machine guns.

Is such a law enforceable? Not completely. There are too many handguns already in the country to ever get rid of all of them. But most people who own handguns would obey the law, and in time even the number of illegal guns would decrease. Will such a law be passed nationally? Probably not. Even through bans have been passed on a local level in several cities, and Japan has had great success with its ban of handguns, most Americans don't see handguns as a threat and so see no need for a ban. Eventually, when the situation gets completely out of hand, legislation will be passed. But sadly, many more people will have to die before the nation realizes that such a measure is necessary.

Many Paths to the Same Goal

SCOTT KENWORTHY

The religions of the world: a vast, complex maze of beliefs, rituals, traditions, philosophies and practices. They are very often a very important part of people's lives but are often pitted against each other in fierce competition, often the cause of much prejudice and even violence. Although the major religions as they exist today are extremely diverse and often contradictory, the founders of all religions were saying essentially the same thing.

The great teachers of the world, such as Christ, Buddha, Krishna, Ramakrishna, Mohammed, Lao-Tzu, Moses, and others, were all enlightened beings or prophets of a high order. They knew the sublime truths of Reality, but they had to keep in mind the audience whom they were speaking to. Therefore, there are generally two sets of teachings: those given to the masses and those given to the direct disciples. For example, Christ spoke to his Apostles that "Blessed are the pure in heart, for they shall see God," and he told them "Be ye therefore perfect, even as our father in Heaven is perfect." He told them to find the Kingdom of God within. To the multitudes, on the other hand, he spoke in parable and spoke of the treasures of Heaven as a reward for good deeds. Oftentimes, a teacher will tell a disciple one thing and another disciple a completely contradictory thing, depending upon individual needs. This is part of the reason contradictions arise among the followers of a faith. For instance, many Christian denominations vary and contradict each other, even though they are based on the teachings of Christ, and this disagreement is due to the emphasis of certain teachings as well as differences in interpretation.

As far as the higher teachings, though, most are saying much the same thing. Patanjali, a great Indian sage, said: "Cultivate friendliness toward the happy, compassion for the unhappy, delight in the virtuous, and indifference to the wicked." Christ: "Resist not evil: but whosoever shall smite thee on thy right cheek, turn him to the other also. . . . Love your enemies, bless those that hate you. . . ." The Buddha: "Hatred does not cease by hatred at any time: hatred ceases by love. . . ." to Lao-Tzu, the founder of Taoism: "The Sage. . . is gentle to the gentle; he is also gentle to the harsh: For Virtue is gentle." Sri Krishna: "A man should not hate any living creature. Let him be friendly and compassionate to all. . . . His attitude is the same toward friend and foe."

These teachings are not contradictory but rather are different approaches to the spiritual life. Many beliefs that are contradictory in the religions of today may not have originally started as such. For instance, the belief in reincarnation as opposed to the doctrine of Heaven: there is no reason to believe that Heaven is an actual place, for Christ speaks of the Kingdom of Heaven that is within, and it is entirely possible that Jesus spoke of an experience or state of being such as the mystical experience. In fact, reincarnation was believed by many Christians until the Conference of Constantinople in 532 AD., when it was declared a heresy by the Church. So it may not contradict the basic teachings of Christ himself.

Christians believe in God as the Holy Trinity, the Jews and Muslims as the supreme personal creator, and the Hindus as an impersonal Spirit that is the ground of all existence; the Buddhists speak of no God at all. Although these teachings seem to oppose each other, one must understand that this difference is due to the limitations of the human mind. All religions teach that God is infinite and eternal, and beyond the grasp of the human mind. Therefore, those who have gone beyond the mind and experienced God, when they try to put the experience into words, must limit their expression of God. Each man will describe it differently, according to his preconceptions, mental make-up, and cultural beliefs. As Sri Ramakrishna says, "The Hindus, who drink water at one place, call it 'jal.' The Muslims at another place call it 'pani.' The English at a third place call it 'water.' All three denote the same thing, the difference being in name only. In the same way, some address the Reality as 'Allah,' some as 'God,' some as 'Brahman'. . . ." Therefore it seems that a prophet will describe the divine in the way that his people will most understand.

Oftentimes Christians quote sayings of Jesus that He is the "light" and "the way," that one can reach the Father only through the Son, as their proof that one can be saved only through Christ. Virtually all the *avataras,* or divine teachers such as Buddha or Krishna, said nearly the same exact thing. Does this mean that they were denying each other? No. It must be understood that they are speaking as the Spirit, not as historical personalities, and that it is by their example and teachings that one may find God.

One could argue endlessly over the philosophical differences among the religions, but on the essence of religion itself, that of our spiritual growth, all religions seem to be in harmony, in fact quite complementary. The XIV Dalai Lama, the spiritual leader of Tibet, put it perfectly: "There are many religions that set forth precepts and advice on how to adjust one's mental attitude, and all, without exception, are concerned with making the mind more powerful, disciplined, moral, and ethical. In this way the essence of all religions is the same, even though in terms of philosophy there are many differences. Indeed, there would be no end to argument if we concentrated just on philosophical differences. . . . Far more useful and meaningful is to try to implement in daily life the precepts for goodness that we have heard in any religion." And it is just this universal message of goodness that all the great teachers have brought to us.

Stream of Consciousness

For about 15 minutes write down pell-mell everything that comes into your head, noting thoughts down in a telegraphic style for yourself only. Choose a quiet time and place that will least draw your attention to the outside world. Find out what's on your mind or under your mind once you suspend activity and sensations for a while. You may not be able to record all thoughts or do justice to each, but you can sample at least by just letting your mind go and witnessing it on paper. You might do this on several occasions to be sure of getting out a lot of material.

Now look over your notes and try to find a thought or image that you might want to develop, that may be connected to further thoughts that had not emerged before. Or see if you can see recurring motifs or connections among thoughts that you at first regarded as discontinous and jumbled. Make some more notes to expand or extend or link up ideas. Then shape these into some sort of essay that will allow some audience you have in mind to understand and enjoy your thought train.

Window

SUE HOLZ

The shade in the window that faces mine in the house next door is halfway down. The light is on and I think someone's in there. No one should be in there. That's Mr. Perri's reading room. He used to read every night. Most of the time when I turned out my light at night his would stay on. He really liked to read, I guess. Mr. Perri died last year. But our myrtle tree died years before that. You can't even see the patch where the stump used to be any more. You can still sort of see the "pitcher's mound" in the yard—the little grassless spot trod away by little feet in their nightly baseball games.

It was kind of funny how I used to play baseball with my brother. He would give me three outs, but I had to get him out just once each inning. It was hard! I never won. I used to complain and even cry sometimes. I guess it was fun though. I would go outside and have a game right now if I had the chance. But we're all so busy right now. Even at this very minute, 7:54 PM, I'm doing homework, my brother has a class at school, Dad's at the dentist, Mom's catching up on the house after a long day at work. We still have a very neat house (downstairs and Mother and Dad's room, anyway). I'm gonna be a supermom too, if I'm ever a mom at all.

Housewives are a thing of the past, and I'm certainly glad for that. My distant relative in Italy was born one day after me, August 12, '68, but when she graduates this year she has to stay home and take care of her little brothers and cook and sew and stuff. No way would they send her to school! Even if they had the money I really don't think there's much opportunity. If there's anything I'm really grateful for it's that there is an opportunity for me out there somewhere. I just have to find it.

My penpal from Finland is a lot smarter than I am (he speaks three languages fluently and won an award for Best Writer in Finland!) but he couldn't pass the exam to get into the University of Tampere the first time he took the entrance test. You've got to be good over there. Really, REALLY good to even get a chance. I wish my penpal would come here for a visit. But he hasn't even written in the longest time. . . . I wonder what I would show him. The shore, New York, the school, the college I'm going to . . . supermarkets, the mall, Route 22.

I drove on Rt. 22 two weeks ago in the rain. It wasn't that bad. I'm still not such a good driver. I really like walking anyway. I walked to the village last week, to make my deposit, and I had to make some copies too. I stopped in to see Charlie, and it was fun talking to him. His mother works in the same place as Mom does. It's in Union. I was in Union yesterday. Besides seeing a good show and eating ice cream cake and seeing two bad accidents and having a great disappointment (I hate you, Joe!), I met someone really cool. I told Mom about him when I got home. They were still up, it was only 10:30. They had a full day too though. At one point they were over at Mrs. Perri's house. She's moving, and we're helping her out with her garage sale. But she gave us some of her late husband's books.

Yeah, Mr.Perri really did like to read, I could see that from my window. I wonder what he thought about me when he saw me from his window, playing baseball with my brother or sitting alone in the branches of the myrtle tree.

Advice Letter

Ask and give advice for personal problems by letter. Set up an advice column in a school newspaper, or just arrange a box or other place where request letters may be left. Letters asking and giving advice can be printed or posted together so that others can read whole exchanges. Traditionally, names are made up to keep advice-seekers anonymous. Alone or with partners, you can write responses to the letters, perhaps after discussing some of the problems first with others when you are uncertain about which advice to give. Or take advantage of others' ideas by writing in for advice yourself.

Dear Debbie

DEBBIE SEMPLE AND ABBE HALPERT

Dear Debbie,

The other day, my best friend and I were shopping. Suddenly, my friend shoved something into my purse and then pushed me out the door. I wanted to go back and tell the clerk about it, but I was afraid I would have looked like the one who had stolen the item. Also, my friend never would have spoken to me again if I had.

What should I do? I want to do what's right, but I'm afraid.

"Shoplifter"

Dear "Shoplifter,"

Technically, by walking out of the store with an item that was not paid for in your purse, you, and not your friend, are the one who shoplifted. That doesn't make what your friend did right or excusable, however.

It's important that you realize what a serious offense shoplifting is. Stores now protect themselves with security guards and expensive electronics. They don't take crime lightly. In many states, you can be fined several hundred dollars and spend six months in jail even if you're accompanying someone who's stealing.

A "friend" who would risk involving you in such an escapade is no real friend, and you should realize that by associating with her, you're headed for danger. Confront your friend and urge her to return the stolen goods. If you friend continues this behavior, you'd be wise to avoid her in the future.

Deb

Dear Debbie,

I'll be going to a new school soon and I'm very nervous about it. I'm trying to lose some weight so I'll look better and be more popular, but my mother doesn't want me to diet. She says that not only do I look fine the way I am, but also it won't help me become popular. The problem is that in order to feel good about myself, I want to be thinner. Do you have any advice?

New-Girl-To-Be

Dear New-Girl-To-Be,

The best advice I could give you is the advice you've already received—from your mother! Many teens believe that automatically they'll be happier and more popular if they lose or gain weight, when rarely does this turn out to be the case. Instead, it can create a great deal of frustration and unhappiness for the teen who's struggling to achieve unattainable results.

If you're in good health and your weight is normal for your height and build, don't waste vital energy by trying to diet. Concentrate instead on your good and special qualities which are certain to have much more influence on your popularity than how high or low the needle climbs on the bathroom scale! Good luck!

Deb

Dear Debbie,

I am sixteen years old and presently a junior at Columbia. Because of my age I don't have a driver's license, but many of my friends, who are seniors, do. I feel guilty because they drive me many places and I can't return the favor. What can I do to make them realize that I appreciate these favors?

Signed,
Too Young to be Licensed

Dear "Too Young,"

Unless your friends voice an objection openly or obviously hint about the inconvenience, I don't think you should feel guilty. After all, it is a group of friends who is giving you rides. I'm sure that they know the difference between someone who becomes an instant friend when they need a ride and a true friend asking for a favor.

Since you feel guilty enough to ask for advice, you don't seem to be a fair-weathered friend at all. As long as your friends know that you would hang out with them whether they drove or not, they won't make you feel like you owe them anything. One thing that might relieve your guilt is trying to think of all the rides you can give them when you get your license. After all, that's what friends are for!

Deb

Dear Debbie,
I'm a senior and I'm having a problem with my grades. For the last three years I've been doing okay in school, usually ending up with a "C" or "C+" average. I plan on going to college, in fact my applications have already been sent out. But since I sent them in, my grades have slipped so much that I'm scared of what my mid-year report card is going to look like. I've hit "senior slump" and not just because I'm a senior. I've had some personal problems lately and I really don't know how to keep them from ruining my grades. Do you have any suggestions?

Signed,
Victim of S.S.

Dear "Victim of S.S.,"
I do have one suggestion for you that has worked with some people I have known to have a similar problem. Try to think of something that you would like to receive as a small reward, within reason, that could be tangible or intangible. For instance, it might be a couple of extra dollars of your choice or what you and your boyfriend/girlfriend will do on the weekend. Then think of a reasonable goal to aim for. If you've been getting "D's" on every math test, don't bet on getting an "A" from now on. Shoot for a "C," then a "B," and so on. Pick a goal to reach in every subject and something you would like to have for reaching each goal.
Then designate a person close to you to keep track of how many goals you reach and what you get for reaching them. Soon you will find that improving your grades can be almost automatic when you have something else to gain. The most valuable reward you'll receive will be the better grades you'll see on your next report card!

Deb

Dear Debbie,
I've been going with a guy for three months and all he talks about is my ex-boyfriend and his new girlfriend. He knows I don't like it. Is he doing this to get back at me for having had boyfriends before him?

In Love

Dear In Love,

Your boyfriend may be jealous of your past boyfriends and vent his feelings by doing this. But whatever the reasons are, there are no excuses for his hurting your feelings.

You need to sit down with him and explain that this talk hurts you. Tell him that you care for him, but that you will not put up with him harping on the subject. Be sensitive but firm and ask him to put a stop to it.

If he still doesn't get the message, you just may have to look elsewhere for a guy who is more mature and doesn't need to say things to hurt you deliberately

Deb

Dear Debbie,

I'm a senior and I haven't been dating anyone recently. But in the past, all of my boyfriends have been in the same grade or older than me. Lately, I've been spending time with my friends going to parties. A few weeks ago I met someone at a party who I really seemed to hit it off with. He's friendly and good-looking and has a good sense of humor. He's also a freshman. Since the party we've talked on the phone, but a mutual friend told me that he's afraid to ask me out because I'm a senior and he thinks pressure from my friends will keep me from saying "yes." The truth is that my friends don't really care and it doesn't bother me either. Should I bring up the subject with him or should I wait until he feels comfortable enough to ask me himself?

Signed,
Assenting Senior

Dear "Senior,"

If you really like this boy then bring up the subject yourself. It sounds like you're sure of his feelings for you more or less so you have less of a risk to take in this situation than he does. Pressure from friends, unfortunately, can keep a prospective relationship from ever getting off the ground. That's not your problem. The only issue for you to deal with is this boy's shyness and apprehension. Everyone is afraid of rejection, and in his position he probably feels twice as nervous about being let down since you're older. If you have to wait for him to make a move you might have to wait forever, no matter how much he likes you. So take the initiative and ask him what he thinks about the two of you. It will resolve each of your feelings and might lead to the beginning of a great relationship. If this happens and you do end up together, always remember that some of his insecurities about you will always be there so you'll know how to react when they surface.

Deb

Dear Debbie,

I am very involved in a lot of school activities which take up most of my time. Lately, many of my friends have been complaining that I never call them and never have time to spend with them. I feel myself drifting from my friends and I don't want that to happen. I try to make them understand that school, my job, getting ready for college and my other activities take up all of my time. I am afraid that my friends will end up getting very upset with me. I'd love to spend time with them, and I do as often as possible, but I can't afford to give up any of my activities.

Signed,
Pressed For Time

Dear "Pressed,"

It's understandable that you feel worried about losing friends that you hardly ever see. However, almost everyone goes through a period when they have no extra time to spend socializing. Many of the friends that you're afraid of losing have probably survived such times. It seems that you feel your situation is only temporary. No matter how busy you are, it's important thay you find a few minutes to tell your friends what's going on. You may remember what it felt like when one of your friends neglected to explain his situation to you in busy times.

After all, the only way in which you could drift away from your friends is if you lost touch completely. Let them know that for the time being you have to concentrate on other activities before you can socialize. That way you can set your mind to work without worrying about losing your friends, and your friends will know that you're concerned about the time you spend together. Before you know it, some of your obligations will fade and you will be able to get back to having fun. If you talk to your friends now, they'll be there when free time fits into your schedule again.

Deb

Statement Through Story

Narrate any true happening that illustrates a general point you want to make. In other words, you are telling a story not only for its own sake but also to show something that the reader could apply to people and events he or she knows. Through your story make a statement. Whether you state the generality directly or leave it to your reader is your decision. A good title can provide direction for both you and your readers.

*This can be in first or third person and drawn from any source.
It could be included in a collection of other writings on the same
theme or could be incorporated later into a larger paper dealing
more comprehensively with the point. Or post or print up.*

How Many Veras?

BETH MORLEDGE

I am sitting on the front porch of our house in Wisconsin. The
sun is shining brightly in the clear sky, a cool breeze dancing through
the treetops. On the white cement pathway leading up to the porch,
my yellow labrador retriever, Duke, is getting a bath from a neighbor
girl, eleven years old. Her chocolate-colored hair contrasts with the
gold of Duke's shiny, wet coat.

Earlier that day the girl had placed in each of the neighbor's
mailboxes a xeroxed note: "Vera Buffet's Pet Care Service: Feeding
10¢, Bathing 50¢, Walking 25¢, Love them no charge." I called her, and
she was overjoyed at receiving her first business call. She was at my
house within minutes. I am watching her now, admiring the gentle-
ness and care she displays as she rinses Duke and towels him dry.

"I want to be a vet when I grow up. The reason I like animals so
much," she tells me matter-of-factly, "is because they like me." Her
face glowed as she bent down to Duke's face and received his highest
form of compliment—a sloppy kiss.

"Well, Vera, I think everybody must like you," I say. Her only
reply is a shrug of her shoulders.

* * *

This scene which occurred three months ago has been a persistent memory in recent days. Last weekend I got a call from my
father, who told me something I didn't want to believe. Vera was dead.
She came home from school one afternoon last week and hanged
herself. "Why?" I ask myself. "What horrible feelings could there have
been in the heart of someone so young? Were there feelings of such
despair that she couldn't stand to live even with hopes that life might
get better? The many memories I have of Vera and this incident are
significant to me. Lately, I have been more appreciative of life and the
good things it has to offer than I have ever been before. I also realize,
as should others, that there are Veras everywhere, faces displaying a
smile, yet hearts filled with pain.

A Bigger View

ANN SIEGEL

My friend Julie and I had just gotten into a big fight over which tape to listen to next. I wanted to hear Billy Joel, but Julie wanted David Bowie. Seething with anger, I stomped out of her livingroom. "I'm not going to give in to her again," I mumbled. To cool down I took refuge in the newspaper. I was flipping through the pages, looking for the comics, when my eye caught a familiar face. I didn't know his name or anything about him. He was just a guy I had seen walking up and down the school halls many times.

But I was looking in the obituary column! As I read on I learned that this boy, a San Marcos sophomore, had died of injuries in a fall off the Goleta Valley Community Center roof. In his picture there was a big grin on his face. He looked as if he was enjoying himself—perhaps at a party. His eyes were bright and clear. His blond hair was carelessly parted and combed. No razor could have achieved the smoothness of his cheeks. He looked energetic and ready to deal with the problems of life.

With a start I heard Julie shouting from the next room, "Anne, what are you doing in there?" Wiping my eyes, I said, "Let's hear some David Bowie."

Children and Animals

KAREN CAMPBELL

One thing I've noticed about little kids is that they can be really cruel to animals. They're just not quite old enough to realize that animals feel pain, just like people do.

During the cold, rainy days of winter, a little kid can sure get bored. I wandered aimlessly around the house, searching for *something* to do. My eight-year-old sister was too sophisticated to play with me. My dad was taking a nap, and my mom was curled up on the couch with a book. I sat down on the green carpet and amused myself by trying to pull up the pieces of yarn that seemed to be rooted to the material beneath. Suddenly I glanced over at the open umbrella that was propped on the floor to dry. I was filled with excitement at my new idea. I went into the laundry room and took my hamster out of his cage. "Winkie must be really bored too," I thought. "I'll bet he'll just love the fun ride I got for him." I held the squirming hamster in one hand, and held the umbrella upright. I gently set him into the basin of the umbrella. Then I twirled it around and around as fast as I could.

Winkie scratched and clawed at the rounded sides but only slid back down to the middle of the umbrella.

My sister walked into the room and screamed, "Karen! What are you doing?! That's mean, you little brat! How would *you* like it if I put you in our umbrella and twirled *you* around?!"

"But Winkie likes it, see?" We looked down into the umbrella. Winkie still clawed at the tightly stretched nylon.

"No he doesn't! Look! He wants out!"

"How'd you know, maybe he likes it!" I screamed back. My sister picked up the scared little hamster with one big sweep of her arm.

"I'm gonna put him up so you can't reach 'im."

I knew if I tried to hit her, she would hit me twice as hard, so I decided not to argue. I sat back down on the carpet and stared morosely into space. Big sisters have to spoil everything!

The Power of Negative Thinking

BRUCE McFADDEN

The picnic is over. Tina and I walk up to the parking lot from the beach to get into my car and drive home. Wait—the car isn't there— was it stolen? No! A quick glance over the edge of the cliff where my car was parked confirms my deepest horrors. The car is lying on its side in a creek after falling more than fifty feet off the edge of the cliff. It is dark, and I can just make out the outline of the car and its black tires. Along with feelings of shock and disbelief, I imagine a crane pulling from the creek-bed below the mangled remains of what once was a shiny white 1982 Rabbit convertible.

In my mind I keep telling myself this could not be real, but the fact that I was involved in an accident two weeks earlier only added to the reality of the moment. The insurance company, the hassle with my parents, the cost, the embarrassment—these and a million other reasons make me wish and pray that I would just suddenly awaken to that wonderful feeling one gets when one realizes some terrible misfortune is only a nightmare.

Walking down the hill to the beach, holding back my desire to yell, "Why me!!" I decide to tell my parents what happened. "Where's Dad?" I ask my mom, to which she casually replies, "Oh, your father took your car to the hospital; he had to see a patient." I slowly repeat this sentence in my mind several times before fully understanding it. Barely self-contained outrage races through my mind, before I am suddenly hit with waves of trembling relief.

Still not believing that what is in the creek is not my car, I run up the hill and peer over the cliff. Sure, it was still there—the wheels made of two dark boulders, the body a piece of white, painted wood, the glistening windshield a bunch of broken lightbulbs, and the whole thing held together by my imagination.

Some good has come of this incident. It has helped me take a more relaxed and skeptical approach in evaluating and dealing with life's apparent disasters. It has helped me to stop creating monsters out of shadows (figuratively speaking); on the other hand, the event has also led me to appreciate and value more those possessions of mine which can easily be taken away or destroyed—at least by my mind's eye.

Thematic Collection of Incidents

Tell briefly several incidents that you think show the same thing, that is, illustrate a certain observation you want to make. An incident is an action that happened once. *Draw these incidents from any sources that you trust—memory, books, other people, and so on (including* Statement Through Story). *Narrate each incident just enough to fit your point, and state the point just enough to make it emerge. The result may resemble a familiar kind of feature article that points out and illustrates a trend, for example, or an essay depicting a common condition. So aim toward a corresponding medium.*

Accepting the Fact of White and Black

ROSE ANN HALL

Lisa and the Gavin

I am from South Boston, and some of the people from Southie have told me about their experiences at school with people of different races and colors. For example, five years ago, when I was in the fifth grade, I was over at my girlfriend Holly's house. Her babysitter was going to the Gavin School at the time, and she told us about the experiences she herself had had.

One day when I was at Holly's house, Lisa was telling us about how to fight if we went to the Gavin School next year. Now that really scared me.

About two months later, Lisa was babysitting again for Holly, and I came over. Well, she was telling us about how she went down to the locker room and lit up a cigarette. She was smoking it out the window when two black girls came to her and asked for a smoke. Lisa said, "I don't have any more left."

And one of the girls said, "I do not think you heard me correctly. Give me a smoke."

Lisa started to walk away and one girl grabbed her by her wrist and yanked her down to the ground and took her cigarette box out of her pocket and started to light it and smoke it. The other girl put her hand on Lisa's head, and Lisa yelled, "Get off of me, nigger."

The girls started to beat her up.

Two security cops were passing by the hall and saw them fighting and stopped them.

When Lisa told me what happened to her, I did not want to go to the Gavin or to any school that had black people in it. I was petrified that it might happen to me.

My mother tried to get me in to St. Augustine School. It was down the street from me and was a Catholic school with all white students. But they would not take me in the sixth grade because I did not start in first grade. They claimed that there was not enough room.

So I went to the Gavin after all.

Nancy and Junior High

When it was finally my turn to go to Gavin, I found out that it was not as bad as I thought it was. At first I was scared, but then it seemed to be an everyday thing. I became used to it.

When I was in seventh grade I met a Spanish girl named Nancy Muniz. She was sitting next to all the boys. They would all whistle at her and ask her out on a date, all that stuff kids did when they experienced their first love at first sight. Well, my teacher had to make a seating plan because they all sat around Nancy and talked all period. The teacher put Nancy next to me.

Nancy told me that she hated boys and that they were too much for her. We started to talk and talk. We had our gym classes together, we walked to class together, we shared lockers together. I even took her to my house to meet my parents. We'd go to my home for forty-five minutes. Then I would walk her back to the school to meet her bus.

The eighth grade came. I was in home room 108 and when I walked in the first day of school, who did I see? Nancy Muniz. It was kind of funny, because when she saw me, she yelled, "Rose Ann Hall, where have you been girl?" She came up to Mr. Randall's desk and gave me a bear hug.

All of eighth grade, we hardly ever went to class. We were either in guidance or at cheerleading practice.

Then there was a time when Nancy got into a little bit of trouble with some kids on her bus. They were calling her a honky lover, and she got into a fight with one girl and the whole busload started to jump in.

She did not come in until almost two weeks later. I said, "What happened to you? I called your house and all I got was, 'Nancy's not home.' That was all your mother would say to me before she would hang up on me."

"She was hanging up on you because she did not know what to say to you," Nancy said. "She speaks very little English."

We cut out after sixth period so I could walk her home to Andrew station. She said that the school said there was nothing that they could do to stop the kids from bothering her.

There was about two months left to the school year. Nancy must have gotten jumped at least two times. Someone slipped her a letter that said if she was seen with that white girl again, she would have a tattoo on her head saying, "I AM A HONKY LOVER."

Nancy and I agreed to see each other only after school and out of school. So every morning for the next month I went down to Andrew station to meet her and we would hook school. We went up to Dorchester Heights all day long, then at lunch time we would go get a pizza. For the rest of the year we did that. We both got put up to high school and could not believe it. But we were not about to argue about it.

After the summer was over I went to South Boston High School. So did Nancy. When I talked to her sister, she told me that Nancy had had a baby girl. When she came back to school, I saw her in the hall, but it was just hi and bye. I figured that she did not have the time with the baby and all to get acquainted with me again.

But when she called me one day and told me she did not want to go through what she did up at the Gavin, I was a little upset with her. She did not give Southie High a chance. She did not give me a chance, either. I felt she was ignoring me and the whole situation.

I tried to get her to see me after school or something. But she said no, and hung up on me.

Rita and Derek

When I reached high school I became best friends with Carol Beck. Carol and I were constantly in her house. When I would ask where Rita was, her older sister, Carol would say, "Either Fields Corner or Jamaica Plain or Somerville." I was thinking to myself, "Well gee. Those places are mostly black communities, and Spanish."

It was not until a few weeks later I discovered that most of Rita's friends were either black or Spanish. It was in the cafeteria when I was eating lunch. Rita and I came in the cafeteria early and sat way in the back of the caf. Then when all the students started to come in for lunch, that's when I noticed the back of the caf where we were sitting was filling up with black people.

I got a little nervous at that time. I said, "Rita."

And Rita said, "Jerome, this is my friend Rose." She introduced me to them and then I said, "I think we ought to leave this part of the caf. It's all black people, and the other side is all white—our white friends!"

She said, "I am with all my friends."

That's when I finally realized that all, well, most of her friends were black.

The next Saturday night Carol and I planned to go to Dance Factory and Rita asked if she could come along because she was meeting her boyfriend there and had no one to go there with. We said yes, and it would be the greatest time to meet her boyfriend.

When we got there, Carol and I were dancing when Rita came over to introduce Derek to us. When I turned around and saw a black boy holding Rita in his arms, *I could have died.* All I could think of was, what would her father say? He would absolutely kill her if he ever found out about this. And the people in Southie would bother her if they ever found out.

It bothered me for a little while. But then I know how I would feel if someone was to tell me I can no longer be around the young man who makes me feel good because he is not the same race as me.

So I did not say anything to her about it. But Sunday I asked her if she knew what she was doing and the consequences she would have to pay if anyone in Southie found out. Especially if her father found out about it. Rita said, "I do not care what the people in Southie care or think."

I did not know that Rita was being harassed for having black friends until I saw a piece of paper on her back that said, "I AM A NIGGER LOVER. HIT ME!"

When I peeled it off her back and showed it to her, she said, "That's nothing. It happens all the time."

I said, "Well, what do you do about it?"

She said, "Nothing."

I said, "Do you know who it is?"

"It's a few white girls that like to cause trouble."

I said, "Well, what are these few white girls' names?"

She told me, but she made me promise not to say anything to them because it would only make things worse. She said, "And besides, they will have their fun and it will wear off and they will stop aggravating me."

I said, "When do you think they will stop? Who are you trying to kid? They won't stop. You will be lucky if they stop in a few months, or maybe even years."

She said, "Well, I can live with it. I'm used to it."

In December of the next school year she was beaten up by two of the white girls, just because of her affection toward black people. I was really hurting for her.

I wanted to kill Betty and Marie for doing that to her. I went up to the both of them at the same time and said, "Do you two have a problem with Rita Beck? That is going to be settled right here and now. Or I will personally kick you both."

Marie did not say anything. But Betty said, "What, are you a nigger lover too?"

I got really bull and said, "If anyone gets that idea, then I am coming after you."

She said, "Then what do you care?"

"First of all," I said, "I do not think it is any of your business who she can and can't hang out with. Second of all, it is *her* choice."

We just kept arguing back and forth about where she goes to hang, and the people of different races. Then it was broken up by aides. They said to get to class.

That was a few months ago. No one's bothered her since then. Right now Rita got a few white girls a job at her work. So I think everything's back to normal.

Personal Essay

Set down thoughts triggered in you by a particular object, locale, or event that has stayed in your mind recently. Refer in your essay to this stimulus itself, and retain some of the mood and circumstances in which the thoughts occurred so that you convey the thinker and the thinking along with the thoughts. Print it up with personal essays of others or in a collection of other pieces of your own aimed at a similar readership.

Visualizations of the Future

STEVE ATKINS

The sport of baseball had not been going well for me. Over the past few games I had a very poor batting average as well as doing a poor job in the field. Concentration on the game had become increasingly difficult, especially at the plate. Somewhere between seeing the ball leave the pitcher's hand and hearing it in the catcher's glove I would lose track of what I was up there to accomplish. It seemed as though I wanted to swing the bat but couldn't, as if a small hand suddenly reached from behind me to hold the bat back. The net result was something between no swing at all and a check-swing. In the field my thoughts had begun to drift from watching my own pitcher throw the ball to watching what was going on in the bleachers. My feelings toward baseball got steadily worse from game to game, to the point where I decided that if things didn't improve drastically soon, I would give it up altogether.

Recently, though, during psychology class, I learned of an interesting technique which caught my attention right away. The psychology teacher, Mr. Weinstock, spoke of a relaxing process which has been used by many people including professional athletes. This process, informally called a "mind-body visualization," is used by the athlete to picture himself doing good things in his sport. The technique seemed a good idea to try, since I had nothing to lose either way. I had a game the following day, so I assumed it would be a good time to try it.

I began the routine fully dressed in my baseball uniform, lounging in a comfortable chair, as my teacher had directed. Starting by closing my eyes and taking deep breaths, I succeeded in relaxing my mind and body. From there I started to visualize each different part of my body from my head downward. While on my downward inventory, I felt a tingling begin in my fingers and toes, indicating the release of pentup tension.

After completing that portion of the exercise, I mentally watched a series of numbers appearing before me, beginning with the number ten. The ten, bright red in color against a black background, stayed for an instant and then was replaced by the numbers nine progressing down through one. The zero was last, and it appeared in my mental image large enough to climb through, so I did.

What was on the other side pleased me a lot, because what I saw was myself playing baseball, but not baseball as I usually saw it. In this game, it seemed that I was the only one playing. There were no bleachers full of people, no umpire, no catcher, and even no pitcher. Only the baseball was visible, but it too was not the same as usual. No longer did it seem the evil and wicked golf-ball-sized pellet trying to avoid the bat. Rather it seemed large and more attracted than repelled. With nothing in terms of distractions to affect me, I swung hard and watched as the ball sailed out of sight.

I returned from my state of semi-consciousness by reversing the counting process and counting from one to ten. When I reached ten, I felt, for the first time in months, a feeling of confidence. I knew then that it would be easier to concentrate on the game and what I wanted to accomplish, so I gathered up my gear and left for the game.

I thought of my previous two times at bat when I stepped up for the third time. Visible only to me was the ball in the pitcher's hand. It was suddenly hurled toward me. Without thinking this time, I gave a quick swing and sent the ball over the third base man for a hit. It was my third hit of the day.

Philosophers and Chimps in the Computer Age

LISA HEILBRON

A few years ago I had my first person-to-computer encounter. It left me frustrated and awed. My father, who uses the University of California computer system, has a terminal connected with the main UC network. Once when it was unoccupied I decided I'd try to talk to the computer. I first punched in my name:

—LISA—

and received an impersonal

—SYSTEM NOT RECOGNIZED. PLEASE SPECIFY ACCOUNT NUMBER—

I punched in

—WHY?—

—SYSTEM NOT RECOGNIZED. PLEASE SPECIFY ACCOUNT NUMBER—

Okay, fine. "Dad, what's your account number?"

I punched it in. Great, I thought, now I'll discover the inner workings of this computer!

—WHAT IS 2 + 2?— I figured I'd start easy.

—ERROR— responded the computer. Wait, I thought, I only asked the question; I haven't given the wrong answer yet.

—WHAT IS GOING ON?— I asked.

—ERROR—

—BUT PLEASE—

—ERROR—

Though the computer was speaking in my language, I certainly wasn't communicating in its! Because I knew the computer was able to perform incredible calculations, I had been deluded into thinking it was intelligent and could respond to me in an intelligent manner. While a computer can be very smart when it comes to solving sets of differential equations, it can also be quite stupid when forced to communicate in natural language. We need to be careful that the rigid way we are forced to converse with computers does not come to affect the way we communicate with each other. It is not impossible that sometime in the future we might hear *people* spewing lines like, "System not recognized," and "illegal operation!"

We seem to rely more and more on computers to do simple tasks that were once performed by human beings. In my trigonometry class, I often thank "modern technology" for providing the hand calculator which gives me the square root of pi instantaneously. My math teacher calls grinding out problems in the old way "good mental exercise," but few of his students agree.

What the calculator has done for math, the word processor can do for English. A person can punch a paragraph full of grammar and spelling mistakes into a word processor and receive an error-free copy. If the computer can spell for us, why should we learn to spell in the first place? If we come to depend on this type of program, writing skills will decline, and the thought processes associated with good writing will wither.

But the technology goes further. Some programs not only correct mistakes, they also write. They go far beyond simple performing of functions to the synthesizing of information which previously required human intellect. An article in the *San Francisco Chronicle* describes one such computer program. The program allows the "writer" to pour in his unorganized thoughts and receive in return a logical, organized, correctly written paragraph. The program does such a good job that it is now being hired to write speeches for politicians. One politician requested a speech that would be effective in "Middle America." The researchers went to Peoria and sampled a cross section of the populace to determine Peoria's views on foreign policy. The results of their survey were fed to the IBM 370, which promptly returned a seven-minute speech on foreign policy with which few Middle Americans, and few of the rest of us, for that matter, would disagree. It began:

> The United States is not a failure. For 200 years we have provided the world, through the great experience of democracy, a model—a model that the world is free to follow, but one that we will not impose. Ideally, we would prefer merely to be this model. Unfortunately, the pragmatic realities of the international scene force us to play other roles. . . .

Imagine the potential effect of these word-synthesizing programs. Theoretically, a person using minimal intellect or reasoning can punch in the crudest of thoughts and receive back a clear sentence. I envision a three-year-old screaming at a computer, "I want my mama, I want food," commands the computer would translate as, "I would appreciate it if my mother would bring me some dinner."

I saw a movie in psychology class about a chimpanzee named Pumpkin who was being taught through a computer using symbols. According to the research scientists working with her, Pumpkin was using structured language much the same way we do. With the help of a word-synthesizing program, Pumpkin could write sentences we write.

The computer is capable of making a monkey look human, but can it also make a human being look like a monkey? We don't know how the computer's ability to do human work will affect us. Will we use the freedom we gain to take on tasks that challenge our potential? Or is it possible that with so much of our work done by computers, we might become lax and indolent?

The computer revolution will affect everybody in a different way. It will give the lazy a pillow to lean on and the energetic a ladder to climb. We can use the computer to become more like Aristotle and Shakespeare. We do not need to use it to become more like Pumpkin, the chimp.

The Paladin

KARL LARSEN

"All right, Karl, what does your Paladin do?" the Dungeon Master asked me.

"Sir Allen challenges Jarl for the life of the princess," was my reply.

"You mean you're going to fight a twenty-foot-tall Frost Giant!"

"Yes, I'm a Paladin, I defend those who cannot defend themselves against stronger opponents."

"OK. Roll to hit." The D.M. was stuttering, fearing my wrath if my best character were killed. I rolled my dice.

"Twenty! Critical hit! Percentage . . . Ninety-nine."

"The Paladin Sir Allen pierced the heart of the Frost Giant King Jarl and saved the frightened princess of Greyhawk!" the Dungeon Master exclaimed to all.

As I left the room where we had been playing "Dungeons & Dragons," I was aware that someone was following me. A hand kindly but firmly tapped me on the shoulder, and I turned to see my image of the Paladin Sir Allen. Perhaps you are wondering what I am talking about. Paladins are knights of various orders who dedicate their lives to the destruction of evil and the betterment of mankind. They are Holy Warriors, the kind of people that children look up to as role models. I had always hoped for the existence of Paladins in today's society. Since I recognized him for what he was, I decided to ask the Paladin about his background.

He told me that a knight is usually well versed in religion, having been raised as a humble person, probably a member of an altar boy group of some sort. Courtesy, honor, respect for all, and the improvement of humanity dictate the actions of a knight. In J. R. T. Tolkien's *The Lord of the Rings* series, a man named Aragorn is the perfect Paladin. He follows all the Paladin codes; he is brave, being the first one in and the last one out of danger, and he is faithful to the woman he will one day wed.

As I talked with the Paladin, I began to wonder if there were any Aragorns in today's society. Surely not according to the exact description, but there are parts of him in many places. Every Nobel peace prize winner is an Aragorn. They all strive for the betterment of mankind. The Boy Scouts practice Aragorn's courtesy and respect. The Police and Neighborhood Watch carry the fight against crime and evil.

The Salvation Army and other charities all seek improvement of health and welfare. As you can see, the ideals are there, and they are good. Why, then, aren't they universally practiced?

People obviously like the knightish ideals as seen by what they like for entertainment. They watch "The A-Team," a group of underground Paladins on a crusade against crime. One of the most popular movies of all time, *The Return of the Jedi*, was about being a knight. Most stories usually have a conflict between good and evil with the good winning. So we see that people *aren't* inherently bad and that they want to see good things happen. So where are all the good deeds?

Perhaps the will is there and it is simply being misapplied. In college, people join fraternities and sororities which appear to resemble organizations of knights. The problem is that these groups do deeds for the *organization*, not for humanity. When I was in junior high school, there was a loosely organized group of teenagers who called themselves the Ishi club. They did things for their own clique, a selfishness which is a shame because they had a lot of potential for helping others.

In fact, there are fewer service organizations than self-indulgent ones. People are misapplying themselves. Everybody has the ability to think like the Paladin Sir Allen; they just need to consider others first and put themselves second. There would be no fear of being left out because there would always be someone else striving for the same goal, acting the part of a knight.

The best starting place would be etiquette, which involves many of the social customs which include holding a door open for a lady, being respectful of elders, and being kind to all. By following these codes, the modern Paladin isn't saying that he is better than others, he is showing respect. We have Paladins today; most of them just need to apply themselves to the right deeds.

My thoughts had left me oblivious to the speech of the Paladin Sir Allen, or maybe they were influenced by him. However, when I looked up, he was gone. All that remained was a small parchment. I picked it up and noted the fine Gothic script that I would expect a Paladin to use. The parchment bore a few words that have changed my whole life: "You too are a Paladin."

The Feeling of Nothingness

JOHN WICKENHAEUSER

I have climbed to its peak four times, twice on foot and twice by bike, and all these times the weather has been different: every time the peak and the path to it show different faces. Once it was so foggy in the city that when at the top of the mountain one could see nothing but a sea of clouds; it was just like being on top of everything, since you could not see much. The peak I speak of is La Cumbre Peak. On this foggy day I biked up Gibralter Road through the mist and into a place of nothingness. Upon arriving at the top, which stands around 3950 feet above sea level, I had the strangest view of Santa Barbara, or rather not of Santa Barbara but of its substitute for the day, a complete blanket of seething, steaming, puffy fog while I was in total, hot, blinding sunlight. This sight was truly awesome and it gave a feeling of complete removal from everything; I was made to feel completely alone when I was only twelve miles from town. It was great!

I spent almost an hour above, as far as I could see, nothing. I would have been convinced that there was nothing down below me if I had not come from that nothingness below. The fact that the whole city that I called home was invisible allowed me to forget about my problems and concentrate on more important things like nothing. It is rare that you can think of nothing, but it is the most wonderful thing to think of in the whole world. The feeling I experienced that single day was ten times better than sleep and thousands of times better than being awake and aware. I was able to concentrate on nothing, and in doing so I found that nothing was really something. It was something intangible, something that one is unaware of until one can experience nothing firsthand. This is becoming increasingly hard to do, as our national wilderness continues to dwindle. This wilderness is the only place most people can find to be alone with their thoughts of nothingness. It is truly a shame that our government cannot get its act together and do something serious about preservation instead of just talking about it. In the hour I spent pondering nothing I gained a sense of complete relaxation, and though my mind was not calm, it had nothing in it; it was finally doing something important, thinking of nothing.

When I finally descended the grade, I began to slip back into the fog and the nothingness, and I realized that there were two kinds of nothingness, the kind in each person's mind and the kind that we commonly think of as nothing, a void. The nothing in one's mind is as intangible as the one in a void, but it contains something, something wonderful and something important to one's well-being and to one's interpretation of the world around. By my mind's definition of nothing the whole town of Santa Barbara was nothing, but by the common definition of nothing, the town *was* something; it was what was going on in my mind that was nothing.

The incident at the sunny peak of a familiar mountain is forever important to me because it caused me to realize how much there is in the world yet truly there is nothing. It all depends on how one looks at it; when I am in a bad mood I can always think of nothing, and nothing will cheer me up, and when I am in a good mood I don't have to think about nothing, for then I am not thinking a thing. And now that I think about nothing I realize that to have two definitions of nothing, one must have two definitions of something.

Generalization Supported by Instances

Frame a generalization about anybody or anything from observations you have made. You might illustrate this with some of the very instances that led you to conclude your generalization. These may include some that you developed in greater detail for previous assignments such as **Memories or Case Study or Statement Through Story.** *But you may draw on any sources and mix in any combination: (1) first-hand experience, (2) testimony by others of their experience, (3) reportage and research, (4) statements by experts, (5) facts well accepted in a certain community or specialty, and (6) logical demonstration. Qualify as to the people or conditions for which the generalization holds true.*

Read it to an interested group or submit it to a publication specializing in your subject. Or include it in a collection of your other writing.

Left-Handers vs. Right-Handers

JANE COLLINS

I have spent a great deal of time studying the difference between left-handed people and right-handed people. As a card-carrying south-paw myself, I speak with experience when I say that left-handed people are generally more interesting, more intelligent, more creative, more intuitive, and more persevering than right-handed people. This statement is not to be taken lightly, for it is the conclusion of many years of research and observation.

The high incidence of left-handedness in geniuses is proof in itself of the high I.Q. level of southpaws. Tests have shown that the brains of left-handers are much better developed than those of right-handers. This is thought to be in compensation for the education discrimination that left-handers invariably must overcome. Starting in their first year of school, left-handers are handicapped by right-handed scissors, right-handed penmanship, and right-handed teachers. As the years go on, right-handed binders, right-handed desks, and, again, right-handed teachers contribute to the hardship that left-handers must face to be educated.

Since the right side of the brain controls the left side of the body, left-handers are also more creative and intuitive than their right-handed counterparts. Left-handers are known to be more emotional and sensitive to the needs of others. Consequently, left-handers are generally very popular. This is partly because of the right brain dominance. Since the right side of the brain is more multi-faceted than the factual left side, left-handers tend to be more multi-faceted, interesting people.

Finally, left-handers grow to be very determined and persevering. This is due to the discriminations that they face in all walks of their lives. Some of these have already been mentioned: binders, scissors, desks, books. From a left-handed point of view a ladle's pouring spout is on the wrong side, the writing on the sides of pens and pencils is upside down, the printing on a mug faces away from the drinker. The list is endless. Most irritating of all, left-handers are forced to write unnaturally, from left to right. This causes the writing to smear, of course, since to continue on the same line the left hand must rest on fresh ink. In overcoming these and other left-handed discomforts, left-handers have learned the importance of patience, diligence, and tolerance.

Left-handed people are determined to leave their mark on the world, even if it is a left-handed mark, which a right-hander would consider to be wrong. Left is actually right, and right is wrong. However, left-handers never say that to right-handers, because besides being interesting, intelligent, creative, intuitive, persevering, determined, sensitive, multi-faceted, patient, tolerant, and diligent, left-handers are generally much more modest than right-handers.

Right? Left.

Crossroads

WILL ROBERTSON

In a lifetime many roads are traveled and few are smooth and easy. Each has its own particular dangers, but inevitably every traveler comes to a crossroad at which he must decide between the dictates of society and his own system of ethics. To travel the well beaten path of society's approval may mean betraying one's beliefs, while attempting to blaze a trail through the wilderness of societal censure may carry the risk of bringing down society's wrath. In the novels *Billy Budd* and *Huck Finn*, the characters of Captain Vere and Huck come to a moral crossroad from which Vere travels the paved pathway of society while Huck chooses the thorny path of individualism, the two alternatives that we as individuals face today.

Huck's decision to break away from the ethics of society is

foreshadowed during his journey down the Mississippi. Huck becomes relatively inured to the regulations of Southern society during his stay with the Widow Douglas, until he is kidnapped by Pap. Once free of civilization's restraints, however, he quickly reverts to his independent mode of life to the point that he says, "I don't see how I'd ever got to like it so well at the Widow's. . . . I didn't want to go back no more." As soon as he gets away from Pap, he sets his course down the river and away from civilization.

After he joins up with Jim, Miss Watson's escaped slave, his estrangement from the morality of his society progresses at an ever increasing rate. When he discovers that some men are going to the island that he and Jim are living on, to look for an "escaped nigger," Huck wastes no time in warning Jim and preparing to leave. Although Huck begins to take an active role in preventing Jim's capture. he still has to struggle with his conscience. He believes that he is committing a sin by helping Jim avoid the slave hunters, and, according to society, he is guilty. The ultimate break with society comes when Jim is captured and turned over to Silas Phelps. Huck must decide between writing to the Widow and helping her recover Jim, and thus being redeemed in the eyes of society, or helping Jim escape and receiving the condemnation of society. His declaration, "All right then, I'll go to hell!" signals his complete break from society and his acceptance of all the risks that the break entails.

Like Huck, Captain Vere in *Billy Budd* is the product of an extremely rigid society, in Vere's case that of the British navy. Vere's indoctrination into and acceptance of his society, however, are so complete that when the crucial decision must be made between his society's dictates and his personal beliefs, he allows his society's convictions to override his own. Vere is described as a man who "had seen much service and been in various engagements, always acquitting himself as an officer mindful of his men, but never tolerating an infraction of discipline." Obviously Vere's dedication to the codes and regulations of naval life was absolute. Vere's inability to function outside of his society's ethical boundaries is supported by the statement, "his settled convictions were as a dike against those wandering waters of novel opinion, social, political, and otherwise. . . ." His dependency on naval protocol to dictate his actions left him no recourse but to condemn Billy Budd, who had unintentionally killed the villainous Claggert. Even though Vere believes that Billy intended neither mutiny nor homicide, his adherence to naval policy will not allow him to give Billy anything less than the death penalty.

Even as Huck took one road and Vere the other, I as an eighteen-year-old am faced with similar decisions in my life, for example, in regard to registering for the draft. Do I follow society's lead and register, accepting the responsibility for saying, "Yes, I will go wherever you send me and kill someone I don't know for a reason that I may not completely understand"? Even if it is not a matter of objecting to taking a life, should I allow myself to be registered to go fight for a cause that I may not believe in but am nevertheless compelled to fight for? Here, the fork in the road lies before me, the choice between what society believes is right and what I believe separating into two different roads.

Which road would Huck take? Which would Vere take? Robert Frost once wrote of two roads diverging in a forest: "I took the one less traveled by, and that has made all the difference." Although the one "less traveled by" has its temptations, I have chosen the well-paved path of conformity, just as Vere has. Perhaps if I had the will and strength to fight society, regardless of my convictions, I would take Huck's path, but like Vere I am torn between what I myself believe and what I have been taught to believe and thus am only a product of my society. I may wish to be Huck, but I am afraid that Vere's society may prove too strong for me. Vere's way? Huck's way? The crossroad lies ahead of me.

Editorial

Make a proposal for some kind of action that ought to be taken regarding a current problem of concern to readers of a magazine or newspaper you have in mind. Or simply argue a position you think appropriate to take by way of reacting to a recent event, trend, or issue. You might write as an "in-house" editorialist or put your case in the form of a letter to the editors of some publication. Set up the matter in the terms and framework you see it in, and marshall the facts and reasons for the solution or position. Fix the length according to some editorials you have seen in publications or to the format of one you are writing for.

Navajos Should Install Solar Collectors, Solar Greenhouses to Heat Their Homes

CHARLENE GATEWOOD

I noticed that few people on the Navajo Reservation are using solar systems to heat their homes. I inteviewed Joseph Orr, who published an article called, "Mud-Heat Storage Solar Greenhouse," in the May/June, 1978 edition of *Mother Earth News*, about a solar green-house he built to heat his home. He thinks that people in the U.S. shouldn't use fossil fuels, like coal, as the primary energy source for heating their homes. He feels there are more efficient ways to use fossil fuels. He thinks that the sun's rays should be the main source of energy used in home heating systems. I agree with Joseph Orr. It is smart for people on the Navajo Reservation to use solar energy systems to heat their homes.

I think people on the Navajo Reservation should use a flat-plate collector to heat their homes. This collector is easy to install for those people on the Reservation who build their own homes, because the design is simple and requires few materials. The flat-plate collector is a wooden box with a glass cover on the top. Inside there is a coiled pipe. The interior of this box is painted black. The dark color absorbs the sun's rays. When the sun's rays pass through the glass cover and warm the air in the flat-plate collector, the hot air will travel through a metal duct system. This metal duct is insulated to keep the heat in. There should be a vent in every room to let the heat in. There is a blower next to a heat storage tank that pushes air into the tank located in the basement. At the bottom of this tank are rocks which absorb the heat. This is called a rock storage tank. The tank traps heat and stores heat in the rocks. There is another blower on the other side of the rock storage tank which forces the air to travel through the ducts and out through the vents.

With a flat-plate collector system as the primary heating system, there should also be a back-up heating system. On cloudy days and during the night the back-up heater will take over to heat up the rooms.

There are four advantages to using a solar heating system. One, the energy of the sun is free to use. You don't have to pay to use the sun's energy. In Arizona, most of the days are sunny. We hardly ever get clouds in the sky that would prevent the flat-plate system from collecting enough heat to heat our homes. Two, there is an endless supply of solar energy. Three, I think people on the Navajo Reservation shouldn't use large quantities of fossil fuels to heat their homes because the smoke is unhealthy. It makes the air outside and inside the home dirty. The air we breathe in contains burned particles from coal. That causes us to be sick. We catch colds from it, get headaches and get runny and stuffy noses. Solar energy heating systems are cleaner and healthier than coal heating systems. Four, fossil fuels should be used for other purposes. Joseph Orr explained that it would be better to use fossil fuels as an energy source for a back-up heating system or for plastics made in the petrochemical industry than as a primary source for home heating systems. In addition he stated, "When we burn coal, it's gone." He is not comfortable using a nonrenewable energy source when there is a solar energy heating alternative.

There are also two disadvantages to using a solar heating system. One, on cloudy days a back-up system is needed. The flat-plate collector needs direct sunlight to collect heat. Two, the passive system requires initial capital. You have to buy the materials before installing the flat-plate collector.

Some people on the Navajo Reservation might think that paying for all of the materials to install the system is too expensive. Those people should realize that once the materials for the system are purchased, the home owners do not have to keep paying for the energy the system uses. People can use this system for a very long time without putting more money into it.

I think a solar heating system can save money over a period of time. People on the Reservation can save a lot of money by saving their trucks from depreciating as quickly as when they haul coal over long distances to heat their homes.

Why not use electricity to heat homes? People who live on the Reservation have to pay too much for electricity. They will save money in a short period of time with the flat-plate collector.

There is another way to heat homes with solar energy on the Navajo Reservation. This method uses a solar greenhouse. It is ideal for people on the Reservation who have trouble hauling coal to their homes or who have trouble getting fresh fruits and vegetables from stores.

If people who are living on the Reservation use greenhouses to heat their homes, then they can heat their homes while growing fruits and vegetables.

The greenhouse is attached on the south side of the house that people live in. It traps heat when the sun's rays pass through a glazed plastic roof or window. Black rocks which are located at the bottom of the greenhouse absorb the heat. When air blows over the rocks the air is heated. Doors or windows can be put between the greenhouse and the house where people live. When the greenhouse heats up they can open the windows or doors to allow the heat to enter the residence, or a fan can blow the warm air into the interior of the house.

One advantage of this system is the money people save from reduced grocery bills. People who eat the food grown in the greenhouses will not spend as much at the supermarket as those who buy their produce from stores. They can grow their own food like carrots, lettuce, onions, chili peppers or tomatoes. Freshly picked vegetables are healthier than vegetables trucked to grocery stores because vine-ripened vegetables contain more vitamins and nutrients. If greenhouse builders grow too much they can sell the extra product to their neighbors or give the extra to other members of their families.

There are three more advantages to using the solar greenhouse heating system. One, heating expenses are reduced. People with solar greenhouses do not pay a lot of money for their heating because they are using the sun's free energy. Two, some of the materials they need can be found around their houses or at local hardware stores. People living on the Reservation can buy the materials, like the glazed plastic, from stores in border towns like Farmington, Gallup or Flagstaff. If people live far from border towns, they can special-order the materials from the hardware stores on the Reservation. Third, the greenhouse pays for itself quickly. As Joseph Orr said, "Your greenhouse pays for itself five times faster through food savings than through heat savings."

I advise people on the Navajo Reservation to use a solar collector or a solar greenhouse connected to their houses to heat homes. It is simple for people on the Reservation to heat their homes with the sun's energy. If people on the Reservation follow my advice, in time they will be able to use the money saved from reduced heating costs for other activities.

Porpoise Lives for Tuna Cargo?

ANNE SCALAPINO

The ocean was rough as the storm quickly gained on the boat. The fishermen had been out for days; and at four o'clock in the afternoon of the final day, they were loading up to go in. Pulling in the net of yellowfin tuna, the tired fishermen brought in more porpoises than usual. Exhausted and overly anxious to get home, they pulled in the net, porpoises and all. Eighteen porpoises had to pay with their lives for the fishermen's long, tiring week.

Unfortunately these are not the only fishermen who haul in porpoises with every tuna cargo. In fact an average of 18,000 porpoises were killed in 1979. This was about half of the 1977 porpoise killings. Although there is a marked decrease in porpoise deaths, there is no excuse for any porpoises to be killed in such a careless way.

These creatures are considered to be the mammals closest to man in intelligence. It is a crime for these innocent, gentle animals to be killed and thrown away for tuna cargo. Many species of mammals have become extinct, proving the great necessity to preserve all of our wildlife.

One is sympathetic with the fishermen's long hours and hard work, but why should their burden be placed on the porpoises— especially when there are precautions that can be taken to save the mammals? Fine mesh nets with floating rims, for example, would prevent many porpoises from becoming entangled and drowning. Another precautionary effort is pulling the net out from under the porpoises swimming near the surface, a practice called backdown.

Some fishermen do this, but many do not usually because of the loss of tuna. The precaution most effective and least used is the method of spotting the tuna without the aid of the porpoises. The reason this method is so unpopular is that porpoises swim above the schools of tuna, near the surface. The visible porpoises provide an easy way for the fisherman to spot the tuna, and it would be more time-consuming to look just for the school of tuna. Fisherman may lose some of their hard-earned catch, but aren't porpoise lives worth the loss of some cargo?

Efforts by the government have been made toward decreasing porpoise death. A fine of $20,000 and/or one year in jail for the death of porpoises by tuna nets has been enforced. Recently the crew of the *Carol S*, a tuna boat, caught only one-fifth of the usual cargo because the fishermen had to avoid killing porpoises. The price of tuna does go up, but saving porpoises' lives is worth the price.

The public can get involved by writing the Secretary of the Interior and asking him to support the Endangered Species Act. There are many ways to get involved; it all depends on how much you care about saving the porpoise.

Review

Review a book, movie, or performance to let others know what it is like and whether they might like to experience it also. This involves more than summarizing the action. You might compare it with others of its kind, give background information, or analyze the technique by which it was done. Try to convey both an objective description and a personal evaluation. Think of a kind of magazine or newspaper that such a review might appear in, and fit style and focus to its audience.

Reading The Right Stuff

STEVEN FRIEDLAND

In *The Right Stuff,* author Tom Wolfe tells the story of the test pilots who risked their lives breaking the sound barrier during the late forties, and then the story of the first American astronauts. The stories are told through the eyes of the main character or characters involved, and this provides a unique insight into those chapters in American history which are recent enough to be parts of people's memories but far enough past to leave some questions into what really happened.

Wolfe starts with the story of Chuck Yeager, the first man to break the sound barrier, on October 14, 1947. Yeager was the definition of the true test pilot at that time. A person who would do his work to the best of his ability, and not accept anything special for that work. He became a god to the pilots with whom he came in contact. Many tried to beat Yeager: few succeeded, sometimes they lost their lives doing it.

While Yeager and the other hot test pilots were flying their hot planes, their wives waited home to hear that their husbands were dead. Wolfe shows the whole family aspect of the main characters, proving that they were no superhuman beings but people just like ourselves in one of the most dangerous jobs in the world. This softens the story, making it not the same as all the stories that had been told previously about the pilots, less merely factual and more human.

Following the stories about the test pilots, Wolfe recounts the selection of the first astronauts, a group of military test pilots who had volunteered for something no one had done before: travel into space. These test pilots were not the top ones, because the "Yeagerites" felt that these missions would be suicide, and the astronauts wouldn't be piloting, just tagging along for the ride on a mission that a monkey had done before. We are kept updated on the feelings of the top test pilots as the national spotlight shifts throughout the book from them to the astronaughts, as Wolfe doesn't let the two major stories go their own ways.

As the astronauts train and eventually take their flights into space we are shown how the government and the press covered up problems with the astronauts so that the country would have one thing to look up to in a time when there were many problems (Bay of Pigs, the Powers incident, Cuban missile crisis). Wolfe, though, tries to tell the true story that in most cases he had gotten from the people involved themselves.

The book ends just as it had started, with Chuck Yeager trying to break a world record. Only this time, the "perfect" Yeager messes up and shows that even the "super-humans" of the test pilot world are only human, and can make mistakes, too. Wolfe leaves us looking to the future in the conclusion, which in this case is today, and keeps us thinking of the things to come.

All Quiet on the Western Front

DAVID WYNER

The 1930's marked an important turning point in the film industry. The first "talkies" started to apprear during this decade, *All*

Quiet on the Western Front being one of them. Most of the actors of the 30s were trained in and used to silent movies, and few made the transition to sound. During the silent movie era, actors used exaggerated gestures and facial expressions to convincingly convey a situation. However, sound gave the actors an opportunity to decrease their body language and use speech variations to convey the idea. In *All Quiet on the Western Front* the actors seemed unaware of this opportunity. They acted as if they were unaccustomed to speech and did not know how to use correct emphasis. Their body and facial gestures were so flamboyant by today's standards that it is impossible for a modern audience to view the acting without laughter.

Another major difference in the filming techniques of the 1930s and the 1980s is the amount of censorship. In the 1930s morals were very refined, and therefore, movie censorship was much stricter than that of modern films. Much of the blood and gore of the book had to be edited for the 1930 movie version. Also, one scene in the book contained some sexual implications. However, the movie never dealt with more than a shadow of a bed and the voices of Paul and the girl. On the other hand, editors today seem to have no problem with blood and sex. If *All Quiet on the Western Front* were to be remade in this decade, it is doubtful that any of the gore appearing in the novel would not appear in the movie. This change has taken away much of the viewer's ability to use his imagination, and therefore may not be considered beneficial.

The directing and editing of the 1930 film illustrate still another way in which the movie industry has advanced. Contrary to modern techniques, almost all the scenes in the movie were short and concise, with a blackout at the end of each. These kinds of scenes and transitions tend to break up the flow and continuity of the film. In Erich Maria Remarque's novel, the majority of the scenes were long and complex and thus helped to keep the reader's interest focused on theme. In today's movies as well, long unified scenes with easy transitions constitute much of effective filming.

In comparing the 1930 movie-making techniques with those of today, one discovers many differences. The 1930 version of *All Quiet on the Western Front* is a fine example of these changes. To a 1930 audience, the movie represented the finest in film making and won many awards. On the other hand, the same movie is viewed by a modern audience as a low budget attempt to bring images to a classic novel. Perhaps the audience is partially responsible for this change. With the ever advancing special effects and filming methods, audiences have grown used to, and come to expect, a high level of effects. It is not possible for most modern day viewers to consider what a remarkable achievement this movie was in 1930. Have we become too desensitized?

British Bedlam

CRAIG PARKER

What is it that is so unique about British comedy? There are many popular examples, like Benny Hill and Monty Python, just to name a few. I believe it must stem from the prim and proper society of England. The British have mastered the use of sarcasm and social *faux pas* that cause the audience to laugh at the society in which they live. The British also use confusion and disorder to spark comic relief.

Michael Frayn's *Noises Off* is another perfect example of a British comedy. In Act I, a British acting company is practicing for a production that is to open the next day. There are two story lines going on at the same time: a play within a play. So not only does the audience laugh at the production that the company is producing but also at the interaction between the actors and the director. Brian Murray plays the exasperated director who cannot seem to get the play together. Dorothy Loudon plays the maid who can't remember to take the sardines when she goes to the study. These problems set up the perfect environment for sarcasm and confusion between the actors and the director. Act I really sets the scene for the play and gives the audience a background of the plot and characters.

Act II takes place backstage and develops some of the relationships between the characters. Garry and Frederick are always quarreling, which causes Frederick to get a bloody nose at the sight of violence. Dotty, Lloyd, and Poppy are caught up in a love triangle. Belinda has a responsibility to make sure Selsdon is on the stage, but he always wanders off. They all are trying to keep the booze out of the reach of old Selsdon. Poppy and Tim fight back and forth on giving the curtain call. All of these events combine to create havoc and contention backstage. Act II is the high point of the play. I think it is the most entertaining part of the production. It leads the audience very well into Act III.

If Act II sounds like a nightmare, Act III is the ultimate nightmare of any director or producer. The stage returns to the way it was in Act I, the audience viewing the props from the front. The play begins again for another showing. However, noises offstage are heard as the actors argue and fight. The actors begin to miss their entrances and forget their lines. Props are misplaced. The phone continues to ring even after it is picked up and eventually is smashed backstage in the fighting. At one point there are three thieves on stage, because Selsdon misses his cue. The mishaps snowball to the point that the actors are all making up their lines, and the story is completely lost. The action finally comes to a standstill, but by that time the audience is roaring with laughter.

I really enjoyed *Noises Off*, because I thought the acting was outstanding. Deborah Rush's lines, as Brooke, "fantastic!" and "sorry?" were great! The timing in the play was excellent. The moment that will stick in my mind forever is when Frederick makes a dash to catch the plate of sardines before they hit the floor. That kind of superb coordination is scattered throughout the production. All of those that enjoy British humor take heed, this is the play to see! Anyone that has been involved in theater would be able to relate to the funny mishaps of *Noises Off*. I was thoroughly entertained, and I think that this type of humor would be appreciated by a wide audience.

White Knights

DAVID GURLAND

White Nights is the story of two frustrated men. One is a famous Russian defector/ballet dancer, now an American "patriot." He has crashed, while on tour, into Communist Russia. The dancer (Nikolai Robchenko) feels threatened because defectors are considered criminals in their native country.

The other is what you may call an American defector. Raymond Greenwood is a young, talented, black tap dancer who, due to an unhappy experience in Vietnam, defected to Russia, where he feels his tap dancing will be more appreciated.

Since the two characters both have some American involvement, and are both dancers, they are paired together by the KGB. Apparently, the KGB wants Robchenko to dance in Moscow, and feels that Greenwood can help them attain their goal. The two dancers start out as fierce enemies but end up as great friends. And that's what the movie is all about. The growth of a friendship between two very different people. The story could have taken place anywhere, but because it took place in the U.S.S.R. it made the film into something of a propaganda documentary.

The entire motion picture is filmed with a subtle anti-Soviet bent. Robchenko's stories about his Soviet oppression, the scenery of the film, and especially the actors playing the KGB agents give the film a sinister mood. The agents were such rotten people, so soulless, I found it very hard to believe that the Soviets depicted in the film were so totally evil. The entire film had the audience believing that Russia makes Hell look like Disneyland. That bothered me. But all of Greenwood's monologues were so anti-American that I suppose all the "antis" cancel each other out.

Despite the underlying themes in the movie, it was quite an entertaining show. The plot moves very quickly and you're never bored nor confused (except sometimes when the characters are speaking Russian, French, and English at the same time) which is due to the marvelous direction by Taylor Hackford. He's the man who brought us *An Officer and a Gentleman* three years ago. He uses a lot of the same plot elements in this film—a military theme, a racial theme, strong friendships, and love interests. Hackford uses the *White Nights* as symbolism. The *White Nights* are periods of time in Russia when the sun never sets, therefore making the nights . . . white. If you do see the film, which you should, you'll see the symbolism.

You'll also see some good acting and some amazing dancing. Mikhail Baryshnikov as Robchenko and Gregory Hines as Greenwood are so good at what they do best, it's unbelievable. The supporting actors are also worth seeing, particularly, Helen Mirren, as an aging Russian ballerina in love with Baryshnikov, Geraldine Page as Baryshnikov's agent, and Isabella Rossellini as Greenwood's Russian wife. She looks exactly like a young Ingrid Bergman; in fact, she's her daughter. And if you can't go see the movie, buy the soundtrack. The music by Lionel Richie and Phil Collins makes the film worthwhile. Recommended.

Description/Definition

Describe what something is or is like. This could be an informative article as for a newspaper or magazine, an item in a manual, or an entry in an encyclopedia. Maybe a new product or invention or organization has come into existence or into prominence that some people would want, or ought to know more about. What is it like. Maybe confusion exists about something familiar that needs redefinition. Your subject could be an action like a process for making something, a procedure for getting something done, or some art or craft. Who might want your subject described or defined? For what purpose? Aim accordingly.

Fashion Tribes

TANJA KAMPE

As I sat on the cold concrete bench eating my lunch, I noticed a new girl walking down the hall. She was stylishly dressed from head to toe except for one thing. There was something that ruined her total look. The girl's hair was cut and styled in the latest fashion, her clothes were right off the pages of a fashion magazine, and her shoes matched perfectly to her outfit. It took me a little while to pinpoint the small detail that ruined her look. It was her socks which were pulled up to her knees. How could she destroy her outfit like that? Did she not know that she had to crinkle her socks down around her ankles to be cool?

As soon as I realized what was wrong with the new girl, I categorized her with the geeks, the people at my school who try very hard to be in fashion by buying all the latest styles and cutting their hair like everyone else but do something wrong to ruin their look. If you tuck your shirt in too tight or roll your pants up too much or pull your socks up you are placed in the geek group and are usually only accepted by them. Geeks do not plan on being what they are, and I am sure that they would change if someone told them what they were doing wrong. Most people pity the geeks somewhat.

Geeks are one of the many tribes of people who exist on every school campus. I use the term tribe because the people who dress and look the same stay together in groups as did the Indian tribes. Each tribe has its own costume, special characteristics, and sometimes even warpaint. The geeks for example, are usually smart but not smart enough to fit in with the intellectuals. They try hard to be like everyone else, but then they try too hard and end up forming their own tribe with its own special rituals. Geeks are looked down upon, and one's "coolness" is questioned if you are ever seen talking to one.

The intellectuals are the smarter students who spend all their time buried in books or in front of a computer. They can be found in the library or study lounge at any time during the day. The intellectuals are respected for their intelligence, but hardly anyone wants to be like them because they do not seem to have any fun. Their tribal dress is clothes that are plain and will not distract them from their studies.

The jocks and jockettes, on the other hand, are the most envied of all the tribespeople. This tribe contains most of the athletes and cheerleaders, the "popular" people. These students are known for having wild pow wows, being Homecoming queens and kings, and knowing everyone who is important. They are always impeccably dressed, and their hair, especially the girls', is always perfect. You would never find a jockette with her socks pulled up to her knees because that would mean immediate expulsion from the tribe. They are the people who the geeks look up to and want to be.

Speaking of wanting to be like someone else, the wanna-bes are considered some of the worst tribes. Wanna-bes are smaller tribes who try to be like a larger tribe. The wanna-be-intellectuals, for example, hang out by the library with books and papers and pretend to be studying. They dress like the intellectuals and try to become them but never quite meet the requirements. There is a wanna-be tribe for every "normal" tribe that exists.

The free spirit tribe is a combination of hippies, surfers, and artists who concern themselves only with what they are doing, not what others are doing. These people dress in whatever is comfortable and usually could not care less if they were in or out of fashion. They value the person more than the outfit.

Last but definitely not least we have the tribe of bizarre people. With the use of warpaints and headdresses these people show their nonconfirmity to society. Members of other tribes are often afraid or intimidated by them because of their unique dress. They wear strange clothes, different hair colors, and any accessories that they like. These styles sometimes resemble the war costumes of Indian tribes. Instead of using feathers and animals hides, the bizarre people use chains and spikes to complete their outfits.

Today the way you dress is not only what you are wearing but also who you are. Clothes are now used to categorize your lifestyle. People examine and judge your outer appearance before looking at what is inside the person. This kind of analysis is very misleading because the person within sometimes has nothing to do with the clothes on the outside. Clothes have developed from articles that cover and warm you to a personal statement. It is obvious that there is a silent fashion battle among all of the tribes. A diversity in dress is good, but when it leads to conflicts it becomes a problem, for when people concentrate too much on their image they lose sight of the person that they really are.

Comparison

Compare two or more things with one another as a way of bringing out the qualities or traits of each. What are the similarities and differences? What is the value of this comparison? It might be to clarify or redefine the reader's understanding of what the things are or do. Or you might evaluate the things by contrasting them. If the items are commercial products, this could be a consumer report. If you are comparing alternative ways of doing or making something, you could show how the process or procedure could be improved. Maybe you want to stress similarities to show, for example, that two behaviors that we usually don't consider together are in fact alike in some important way. Often comparison helps to reclassify phenomena so as to allow fresh thinking about them.

Tale of Two Cities

ANDY MAXWELL

At 7:00 in the evening of July 7, 1982, at Royals' Stadium in Kansas City, Missouri, the stands were slowly filling. Some of the fans sitting near me were elderly men with scruffy beards and short hair; they wore dirty, worn-out overalls. When someone delivered a base hit, a mild cheer went up in the stands. In a group of high school girls, a brunette stood out from the rest. During the game, she moved around the stands yelling at different players. In the seventh inning, she cautiously leaned over the railing and, as if she were dropping a handkerchief, gently tossed a newly-bought cotton candy cone at the left-fielder. Ignoring her, he called for the bat boy to remove the offering.

At 2:00 in the afternoon of August 8 at the Dodger Stadium in Los Angeles, I sat among some thoughtless Dodgers rooters. The beer guzzlers to my left had beards and long hair. Even though they weren't Atlanta rooters, they wore dark blue Atlanta hats just to be different and cause an uprising. One of them kept waddling passed me, talking to himself as he went to buy more beer. Through their cupped hands, his friends kept yelling at the plays and players. When Pedro Guerrero smacked a base hit and Ken Landreaux scampered in, the Dodgers fans went into a wild, unnecessarily deafening uproar that shook the stands.

Sitting in the stadiums of two United States cities, I was aware of a difference; it was as if I were visiting two different countries. I entertained the thought of how, even within one country, a baseball fan can have culture shock.

I've observed baseball fans in San Francisco, San Diego and Los Angeles, but I was much more impressed with the people in Kansas City. A youthful vendor, peddling programs, thought I was kidding when I said I wanted to buy three programs. He chuckled and nonchalantly handed me one program. When I told him I wanted them for my friends, he hurriedly handed me three and exclaimed, "Well Jimminy Crickets, that's great!" With praise a man in back of me said to his wife, "That rookie catcher got two hits last night in his first appearance as a major leaguer; not too bad for a rookie!" A tomboy in the group of schoolgirls, with an ear-piercing voice, bellowed, "I think George Brett sure is purty!" As I was eating my second mustard-covered Polish sausage sandwich, a friendly lady in front of me smiled and said "My God, you must be a growing boy; look how much you eat!" Those people really made me feel at home.

The Dodger Stadium dialogue, however, was different. Those pugnacious Dodgers fans wearing Atlanta hats were making paper airplanes from pages of their programs. For some reason, the young Atlanta hat wearers despised Steve Garvey. When Garvey struck out, the young troublemakers cried "Garvey's a bum! He can't even hit the ball; what's he doing in the major leagues?" An elaborate old lady sitting in front of me turned around and ordered, "Let me see your program!" And before I could say yes, she snatched it from my hands. Sitting in Dodger Stadium is like sitting in a junior high cafeteria.

As the last out was recorded in Kansas City, the fans felt proud that their team did well and they gave the Royals a well deserved round of applause. As I left my seat and was walking out of the stadium in the beautiful evening, I realized how lucky I was to become a Royals fan.

The Dodgers game had a happy ending too, but it wasn't a happy ending for the Atlanta hat wearers; when they realized Atlanta had lost, they screamed even more rude comments. At that point I wondered what they would have said if they wore Kansas City hats?

Mark and Timmy:
Two Cultural Consumers

ALEXIS HORANZY

A couple of summers ago, I babysat with three little boys while their parents were at work. Mark (7) and John (7) were brothers, and Timmy (7) was a neighbor from down the street. Right off, I noticed big differences between Mark's behavior and Timmy's behavior. Mark liked to draw landscapes, construct Leggo spacemobiles, and make paper airplanes. He finished any project he began, working intently to its completion. When we talked he expounded on the virtues of beeswax crayons and explained why plants grow. Timmy, on the other hand, always wanted to play "The Incredible Hulk." The rules of the game were simple. Timmy would play the Hulk and beat up Mark and John. However, since Mark and John had never had a T.V. in their house, they had never seen "The Incredible Hulk" and were not much interested in being beaten up in the name of this strange creature, whoever he might be. I would try to interest Timmy in Mark's activity, but after two minutes, he would want to start a game of "Hulk " and after five minutes of that he would wander into the living room and do something like pull a basket full of shells off the shelf.

Timmy's attention span was incredibly short, but he was not sick or stupid. He was like millions of other kids raised on television. He knew that only the Nightrider Race Set or the Star Wars Action Figures were fun because T.V. had told him so. He told time by which shows were on the television. Once, when we passed a T.V. store window, Timmy turned to me and said, "*The Flintstones* is on. My mommy should be getting home."

Mark, by contrast, though only seven years old, liked to read. His books already filled one shelf in the living room: *The Otter Twins, A Fox in One Bite, Harry, the Wild West Horse. The Chronicles of Narnia* and Homer's *Odyssey* were there when he was ready for them. When we talked, he told me about *King Midas's Touch* and *The Caboose That Could*, and asked me to read new stories.

Mark and Timmy were a beautiful contrast: The Word Whiz and The Video Kid. I thought about the differences between Mark and Timmy and about how the two different mediums—books and T.V.— had affected them so differently. In a world going video, Mark's parents had opted to raise him differently. The family did not own a T.V. Mark attended a special school which focused on creativity and reading. At this school, Mark, at the age of five, began to learn to play the recorder and to speak German. He learned numbers through pictures he drew to accompany stories he read. These teaching methods appealed to Mark's parents, but they were more interested in a teaching tool the school did *not* have: the school did not own a T.V. Mark's parents wanted their son to develop his own creative skills and imagination; they were not interested in inundating him with society's "looney tunes." As a result, many doors opened to Mark.

As he grows he will journey to many different places through the books he reads. The places may be real or the creation of someone else's mind. Others may read the same books, taking the same journeys. Yet, his journeys will not really be the same as everyone else's. He will cast his own stars in his private adventures. A part of him will interact with each book to produce something that is a lot of him and a lot of the book. Timmy won't experience this shared product when he watches television.

As I worked with these kids I recalled my experience with *Wuthering Heights*, how the wonderful story drew me in until I was right there on the heath sharing Cathy and Heathcliff's struggles, and how later I saw the "classic" motion picture, *Wuthering Heights*, and I laughed all the way through it. The actors were caricatures of my mental creations. They reduced the strong-willed, vibrant Cathy and Heathcliff into the insipid clichés of lovers doomed to separation. I felt none of the intense love, hatred, anguish, fear, or uncertainty that surged from the pages of the book.

I envisioned at the beginning, a dark, brooding, sexy Heathcliff, unkempt, his clothes in filthy tatters, later transformed into a Heathcliff dressed only in the finest silk shirts and wool suits. Laurence Olivier, who admittedly is one of the world's greatest actors, was not great enough to replace my Heathcliff. Compared to my sharpminded wary Heathcliff, Olivier was a dolt. During his heated discussions with Cathy, I wanted to shout at the screen, "You're Heathcliff, you're

angry, you're jealous! Stop looking like a wounded puppy!!" My Heathcliff wore a sweat-soaked, white cotton shirt, a castoff from Hindley,
and breeches, clumsily patched. Olivier dressed in Hollywood's poor
man costume, neatly stained.

Edward I imagined as slightly frail but a gorgeous blond always
impeccably dressed. Although the movie had the clothes right, Edward
was wrong. He was utterly wimpy—very plain, a real Mama's Boy.
Cathy would not have married HIM.

My image of Cathy was strange. I knew she was devastatingly
beautiful; yet I never saw her, I was so involved with her emotions; I
shared her tension, aware of her feelings exposed like raw nerves,
sensitive to the slightest touch. Merle Oberon had the beauty to be
Cathy, but compared to my Cathy she had all the emotion of a clam.

I suppose the most memorable disappointment, though, was the
moors. I smelled the heather and caught a chill from the cold wind as I
read the book. In the movie, at Cathy's death scene, Heathcliff carried
her to the window so she could see the moors one last time. As she
sighed and said, "Oh, Heathcliff! Look at the moors! Aren't they
lovely!" the camera panned out to the most beautiful view I have ever
seen of a heath painted on a backdrop!

I was disappointed with the visual shortcomings of this "classic"
film. But I have not been trying to give a movie review. My point is that
no film could replace the images I had created.

Mark will have the experiences like mine too. Many times he will
derive more pleasure out of his own images than out of a director's.
Timmy will never know what he is missing.

No matter how video-oriented the world becomes, people will
always exist who, like Mark, prefer creating their own images to
relying on the images others bombard them with. These people refuse
to limit themselves to the beauty of a backdrop.

Evaluation

*Tell what something is worth by setting forth its good or
bad points. Your subject could be an enterprise or operation,
someone's work or behavior, an object of art or manufacture, a
program, and so on. Within what framework of values are you
making your assessment? You might just praise or condemn or
make a mixed judgment. How general or specialized an audience will be interested in knowing what you think of your
subject? You might think of readerships for certain publications
for which it would be suitable. Your evaluation could be one
kind of consumer report.*

Growth and the Art of Automobile Maintenance

TIMOTHY M. SHEINER

The green and white building sits unobtrusively at the bottom of the hill. Some people never notice it; others are immediately drawn to the modest self-confidence, calmness, and quality exuded by the fifty-year-old structure. Cars surround the building and litter the yard. All are in various stages of disembowelment, but the bustle and activity of the place causes the observer to assume that they will all be back on the road shortly. The interior of the shop is confident and organized, containing a lathe that was old before it came to the garage forty years ago, a homemade boiler, piles of dead parts from long-forgotten cars and the unavoidable clutter of a half-century of skilled use—tools, grease, personalities, jokes, and history. This is Graham's Garage, and it has become an important part of my life.

More than anything else, Graham's Garage is Ed Graham. A remarkable man of sixty, he happily spends fifty or more hours a week at the garage. Although always busy, he is warm, open and relaxed. I have arrived at work Saturday morning a few times to find that he hasn't gone home yet: a faithful customer's car, an interesting problem, and he forgot what time it was. I have seen him discuss a customer's recent vacation for twenty minutes while showing no sign that he urgently needed to go back to work. He is very interested in and supportive of other people's pursuits. He ran track at my school forty-five years ago. When he found out I was on the track team he asked me for my meet schedule. There he was, in spite of all the work he had to do, at my next meet cheering for me and my school. Consider the man and it is obvious why the garage has prospered for all these years.

This remarkable place and this remarkable man have taught me many things, one of them being that in order to be a successful mechanic one has to be patient. Yelling at a frozen nut won't break it free. Cursing the man at the parts store because he sent the wrong part is not a way to develop a good relationship with him. Becoming exasperated with a customer for not understanding his car is not good for business. Because these types of problems, mechanical and personal, occur so often I have become quite adept at dealing with them. Mechanical problems require patience, calmness and the firm faith that the problem can be solved if approached in a careful, methodical way. And if that doesn't work, a hammer and a cold chisel will.

Problems that deal with people are more complex. They also necessitate patience, but it must be combined with skills of listening, understanding and a sense of humor. Once, a customer decided to remain and watch me fix her car. The job was difficult and her breath on my neck made it that much harder. Suddenly, she started a long rambling discourse on her very personal problems with men. Shocked, bored, and embarrassed, I wanted to ask her to be quiet, but as she was the customer I laughed at her jokes, sympathized with her position, and made the proper clucking noises. She departed with a repaired car and the added bonus of a cleansed psyche.

Besides mechanical skills and patience, the garage has developed my sense of independence. This development has come partly from my reaction to being the brunt of good-natured jibes about my age, supposed innocence, or anything that strikes the veterans of the place as funny, and partly from the amount of responsibility I have taken. As an unsure apprentice reluctant to take responsibility, I was the perfect target for the teasing, which bothered and embarrassed me, but as I learned more, I became more self-confident, taking more initiative and greater responsibility. I soon became able to laugh at myself and my rookie ways while returning the wisecracks tit for tat. Only then was I recognized as an equal by everyone at the garage.

A beautifully-engineered, finely-tooled, flawlessly operating machine causes me as much elation as the brilliant colors and deft brushstrokes of the masters. This commonality of feeling stems from the superb craftmanship I perceive in both. This craftmanship is, for me at least, a frustrating rarity these days. Things break far too easily, and the repair work is nearly always expensive, inexpertly done, and only marginally effective. The expensive and modern way of fixing something that has broken is to replace it. This is not true of Graham's, where we do things the old way and the right way. We have lathes, drill presses, taps and dies; we can and actually do fix broken parts. Therefore, the garage is not just a place where I sweat, strain, learn, laugh, and socialize, but it represents, to me, the old-world ideals of quality, skill, and pride in one's work. I have become a part of Graham's garage, but, more importantly, it has become a part of me.

Causal Analysis

Explain why something is true or has come about. What are the causes for a certain current trend, for example, or for the success or failure of some endeavor? Analyze the way some enterprise or group, process or procedure works to show why it produces certain results. Connect effects with their causes. What is the importance of your causal explanation? For whom? This could be a way to increase understanding of the good or bad effects of some agency or custom, trace some effects to their hitherto unexplained causes, or show some hidden side-effects of some actions not ordinarily associated with them. You might think of what ordinarily unconnected things should in fact be connected causally or of what common phenomena might be better understood by causal analysis.

What Makes for School Success?

CARIN HANSEN

As a student, I have often wondered why some kids do well in school while others seem to struggle and get bad grades. One particular friend of mine is an example of the problem I want to research. Although we are equally intelligent, her grades are lower than mine. I am looking for some kind of theory that would explain the difference. The only factor that I can think of, hindering her but helping me, would be our home environments. More specifically, I think that unsupportive parents who were insensitive to her needs could cause her to dislike school. My parents are much more helpful and encouraging. Could a student's parents be rightfully blamed or praised for their child's performance in class?

I recalled a section on attitudes in the book *Exploring Social Psychology*[1] that seemed to answer yes. First, people have affective feelings on a subject, which include liking or disliking. From these feelings, they form beliefs which are acted out in specific behaviorial tendencies. This means that students with a negative idea about school, possibly from their parents, would begin to act against attempts made to educate them, causing poor performance.

To begin searching for other possible explanations, I went to Cliff Purcell, a counselor at San Marcos High[2]. I asked him what factors he thought would influence school performance. First, he said that parents were most important. Successful parents, he said, would have a higher socio-economic standing, and this group tends to lend more support to their children. Kids in this group get a more positive self-image and see themselves as capable of doing good work. He continued by saying that these students would become friends with others relatively equal to themselves and form a strong peer group.

I had collected many ideas by now but needed to test them. I did this by writing up a questionnaire to be given to high school students, which asked about many variables, including home environment, personal interests in school, and educational habits[3]. Finally, I ended by asking about grade-point average and goals for the future. I hoped that when I analyzed the papers, I would find some consistent reason why good students did well and some explanation of what held back the poor students.

Although I distributed the questionnaires only in advanced English classes, the results represented a very wide variety of students. The grade-point averages alone ranged from 1.5 to 4.0. There were several factors which turned out to be relatively good determiners of the students' grades. To begin with, only 2% of the students surveyed with above a 3.2 grade point answered *no* when asked if they liked school. However, about 20% of the students below a 3.2 ansered *no*, they did not like school. This could be a result of their not doing well, or it could be a negative outlook which causes non-interest, boredom, and therefore bad performance.

Rather than parents, the second determining factor of a student's performance was his/her extra-curricular involvements. Almost all of the A and B students were in some way involved in school outside of the academic classroom. This is important because these people can see themselves as part of the school, rather than someone who is forced to go. Those who participate feel that they belong, and this causes them to want to succeed.

This involvement theory comes from a lecture by D. Bielby, a sociology professor.[4] She compared Japanese techniques of operating a working group with the American process. The Japanese companies are successful because everyone sees himself as a member of a group, just as involved students would see themselves as a part of San Marcos High. Secondly, it has been shown that Japanese workers become self-motivating because of their involvement and personal stake in what happens. When applied to high school, it shows that students who participate also become self-motivated, enabling them to perform well.

Parents do influence their child's attitudes. However, the final determinant of success lies with students themselves. They should become involved or be able to motivate themselves. Finally, students who were not lucky enough to have helpful parents must want to work for their own benefit.

Sources

[1] Robert A. Baron and Donn Byrne, *Exploring Social Psychology*, p. 58.
[2] Cliff Purcell, Counselor, San Marcos H.S., January 8, 1986.
[3] "How People Learn," San Marcos H.S. (a questionnaire), January 13, 1986.
[4] D. Bielby, University of California at Santa Barbara professor. "Japanese Attitudes" (a lecture), October 17, 1985.

Textual Interpretation

Say what you think is the full meaning an author intended to express in some text that you think the reader is meant to fill out. Most fiction, poetry, and drama leave much to the reader to infer on his or her own by putting together all the images, ideas, or actions into some whole that accounts for the parts. But your text need not be from literature if you feel that its subtlety, symbolism, or complexity require the reader's interpretation; it could be a true narrative or an essay. Choose some text that you have been drawn into and have thought about and that you think you could interpret to increase others' understanding and appreciation. Quote or refer to the text wherever you think it needs elucidation or whenever you think your interpretation needs support. Presumably all your evidence lies in the text, except perhaps for certain outside information that you think is fair to bring to bear on the work.

You might aim your interpretation at a literary periodical or at an audience interested in such subject matter as psychology, sociology, or philosophy. To the extent that your interpretation brings out how the author makes us feel or think something, your remarks might interest people concerned with writing or artistic technique.

Truth Abused

MARY POWERS

In the play *A Streetcar Named Desire* the author, Tennessee Williams, shows his preference for Blanche's world over Stanley's. Although Williams appears to favor Blanche's world, he does not approve of her behavior. Williams is also critical of Stanley's brutal use of the truth. Therefore, Williams seems to favor a world combining the *favorable* qualities of Blanche's world and Stanley's *harmless* use of the truth.

Williams apparently favors Blanche's world; he conveys this idea by assigning Blanche favorable qualities and Stanley less favorable qualities. In the areas of nationality, color symbolism, astrological symbolism, and occupation, the contrast between Blanche and Stanley is evident. Blanche is of French descent, shown by her French name, DuBois. The French nationality traditionally represents emotion, culture, poise, and sensitivity, all fine qualities. Other fine qualities are shown by the fact that Blanche wears soft pastels; this choice of colors represents her aura of sensitivity as well as her innocence and purity. Blanche's innocence and purity are again symbolized by her astrological sign—Virgo, "the virgin." The fact that she was born under this sign hints at her innocent qualities. Blanche's occupation as an English teacher also implies that she is sensitive, cultured, and proper. Altogether these facts hint at the fine qualities which Blanche possesses.

In contrast to Blanche's favorable qualities, Stanley suffers from undesirable traits. In the play's scheme of things, Stanley's nationality, as shown by his name, Kowalski, is Polish. The Polish stereotype represents stupidity, ignorance, uncleanliness, and stubbornness, all definitely poor qualities to possess. Stanley also tends to wear flashy, brilliant primray colors, further displaying his unrefinement. In addition, Stanley's astrological sign of Capricorn, "the goat," is also symbolic of his stubbornness. Finally, Stanley's occupation as a salesman shows the stubborn force and pushiness he uses to monopolize and pressure others in order to get what he wants. Collectively, the ways Stanley is represented in the play show the bad traits he possesses which make up his personality.

Though evidence in the play indicates that Williams prefers Blanche's world over Stanley's, the author does not support Blanche's present behavior. In order to live in her favorable world, Blanche has become a prostitute, an alcoholic, and a liar. Blanche's activity as a prostitute is subtly hinted at throughout the first half of the play, through Stanley's suspicions and also through Blanche's behavior. Her mysterious "leave of absence" from the school is one of the first indications that Blanche may be up to no good. Blanche's expensive clothes and jewelry add to this suspicion, especially in Stanley's eyes. When Stanley raids Blanche's wardrobe, he shouts to Stella: "Look at these feathers and furs she came to preen herself in! What's this here? A solid-gold dress, I believe!. . . Genuine fox fur-pieces, a half a mile long!" Stanley also comments, "Open your eyes to this stuff! You think she got them out of a teacher's pay?" Blanche's subtle comments arouse Stanley's suspicions even more. When Blanche comments that her sign is Virgo, "the virgin," Stanley laughs contemptuously and asks if Blanche knows a man named Shaw. Stanley is further intrigued by her nervous response and tells Blanche, "Well, this somebody named Shaw is under the impression he met you in Laurel, but I figure he must have got you mixed up with some other party because this other party is someone he met at a hotel called the Flamingo." When Blanche comments that she would "not dare to be seen in [the Flamingo]," but has "seen it and smelled it," Stanley comments, "You must've gotten pretty close if you could smell it." Blanche then dabs her forehead with a handkerchief and trembles; her nervous reactions show the truth of the matter. After this encounter with Stanley, Blanche comments to Stella, "I wasn't so good the last two years or so, after Belle Reve had started to slip through my fingers."

Not only Stanley's suspicions but also Blanche's behavior indicate her prostitution. Blanche attempts to seduce almost every man she meets, including the newspaper boy, Stanley himself, and Mitch. Blanche's attraction to the paper boy comes as a result of her experiences with the young man she loved, Allen, who betrayed her. She asks the paper boy for a kiss, then, after kissing him, says, "Now run along, now, quickly! It would be nice to keep you, but I've got to be good—and keep my hands off children." Blanche also flirts with Stanley; when she first meets him, "she sprays herself with the atomizer, then playfully sprays him with it," to which Stanley angrily replies: "If I didn't know you was my wife's sister I'd get ideas about you!" Blanche's flirting with Mitch is even more obvious. She asks him into the house for a drink, asking him to "Sit down! Why don't you take off your coat and loosen your collar?" They are also sitting in a room lit only by one dim candle; Blanche explains by saying, "We are going to pretend that we are sitting in a little artists' cafe on the Left Bank in Paris." But the most obvious part of her seduction comes when she speaks French to Mitch: "Voulez-vous coucher avec moi ce soir? Vous ne comprenez pas? Ah, quelle dommage!" Mitch does not understand French, so he does not realize that she is saying, "Do you want to go to bed with me tonight? You don't understand, do you? Oh, what a shame!" Eventually, after tracking down Blanche's past, Stanley finally uncovers the truth of her behavior to Stella: "She moved to the Flamingo!...The Flamingo is used to all kinds of goings-on. But even the management of The Flamingo was impressed by Dame Blanche...so impressed...that they requested her to turn in her roomkey—for permanently!" Stanley also tells Stella of Blanche's attempts to seduce other men of the town and of Blanche's affair with her seventeen-year-old pupil. Blanche herself finally verifies the truth of the story in her discussions with Mitch. She cries hysterically:

> Yes, I had intimacies with strangers. After the death of Allen—intimacies with strangers was all I seemed able to fill my empty heart with. . . . I think it was panic, just panic, that drove me from one to another, hunting for some protection . . . in the most—unlikely places—even, at last, in a seventeen-year-old boy but—somebody wrote the superintendent about it—"This woman is morally unfit for her position!

Blanche's secret is revealed, thus causing her to lose the trust and respect of those she was so close to, both Mitch and Stella.

Because Blanche is a prostitute, she is also a heavy drinker, hoping to cover up her problems. She steals Stanley's liquor constantly yet will not admit to her alcoholism. She makes up excuses for her drinking, telling Stella that "your sister hasn't turned into a drunkard, she's just all shaken up and hot and tired and dirty." And when Mitch questions Blanche about the ownership of the liquor she is drinking, she replies, "It isn't Stan's. . . . Some things on the premises are actually mine!" Blanche's alcoholism is made even more evident by Mitch's comment to Blanche: "You ought to lay off his [Stanley's] liquor. He says you been lapping it up all summer like a wild-cat!" After their discussion, during which Mitch rejects Blanche and she throws him out, she drinks steadily until Stanley's arrival, again showing her attempts to drown her problems with alcohol.

As a result of her heavy drinking, Blanche also lies in an attempt to hide her alcoholism. Her excuses to Stella for her drinking and her lies to Mitch are evidence of this cover-up. Blanche also lies about her past in order to hide the fact that she is a prostitute, as well as other facts which would hurt her reputation. Blanche lies in order to protect herself and when her lies are exposed she is betrayed by the truth. Blanche cannot live by the truth; this idea is apparent when Mitch tears the paper lantern off the light bulb. Blanche cringes in fear from the exposed light as she cringes from the exposed truth, for light in this play symbolizes the truth. Therefore, rather than face the light of truth, she prefers to live in the darkness of her dream world. She tells Mitch, "I don't want realism. I want magic!. . . I try to give that to people. I misrepresent things to them. I don't tell the truth, I tell what *ought* to be the truth. And if that is sinful, then let me be damned for it!"

Williams is critical not only of Blanche's behavior, but of Stanley's cruel use of the truth as well. Stanley actually *mis*uses the truth—his brutal honesty destroys those people he loves, Stella and Mitch, as well as Blanche. His honesty in his emotions and in his speech are what destroys Stella. Stanley communicates *physically* with Stella—by throwing the radio, slapping her, etc. Stella eventually realizes by the end of the story that her and Stanley's relationship is merely physical, with no mental attraction. This idea is shown when Blanche is taken to the asylum; Stella then seeks *physical* comfort from Stanley; she cries in his arms, and he murmurs Stella's name to her while fingering the opening of her blouse.

Stanley also destroys Mitch and Blanche through the same brutal revelation of Blanche's past. Through the discovery of what Blanche really is like, Mitch loses all respect for her and, as a result, loses his hope for a future with someone he loved and trusted. Mitch can no longer feel the same toward Blanche after his talk with Stanley; he tells Blanche, "You're not clean enough to bring in the house with my mother." When Mitch then sees Blanche again he drops his head to the table and cries, for he recalls his loss of hope.

Blanche herself is ruined not only by her unveiled secret, but also by Stanley's raping her. Stanley's brutal honesty is shown when he openly displays his lust for her in this episode. He admits his lust when he shouts at her: "We've had this date with each other from the beginning!" Stanley's brutal honesty obviously destroys Blanche; his revelation of her past destroys her reputation; then, through his rape, Stanley forces Blanche into insanity. The destruction caused by

Stanley's brutal truth shows that Williams disfavors Stanley's use of the truth.

If Williams disfavors Stanley's use of the truth, then he must favor *harmless* use of the truth plus the positive qualities of Blanche's world. Stella is something of a symbol of this combined world. She possesses the innocence and sensitivity of Blanche's world: she cares about the feelings and emotions of both Blanche and Stanley. Stella sacrifices her time and labor for the benefit of Blanche and Stanley; Stella herself comments to Blanche, "People have got to tolerate each other's habits, I guess." Stella also acts as a peacemaker between the two, defending Blanche against Stanley, and Stanley against Blanche. Stella is also ready to forgive and forget when someone she loves hurts her. After Stanley's outburst at the poker game, Stella calms the frightened Blanche by saying, ". . . it wasn't anything as serious as you seem to take it. . . . He was as good as a lamb when I came back and he's really very, very ashamed of himself."

Stella possesses these fine qualities because she is a DuBois; she also possesses a positive use of the truth in addition to these fine qualities. Because she is a Kowalski, truth is important to her, but, while Stanley's truth is harmful, Stella's truth is positive. This positive honesty is symbolized by her nickname, "Stella for Star." Since light is a symbol of truth in this play, and a star is a guiding light, Stella's nickname indicates that Stella is able to effectively use the truth, something which neither Blanche nor Stanley can do. Stella is also a "guiding star" in that she will evidently attempt to guide her new-born baby down the proper pathways as he grows up so he may achieve the combined world that Williams supports so heavily. This will take a lot of effort on Stella's part, but she will be able to do it because of her determination and love for others.

The outcome of Blanche, Stanley, and Stella's lives may be interpreted through the outcome of the story. Blanche went insane because she could not accept honesty when it was presented to her. Her move to the asylum is the best thing for her because, as a result, she escaped Stanley's brutal honesty and could live in her own enjoyable dream world of insanity. This insanity provides a paradise for Blanche, a place where she can escape criticism, brutal truth, and, thus, her own destruction. Like Blanche, Stanley cannot accept honesty either and will lie to cover up what threatens him. He must stay with Stella in order to survive, for he is dependent on her. This dependency is apparent when Stella leaves the house after he rages at her; then Stanley cries, "Stella! My baby doll's left me!" Stanley then runs outside to try to win Stella back. Stella is one of the few people Stanley can positively communicate with, even if this communication is only physical, and he needs Stella for this reason.

Stella herself will be able to survive the best of the three characters since she possesses most of the good qualities of both the

DuBois and the Kowalski worlds. She will continue to be a guiding force for the other two and especially for her baby, and, since she is able to accept the truth, she will also be able to accept her future, whatever it contains. Even a break-up with Stanley will not ruin Stella, for she realizes that her marriage is based on physical contact rather than mental contact. This knowledge, added with her strength to accept the truth, will bring her through a break-up with Stanley, should it happen. Stella's own inner strength and guiding force will help her build a good life for herself and also for those she loves.